BUDDHA GAYA

THE HERMITAGE OF SAKYA MUNI

BUDDHA GAYA

THE HERMITAGE OF SAKYA MUNI

BY

RAJENDRALALA MITRA, LL.D., C.I.E.

PUBLISHED UNDER ORDERS OF THE GOVERNMENT OF BENGAL

GYAN

Published by

Gyan Publishing House
5, Ansari Road
Daryaganj, New Delhi-110002
Phone: 011-47034999, 9811692060
E-mail: books@gyanbooks.com

Distribution Network
gyanbooks.com
India, USA, Canada, UK, Australia, France

ISBN : 978-81-212-2706-3 (HB)
First Published, 1878

2nd Impression 2021

Printed at: Gyan Press, Delhi.

Buddha Gaya
Author: Rajendralala Mitra

BUDDHA GAYÁ,

THE HERMITAGE OF SÁKYA MUNI.

BY

RÁJENDRALÁLA MITRA, LL.D., C.I.E.,

HONORARY MEMBER OF THE ROYAL ASIATIC SOCIETY OF GREAT BRITAIN AND IRELAND, AND OF THE PHYSICAL CLASS OF THE IMPERIAL ACADEMY OF SCIENCES, VIENNA; CORRESPONDING MEMBER OF THE GERMAN AND OF THE AMERICAN ORIENTAL SOCIETIES, OF THE ROYAL ACADEMY OF SCIENCE, HUNGARY, AND OF THE ETHNOLOGICAL SOCIETY OF BERLIN; FELLOW OF THE ROYAL SOCIETY OF NORTHERN ANTIQUARIES, COPENHAGEN, ETC., ETC.

PUBLISHED UNDER ORDERS OF THE GOVERNMENT OF BENGAL.

Calcutta:

PRINTED AT THE BENGAL SECRETARIAT PRESS.

1878.

PREFACE.

In the winter of 1876 the late king of Burmah deputed three of his officers to superintend the repairs of the ancient temple at Buddha Gayá. The men arrived at the place in January 1877, and immediately set to work. With the permission of the Mahant, in whose charge the temple is kept, they cleared away a large space around it, built an enclosing wall, renewed the retaining walls of the terrace of the temple, replastered its interior, and took some steps for preserving the sacred Bodhi tree. In the course of their work they brought to light a great number of votive stúpas, images, friezes, impressions of the sacred feet, and other objects of antiquarian interest. Some of these they built into the new wall, others lay scattered about the place.

The subject was brought to the notice of the Government of Bengal in the middle of last year, and suggestions made to prevent the masking and modernizing of the ancient temple. Thereupon a demi-official letter was written to me by Sir Stuart Bayley, then Secretary to the Government of Bengal, and in it the wishes of the Government were thus set forth:—"It is not desired to interfere with the Burmese gentlemen beyond giving them such guidance as may prevent any serious injury being done to the temple, of which there seemed at one time some danger from their laying bare a portion of the foundation; and to arrange for such of the antiquities as are worth preserving being properly taken care of. They are at present building them into walls, and sticking foolish heads on to ancient torsos, &c. Mr. Eden wishes to know if you can make it convenient to pay a visit to Buddha Gayá to inspect the work and the remains collected, and to give advice as to their value and to their disposition, and whether there are any that should go to the Asiatic Society; and generally to advise the Government in regard to the manner in which the operations of the Burmese excavators should be controlled."

In compliance with the wishes of His Honor the Lieutenant-Governor of Bengal, I visited Buddha Gayá in the autumn of 1877, and in the course of my inquiries collected much information and many drawings, maps, and plans, which could not be conveniently embodied in the report I submitted to the Government on the results of my researches. These have since been utilised in the following pages.

The temple of Buddha Gayá attracted the attention of antiquarians from a very early period in the history of British rule in India, and many notices had been published long before I visited it last, but no attempt had been made to compile a complete record of its archæology.

One of the earliest papers published by the Asiatic Society of Bengal was a translation of an inscription found at Buddha Gayá. Its author was Sir Charles Wilkins; but it appeared without any note or comment, and no information was given in it of the holy spot.

Dr. Buchanan-Hamilton came to the place in 1809, but the results of his inquiries were not published until 1830; and the paper he then contributed to the 'Transactions of the Royal Asiatic Society of Great Britain and Ireland' (Volume II) was devoted principally to the legendary information he had collected from the mahants of the local monastery. A summary of this paper subsequently appeared in the first volume of Martin's 'Eastern India,' along with a few illustrations, but with no addition to the descriptive matter.

In 1832 Mr. Hawthorne, then Judge of Gayá, forwarded to James Prinsep copies of some inscriptions found in and about Buddha Gayá. These were published in the first volume of the 'Journal of the Asiatic Society of Bengal,' but without any detailed description of the temple. About the same time Colonel Burney sent to him a revised translation of one of the inscriptions, and it appeared in the last volume of the 'Asiatic Researches.'

The late Major Markham Kittoe was appointed Archæological Surveyor to the Government of India in 1846, and the first field to which he directed his attention was the district of Gayá. He saw most of the places of antiquarian interest in the district, and collected a large number of drawings, inscriptions, and sculptures; but his premature death prevented him from digesting them into a presentible report. The only paper he communicated to the Asiatic Society of Bengal on the antiquities of Buddha Gayá was confined to the character of the sculptures he had seen there. On his death his papers were dispersed, and no use could be made of them. Of the sculptures he had collected, some were sent to the India House Museum, and the rest made over to the Museum of the Asiatic Society of Bengal.

General Cunningham visited Buddha Gayá in 1861, and the notes of his researches were first published in the 'Journal of the Asiatic Society of Bengal' (Vol. XXXIII), and subsequently embodied, along with a number of valuable illustrations, in the first volume of the Reports of the Archæological Survey of India. Immediately after his visit he recommended that measures should be adopted to carry on excavations round the temple, to trace the sites of the different edifices which at one time surrounded it, and to bring to light such objects of antiquarian value as may be found buried there. The work of excavation was undertaken by Major Mead, but no report of his operations was ever published.

While Major Mead was carrying on the excavations, I was invited by him to go and see the antiquities he had brought to light. Unwilling to anticipate in any way the report which that gentleman then intended to submit to Government, and which, I understood, was to comprehend a complete description of the village, I obtained his permission to notice only some radiating arches which I saw there, and which I supposed would be particularly interesting to the Asiatic Society of Bengal. My note on the arches appeared in 1864, and remarks on those arches by the late Mr. C. H. Horne, then Judge of Benares, Mr. Peppe of the Opium Department, and Mr. James Fergusson, appeared in the following years. The last named gentleman had before that also published a brief account of the temple in his 'History of Architecture.' He has since published an amended note about it in his 'History of Indian and Eastern Architecture.'

General Cunningham visited the place for the second time in 1871, and published a comprehensive essay on its antiquities in the third volume of his Archæological Survey Reports. His two notices, as the works of a distinguished scholar who has devoted well nigh half a century to the study of Indian antiquities and is unrivalled in his thorough familiarity with the subject, are worthy of the highest praise. They embrace almost every topic of interest, and throw a large mass of light on a subject which was till then but little known. They have not, however, set aside the necessity for further research, and hence the present undertaking.

Coming to the field after so many distinguished inquirers, I could only hope to glean where they had reaped the harvest. In the following pages I have, therefore, attempted to follow their footsteps, to elucidate questions left doubtful by them, to elaborate where they are brief, to fill up lacunæ, and to summarise all that is worth knowing of a locality which occupies a most important position in the religious history of India. My task has, therefore, been more of a summarist and compiler than that of an original inquirer, and I feel myself under great obligation to my predecessors for the assistance I have derived from their researches. If in the discharge of my self-imposed task it has become necessary for me occasionally to question the correctness of their opinions, my object has been to serve the cause of truth, and not to find fault with them. As pioneers traversing a new and untrodden path, they had grave difficulties to overcome, and mistakes and misconceptions were under the circumstances unavoidable; but the tact and talent they brought to bear upon their work proved eminently successful. Every credit is, therefore, due to them for the services they have rendered to the study of Indian Archæology, and I feel bound to record the expression of my sense of respect and admiration for their zealous and arduous labours.

CONTENTS.

CHAPTER I.

BUDDHA GAYÁ.

CHAPTER II.

THE PENANCE OF BUDDHA.

CHAPTER III.

ARCHITECTURAL REMAINS.

CHAPTER IV.

SCULPTURES.

CHAPTER IV—concluded.

SCULPTURES—*concluded.*

CHAPTER V.

INSCRIPTIONS.

CHAPTER VI.

CHRONOLOGY.

ILLUSTRATIONS.

PLATE.

PLATE.

WOODCUTS.

ERRATA.

Page 114, line 4, *for* spine *read* spire.
" 119 " 12, " Rama " Dasaratha.
" 131 " 13, " sculptures " sculptors.
" 131 " 14, " is " are.
" 133 " 1, " this " the wheel.
" 133 " 22, " square " straight.
" 154, lines 23 & 25, " XLV " XLIV.
" 168, line 6, " three years " the year.

Page 190, line 23, *for* him *read* them.
" 191 " 4, " stones " stone.
" 191 " 9, *omit* the plate reference.
" 201 " 15, *for* [illegible] *read* [illegible]
" 206, marginal note, *for* No. 13 *read* No. 14.
" 207, line 23 " have " has.

THE HERMITAGE OF ŚÁKYA MUNI.

CHAPTER I.

BUDDHA GAYÁ.

BUDDHA GAYÁ—ITS SITUATION—BOUNDARY—RIVER—EXTENT—PRESENT CONDITION—POPULATION—HOUSES—PRINCIPAL BUILDINGS—MONASTERY—CEMETERY—MONKS—PUBLIC OFFICES—PRESENT OWNERS AND THEIR HISTORY—PRESENT REVENUE—ANCIENT NAME—STORY OF GAYÁSURA—MODERN NAME, HOW DERIVED AND WHEN USED.

The four most sacred places noticed in the annals of Buddhism are Kapilavastu, the birth-place of Buddha; Buddha Gayá, his hermitage; Benares, where he first promulgated his doctrine; and Kusi, the place of his *nirváṇa*—the *summum bonum*, to the attainment of which he had devoted his long and arduous life. Of these, the first and the last, which too prominently set forth his human failings, were perhaps not quite so much respected as the other two; but they were, nevertheless, all places of great sanctity, and for full fifteen hundred years were held, in the estimation of his followers, as the holiest places of pilgrimage on earth. With the expulsion of Buddhism from India three of them have fallen into oblivion, and one has been appropriated to Hindu worship. It is the object of the following pages to supply an account of one of them,—that which is most intimately associated with the sanctification of the great reformer.

Buddha Gayá is now a large thriving village, bounded on the north by Hariharpur; on the west by Mastipur, Dhoṇḍowá, Bhuluá, and Turí; on the south by Rámpur; and on the east by the river Liláján. Lat. 24° 41′ 45″ N., long. 85° 2′ 4″ E. It is accessible from Gayá by two roads: one, the old trunk road from Calcutta to Gayá, and the other, the new road to Sherghâṭi. The distance by the former is just five miles, over an unmetalled road much out of repair; and by the latter, seven miles, and then two miles across paddy-fields to reach the inhabited portion of the village on the east side.

The river Liláján, which runs along the eastern boundary of the place, is about half a mile broad. During heavy rains the whole of this surface is covered by water for a few days, but for the rest of the year it remains a dry bed of sand with a silver streamlet, scarcely 80 yards in breadth, on the off side.. Its name is a corruption of the old Sanskrit *Nairanjaná*, or 'the immaculate.' About a mile below Buddha Gayá, near the Morá Hill, it comes in contact with the Mohaná, and the united stream assumes the name of Phalgu. Its character, however, remains very much the same throughout its whole length.

In the revenue records of Government Buddha Gayá is reckoned under two names,—Buddha Gayá proper and Mastipur Táráḍí, which last is also known by the name of Táráḍí Buzurg. The former comprises an area of 2,152 acres 3 roods and 37 poles, and the latter 647 acres 2 roods and 18 poles, making a total of 2,800 acres 2 roods and 15 poles. The name of Táráḍí has evidently originated from the circumstance of the area around a mediæval temple of Tárá Deví having been dedicated to her worship. The area of the two villages is one fertile plain, studded with tanks, fringed on the river-side by large and umbrageous mango topes, and broken here and there by one large and several small mounds, parts of which are covered by human habitations. The boundary line between the two villages is marked by a village road, which runs from the south of the big mound to the hamlet of Kohlurá (*see* Plate I).

The mounds are mostly on the east side, the largest being on the middle of that side. They mark the sites of ancient buildings, which have long since crumbled to dust. The largest mound covers an area of 1,500 × 1,400 feet, and is divided into two unequal parts by the village road aforesaid. The southern portion is about one-third the size of the northern one; but it is the most important from an antiquarian point of view, as in the centre of it stands the most ancient monument in the village. This monument I shall in this work name the Great Temple. The northern portion, according to General Cunningham, (a) measures 1,500 × 1,000 feet. At the beginning of this century, when Buchanan Hamilton visited the place, it was called the *Rájasthán*, or 'palace,' and there were, "on the east, north, and west

(a) 'Archæological Survey Report,' Vol. I., p. 11.

faces, traces of a ditch; and on the west and south, remains of an outer wall or rampart, with the appearance of there having been a ditch between it and the palace; but by far the greater part of the building seems to have been a large castle or palace, which probably contained many small courts, although these have been entirely obliterated by the expiration of time."(a) Except where there were traces of a double wall and ditch, the whole was then a uniform terrace, consisting chiefly, as is said, of bricks, but covered with soil. The remains of the outer ditch are still visible, and foundations of walls and houses, and the debris of ancient dwellings, abound every where under the soil; but the popular name in the present day for the place is *Garh*, or 'fortress,' and not *Rájasthán*, or 'palace.' As will be shown hereafter, it was originally the site of a large monastery, but might have been afterwards converted into a fort. Its height varies from 10 to 15 feet above the level of the surrounding country.

According to the Census papers of 1872, the two villages together comprise 497 houses and a population of 3,050 persons, of whom 1,582 are males and 1,468 females. The people are mostly Hindus, only 392 being Muhammadans. Most of the houses are tiled huts with mud walls, such as are common all over the district; but a few are of masonry, including a dozen temples and several sepulchral monuments.

Next to the Great Temple, which will be noticed further on, the largest building in the village is a monastery, or maṭh. It is situated on the left bank of the Liláján, in the midst of a garden extending over an area of about 20 acres, and surrounded by a high masonry wall. It is four-storeyed in some parts, but three-storeyed all round a small quadrangle. The ground floor round the quadrangle is faced by a one-storeyed verandah built on sculptured monolythic pillars on three sides, and on wooden pillars on the fourth side. The roofs are low, and the windows very small and few in number; but the building is very substantial, and in excellent repair. To the north of this there are three two-storeyed buildings of moderate size, and long ranges of out-offices and stables in front on the east. On the south there is a commodious three-storeyed building, called *Báradwári*, with a terrace in front of it. There are also four temples, one of which contains only a marble slab, originally designed for a chiffonier, but now bearing an inscription partly in Sanskrit and

(a) 'Transactions, Royal Asiatic Society,' Vol. II., p. 45.

partly in Burmese: a second contains some Buddhist statues. Outside this monastery, towards the west, on a part of the large mound aforesaid, there is a two-storeyed building of good make and size (*see* Plate XIV). It belongs to the monastery, and around it are four Hindu temples, one of which is dedicated to Jagannátha, one to Ráma, built by Gangá Bäi, who died at the beginning of this century, and the rest to Śiva. The positions of the several temples in Buddha Gayá are shown on the annexed map of the place (*see* Plate I).

Towards the south-west corner of the outer wall of the monastery there is a cemetery, also attached to the monastery. The dead bodies of the monks, unlike those of other Hindus, are buried, and the cemetery contains the graves of about two hundred persons. The body is buried in a sitting posture; and in the case of mere neophytes a small circular mound of solid brickwork from three to four feet high is all that is deemed necessary for a covering for the grave. For men of greater consequence a temple is held essential; and in it, immediately over the corpse, a lingam is invariably consecrated. For Mahants the temple is large and elaborately ornamented. It would seem that even for neophytes a lingam was held essential; but in the majority of cases its place was supplied by a miniature votive stupa picked up from the Buddhist ruins in the neighbourhood. Half-buried on the top of the mound, it passes very well for a lingam. In the way from Gayá to Buddha Gayá there are several monasteries of Hindu Sannyásis, and everywhere the graves are alike.

The place enjoys the benefits of a police outpost, a post-office, and a vernacular school, as also an alms-house, attached to the monastery, where rice and pulse are daily doled out to three hundred to five hundred persons, mostly poor pilgrims from Gayá. There are also a sufficient number of shops for the supply of the necessaries of life to the people, and one among them struck me as remarkable for such an out-of-the-way place: it was that of a book-binder.

The two villages now belong to the monastery described above, and are owned by the head Mahant. It is said that the monastery was first established here in the early part of the last century. According to a memorandum supplied me by the present head of the establishment, one Dhamandináth, a mendicant of the order of Giri,(a) one of the ten orders of the followers of Śankara Ácháryya's Śivite

(a) *Vide passim* 'Wilson's Essays on Hindu Sects,' Vol. I, p. 202.

School, first took up his abode in the village of Buddha Gayá, and built a small monastery for the accommodation of the itinerant members of his order. He was followed by his disciple Chaitanya Giri, whose remains were buried within the enclosure of the great Buddhist temple, and a small temple built thereupon. The Buddhist temple at the time had no priest, nor any worshipper; and such an appropriation of it by a saintly hermit in a small village during the Muhammadan rule was an act which none would question. Chaitanya was followed by his disciple Mahádevelva, who was renowned for his learning and austerity. He worshipped Mahádevi for several years in front of the Buddhist temple, and through her special favours was enabled to build the present large monastery of his order. It is said he obtained from the emperor Shah Alum a *firmán* to hold the Buddhist temple in his possession, and to be recognized as the chief Mahant of the place. He was followed by his disciple Lála Giri. He was noted for his beneficence, and to him is due the credit of establishing the alms-house. His successor was Rághava Giri, the only especial epithet in whose favour, in the memorandum before me, records his personal beauty. His successor, Rainahita, is described to have added to the accommodation of the monastery. He died at Kásí, leaving three disciples, of whom the first two died early, and the youngest was Śiva Giri, whose successor is the present Mahant, Hemanátha Giri. This account does not agree with the entries made in General Cunningham's plan of the Great Temple, attached to his first report. There Mahádeva is described as the first Mahant, and the second, Chaitanya, occurs under the name of Chait Mull. The Mahant living at the time of Dr. Buchanan Hamilton's visit informed that gentleman that "Chaitan" was the first who came to the place, at a time when it was overrun by bushes and trees, and the sect of Buddha in its neighbourhood was entirely extinct.(a) I also find, from an extract furnished me from the Gayá Collectorate, that there was a Mahant of the name of Golá*p* Giri; but his name does not appear in my list. It is probable, however, that Goláp was an *alias* of Śiva Giri, who obtained a *mukarrari* lease from Government of the village of Mastipur Táráḍí.

The Mahants are pledged to lifelong celibacy, and according to the rule of their order the most pious and learned among their disciples (of whom there are always from thirty to fifty) is expected to succeed; but as a matter of fact I have elsewhere

(a) 'Transactions, Royal Asiatic Society,' Vol. II, p. 40.

seen that only the youngest, and he who bears the strongest personal resemblance to the abbot, generally succeeds to the high rank. The monks lead an easy, comfortable life; feasting on rich cakes (*málpuyá*) and puddings (*mohanbhog*), and freely indulging in the exhilirating beverage of *bhánga*. Few attempt to learn the sacred books of their religion, and most of them are grossly ignorant. The present Mahant is an intelligent man, but not particularly well versed in the Śástras. He has, however, a fine collection of Sanskrit manuscripts, and employs the more intelligent among his disciples to copy manuscripts for him. Some of the books of their faith are, however, occasionally expounded to the monks by one of their seniors, rarely by the Mahant himself.

The present revenue of the village of Buddha Gayá is Rs. 3,308, and of Mastipur Tárádí Rs. 344; the road-cess on the two villages being Rs. 57. For so extensive an area as 2,800 acres the revenue fixed is light, and it leaves a large net profit to the monastery. The Mahant has also other lands, and a steady income from the offerings made by Hindu pilgrims to the sacred pipal-tree in the enclosure of the Great Temple. Altogether his annual income is reckoned at upwards of Rs. 80,000. The number of Sannyásis who live on this income varies from fifty to a hundred daily, and the alms-house and the vernacular school are also supported by it.

In an apochryphal inscription of the tenth century, published by Wilkins(*a*), Buddha Gayá is described to have been "a wild and dreadful forest," where Vishṇu, in the form of Buddha, first made his appearance; and Spence Hardy, on the authority of Singhalese records, calls it "the forest of *Uriwela*."(*b*) The *Mahávanso* does not, however, call it a forest, but simply Uruwelaya, in the kingdom of Magadha.(*c*) Commenting on these passages, General Cunningham observes:—"But from other authorities we learn that *Uruvilwa* was the name of one of the three Káśyapa brothers who resided at Buddha Gayá, and who were there converted by Buddha."(*d*) This would suggest, though it is not said in so many words, that the village owes its name to one of the Káśyapas. This, however, does not appear to have been the case. The village could not have received the name from one of the disciples when Buddha selected it for his hermitage, before attaining the rank of a

(*a*) 'Asiatic Researches,' Vol. I, p. 284. The character of this inscription will be discussed at length further on.
(*b*) 'Eastern Monachism,' pp. 3, 213; 'Legends and Theories of the Buddhists,' p. xli.
(*c*) Turnour's 'Mahavanso,' p. 2.
(*d*) 'Archæological Survey Report,' I, p. 50.

saint. That the name of the place was Uruvilvá when Śákya retired to it is certain from the Gáthá portion of the 'Lalita Vistara,' where it is named; and as that portion of the work was composed immediately after the reformer's death, (a) it is impossible to suppose that any mistake was then made about the name of a place which was so intimately connected with his life. The Gáthás describe the place as the "old Uruvilvá (*Práchina Uruvilvá*), with its charming woods, herbs, and creepers, on the banks of the Nairanjaná," (b) and elsewhere add that when the saint was engaged in his profound meditation "the village girls, cowherds, wood-cutters, and grass-cutters, would take him to be a hobgoblin fond of filth, and cast dust on him." (c) The prose portion of the work goes further, and describes the place as a village belonging to a military commander. It says:—"Thus, when Bodhisattva had sojourned, according to his choice, on the Gayaśirsha Hill, he proceeded, walking all the way, to the village of Uruvilvá, belonging to a general (Senápati), and arrived thereat. There he beheld the river Nairanjaná, with its clear water, with a holy spot on its bank, and the village decorated with masonry houses, trees, herbs, and pastures. There the mind of the Bodhisattva was greatly delighted, and he said:—'Friends, verily this is a charming place, well worthy of myself and of the respectable youths who wish for salvation: let us abide here.'" (d)

These extracts clearly show that the place was not a "wild, dreadful forest," nor a forest of any other kind, but a quiet, retired village, with its woods, groves, and pastures, such as are now to be seen in many parts of India, and which two thousand and four hundred years ago must have been common everywhere. Hermits generally select such retired places for their abode, but rarely "dreadful forests," altogether away from human habitations. Anyhow this much may be accepted as certain, that the ancient name of the place of Buddha's

---

(a) *Vide* my edition of the 'Lalita Vistara,' Introduction, p. 47.

(b) [illegible] ।

—'Lalita Vistara,' p. 327.

(c) [illegible] ।

—'Lalita Vistara,' p. 325.

(d) इति हि भिक्षवो बोधिसत्त्वो [illegible] ।

—'Lalita Vistara,' p. 311.

hermitage was Uruvilvá, and not Buddha Gayá, for it could not have taken the epithet 'Buddha' before a Buddha had come into existence; nor Gayá, for that name belonged to a town in its close neighbourhood. It was held in fief by a Senápati, or Commander in the service, most probably, of the potentate who ruled at Gayá, which was then the capital of a kingdom called Kíṭaka.(a)

Now for the meaning of the name. In the Thibetan version of the *Lalita Vistara* it has been given in words which the accomplished French translator of that work renders into *abondant en étangs*.(b) In Sanskrit, however, neither *uru* nor *vilvá* can be in any way made to stand for a tank. Turnour, in the *Maháwanso*, derives it from *uru* 'sand,' and *weláya* 'waves' or 'mounds;'(c) but both the words are of Sanskrit origin, and in that language they have no such meanings; nor are there such mounds of sand at Buddha Gayá, except in the bed of the river, as would justify the designation. According to the *Abhidána Appadípiká*, quoted by Childers, *uru*, in the feminine gender, means 'sand;' *velá*, both in Páli and Sanskrit, means the 'seashore' or 'boundary;' and the two together may mean the village bounded by a sandy bank. But all the places on the Phalgu and the Liláján being in the same predicament, the name would not be at all distinctive. In Sanskrit *uru* does not mean 'sand,' but *uras* means 'big,' 'high,' 'large,' 'broad,' 'extensive'; and *vilvá* 'a fruit,' the *Ægle marmelos*, or *bel* fruit: and the two together can only imply a species of large *bel*. I am, however, aware of no such species, unless the epithet be made to qualify the tree, and not its fruit. The kathbel-tree (*Feronia elepantum*, Codr.) grows to about twice the size of the ordinary bel-tree, and may well be indicated by such a name. The tree is common all over the district, and I noticed several large specimens of it at Buddha Gayá. It must, however, be added that no Sanskrit dictionary, either general or botanical, gives the word as the name of that tree. If we could change the second word to *villa*, it might stand for a hole or pond, and thence a tank, as in the Thibetan version; but in the six manuscripts of the Lalita Vistara which I have before me the second word is written *vilvá*, and the *Maháwanso* supports this reading. I can, therefore, attribute the Thibetan version to a misreading of, or an error in, the text from which it was rendered. Of the three Káśyapa brothers, the eldest was named

(a) Kíṭaka is now accepted as a synonym for Magadha; but it was evidently the name of the southern portion of it. Its area, given in the *Déśávali*, a mediæval work, would barely cover the district of Gayá.

(b) 'R-gya-Tcher-rol-pa,' p. 238.

(c) 'Maháwanso,' Index, p. 27.

Gayá Káśyapa, or Káśyapa the mountaineer, from Gayá, the name of the most prominent hill in the district; the second was named Nadi, or Sarit, Káśyapa, or Káśyapa of the river, meaning the Nairanjaná or the Phalgu; and the third, Uruvilvá Káśyapa, or the Káśyapa of the wood: all three deriving their names from prominent places in the locality, and not giving their names to them.

The word 'Buddha Gayá' does not occur in such of the Buddhist manuscripts collected by Mr. Hodgson in Nepal as I have seen; nor is it to be met with in any Hindu work. It is obviously, therefore, a modern name, given by the Hindus to distinguish it from their own sacred place in its neighbourhood, and at a time when the old name had become obsolete. It is, however, mentioned in Mr. Wilkins' inscription; and if the authenticity of that record could be established, the name would be at least eight hundred years old. I feel, however, pretty certain that it is a forgery, and the name much more recent. General Cunningham says "the name is usually written Buddha Gayá; but as it is commonly pronounced Bodh-Gayá, I have little doubt that it was originally called Bodhi-Gayá, after the celebrated Bodhidrum, or 'Tree of Knowledge.'" This conjecture, however, is not acceptable, as the name was used to distinguish the place from Brahma Gayá, or Gayá proper, and not to denote any of its peculiar features. The *Ain-i-Akbary* is silent on the subject: it only says—"Gayá, the place of Hindu worship, is in this sircar. They call it Brahma Gayá, being consecrated to Brahma." (a)

To explain the manner in which that name came into vogue, it would be necessary to advert to the history of Gayá, with which it is connected. It is evident from the Lalita Vistara that Gayá, as a town, existed at so early a date as the youth of Śákya Siñha, at least two thousand and four hundred years ago. It was to that place he first went on his way to the south-west from Rájagriha, the capital of Magadha at the time; and it was then that he first conceived the idea of devoting himself to the particular form of meditation which would secure to mankind the highest blessing. He was invited to the place by certain householders, who received him with cordial welcome. (b) It was, besides, one of the first places which received the doctrine of the reformer, and became the head-quarters of the faith. But it did not long retain that pre-eminence, for at the beginning of the fifth century it

(a) 'Gladwin's Translation,' Vol. II, p. 25.
(b) 'Lalita Vistara,' p. 309.

had altogether lost its Buddhist character; and when Fa Hian came to it in 404 "all within this city was desolate and desert." In the middle of the seventh century, when Hiouen Thsang visited it, it had relapsed into Hinduism, and the Gowáls were fully in the ascendant. Buddhist records do not show when this relapse took place, and in the Hindu writings we have only a wild story to describe it. This story occurs in the *Gayá Máhátmya* section of the Váyu Puráṇa. (*a*) It affords a striking illustration of the manner in which Buddhism passed into Hinduism, and I shall quote it entire, as that will better explain the circumstances of the case than the abstract of it given in Martin's 'Eastern India.'(*b*) It runs thus:—

"The Great Father of the universe, Brahmá, born in the lotus-navel of Vishṇu, created all living beings by order of Vishṇu. From his fierce nature that Lord brought forth the Asuras, and from his humane disposition he produced the noble-minded Devas.

"Among the Asuras, Gayá was endowed with great strength and vigour. In height he measured 125 *yojanas*, and in girth 60 *yojanas*. He was distinguished as a devout Vaishṇava. With his breath held back, he practised the most rigorous austerities for many thousand years on the noble hill of Kolâhala. The Devas were oppressed by his austerities, and dreaded serious misfortune. They repaired to the region of Brahmá, and there prayed to the first Father of Creation:—'Pray, protect us from the demon Gayá.'

"Brahmá said:—'Let us proceed to Śankara for help.'

"Preceded by Brahmá, they all went to Śiva, on the Kailáśa Mountain, and, saluting him, said:—'O Lord, protect us from the great demon.'

"Sambhu said:—'Let us seek the help of Hari, the great God, sleeping on the milky ocean; he will design some means of relief for us.'

"Brahmá, Maheśvara, and the Devas, satisfied Vishṇu by the following hymn:—

"'Our salutation to Vishṇu, to the Lord of all, the Creator of all, and the Sustainer of all; salutation to the Destroyer of all and the Extinguisher of all; to the Sustainer and the Supporter; to the Destroyer of Rákshasas and other evil spirits; to him who promotes the prosperity of the creation and is the redeemer

(*a*) The 'Agni Puráṇa' gives an account of Gayá, but not the story.

(*b*) 'Eastern India,' Vol. I, pp. 51f.

of Yogis.' Thus praised, Vishṇu became manifest to the Devas, and inquired—'Why have you all come here?'

"They prayed:—'Save us, O Lord, from the demon Gayá.'

"Hari said:—'Do you, Brahmá and others, proceed to the Asura, and I shall follow you.'

"Keśava, mounted on his *Garuḍa*, and the others, each on his exquisite vehicle, repaired to bless the demon. They addressed the demon, saying:—'Why are you continuing your austerities? Well satisfied with your devotion, we are come to grant you any favour that you may desire. Say, Gayásura, what do you wish.'

"Gayásura said:—'If you are really satisfied with me, render my body purer even than that of Brahmá, Vishṇu, or Maheśvara; purer even than all the Devas and Bráhmans; purer than all sacrifices and sacred pools and high mountains; purer even than the purest of gods.'

"'Even so be it,' responded the gods, and repaired to heaven.

"[The result of this blessing was that] mortals who beheld or touched the demon at once ascended to the region of Brahmá. The thirty-three regions [of the universe] became empty, and the domains of Yama were deprived of their inhabitants. Thus deprived of their subjects by Gayásura, Yama, along with Indra and the other gods, repaired to Brahmá and addressed him, saying:—'O Father of Creation, take back the offices that you had bestowed on us [for we can no longer hold them].'

"Brahmá replied:—'Let us repair to Vishṇu, the undecaying.'

"To Vishṇu they thus addressed:—'Lord, by the sight of the demon whom you have blessed all mortals are being translated to heaven, and the three regions have become empty.'

"Vishṇu, thus implored by the gods, said to them:—'Do you go and ask the demon to give you his body, so that you may perform a sacrifice (*yajña*) thereon, and you will be able to overcome your difficulties.'

"The gods accordingly went to Gayá, the demon, who, beholding before him Brahmá with his companions (*lit.* 'three times ten,' meaning the other gods), rose from his seat, saluted them with reverence, and, having welcomed them in due form, said:—'Blessed is my life this day; blessed is my penance: verily I have attained all my objects, since Brahmá has become my guest. Say, wherefore are you come, and I shall at once execute the task for you.'

"Brahmá said:—'Of all the sacred pools that have been seen by me in my rambles, there is none that is, for sacrificial purposes, purer than thy body, which has attained its purity through the blessing of Vishṇu. Do you, therefore, O Asura. present me thy holy body for the performance of a sacrifice?'

"Gayá, the demon, said:—'Blessed am I, O god of gods, since thou askest me for my body: my paternal ancestors will be sanctified shouldst thou perform a sacrifice on my body. By thee was this body created, and well it is that it should be of use to thee: it will then be truly of use to all.'

"Having said this, Gayá, the demon, leaning towards the south-west, fell prostrate on the ground on the Koláhala Hill; his head lay on the north side, and his feet extended towards the south. Brahmá then collected the necessary articles for the sacrifice, and, having created from his mind the officiating priests (Ritvijas), duly performed a sacrifice on the body of the demon. Having bathed and offered the concluding *avabhritha* oblation to the fire, he gave adequate fees to the priests. On the completion of the sacrifice, he, with his divine companions were, however, surprised to find that the demon was still moving on the sacrificial ground. He thereupon said to Yama:—'Do you go and quickly fetch from your house the stone of religion [Dharmaśilá](a) that is lying there, and place it on the head of the demon by my order.' Yama, hearing this, immediately placed the stone on the demon's head to keep it immovable; but even after the stone was so placed the demon moved along with the stone. Then Brahmá ordered Rudra and the other gods to sit upon the stone to keep it fixed; and they did as they were directed. But even after being pressed down with the feet of the gods the demon still moved. Greatly distressed, Brahmá then ran to Vishṇu asleep on the ocean of milk, and, saluting that Lord of the three regions, thus addressed him:—'O Lord, great master of the universe, and ruler of creation, thou master of virtuous beings and giver of blessings and salvation, I salute thee.'

"Vishvaksena said to Vishṇu:—'Lord, the lotus-born (Brahmá) is saluting you.'

"Vishṇu said:—'Go and bring him here.'

"Vishvaksena did as he was ordered. Vishṇu said to Brahmá:—'Say, wherefore are you come.'

(a) The stone is described as the fossilised body of a pious woman who had offended her irate husband by giving up shampooing his feet in order to welcome Brahmá, who came to her house.

"Brahmá replied:—'Lord of Lords, on the completion of the sacrifice Gayásura began to move, and thereupon we placed the sacred stone (Dharmaśilá) on his head, and Rudra and the other gods sat upon it, but still the demon moves. Now help us, O destroyer of Madhu, to make him immovable.'

"On hearing the words of Brahmá the Lord Hari drew forth from his person a fierce form, and gave it to Brahmá, in order to help him to make the demon motionless. Bringing that form, Brahmá placed it on the stone, but it nevertheless moved; so he again sought the aid of Vishṇu. Vishṇu thereupon came from the milky ocean, and, under the form of the wielder of the mace, (Gadádhara,) sat upon the stone to prevent its moving. Moreover he, in the five forms of Prapitámaha (the great grandfather), or the first; Pitámaha (grandfather); Phalgvíśa (the Lord of Phalgu); Kedára, and Kaṇakeśvara, rested thereon. Brahmá, too, sat there; so did the elephantine Vináyaka (Gaṇeśa). The sun, in his threefold form of the sun of Gayá, the northern sun, and the southern sun; Lakshmí, under the name of Sítá; Gaurí, under the name of Mangalá; Gáyatrí, Sávitrí, Trisandhyá, and Sarasvatí, likewise sat there. And, since before sitting down, by plying his mace, Hari rendered the demon motionless, he is therefore called the first or sovereign wielder of the mace (*ádigadádhara*).

"Gayásura said to the gods:—'Why should you, after I have given my sinless body to Brahmá, treat me thus? Would I not have become motionless at the request of Hari? Why, then, should he thus torture me with his mace, and the gods should join him? And now since you all have so cruelly treated me, do you show your mercy to me.'

"The gods were delighted and said:—'We are fully satisfied with you. Do you ask a blessing from us.'

"Gayá prayed:—'As long as the earth and the mountains, as long as the moon and the stars, shall last, so long may you, Brahmá, Vishnu, and Maheśvara, rest on this stone. May you, the Devas, rest on it too, and call this place after me the sacred Kshetra of Gayá, extending over five *kro'a*, of which one *kro'a* would be covered by my head. Therein should abide, for the good of mankind, all the sacred pools on earth, where persons, by bathing and offering of oblations of water and funeral cakes, may attain high merit for themselves, and translate their ancestors, blessed with all that is desirable and salvation, to the region of Brahmá. As long as Vishṇu in his triple form shall be adored by the learned, so long should this be renowned on earth as the sacred place of Gayásura, and resort to it should rinse men of even the sin of killing Bráhmans.'

"Hearing this prayer of Gayá, the Devas, headed by Vishṇu, replied:—'Whatever thou prayest, that shall for certain be accomplished. By offering the *pinḍa* and performing *śráddha* here, persons will translate their ancestors for a hundred generations, as also their own selves, to the Brahmaloka, where exists no disease. By worshipping our feet, they will attain the highest reward in after life.'" (*a*)

The Hindus believe this story to be literally true, but Dr. Buchanan Hamilton calls it "a monstrous legend;" and well he may. At first sight nothing can appear more absurd and stupid than this story: it offends every sense of propriety, and has not even the merit of ingenuity in its narration. The Brahmayoni Hill, which

---

(*a*) विष्णोर्नाभ्यम्बुजाज्जातो ब्रह्मा लोकपितामहः । प्रजाः ससर्ज संप्रोक्तः पूर्वं देवेन विष्णुना ॥
आसुरेण तु भावेन असुरानसृजत् प्रभुः । सौम्यकेन भावेन देवानसृजदथोऽपुनः ॥
गयासुरोऽसुरस्तत्र महाबलपराक्रमः । योजनानां सपादञ्च शतं तस्योच्छ्रयः स्मृतः । स्थूलः षष्टियोजनानां येनोऽसौ वैष्णवः स्मृतः ॥
कोलाहले गिरिवरे तपस्तेपे सुदारुणं । बहुवर्षसहस्राणि निरुच्छ्वासं स्थितोऽभवत् ॥
तत्तपस्तापिता देवाः संक्षोभं परमं ययुः । ब्रह्मलोकं गता देवा अब्रुवंश्च पितामहं ॥
गयासुराच्च देव ब्रह्मा देवांश्चैतोऽब्रवीत् । ब्रह्माद्याः शङ्करं देवा ब्रह्माद्याश्च गताः शिवं ।
कैलासे चाब्रुवन्सर्वे रक्ष देव गयासुरात् ॥
ब्रह्मादीनब्रवीच्छम्भुर्गच्छामः शरणं हरिं । क्षीराब्धौ देवदेवेशः स नः श्रेयो विधास्यति । ब्रह्मा महेश्वरो देवा विष्णुं गत्वा तु तुष्टुवुः ॥
॥ देवा ऊचुः ॥ ओंनमो विष्णवे भर्त्रे सर्वेषां प्रभविष्णवे । रोचिष्णवे सुमनसाम् नमो भ्राजिष्णवे नमः ।
सहिष्णवे जिष्णवे च रावणादिमहिष्णवे । वर्धिष्णवेऽक्षिप्रसाक्ष योगिनां चारयिष्णवे ॥
सनत्कुमार उवाच ॥ एवं स्तुतो वासुदेवः सुराणां दर्शनं ययौ । किमर्थमागता यूयं देवैर्ब्रह्मादिकमब्रुवन् ।
गयासुरभयादेव रक्षास्मानब्रवीद्धरिः । ब्रह्माद्या यान्तु तं दैत्यमागमिष्याम्यहं ततः ॥
आयान्तो गरुडारूढो वरं दातुं गयासुरं । सर्वैः सह समायाता अपृच्छत्कथमुच्यतां ॥
ऊचुर्वा वासुदेवाद्याः किमर्थं तप्यते तपः ॥ प्रसन्नाः सगणाः सर्वे वरं ब्रूहि गयासुर ॥

गयासुर उवाच ॥

यदि तुष्टाः शरीरं मे ब्रह्मविष्णुमहेश्वरात् । सर्वदेवद्विजातिभ्यो पवित्रं विष्णुलोकयात् । देवेभ्योऽपि पवित्रोऽहं पवित्रतमकस्तु च ॥

सनत्कुमार उवाच ॥

पवित्रमस्तु तं देवा दैत्यमुक्त्वा दिवं ययुः । दैत्यं दृष्ट्वा च स्पृष्ट्वा च नराः ब्रह्म परं ययुः ॥
शून्यं लोकत्रयं जातं शून्या यमपुरी ह्यभूत् । यम इन्द्रादिभिः साधं ब्रह्मलोकं ततोऽगमत् ॥
ब्रह्माणमूचिरे देवा गयासुरविलोपिताः । ब्रह्मा दत्तोऽधिकारो वै गृहाण त्वं पितामह ॥
ब्रह्माऽब्रवीत्ततो देवान् ब्रजामो विष्णुसन्निधौ । ब्रह्मादयोऽस्तुवन्विष्णुं यथा दत्तवरोऽसुरः ॥
यद्दर्शनात्सुराः सर्वे शून्यं लोकत्रयं ह्यभूत् । देवैरुक्तो वासुदेवो ब्रह्माणमिदमब्रवीत् ॥
गयासुरं प्रार्थय त्वं यज्ञार्थं देहि देहकम् । विष्णूक्तः स सुरो ब्रह्मा गयासुरमथाब्रवीत् ॥
गयासुरोऽब्रवीद्दृष्ट्वा ब्रह्माणं सिद्धैः सह । संपूज्योवाच विधिवत् प्रणम्य कृताञ्जलिः ॥

is the same with the Koláhala Mountain, is scarcely three miles in length, and the idea of locating on it a being 125 *yojanas*, or 576 miles, in height and 268 miles in girth would never strike the poorest fabler. A head a mile in circumference on a body 576 miles high would bear to each other about the same relation which a pin's head would to the ordinary human body. The helplessness of the gods to keep down a prostrate monster, and their futile attempts to prevent his moving, are as childish as possible. And such being the case, the question suggests itself, How is it that the author of the *Váyu Puráṇa*, of which the *Gayá Máhátmya* professes to be a part, invented so puerile a story for ensuring the respect and devotion of the people at large to this place? He was not wanting in intelligence, for he discusses many abstruse questions of philosophy with considerable tact and ingenuity; he possessed,

---

गयासुर उवाच ।

[illegible] ।

ब्रह्मोवाच ॥

[illegible] ।
[illegible] ॥

गयासुर उवाच ॥

[illegible] ॥
[illegible] ॥

सनत्कुमार उवाच ॥

[illegible] ।
[illegible] ॥
[illegible] ॥
[illegible] ॥

ब्रह्मोवाच ॥

[illegible] ॥

सनत्कुमार उवाच ॥

[illegible] ॥
[illegible] ॥
[illegible] ॥

ब्रह्मोवाच ॥

[illegible] ॥

too, sufficient insight into human character to know what would command ready credence and what would be rejected at first sight as worthless. It would be illogical and untrue to say that he could not distinguish the reasonable from the puerile and absurd. To reject, therefore, the story as absurd would, in my mind, appear hasty, and indicative of idle impatience. It would much more become the philosophic historian to assume that something esoteric is hidden under the garb of an extravagant fable; and that esoteric meaning, I believe, is easily found, if the legend be taken as an allegory of the success of Bráhmanism over Buddhism.

Gayá is called an *Asura*, which ordinarily means a Titan, a demon, a vicious monster, a reviler of gods and religon; but he has not been pourtrayed as such. He revels not in crime, he injures none, and offends neither the gods nor religion by word or deed. On the contrary, he is described as a devout Vaishṇava (*śreshṭhah vaishṇavah*), who devoted himself to rigorous penance, to long protracted meditations, and to the acquirement of the highest purity of body and soul; one whose very touch sufficed to cleanse mankind of the greatest sin, and to translate them to heaven. The most serious charge brought against him was that he made salvation too simple and

---

सनत्कुमार उवाच ॥

विष्णुदेवो यदोविष्णुं देव मां पीडि यज्ञकः । हरिराकाशग यं हं विष्णुः स समाकथत् । समुदाय हरिः गयासुरमसोऽपि वद्धक तत् ॥

ब्रह्मोवाच ॥

देव देव सतो याते ब्रह्माण्ड महासुरः । शिलायां देवरूपिण्यां यथायां तस्य ब्रह्मणे ॥
यज्ञादिषु च देवेषु पं शिलेषु सुरोऽप्यभवत् । इदानीं शिलयायांस्तु प्रसादं कुरु माधव ॥

सनत्कुमार उवाच ॥

ब्रह्मणो वचनं श्रुत्वा धर्मज्ञ स्वशरीरतः । मूर्तिं ददौ शिलायां च अचलां ब्रह्मणे हरिः ॥
धारीत्वा मूर्तिं तथापि शिलायां नामधारणाम् । तथापि चलितं वीक्ष्य पुनर्देवशिलाकृतम् ॥
धारितं विष्णुः शीरान्धेः शिलायां वं स्थितोऽभवत् । अनादिनिधनः स्वेन पुण्डरीकाक्षनामकः । शिलायां विष्णुरावि च स्वयेन महाधरः ॥
शिलायां यथा देवैः शिलायां प्रतिष्ठितः । पितामहोऽपि चतुर्मिः केदारः कनकेश्वरः । ब्रह्मा स्वयं शिलायां स्वस्वरूपे शिलामयः ॥
गयादित्यरूपेणायैः दक्षिणार्कशिला रविः । लक्ष्मीः सीताभिधानेन गौरी च मङ्गलाख्या । गायत्री चैव सावित्री त्रिसन्ध्या च सरस्वती ॥
धात्मा महता धारो गजादित्यः शिरोगतः । शिव इत्येन हरिणा गदाधरो महाधरः ॥
रचे गयासुरो देवान् किमर्थं वञ्चितोऽप्यहम् । यज्ञार्थं ब्रह्मणे दत्तं शरीरममलं मया ॥
विष्णोर्वचनमात्रेण किं न स्यां निश्चलो ह्यहं । स सुरैः पीडितोऽत्यर्थं गदया हरिणा कथं ॥
तीक्ष्णेन मर्द्धं देवाः प्रसन्नाः सन्तु वै यदा । महाधरादयस्तुष्टा ऊचुः वाहि महासुर । वरं वृणु प्रसन्नाः स्मो देवान् प्राह महासुरः ॥

summary. The epithet in his case can, therefore, only mean that he did not profess the faith of the Bráhmans, nor follow their ways: in short, he was a heretic. This character has always been assigned to the chiefs among the Buddhists. They were pious, they were self-mortifying, they devoted themselves greatly to penance and meditation; but they did away with the sacrifices and ceremonies of the Bráhmans, and Gayá therefore may safely be taken to be a personification of Buddhism. His body measured 576 × 268 miles; and the country from Kalinga to the Himalaya, and from Central India to Bengal—the area over which Buddhism had spread at the time when the legend was written,—covered fully that space, and a great deal more. The head-quarters of Buddhism were then at Gayá; and the town of Gayá is even now barely a mile in extent. The attempt of the gods to put down the head of the monster typifies the attempts of the Hindus to assail Buddhism at its inspiring centre, the head-quarters; and the thwack of Vishṇu's mace indicates the resort which had been made to force when religious preaching had failed to attain the end. The rock of religion was placed on the head of the infidel, and the force of the gods kept it fixed and immovable. It was the blessing of the gods, too, which sanctified the seat of Buddhism into a principal sanctuary of the Hindu faith. We are well aware of the means resorted to at Puri, Bhuvaneśvara, and elsewhere to render Buddhist emblems, Buddhist shrines, and even Buddhist idols, subservient to Hindu worship; and it would not be at all unreasonable to suppose that the same process

---

गयासुर उवाच ॥

[illegible] ॥

[illegible] ॥

[illegible] ॥

[illegible] ॥

[illegible] ॥

सनत्कुमार उवाच ॥

[illegible] ।

देवा ऊचुः ॥

[illegible] ॥

[illegible] ॥

—'Gayá Máhátmya,' Chap. II.

had been resorted to at Gayá. At any rate, this assumption offers the most satisfactory explanation of a legend which would otherwise be absurd and inconsistent, and converts it into a complete and very expressive allegory.

The prominent position which the impression of Buddha's feet occupies in the most sacred temple of the place, the Vishṇupad, affords a strong proof in this respect, for nowhere else within the length and breadth of India has the worship of foot-marks received so high a place in the cultus of the Hindus. Nor were the Hindus satisfied with appropriating the Buddhist sanctuaries of Gayá to their worship. They repeatedly assigned to Vishṇu epithets which were purely Buddhistic, and did not even let alone the term Buddha itself. (a) They likewise attempted to take all the leading Buddhist places of note, such as Rájagriha, Gidhrakúṭa, Buddha Gayá, as sacred in their creed. In the *Gayá Máhátmya* there is a verse which enjoins that before offering the funeral cake on the Vishṇupad the pilgrim should go to Buddha Gayá and salute the bodhi-tree there. A special *mantra* has also been provided for the purpose. It says:—"I salute, repeatedly salute, thee, Aśvattha-tree, the tremulous-leaved, the *yajña* (sacrifice personified), the Bodhisattva, the eternal source of permanence. O pipal-tree, the most noble among trees, thou art the eleventh among the Rudras, Pávaka among the Vasus, and Náráyaṇa among the Devas. O noble pipal-tree, since Náráyaṇa always resides within thee, therefore art thou the most beneficent among trees. Thou art blessed, thou destroyest [the evil consequences] of bad dreams. I salute the god who has assumed the form of the Aśvattha-tree, and is the holder of the conch-shell, the discus, and the mace. I salute Hari, of the lotus eyes, who has assumed the form of a tree." (b)

In laying down this rule, the text does not look upon the tree as existing apart from Gayá, but in a part of it. In fact, everywhere in the *Máhátmya* Gayá

(a) एतस्मिन्नेव काले तु प्रबुद्धो भगवान [illegible] ॥—'Gayá Máhátmya,' p. 40.
[illegible] ॥—Ibid, p. 70.

(b) [illegible] ।—

चलदलाय वृक्षाय सर्वदा स्थितिहेतवे । बोधिसत्त्वाय यज्ञाय अश्वत्थाय नमो नमः ॥
एकादशोऽसि रुद्राणां वसूनां पावकस्तथा । नारायणोऽसि देवानां वृक्षराजोऽसि पिप्पल ॥
यस्मात् त्वयि वृक्षराज नारायणस्तिष्ठति सर्वकालं । अतः शुभस्त्वं सततं तरूणां धन्योऽसि दुःस्वप्नविनाशनोऽसि ॥
"अश्वत्थरूपिणं देवं शङ्खचक्रगदाधरं । नमामि पुण्डरीकाक्षं वृक्षरूपधरं हरिं ॥—*Gayá Máhátmya*, p. 98.

is assumed to include the whole area from the little hill Pretaśilá, on the north, to the Bodhidruma, on the south, a distance of about 13 miles. Inasmuch, however, as this would have been too large an area to keep strictly sacred, prominence has been given to a small tract midway, forming what is in books called Gayáśiras, 'the head of Gayá.' This tract is not, as has been stated by some, the Brahmayoni Hill, but a low spur of it to the north-east, about a mile in area, forming the site of the old town of Gayá. It is separated from the latter by a narrow defile, about 200 yards wide, which forms the neck, and over it passes the Buddha Gayá road. This spur is the most sacred spot according to Hindu estimation, and Hiouen Thsang calls it Gayá, as the Hindus do. According to him it is a town "well-defended and difficult of access, having a large population, of which the Bráhmans of a particular caste, the sons of a Rishi, alone numbered a thousand families." (*a*) This could not possibly have been predicated of any spot on the top of the Brahmayoni, which bears not the smallest trace of ever having been largely occupied; and from its steepness, ruggedness, and rocky character, could never have formed the site of a large town. There is nowhere on the top of it a level area of a thousand square feet. Formed of a succession of sombre valleys and dangerous summits, it would scarcely be fitted for a town. What the traveller means by the hill of Gayá is evident from the fact he mentions, that the hill in question is "in the kingdoms of India called the Divine Mountain," which is obviously the Chinese rendering of Brahmayoni. The direction and distance of this hill was, according to him, five to six *li* to the south-west, and these are exactly the distance and direction of Brahmayoni from the Vishṇupad. (*b*) Aśoka is said to have built on the top of this hill a stone stupa one hundred feet high; but it had been demolished long before the date of the Chinese pilgrim, showing clearly that the Bráhmans had occupied the place from an early date, and consecrated it to their worship.

(*a*) "Le voyageur fit de quarrante à cinquante *li* au sudouest du couvent de Kiaï-hien (Çilabhadra), passa la rivière *Ni-lien-chen* (Nairanjaná) et arriva à la ville de *Kia-ye* (Gayá). Cette ville est bien défendue et d'un accès difficile. Elle ne renferme qu'un petit nombre d'habitants ; les *P'o-lo-men* (Bráhmanas) seuls forment un millier de familles. Ils descendent d'un Richi. Le roi ne les traite point comme des sujets, et la multitude du people leur témoigne un profond respect." Page 455.

(*b*) Mr. Beal, in a footnote to his translation of 'Fa Hian,' says that "at the base of this mountain, and between it and the river, is built the village of the sahib" (p. 120). The site indicated is that of the old town of Gayá, and not of Sáhibganj, which, on reference to the map, will be found to be to the north of the old town, as also of the Brahmayoni Hill. Professor H. H. Wilson supposes Buddha Gayá to be the site of ancient Gayá ('Essays,' II. 341). The 'Lalita Vistara,' however, leaves no room to doubt the existence of the present Gayá as a town long before the commencement of the Christian era, and of Buddha Gayá having been distinct from the town of Gayá.

Now, the Gayáśiras of the Śástras is ordinarily called Gayá, and in the present day by the people of the place *Purána* Gayá, or the 'old town of Gayá,' being almost exclusively occupied by the Gawál priests, to distinguish it from the portion which is occupied by tradespeople and others, which the Muhammadans called Iláhábád, but, having been greatly extended about the end of the last century by Mr. Law, then Collector of the district, is now called Sáhibganj, or the 'Sáhib's Mart.' The mart itself occupies the site of a deer-park or *rumna*, which the Buddhist monks were so fond of keeping up in the neighbourhood of their monasteries. The names of *old* and *new* Gayá having been thus disposed of, it was necessary to devise specific names for other portions of the more comprehensive Gayá of the Hindus. One portion, a small hill on the other side of the Phalgu, opposite Vishṇupad, which still bears some Buddhist inscriptions, but which had been entirely Hinduised, was named Ráma Gayá, or the Gayá of Ráma; another Vishṇu Gayá: and in the same way Uruvilvá, which was never entirely converted into Hindu worship, was very appropriately named the Gayá of the Buddhists, or Buddha Gayá.

When this change was first made there is no evidence to show, but it is certain that Gayá itself passed from the Buddhists to the Hindus at an early age. When Hiouen Thsang visited Gayá in 637, it was a thriving Hindu town, "well defended, difficult of access, and occupied by a thousand families of Brahmans, all descendants of a single Rishi."(*a*) These families were evidently the Gawáls, who profess to be the descendants of the priest whom Brahmá, according to the legend, created from his mind to officiate at his sacrifice. Their number is now reckoned at six hundred, for it is generally believed that the Gawáls are dying out, because, in order to preserve their purity, they do not marry out of their own caste, and in most instances wed their own near relatives. At the time of Fa Hian, in 404 A.C., "all within the city was desolate and desert,"(*b*) showing that even before that time it had passed away from the Buddhists. On the other hand, the more ancient records describe the town as an important seat of Buddhism; and the scene of a great many Buddhist stories is laid in it. As the stories are, many of them, as old as the commencement of the Christian era, it must follow that the Hindus took Gayá from the Buddhists between the second and fourth centuries. The distinctive name of Buddha Gayá must, however, be of a much later date.

(*a*) See note (*c*), p. 19.

(*b*) Beal's 'Travels of Buddhist Pilgrims,' p. 120.

CHAPTER II.

THE PENANCE OF BUDDHA.

ANCIENT FAME OF URUVILVÁ—OLDEST RECORD ON THE LIFE OF ŚÁKYA—ŚÁKYA'S DEPARTURE FROM HOME—PROGRESS TOWARDS THE EAST—PUPILAGE WITH ÁRÁDHA KÁLÁMA AT VAIŚÁLI—INTERVIEW WITH VIMBISÁRA AT RÁJAGRIHA—PUPILAGE WITH RUDRAKA—PROGRESS TO GAYÁ—SETTLEMENT AT URUVILVÁ—FORMS OF PENANCE COMMON AT THE TIME—THE HEXANNUAL PENANCE—APPREHENSIONS OF THE DEVAS FOR THE SAFETY OF THE SAINT—INTERVIEW WITH HIS MOTHER—THE CHARACTER OF THE PENANCE—MÁRA'S ATTEMPT TO FRUSTRATE THE OBJECT OF THE PENANCE—PENANCE COMPLETED—ŚÁKYA PERCEIVES ITS FUTILITY—DEVAS ATTEMPT TO INVIGORATE HIM WITHOUT THE USE OF FOOD—DESERTION OF HIS COMPANIONS—RESOLUTION TO GO IN SEARCH OF FOOD—TAKING OF A PIECE OF CLOTH FROM A CORPSE AND THE WASHING OF IT—SUJÁTÁ'S PREPARATION OF FOOD FOR THE SAINT AND PRESENTATION OF IT—ŚÁKYA'S BATH AND REFRESHMENT—PROGRESS TOWARDS, AND DECORATIONS OF, THE BODHIMANDA—THE VOW AT THE TIME OF SITTING ON THE PLATFORM—MÁRA ASSAILS THE SAINT—THE RESULT THEREOF—ADORATION BY GUARDIAN DIVINITIES—THE FOUR MEDITATIONS—COMPLETION OF THE MEDITATIONS—THE PHILOSOPHICAL IDEAS WHICH SUGGESTED THEMSELVES AFTER THE MEDITATIONS—SEVEN WEEKS' COGITATIONS—EXHORTATION TO PREACH—DEPARTURE FROM URUVILVÁ TO BENARES—TRUTHS DEDUCIBLE FROM THE LEGEND OF BUDDHA—ANTIQUITY OF THE LEGENDS—SITES AND MONUMENTS NOTICED BY HIOUEN THSANG.

FROM an obscure position as a small village of no interest, Uruvilvá rose to high distinction as the hermitage of one of the greatest religious reformers of the world—of one who exercised the most unbounded influence on the mind of man. For over sixteen hundred years it was held to be the most sacred spot on earth by at least one-fifth of the human race. For centuries the stream of pilgrims flowed towards it without intermission. Princes from all parts of India vied with one another in enriching it with the highest treasures of art that they could command. Every spot where the saint had rested or taken his meal, every pool in which he had laved his person or washed his scanty raiments, every nook and corner connected in some way or other with his long-protracted meditations and self-torture, once had its recording stone; and nothing was left undone to produce an uninterrupted page of monumental history for the period he devoted to the acquirement of perfection in the knowledge of good and evil. The hand of Time has, however, obliterated nearly the whole of this page, and what little remains cannot be deciphered without some idea of what the whole probably was. It is necessary, therefore, before proceeding to describe the archæological remains to be met with at Buddha

Gayá, to glance at the principal events in connection with the life of the saint during his sojourn there, and at the memorials of those events accounts of which have been transmitted to us by ancient authorities.

The highest authority on the life of Śákya is the Lalita Vistara. Parts of it were compiled either in his life-time or immediately after his death, and others within a century and a half of that event. (a) Although legendary in its character, and abounding in descriptions of miraculous events, in exaggerations and hyperboles, which vitiate its testimony, it is the oldest available. I shall therefore give here an abstract of that portion of it which bears upon the hermitage of the saint, and in doing so use the very words of the text to a large extent.

According to it the sights, successively, of a sick man, an old man, and a corpse,—of disease, decrepitude, and death,—wrought a revulsion of feeling in the mind of Śákya; and on the night of the birth of his only son, (b) he abandoned his paternal abode at Kapilavastu to lead the life of a hermit. He had then a firm conviction in his mind about the evanescence and utter worthlessness of all worldly pleasures and enjoyments; but he knew not what was really permanent and salutary. He proceeded, therefore, in search of knowledge, from whatever source he could get it, and not to impart it to others. Clad in the ochre-colour garments of a houseless hermit, staff and alms-bowl in hand, he sallied forth, more to avoid his home and its sensuous surroundings, which he thought were the nurseries of misery and woe, than to carry out any settled scheme as to the course he would follow. There were calm and contentment and peace in the life of a hermit, and so he became a hermit; but he knew not what it was that brought on that calm and contentment. Proceeding eastwards, he first came to the hermitage of a Bráhman lady of the Śákya race, who received him with much respect, and offered him food and raiment. His next hostess was also a Bráhman lady; Padmá was her name, and she lived in a retreat, where the youthful hermit found a warm welcome. He next

(a) *Vide passim* the Introduction to my edition of the 'Lalita Vistara,' pp. 47f.

(b) The occasion has been specially selected by the biographer, probably with a view to give prominence to the fortitude of the sage's mind, which could effect such a renunciation on so auspicious an occasion. The 'Bodhisattva Avadána,' a later authority, however, denies this, and says that the son was born six years after the sage's retirement from home. It narrates, likewise, the details of an attempt on the part of a cousin to carry on an intrigue with Yasodhará, the wife of Śákya, and of the taunts which were showered on the boy for his auspicious birth. This would suggest the idea that the immediate cause of Śákya's retirement was the want of fidelity of his wife; but the authority of the 'Lalita Vistara' cannot be set aside by that of the 'Divya Avadána.' See my 'Sanskrit Buddhist Literature of Nepal,' p. 26.

visited, successively, the hermitages of one Raivata, a *Brahmarshi*, or sage of great renown, and Rájaka, son of Trimadaṇḍika. Proceeding thus from one hermit's chalet to another, he reached the great town of Váiśali (modern Besádh), which was in those days noted for its republican institutions and entire absence of royalty.(a) There lived at the time a great teacher, by name Áráḍha Káláma, surrounded by three hundred pupils and a large concourse of auditors (*śrávakas*), to whom he expounded the doctrine of poverty and the control of the passions. Śákya sought his instruction, and abided in his hermitage. His pupilage, however, did not prove satisfactory. He soon found out that the doctrine taught did not enlighten him in the least as to the means of overcoming the threefold pain incident to human existence, and the ultimate end of man.

Disappointed with his teacher, Śákya left the asylum after a time, and went on to Rájagriha, the capital of Magadha. There he took his abode on a little hill, called Páṇḍava, and procured his food by begging in the city. His youth and handsome appearance, conjoined with his hermit's garb, attracted the attention of every one who saw him; and even the king, Vimbisára, paid him a visit, and promised to receive him as his tutor, should the youthful hermit ever acquire the knowlege he sought. Among the great teachers of the place there lived then one Rudraka, son of Ráma, who taught the doctrine of "qualities and their effects divested from their ideas." He had a retinue of seven hundred disciples, and was highly respected by all for his learning and sanctity. Śákya sought his instruction, and became his pupil. But, as with Áráḍha Káláma, so with this sage, he was soon disappointed. He left him with a view to proceed further on in his search of the unknowable. Five of the pupils of Rudraka, all scions of respectable families, forsaking their tutor, also joined him in his rambles over the country.

Taking a south-westerly course from Rájagriha, the six hermits at last arrived at Gayá, which belonged to King Vimbisára, and formed a part of his kingdom of Magadha. Here they took their seat on the hill named Gayaśírsha (modern Brahmayoni), and passed some time in peace. The mind of Śákya was, however, never at rest, and in the course of his cogitations three ideas vividly presented themselves to him, and they all tended to show that all ceremonies and sacrifices, all fasts and penances, all forms of adoration and worship, impelled by sensuous desires

(a) *Vide passim* 'Lalita Vistara,' p. 23.

(*káma*), lead only to pain and suffering, but never to that knowledge which is superhuman and devoid of rewards and punishments. He resolved, therefore, to adopt that course only which would enable him to acquire the knowledge in question. Neither, however, the city of Gayá, nor the bleak rocky crest of the Brahmayoni Hill, was suited for his purpose; and he proceeded to the neighbouring village of Uruvilvá, whose woods and groves offered a pleasant retreat for a man tired of the vanities of this world, and longing for a peaceful communion with his mind.

While at Uruvilvá, Śákya called to mind all the different forms of penances which people at his time were in the habit of submitting to, and which they thought raised the mind above all carnality. "Here," he thought, "am I, born in the Jambudvípa, among people who have no prospect of intellectual redemption (*ádhi mukti*), crowded by Tírthikas with divers wishes, and at a time when their faculties are riggling in the grasp of the crocodile of their carnal wants. Stupid men, who seek to purify their persons by divers modes of austerity and penance, and inculcate the same! Some of them cannot make out their *mantras*. Some lick their hands. Some are uncleanly. Some have no *mantras*. Some wander after different sources. Some abstain from fish and flesh meat. Some mind not the annual duties. Some abstain from spirit and the water of chaff. Some beg alms from one, three, five, or seven tribes. Some indulge in tubers, fruits, mosses, kuśa grass, leaves, cow's dejecta, frumenty, curds, clarified butter, molasses, and unbaked cakes. Some wash the body of charioteers, parrot-flyers, and news-purveyors. Some dwell in villages, or in woods, for their livelihood. Some adore cows, deer, horses, hogs, monkeys, or elephants. Seated at one place in silence, with their legs bent under them, some attempt greatness. Some speak to only one person, others to seven. Some eat once in a day and night, some once on alternate days, and some at intervals of four, five, or six days; some once in a fortnight performing a *chándráyana*. (*a*) Some put on themselves the feathers of vultures or owls. Some, seated on a board or a munjá mat, wear bark, kuśa grass, valvaja grass (*Eleusine Indica*) or blankets of camel's hair, or of goat's wool, or of hair, or hides. Some sleep more or less in wet clothes. Some sleep on ashes, gravel, stones, boards, thorny grass, or pestles, with the face

(*a*) The ordinary Hindu rules of *Chándráyana* (lunar penance) require the diminution of the daily consumption of food by a mouthful every day during the wane, beginning with fifteen mouthfuls on the day of the full moon, and the increasing of the food in the same ratio during the waxing of the moon. Other forms of fast are also observed under this name.—*Manu* VI, v, 20.

downwards, in a hut on the bare ground. Some wear one, two, three, four, five, six, or seven pieces of cloth; others go naked, making no distinction between fit and unfit places. Some have long hair, nails, beards, and matted hair, and wear bark. Some live upon a single meal of a mixture of sesamum and rice. Some smear themselves with ashes, cinders from altars, dust, or clay. Some carry on their persons and in their hands down, munja grass, hair, nails, rags, mud, or a cocoanut shell alms-bowl. Some drink hot water, or rice-water, or fountain water, or water preserved in earthen jars. Some carry on them cinders, metals, astringent things, three sticks, skulls, alms-bowls, bones, or swords, and by these means they hope to attain to immortality, and pride themselves on their holiness. By inhaling smoke or fire, by gazing at the sun, by performing the five fires, (*a*) resting on one foot, or with an arm perpetually uplifted, or moving about on the knees, some attempt to accomplish their penance. Some seek salvation by killing themselves by entering into a mass of lighted chaff or charcoal, or by suppressing their breath, or by roasting one's self on (hot) stones, or by entering any fire or water, or ascending in the air. The syllables 'om,' 'vashaṭ,' 'svadhá,' 'sváhá,' as also blessings, hymns, lighting of the sacred fire, invocations, repetitions of mystic *mantras*, teaching of the Vedas (*lit.* mantras), or fancying the picture of a divinity in one's mind, afford means of purification to many. Some pride themselves on their saluting Brahmá, Indra, Rudra, Vishṇu, Deví, Kumára, Mátrí, Kátyáyaní, Chandra, Áditya, Vaiśravaṇa, Varuṇa, Vásava, Aśvina, Nága, Yaksha, Gandharva, Asura, Garuḍa, Kinnara, Mahoraga, Rákshasa, Preta, Bhúta, Kushmáṇḍa, Párshada, Gaṇapati, Piśácha, Devarshi, Brahmarshi, or Rájarshi. Some select some of them, others resort to the earth, the water, heat, the air or the ether. Mountains, rivers, fountains, tanks, lakes, long narrow sheets of water (*taḍágas*), oceans, vats, ponds, wells, trees, lotus herbs, creepers, grasses, stumps, pastures, cremation grounds, courtyards, and bowers, afford asylums to others. Houses, columns, stones, pestles, swords, bows, axes, arrows, spears, and tridents, are the objects of salutation to some. In curd, butter, mustard, barley, garland, durva grass, jewels, gold and silver, some seek their welfare. Thus do these Tírthikas, dreading the horrors of mundane life, seek their shelter. Some seek heaven and salvation in their offspring, and resolutely apply to them. They all follow the wrong road; they fancy that to be the true

(*a*) *Pancha-topá*, sitting in summer amidst four blazing fires, with the sun over head for the fifth.

support which is untrue; they hold evil to be good, and the impure to be pure. I shall then commence that kind of vow and penance by which all hostile sects shall be overpowered. To persons deluded by works and sacrifices, I shall show the destruction of all works and sacrifices. To Devas, perceivable by meditation, as also to those who become manifest in divers forms, I shall exhibit a meditation by which they may be overpowered."(a)

Having thus taken his resolution, he commenced the most difficult of all difficult penances,—the dreadful penance of hexannual fast (*shaḍvárshika-vrata*), called *áspháanaka dhyána*. It was a fast which no person, human or superhuman, could perform, except a Bodhisattva. It needed the total stoppage of all inhalation and exhalation of the breath, all emotions, all functions of the body, and all agitations of the mind. One long-continued, uninterrupted concentration of the mind to the contemplation of its own condition was its absolute requirement. "It made the whole of illimitable space manifest to the mind, and was itself illimitable space" (p. 314). "Thus, with a view to show to the world a veritable wonder, to overthrow the pride of the Tírthikas, to revile all heterodox theories, to defeat the Devas, to refute the doctrine of eternity of those who look to works for reward, to enhance the merit of virtue, to display the might of wisdom, to cultivate the power of meditation (*dhyána*), to show to mankind the might of his person and its capacity for endurance, to promote the heroism of his heart, he sat on a bedstead placed on a pure spot on the earth; and in that position squeezed and tortured his body by his mind."(b)

Thus seated he passed eight nights of winter, torturing his body by his mind. His person was bedewed with perspiration, "even as the body of a weak man is when held by the neck by a powerful person;" his breath was stopped; gurgling sounds emitted from his throat; and whizzing sounds issued from his ears. The Devas thought he was dying, and Devaputras, along with the thirty-three Devas, informed Máyádeví of the condition of her son. Thereupon Máyádeví, surrounded by a retinue of Apsaras, at midnight repaired to the bank of the Nairanjaná, and, beholding the condition of her son, burst forth in deep lamentations. Roused by the sound of

(a) 'Lalita Vistara,' pp. 312, *et seq.* Several of these penances have been enjoined by Manu, and they are all strictly Hindu, showing that the Vedic rituals had, long before the time, given place to them.

(b) 'Lalita Vistara,' p. 314.

wailing, Śákya asked her:—"Who art thou with dishevelled hair and disordered toilet, lying on the ground and mourning in grief the loss of a son?"

Máyádeví replied:—"I am thy mother, who bore thy heavy burden for ten months in my womb, and am now weeping for my son."

Śákya encouraged her by saying, "Fear not; you shall have your son. I shall render my labour fruitful. I shall for certain dispel all darkness, and make true knowledge manifest. I shall revive the doctrine of Dipankara. Were the earth to rend into a hundred fragments; were the gold-crested Meru to be submerged in the ocean water; were the sun, the moon, and the stars to fall on the earth, yet shall I never die. Grieve not, therefore, and you will soon behold me possessed of Buddha knowledge."(a)

Śákya then reflected that there were many Śramaṇas and Bráhmanas who prided themselves on their abstemiousness. He, too, therefore should be abstemious. Accordingly he lived on a single plum, nor was that plum of a larger size than an ordinary plum. This regimen sadly reduced his person; his "ribs projected like so many legs of a crab; his spine bulged out like the knots of a bamboo; his eyes sank as water in the bottom of a well in summer; his limbs became lank, like the limbs of a goat or a camel; and altogether he was so completely shrivelled up that he looked like an eel." He nevertheless thought he should reduce his daily allowance of food, and took to a single grain of rice, and that not of a larger size than ordinary rice. This was next replaced by a single grain of sesamum seed per day, and ultimately even that was given up and absolute fast resorted to. "Unflinching in his determination, thus for six long years he, for the good of mankind, remained seated on the bedstead, unsheltered from rain, wind, and sun; unprotected from the bite of gnats, mosquitoes, and other vermin; never stretching his limbs, nor attending to any call of nature. The heavy rains of the rainy season, the scorching heat of summer, the dews of autumn, and the piercing cold of winter, all passed over him, and he did not even move his hands to protect himself. Village boys and girls, cowherds and shepherds, poor women who came to collect dry leaves or grass, or wood or dung, took him to be an imp of dirt, and in sport cast dust on his person."

At this time that sinful demon Mára, the divinity of lust, perceived that Śákya was about to complete his six years' dreadful penance and attain to perfect

(a) 'Lalita Vistara,' p. 318.

knowledge. He dreaded much the consequence of such perfection, as it was sure to deprive him of his supremacy over mankind. He sought, therefore, to unsettle the mind of Śákya by plausible, but wicked, advice. He dilated largely on the horrors of the penance, advised his hearer to betake to a life of ease and pleasure, and, by charity and other easily-accomplishable means, to attain the virtue he sought. But Śákya gave no ear to the soft persuasions, and severely rated the sinful wretch for his wickedness.

Having thus completed his six years' penance, Śákya felt that the measures he had adopted were not the right ones for the attainment of his object; that they could not help him to relieve mankind from the woes of birth, disease, and death; that, by weakening his body to the last degree of feebleness and emaciation, he was rendering himself unfit for that absolute knowledge which was the highest object of his existence. He resolved, therefore, to rise from his seat, and, after refreshing himself with food and drink, to ascend the Bodhimaṇḍa in search of that knowledge. This statement shows that the place of hexannual penance was not, as generally supposed, the Bo-tree at Buddha Gayá, but distinct, and at a considerable distance to the north of it; and Hiouen Thsang supports this statement. (a)

Perceiving the intention of Śákya, certain Devaputras, or minor gods, offered to enter the pores of his body and invigorate him, so that he may be enabled to become a Buddha without tasting food. But he declined their offer. He felt that the people of the neighbourhood knew him to be a fasting saint, but if he got himself invigorated by the aid of the Devaputras, they would suspect his rectitude, and cause a scandal. He therefore said aloud:—"Now that I have completed my six years, I shall seek for some edible grains for food."

When the five respectable youths who were in his company heard this, they said among themselves, "Now that he has failed to attain true knowledge by his austerities, how can he hope to make it manifest by attending to his belly? This is childish." And, saying this, they left him, retired to Benares, and took their abode in the Deer-park at Rishipaṭṭana.

Śákya, having resolved upon his course, rose from his seat and, in order to obtain from them the means of regaining his strength, proposed to go to the ten virgins of the village, who had taken great interest in his penance and provided

(a) 'Memoires sur les Contrées Occidentales,' Vol. I, p. 479.

him with the different seeds which he had taken in the early part of his self-mortification. One of them, named Sujátá,(a) was particularly devoted to his interest. She had done all she could for his comfort, and had likewise fed eight hundred Bráhmans daily in order to promote his welfare, cherishing the fond desire that Śákya should attain his Buddhahood after tasting food prepared by her. But before Śákya could proceed to the virgins, he felt he must renew his vestment, for his old yellow garment had all rotted away during his six years' penance.

How to provide a new suit of clothes was, therefore, his first difficulty; but it was soon overcome. Proceeding on through a cremation ground, he perceived a corpse lying there, wrapped in a piece of coarse cloth. The body was that of Rádhá, a maid-servant of Sujátá. Śákya put his left leg on the body, and with his right hand removed the cloth and took it up. The cloth, however, could not be used without washing, and Śákya was thinking where to proceed to obtain some water for the purpose, when the Devas, with their hands, excavated a tank, and it became full of water. The next idea was where to get a piece of stone on which the cloth could be struck for proper washing, and a stone was immediately produced by Śakra, who offered likewise to wash the cloth for the saint. This offer, however, was declined, and Śákya did the needful for himself. But when he had done so, and attempted to come out of the tank, he found the bank too steep, made so by the wicked Mára, and in his weak, exhausted state could not rise. There was, however, a kakubha-tree (*Pentaptera arjuna*) on the bank, and at his request some Devas bent down one of the branches and thereby enabled him to get out. (b)

Having come upon the bank, he sat under the kakubha-tree, and began to sew the cloth into proper form, when a Devaputra, of the name of Avimalaprabha, brought him an excellent suit of yellow cloth befitting a saint, and solicited his acceptance. The offer was graciously accepted, and Śákya resolved to put on the dress next morning and to go to the village for alms. Information of this resolution was, at midnight, conveyed by the Devas to the village girl Sujátá, who

(a) The name is differently given by different writers. According to Beal, the milk and rice were given by the two daughters of Sujátá, the lord of the village of Uruvilvá (Fa Hian, p. 121); in Burnouf's account the damsels are named Nandá and Nandabálá; but in the 'Maháwanso' and Spence Hardy's 'Manual of Buddhism' (p. 168) one damsel is mentioned, and she is Sujátá. In some works Trapusha and Bhallika are so named; their account will appear lower down.

(b) The sites of the tree and the tank are, by Fa Hian, said to be 3 *li* to the westward of the Tree of Knowledge. Cremation grounds in this part, as in other parts, of India, are, however, generally situated on the bank of a river, and the direction therefore appears to be wrong. Hiouen Thsang places them to the south-east of the tree.

had so long wished that the saint should receive food from her before attaining his perfection, and she immediately set about it.

At early dawn she collected some fresh milk, and seven times extracted the cream therefrom, and over a new hearth, in a new vessel, with fresh rice, dressed a dish of frumenty, and, having seasoned it with aromatic waters, candy, and spices, placed it, covered, in a golden bowl. Then, addressing her maid, she said, "Uttará, go and invite a Bráhmaṇa, to whom I may present this honeyed frumenty."

"Please your ladyship," replied the maid, and then went towards the east in search of a Bráhmaṇa; but she found none. The only person that came to her sight was the Bodhisattva (Śákya). She then went to the west and the north, but with no better result, and reported the circumstance to her mistress, saying, "Wherever I go I meet a handsome Śramaṇa, but no Bráhmaṇa."

"Do ye go, Uttará," said the lady, "and bring him here, for he is the Bráhmaṇa and he the Śramaṇa for whom I have designed this dish."

"Please your ladyship," responded the maid, and did as she was bid.

Śákya was then escorted to the house, and welcomed with every mark of respect. The bowl of frumenty was likewise presented to him. Śákya accepted the frumenty, but said, "Sister, what is to be done with the golden bowl?"

She replied, "Let it be yours."

Sákya said, "Of what use will such a vessel be to me?"

She responded, "Do what you will with it; I cannot offer you food without the vessel."

With the bowl in hand Śákya issued forth from the village of Uruvilvá,(a) and repaired to the river Nairanjaná. There he placed his garments and the bowl in a corner, and entered the river for a bath. The Devas, seeing this, showered powdered agallochum and sandal, flowers of divers colours, and various aromatics and unguents, on the river, so that its waters became redolent with the finest aroma. When Śákya had finished his bath, hundreds of thousands of Devas came to the river to pick up the flowers, in order that they may raise *Chaityas* over them, and

(a) According to Fa Hian, the spot where the frumenty was given was 2 *li* to the north of the cremation ground, where Buddha washed the cloth he had taken from a dead body, and that was 3 *li* to the west; and according to the same authority, he proceeded 2 *li* further north, where he ate it (p. 121), so that the position would lie to the north-west of Uruvilvá, where there is no river within two miles. The directions given are evidently incorrect. The true position is to the south of Uruvilvá.

worship them. Whatever hair of the head and of the beard had fallen in the water, the same was carried away by Sujátá for the same purpose.(a)

When the Bodhisattva ascended from the river, he beheld a charming tope close by, and thither he repaired. A Nágakanyá there placed a jewelled throne(b) for the use of the Bodhisattva, who sat thereon, and, having refreshed himself with the frumenty, threw the golden bowl into the river. Instantly a king of the Nágas, named Ságara, seized the vessel and ran away homewards with it; but the thousand-eyed Purandara (Indra) perceived it, and, assuming the form of a *garuḍa*, attempted to snatch it. He, however, failed in the attempt, and at last got it by begging for it. Having taken it to his home, he caused a *Chaitya* to be built over it, and in honour of it, instituted an annual feast called *Pátrijátrá*, or 'the feast of the bowl,' which is regularly observed by the gods. The throne on which Bodhisattva sat was taken away by the Nágakanyá for a similar purpose.

After this refreshment Bodhisattva regained all his former strength, vigour, and beauty of person, as also the thirty-two signs of a perfect being (Mahápurusha), along with the eighty minor signs; and the glory of heaven became manifest on his person. He then proceeded towards the Bodhimaṇḍa.

The nature of the Bodhimaṇḍa is nowhere fully described; but it was no other than a platform built round the largest Indian fig-tree in the village, which was probably the resort of the elders—the place where they congregated of an evening to discourse on village topics,—and where learned men occasionally delivered lectures on religion and morality to the people. It, of course, then had not its present name. It is not unlikely that the tree had not even a platform round its base.

The road to it was purified by the wind-gods with the most charming zephyr; the rain-gods showered on it delightfully fragrant water and flowers; the trees bent their heads towards the road in token of respect; all the great mountains bent their heads towards it; little herbs settled on the top of it; the road from the river to it, a distance of a *krosha*,(c) was entrenched and guarded by Devaputras; on either side of

(a) How the lady comes here is not explained. It is not stated that after giving the frumenty at her house she had followed the saint.

(b) Fa Hian calls this a stone six feet square, which, as well as the tree, he saw.—*Beal's Translation*, p. 121.

(c) The direct distance from the river to the tree is barely 300 yards; but, as pointed out by Fa Hian, the part of the river where Sákya partook of the frumenty was 2 *li* south of the town, and thence the distance to the tree may be a mile or more.

the road pavilions, bedecked with jewels of the seven kinds, were erected. There were also seven palm-trees, at a distance of an arrow's throw from each other; and thereupon were placed networks of jewels, flags, and umbrellas. In the intervals between every two palm-trees there was a tank, covered with flowers and aquatic animals. Thousands over thousands of Apsaras strewed flowers and aromatic water on the road, scented the place with aromatics and incenses, and filled the pavilions with heavenly music. Brahmá appointed guardians for the protection of the Bodhimaṇḍa, and the whole world was at peace and in the enjoyment of perfect happiness, when the Bodhisattva proceeded along the road and was about to ascend the jewelled seat that had been placed for him on the platform under the Tree of Knowledge. When he approached it a Nága king, named Kálika, with his wife, Suvarṇaprabhá, and a large retinue, approached him and paid their obeisance.

Standing by the side of the Bodhimaṇḍa the Bodhisattva called to mind how seated former Bodhisattvas had attained to perfection, and it struck him that the proper course was to spread some grass on the ground, and to sit thereon. Immediately after he beheld a grass-cutter engaged in cutting tender greenish-blue grass, soft as silk. He went to him, and in mellifluous accents asked for a supply. It was immediately given, for it was no other than Śakra himself, who had appeared as a grass-cutter to serve the saint. Having got the grass, the Bodhisattva came with it to the trunk of the Tree of Knowledge, and, spreading the grass, sat thereon with an erect body, facing the east. Having seated himself, he made this vow:—"Seated here let my body shrivel up if it will; let my skin, flesh, and bones, rot to nothing if they will: but never shall this body rise up from the seat until I have attained that true knowledge which is so difficult of attainment in course of many Kalpas." (a)

Now, when Buddha was thus seated, six Devas of the class called Kámávachara, or those who can roam about anywhere at will, took their stand on each side of him, to guard his person from all accidents. At the same time there issued forth from his body a brilliant light, which illuminated all the quarters of the globe. Impelled by this light, many celestial Buddhas and Bodhisattvas, from each of the ten quarters of the earth, came down with their countless following to behold the

(a) According to Fa Hian, at this time 500 blue birds came flying towards him, and having encircled his person three times in their flight, departed. Hiouan Thsang also refers to this circumstance; but it is not mentioned in the 'Lalita Vistara'. The birds meant are the blue-necked jays, which are held by the Hindus to be very auspicious if seen when starting on a journey. (*See* note, p. 53.)

Bodhisattva then about to attain his perfection, and to pay their adorations to him. Each party performed the usual rites of worship with great devotion, and recited a set of verses in his praise.

When the celestial visitors were gone, the Bodhisattva thought of the wicked wiles of Mára, and of his wishes to frustrate all attempts at goodness. (a) It struck him that it would not be proper to attain to perfection without overcoming the Sinful One. By overcoming him he would overcome the universe, and bring every one to subjugation; so he made up his mind to rouse the author of evil. Thereupon a brilliant flame issued forth from between his eyebrows. It caused a universal agitation, covering at the same time all the regions with an effulgence which was terrible to behold. A voice was also heard announcing that Śákya would soon attain to perfection and redeem all creation for ever, and warning Mára of the doom which awaited him.

Mára, beholding the light and hearing the voice, was overpowered by anger, jealousy, envy, and terror. He had a dream, too, which, in thirty-two dire forms, represented the desolation which would be brought on him and his home. He felt that the time for immediate action was come, and that he must either give up all hope for the future, or at once frustrate the attempt of the Bodhisattva. He, therefore, convened a meeting of all his sons, ministers, and generals, and held protracted council to decide upon what should be done. The council was divided. One of his sons, Sárthaváha by name, strongly advised submission to the lot awaiting them, and pointed out in glowing colours the futility of waging a war which was predestined to bring them to utter disgrace. "Immense," said he, "may be your power and your majesty; each of your chiefs may be a mighty hero, invincible in battle; but were the three thousand regions to be full of fire-flies, a single sun would swallow them all and drown their light." He was, however, overruled, and grand preparations were made for mobilising the troops of the Evil One. Fierce forms of monsters and hobgoblins,— "of gorgons, hydras, and chimeras dire"—armed to the teeth with every implement

(a) Among the Hindus Mára is the god of love, the counterpart of the Greek Eros or Cupid, and the only arms he bears is a bow made of flowers and five arrows of the same material; but the Buddhists assign to him a very different character. According to them he is the presiding divinity of our sensuous desires, and the greatest opponent to goodness. In this respect he plays the same part as an adviser of evil, which Satan does according to the Christian theologians. In his career of mischief he has travelled to Scandinavia, and, without even much altering his name, 'still rides the modern Saxon in his sleep (nightmare) as he did the Yngling King Vanland." He commanded a prominent position in the Odinic mythology, and was known exactly by the same appellation (Mára) and for the same disposition which has given him so infamous a notoriety among the Buddhists.

of war, assembled from all quarters of the universe,—"mighty warriors, dreadful to behold, causing horripilation to all, such as were never before seen or heard of by gods or men. Their faces were frightful in millions of different ways; their limbs and trunks were enveloped by hundreds and thousands of serpents; they were armed with swords, bows, arrows, spears, iron lances, axes, hatchets, rockets, clubs, sticks, lassoes, maces, wheels, thunder-like missiles, and darts. Their bodies were encased in stout armour of hides. They had abnormal heads, bandy feet, and crooked hands and eyes. Their bodies, eyes, and heads, were enveloped in flames; monstrous were their bellies, feet, and hands; dreadfully fierce were their faces; distorted were their mouths and appearance; protruding were their horrid teeth. Thick, big, and protruding were their tongues, like hairy trunks; and their blood-shot eyes were filled with the venom of the black serpent. Some of them vomited forth snakes; some swallowed snakes from their hands; some, like garuḍas, jumping out of the sea, indulged in devouring human flesh, bones, blood, hands, feet, skulls, and ordure." Some were of enormous size. Some had one, three, four, or more arms; others many legs; some had no heads; some no legs; some no arms; some had deep sunken eyes, others far-protruding enormous red ones. Some vomited forth the venom of the serpent; others anointed their persons and weapons with snake poison. Many of them were mounted on horses, elephants, mules, donkeys, and buffaloes, dressed in chaplets of bones, and engaged in frightful acts of cruelty; others came on foot. They surrounded the Bodhisattva and assailed him in a thousand different ways, casting on his person stones, mountains, trees, serpents, and instruments of every kind, and creating the most frightful noises. Their warfare, however, was of no avail: the saint remained unmoved.

A council of war was next convened. Those among the thousand sons of Mára who were inimically disposed stood by the left hand of the Evil One, and those who were favourably inclined towards the Bodhisattva stood on the right; and a protracted discussion followed. The former boasted of their might and vigour, and each offered to destroy the Bodhisattva in a trice. "I," said one, "can, with my hundred arms, cast a hundred arrows at once, and they would mangle the body of the hermit in no time." But he was immediately retorted by another, who remarked that "his arms were worth no more than so many hairs of the body in the case of one whose person was unassailable by venom, or arms, or fire: the fiercest arms thrown on him would all be converted into so many flowers." "I," said another, "can by a single glance reduce the Śramaṇa to ashes." "Ah!" replied his opponent, "were the whole universe to be inflamed by venom, a single glance of the saint would suffice to quench the fire." A third was ready "to pluck the Tree of Knowledge with his hand and cast it to the uttermost bound of the earth;" but he was immediately met by the remark, "Were you, proud one, able with thy hands to pluck the earth along with all the mountains, seas, Devas, Asuras, and Gandharvas on it, and were there as many like you as the grains of sand on the banks of the Ganges, still you could not, with your united efforts, disturb a single hair on the body of the Bodhisattva." Others followed, some vaunting, and some counselling caution; but no decision could be arrived at. The members of the right could not be overcome by argument. The left felt sure that nothing could be done to disturb the saint, and that their attempt would for certain prove most disastrous to themselves. "He who wishes," said one, "to rouse the sleeping serpent; he who wishes to rouse the sleeping elephant; he who wishes to rouse the sleeping lion,—runs less risk than he who desires to disturb this lord of humanity." Even the commander-in-chief of the army could not muster courage to lead the attack, and discreetly advised retreat. The speeches are remarkably pointed, and their tone recalls to mind the council of Satan after the fall, as described in the 'Paradise Lost.' I refrain from quoting them all, as they would occupy too much space.

While the debate was thus progressing, the Bodhisattva opened wide his mouth, which appeared like a lotus with a hundred petals. Mára, seeing it, imagined that the whole of his army was being swallowed up, and, in his fears, felt disposed to run away. But he soon revived his courage, and a fierce and united attack was made on the saint. Missiles of all kinds—arms, stones, and mountains—were hurled against him, and fire and poison showered over him; but they all changed into flowers, the fire forming a halo behind his head.

The Bodhisattva then scratched his head with his right hand.(a) Mára beheld it, and, thinking that the saint had lifted a sword, in very fear ran away towards the south. He, however, soon rallied, and returned to the attack; but, even as

(a) Fa Hian says he struck the earth with his toe; but this circumstance is not mentioned in the 'Lalita Vistara.'

before, his countless missiles all changed into garlands and hung round the Tree of Knowledge. The Bodhisattva then reviled him for his wickedness, and advised him to depart. The goddess of the earth also appeared in person, and, after paying her respects to the saint, advised Mára to retire.

Mára felt greatly crest-fallen. Oppressed by shame and disgrace, he called back his troops and ordered them to await further instructions. In the meantime he sent for his sixteen daughters (a) and deputed them to deploy their most ravishing arts to captivate the mind of the saint. They advanced in the most amatory mood. Some hid one side of their faces with their veil, leaving the other side visible. Some displayed their hard, heaving busts. Some, by gentle smiles, displayed their teeth. Some, as if by accident, lifting their arms, displayed their sides. Some pouted their lips, bright red as the *bimba* fruit. Some glanced at the Bodhisattva with half-closed, languishing eyes, and closed them immediately after. Some, in the attempt to hide them, exposed their busts. Some allowed their garments to fall slack and expose their persons. Some, in the attempt to adjust their waist ornaments, displayed their waists. Some indulged in tinkling the silver bells on their feet ornaments. Some danced, others sang, and others played on musical instruments. Some busied themselves in adjusting their toilet, others in disadjusting the same. In short, in thirty-two different ways did they bring their coquettry to bear on the mind of the saint. They went further, and, in the most ardent amatory addresses, sought to inflame him.

They said:—"Now that the delightful spring has come, let us, dear one, enjoy under the blooming trees your charming and resplendent beauty, so lovely, so enticing, so auspicious, and so variegated.

"We are designed and born expressly for the delight of the gods and mortals. Arise quickly from your seat, withdraw your mind from the unattainable knowledge, and enjoy our glorious youth.

"Behold these well-adorned and well-preserved daughters of Mára, who have come dressed and ornamented for you. Where is the living being, diseased and dried up like a piece of wood though he be, who, after beholding such beauty, is not inflamed by passion?

(a) Fa Hian reduces the number of the daughters to three, and says that a glance of the saint metamorphosed them into old hags. This, however, refers to a subsequent attack (p. 44). The maidens are said to have commenced their attack from the north, and Mára and his host from the south.—*Beal's Translation*, p. 123.

"With hair soft and redolent with the finest perfume; enticing faces adorned with tiara, ear-rings, and leaves of gold; shapely forehead; countenances set off with choice unguents; eyes large and bright as the lotus; faces resplendent as the lunar orb in its fullness; lips of the colour of the fully ripe *bimba* fruit; teeth that rival the whiteness of the conch-shell, or the *kunda* flower, or the driven snow;—here we are, who long for your love. Do you, dear one, cast a glance?

"With hard, heaving busts, persons dimpled with rotundity, and expansive hips, here we are, lord; do cast a glance on these exquisite maidens.

"With limbs taper as the trunk of the elephant, hands adorned with bracelets, and hips set off with golden chains, here we are, lord; do cast a glance on your slaves.

"Moving languishingly like the swan, with speech sweet, endearing, and enchanting, such beauties, so well adorned, so thoroughly versed in love's art, so accomplished in singing, music, and dancing, modelled expressly for love—should you not wish for such suppliants for love, you will be deprived of the greatest pleasures on earth. Even as the fool who runs away from the sight of a jewel—stupid mortal! ignorant of the value of wealth and enjoyment—so are you, unversed in love, spurning us, maidens, who have come to you."

The Bodhisattva said:—"I shall be the king of the three regions, the revered lord of the heaven and the earth, the mover of the wheel of religion, gifted with the ten transcendental powers, surrounded with sons and disciples, and these disciples by tens of thousands bowing before me. Fallen in love with religion, my mind cannot enjoy worldly objects."

The maidens:—"While delightful youth lasts in thy sprouting manhood, while disease and decay do not assail you, while you are in the heydey of youth and loveliness, as we are, do you, of smiling face, no longer delay to enjoy with delight the sports of love."

The Bodhisattva:—"As long as I have not obtained the nectar of immortality; as long as the regions of the Devas and the Asuras are not free from transitory pain; as long as disease, decay, and death, do not appear as angry enemies,—so long shall I think of the blissful path to the fearless region."

The maidens:—"Even as in the region of the Devas, the lord of the three-fold ten (Indra) surrounded by fairies (*apsaras*), bepraised by the greatest among the immortals (Jáma and Sujáma) is free from every and all disagreeable objects, so in the palace of Mára, sweetly overpowered by pleasure, lovely one, enjoy the pastimes of love with us."

The Bodhisattva:—"Love is unsteady as drops of water on the points of grass-blades, or the clouds of autumn, furious as the daughters of serpents, and infinitely dreadful. Adored by Śakra, Sujáma, and the Devas, holding Namuchi in subjugation, who will delight with loving women environed with misery?"

The maidens:—"Behold the trees with tender leaflets in full bloom, listen to the heart-enlivening song of the coel, the hum of bees in the cool breezy bower, amidst groves frequented by the noblest of celestial choiristers (*kinnara*), and enjoy them with these maidens on a soft curling sward."

The Bodhisattva:—"These trees with tender leaves have flowered in accordance with the laws of nature; the bees, drunk with honey, have entered the flowers impelled by thirst; and the sun will dry up the grass on the sward. I have set before me the nectar which former *Jinas* have tasted."

The maidens:—"Behold these moon-like faces, like a garland of sweet faces, with speech sweet and delightful, and teeth white as silver or driven snow! Such beauties are scarce in the mansions of the gods, more so in those of mortals. Even these always long for your company!"

The Bodhisattva:—"I behold bodies impure and defiled, full of vermin, rotten, mere fuel, fragile, and enveloped in pain. I long for that which is beneficial to the whole creation, movable and immovable,—the undecaying, which has been sought by great Buddhas."

The maidens:—"Versed in all the sixty-four devices of love, tinkling the small bells of their anklets and waist-chains, with their garments all slack, struck mad by the shaft of the god of love, these laughing, delightful maidens,—how distorted must be your mind, dear sir, if you do not associate with them!"

The Bodhisattva:—"The whole world is manifest with evil and enveloped in passion; love is like unto the sword, the dart, and the spear, like a razor dipped in honey, like the tinder (*lit.* dried cowdung) before the fire on the head of the serpent. I know these things well, and therefore avoid the company of all women, the charmers who destroy all (moral) merit!"

Thus all their impassioned eloquence was of no avail.

With a smiling face the saint, in mellifluous accents, reproved them as often as they addressed him, and advised them to retire and betake to a virtuous course of life.

The maidens retired; and Mára, disappointed, discomfited, and completely disgraced, in overwhelming grief withdrew his army.

Now eight guardian deities of the Tree of Knowledge came forward and adorned the person of the saint with the sixteen graces peculiar to Bodhisattvas. Mára at the same time came forward and entered into a protracted discussion with the deities and the Bodhisattva; but his logic and sophistry proved as unavailing as his army and the seductive arts of his daughters, and he had at last to give up the contest altogether.

Having thus overcome Mára, the Bodhisattva, at nightfall, entered into the meditation which enlightens the understanding, and completed it at the close of the first watch of the night. He then undertook the meditation of ecstacy, and accomplished it at the close of the second watch. He next entered into the meditation which has no object of thought,—a simple, but absolute, concentration of the mind on itself. This was successfully completed at the close of the third watch. Lastly, he completed the meditation which is devoid of all pleasure and pain, and is absolute knowledge.

Thus was perfect knowledge acquired by the Bodhisattva, and he became a Buddha. What this perfect knowledge was is nowhere described; but it being absolute, it is assumed to have embraced the whole circle of theology and mental and moral philosophy. Some idea of it may be formed from the thoughts which are said to have arisen in the mind of the saint at dawn of day immediately after the completion of the fourth meditation:—

"Verily," he thought, "it is painful that beings should take birth, live, die, fall, and multiply; nor do they perceive that it is a tree of pain that they endure. Alas! they know not that decay, disease, and death, are but the manifestations of that mighty tree of pain,—that of decay, disease, and death."

"But whence do disease and death (*jarámaraṇa*) proceed, and what is their cause?

"Disease and death proceed from birth (*játi*): birth therefore is their cause.

"Whence does birth proceed, and what is its cause?

"Birth proceeds from the world (*bhava*): the world therefore is its cause.

"But whence proceeds the world, and what is its cause?

"The world proceeds from the elements (*upádána*): the elements therefore are its cause.

"But whence proceed the elements, and what is their cause?

"The elements proceed from desire (*trishná*): desire therefore is its cause.

"But whence proceeds desire, and what is its cause?

"Desire proceeds from sensation (*vedaná*): sensation therefore is its cause.

"But whence proceeds sensation, and what is its cause?

"Sensation proceeds from contact (*sparsha*): contact therefore is the cause of pain.

"But whence proceeds contact, and what is its cause?

"Contact proceeds from the six organs of sense (*shaḍáyatana*): the six organs therefore are its cause.

"But whence proceed the six organs, and what are their causes?

"The six organs proceed from name and form (*náma-rúpa*): name and form therefore are their causes.

"But whence proceed name and form, and what is their cause?

"Name and form proceed from consciousness (*vijñána*): consciousness therefore is the cause of name and form.

"But whence proceeds consciousness, and what is its cause?

"Consciousness proceeds from intuition (*sañskára*): intuition is therefore the cause of consciousness.

"But whence proceeds intuition, and what is its cause?

"Intuition proceeds from illusion (*avidyá*): illusion therefore is its cause.

"Thus illusion is the cause of intuition; intuition that of consciousness; consciousness that of name and form; name and form that of the six organs; the six organs that of contact; contact that of sensation; sensation that of desire; desire that of the elements; the elements that of the earth; the earth that of birth; birth that of decay, death, grief, anxiety, misery, distress, and desire for relief, and thence proceeds the whole—verily the whole—of this tree of pain.

"But by what happening can disease and death not happen? By prohibiting what can disease and death be prohibited?

"If there be no birth, there can be no disease and death. By prohibiting birth, therefore, disease and death can be prohibited.

"But how can birth not take place? By prohibiting what can birth be prohibited?

"If there be no world there can be no birth. By prohibiting the world, therefore, birth can be prohibited.

"But how can the intuitions not take place? By prohibiting what can the intuitions be prohibited?

"In the absence of illusion there can be no intuition. By the prohibition of illusion intuition is therefore prohibited. By the prohibition of illusion consciousness is prohibited. So by the obviation of birth, disease, death, grief, anxiety, misery, and longing, the source of diseases, is obviated, and thereby verily is the source of the great tree of pain obviated.

"Thus became manifest to the Bodhisattva the light of religion, unknown before, which always expands by the application of the mind, and produces sense, vision, learning, expansiveness, memory, and knowledge.

"Thus did I, O Bhikshus! at the time learn that this is pain, this is the totality of misery, this is the means of removing it, and this knowledge, which points out the means of removing misery. I learnt that this misery of desire, this of the world, this of delusion, this of sight,—how these miseries may be finally removed; how this misery totally disappears leaving no trace behind. I learnt, too, this is illusion, this the totality of illusion, this the removal of illusion, this the knowledge of removing illusion, how this illusion totally disappears, leaving no trace behind. Enough!

"I learnt these are intuitions, this the totality of intuitions, this the means of removing the intuitions, this is the knowledge of removing the intuitions."

The other categories are recited in the same way; but it is not necessary to reproduce them here. The metaphysical substratum of these cogitations appears to be a system which makes *jñána*, 'knowledge' or 'consciousness' to be the prime source of the phenomenal world, and takes no note of anything beyond, material or spiritual. No God is any where acknowledged. It corresponds so far with the Idealism of Berkeley and the Transfigured Realism of Herbert Spencer, as it denies materiality or realism to the phenomenal world, but it does not, like them, recognize an all-comprehending power. In this respect it approaches nearest to what is called Moderate Idealism, which, according to Viscount Amberley, "agrees with Berkeley in dismissing to the limbo of extinct metaphysical creatures the substance supposed to lurk beneath the apparent qualities of bodies. It holds that there is no such substance, and that these qualities, and therefore bodies themselves, exist only in consciousness. But it differs from Berkeley in omitting to provide any source whatever, external to ourselves, from which these bodies can be derived. Not only are they in their phenomenal aspect the mere states of our own consciousness, but they have no other aspect than the phenomenal one, and are in themselves nothing but phenomena."(a) This is, however, only the philosophy of Buddha as developed in his cogitations, and even as the Moderate Idealist "rather inconsistently concedes to other human beings, something more than a merely phenomenal existence;" so does Buddha. But his disciples have evolved very different schools of thought, and it is difficult to determine what were really his ideas on the subject.

Immediately after these cogitations gods of different classes showered flowers on the Bodhimaṇḍa in token of their great joy at the successful termination of the arduous undertaking of the great saint. "Seeing that the Devaputras had been so disposed, the Bodhisattva, rising in the air to the height of seven palm-trees, rent asunder all the trammels of existence, and proclaimed—'When the road is destroyed the dust is allayed, and the dried up miseries return not again. When the road is destroyed pain comes to an end.' Hearing this the Devaputras showered flowers again and again, so that the earth was covered knee-deep by the flowers. For seven days and nights the Bodhisattva, now Buddha, remained seated on the Bodhimaṇḍa, with the conviction 'now has the eternal knowledge been thoroughly understood by me; 'now has the pain of birth, disease, and death, been brought to a close by me.'"

At the moment when the Bodhisattva attained the perfect knowledge, the whole world was imbued with a sense of supreme felicity; all the regions of the universe were refulgent with a glorious light; the darkness of sin was dissolved everywhere; every living being was agitated by a sense of excitement; all former Buddhas extolled the great achievement; the world was covered by a net-work of jewelled

(a) Amberley's 'Analysis of Religious Belief,' II, p. 421.

umbrellas, and they shed a resplendent light; Bodhisattvas and Devaputras in all the ten quarters of the globe made the air resonant with exclamations of joy, and the clouds showered from the sky auspicious rain to enable the seed of religion to germinate. The glad tidings spread everywhere, and all, who could, repaired to the Bodhimaṇḍa to offer their congratulations to the saint.

The first to come was a body of Apsaras of the class called *Kámávachara*, *i.e.* those who can instantly go wherever they like. These paid their adorations to the saint, and then recited hymns in his praise.

Next came the Devaputras of the class called *Suddhávásakáyika*, *i.e.* pure in body and raiment; then the Devaputras of the class *Ábhásvara*, or radiant; next the Devaputras of the class *Subrahma*; next the Devaputras of the class *Śuklapakshika*, or white-winged; next the Devaputra named *Paranirmita-vasavarti* with his retinue; then Sunirmita Devaputra; then Santusita Devaputra; then the guardian gods of the different watches of the day and night; and each party, in due order, paid their adorations and recited hymns in praise of the saint. Next followed Śakra with his heavenly host of thirty-three gods, and then four celestial emperors (mahárájás), each with a mighty host of Devaputras, and then the gods of the sky and the gods of the earth, and each in succession went through the same ceremony.

Seven days and nights having thus elapsed, on the morning of the eighth day a mighty host of Devaputras brought thousands of pitchers full of perfumed water, and bathed the saint and the Bodhimaṇḍa with the same. On that occasion a Devaputra, of the name of Samantakusuma, asked the saint the name of the meditation he had practised during the seven preceding days. In reply to this query the saint said it was called *Prityáhára-vyúha*, or "the enjoyment of gratification."

After this the saint passed the second week in walking constantly (*Dírgha-chankrama*); the third, in constantly looking at the Bodhimaṇḍa without even the interruption of a wink; and the fourth in traversing by his mind the area from the eastern to the western ocean (*Dahara-chankrama*).

On the termination of the fourth week the sinful Mára approached the lord and said, "Forbear, Bhagavan! forbear. O Sujáta, this is the time for the lord's forbearance."

In reply to this address the lord said:—"O sinful one, I shall never forbear until my disciples become old; until they become able, self-restraining, frank, humble, proficient, experienced, versed in the details of religion, powerful, able to disseminate the knowledge of the teachers among the born and the unborn, competent to overcome heretics by their teaching, and to disseminate virtue. No, I shall not forbear until the light of Buddha and Sangha has been firmly established by me, and infinite Bodhisattvas are made manifest in the peerless Bodhi knowledge. No, as long as my fourfold followers become not self-reliant, humble, frank, and proficient, so long shall I continue to inculcate the invulnerable Dharma."

Hearing this, the sinful Mára retired to a corner, and sat very much mortified, distracted, and helpless, with his face cast down, and scratching the earth with a stick. Thereupon three of his daughters, namely, Ratí, Aratí, and Trishná, thus addressed him:—"Why are you, father, so grieved? (If the cause of your affliction) be a mortal or an elephant, say, and we will tie him up in a lasso and soon bring him to your control."

Mára replied:—"In this world the revered Sujáta is not subject to the passions; he stands beyond what is within my control, and therefore am I in such excessive grief."

Impelled by the volatility and fickleness of their sex, and unmindful of their father's remarks, the daughters assumed the fullness of middle-aged beauty, and appeared before the saint; but he did not turn his mind towards them, and they stood withered and shrivelled-up. Returning then to their father, they said:—"Well have you said, father, that 'he is not subject to the passions; he stands beyond what is under my control, and therefore am I in such excessive grief.' Had he cast a glance on the beauty we had assumed for the distraction of Gautama, his mind would have at once been overcome. Now, father, relieve us of this withered, shrivelled-up body."

Mára said:—"In this world of movables and immovables I can see not the man who can undo the resolution of Buddha. Quickly repair, therefore, to the presence of the sage and confess your guilt, and he will restore you to your former beauty."

The daughters did as they were advised, and the saint benignly forgave them.

The fifth week the saint sojourned near the house of Muchilinda, a Nága king. The weather was excessively rainy and cold, and as the saint remained outside the house, the Nága king coiled himself seven-fold round his body, and outstretched his hood so as to protect the head of the saint from the rain. And like unto him other Nága kings came from the east and the west and the south, and did the same, so that no cold wind could come in contact with the body of the perfect one.

On the lapse of the week the rain ceased, and the Nágas uncoiled themselves, circumambulated the person of the saint three times, and, after prostrating before him with profound respect, retired to their homes.

The following week the saint passed under the shelter of a nyagrodha-tree, belonging to a goatherd. On his way from the house of Muchilinda to the tree, a large concourse of gods and hermits met him on the bank of the Nairanjaná. and congratulated him on his having safely passed through the rainy days.

The seventh week the saint passed under the shelter of a sacred tree (*Tárâyaṇa*) in a grove of khirika-trees (*Memosops kunki*). When he was there, two well-disposed, intelligent merchants, named Trapusha and Bhallika, were returning from the south, after a very successful venture, bringing with them five hundred carts laden with merchandize. They had two bullocks, named Sujáta and Kírti, which had the wonderful quality of moving on over difficulties which no other bullock could face; but if there happened to be any danger ahead, they stopped short, and never would move an inch, even if they were impelled by the severest chastising. When the caravan arrived near the grove, the wheels of the carts sank under the earth up to the nave, and the bullocks stopped and could not be prevailed upon by any means to proceed. They rent asunder all the harness, broke the carts, and stood in fear and amazement. The wonderful yoke of Sujáta and Kírti was tried, but it, too, failed. Thereupon the merchants suspected there must be danger ahead, and sent mounted couriers to survey the ground. After examining every place the couriers returned, and reported that there was no danger ahead, but a very pious-looking and wonderful saint living under a tree. The gifted bullocks now rushed towards the tree, and the whole party beheld the saint seated calmly, dressed in his ochre-coloured garments. The merchants paid him their respects, and offered him a present of honey and sugar, asking him to hold forth a vessel to receive the same.

The thought now struck the saint—how did former Buddhas receive such presents?—and the conclusion arrived at was that an alms-bowl was the most appropriate vessel for the purpose. At this time, knowing that the hour of the saint's repast had arrived, four great kings came from the four quarters, and each placed before him a golden vessel, praying that the saint would deign to accept it. The saint, however, declined the offer. Similarly four vessels, of silver, crystal, and other precious materials, were successively offered, but declined.

The saint then reflected in his mind what was the most appropriate material for an alms-bowl, and what had been used by former Tathágatas, and the conclusion he arrived at was that stone was the best material. Then Vaiśravaṇa, the great king, along with three others, viz. Dhritaráshṭra, Virúdhaka, and Virúpáksha, brought four stone vessels and respectfully offered them to the saint. These were accepted.

Soon after two milch-cows belonging to the merchants, when milked gave, instead of milk, some well-churned butter. The Bráhmans present looked upon this as an evil omen, and ordained an expiatory sacrifice; but a wise man of the party recommended that the wonderful product should be presented to the saint, and this was done.

Having refreshed himself with the offerings presented to him by the merchants, the saint reflected whether, now that he had acquired the perfect knowledge, he should keep it to himself or impart it to others, and he was disposed to adopt the first branch of the alternative, as he thought none could duly appreciate his doctrine. Brahmá, however, felt that such a resolution on the part of the saint would deprive the world of the greatest blessing. So he, Indra, the presiding divinity of the earth, and other gods, repeatedly and earnestly besought him to change his mind, and exhorted him to deign to impart the knowledge to others for the benefit of creation, and ultimately made him accord his assent to the proposal.

The question then arose as to whom he should first impart the knowledge, and where he should do so. He thought of his old tutors, Rudraka and Áráḍha Káláma, but, doubting their faith, ultimately decided upon his five youthful companions, who had left him, but who were likely to prove the most docile recipients. As they were then at Benares, he proposed to proceed thither.

Descending from the Bodhimaṇḍa, he proceeded on his journey. Halting at Gayá, he met a hermit named Ájívaka, who at once recognised in him all the emblems of a perfect being. He approached him and asked, "Tell me, blessed Gautama, what is Brahmacharya?"

The saint replied in verse:—"I never had a tutor, and none exists like unto me: I alone am perfect in knowledge (*sambuddha*), thoroughly purified and sinless."

Ájívaka inquired:—"Respected sir (*arhat*), do you know the soul of Gautama?"

The saint replied:—"I verily am the ruler in this world. I am without a successor; I, a Sura, a Gandharva; I have none to rival me."

Ájívaka again inquired:—"Do you know the soul of *Jina*, the Gautama?"

Tathágata rejoined:—"The *Jinas* are those who have, like me, cleansed themselves from sin. Since all sinful attributes have been overcome by me, I am verily a supreme *Jina* (*upajina*).

Ájívaka asked:—"Where are you going to?"

Tathágata replied:—"I shall repair to Váránasí, and, arriving at the city of Kásí, make refulgent the world immersed in darkness. I shall repair to Váránasí, and, arriving at the city of Kásí, rouse the mute world with the blast of the immortal trumpet. I shall repair to Váránasí, and, arriving at the city of Kásí, turn the wheel of the law in this world."

After this conversation, each turned his own way. The conversation is pointless, but it is worthy of note as affording a clear proof of the existence of Jainism before the composition of the Lalita Vistara.

With the departure of Śákya for Váránasí, the description of his penance comes to a close. The description is obviously legendary to a great extent, and too full of palpably fictitious, miraculous, and supernatural occurrences to be worthy of any confidence. But within this dense mass of cloud it is not difficult to perceive an outline of the true character of the saint, which has all the elements of genuine history.

Early in the fourth quarter of the last century a feuilleton appeared, which, by dint of *à priori* arguments and sophistic reasoning, attempted to prove that the accounts published of British successes in the American war of independence were all false. The success which attended this venture led to the origin of similar feuilletons disproving the existence of Napoleon Buonaparte and other personages. The object in these cases was fun, and this was fully attained; but of late this system of reasoning has been, with sober seriousness, brought to bear upon ancient history, and, among others, Buddha has been shown to be a myth. It would be out of place to enter into a discussion here on the subject, or to refute this assumption. Believing as I do, with some of the most distinguished scholars of the day, in the historical entity of the author of the Buddhist religion, I shall note briefly the circumstances which appear to me to be mythical or legendary incrustations on an historically probable substratum.

That such a tribe as that of the Śákyas did once exist on the north of the Ganges none will, I fancy, question. At the time of Buddha's birth, India was divided into many small kingdoms, each held by a tribal chief, and Kapilavastu, under Suddhodana, was one of them—a small principality, perhaps not quite so large as the Bettiah or the Darbhangá Ráj of the present day. Its chief unquestionably exercised full regal powers, but his income in those days could scarcely have been more than a fourth or a fifth of that of modern Darbhangá. Wassiljew is of opinion that the royal parentage of the saint is an invention, designed to shed additional glory on him; but seeing how many royal personages with extensive dominion and absolute power have, in mediæval and modern times, both in Europe and Asia, voluntarily exchanged the throne for a monk's cell, there is nothing extraordinary in a petty Indian prince, in a sudden fit of a capricious revulsion of feeling, or from domestic discord, or from satiety after over-indulgence in the pleasures of the world, (a) or from a naturally religious disposition, forsaking his home and betaking to an ascetic life; and I see no reason to reject the united testimony of all Indian writers on the subject. An invention of the kind is possible, but it is not probable. Certain it is that no such invention has been attempted in the case of Nának, Guru Govind, Kabir, Chaitanya, and other later religious reformers in India. Religious glory was in their cases so supreme that it could gain nothing by exalted birth. The latter would pale before the former; not to advert to the shortness of time between the death of Śákya and the composition of his biography to admit of an invention, trifling in itself, and involving a question of fact, to be easily made current.

Leaving out of consideration the circumstances under which Śákya obtained his hermit's garb as unworthy of notice, his peregrinations and pupilage under different tutors are perfectly natural. That he should be received with welcome by Vimbisára of Magadha, a neighbouring chieftain, who was most probably aware of the young hermit's birth and parentage, is nothing extraordinary; the conversation between the two, and the promise to become a pupil should the youth ever attain success in his mission, being mere poetical embellishments. The account of the journey from Magadha to Uruvilvá contains nothing legendary or

(a) See my 'Sanskrit Buddhist Literature of Nepal,' p. 68.

supernatural. In the present day hermits are passing from place to place by hundreds and thousands, halting under the friendly shelter of trees when tired, and living upon the alms of the charitable. Nor is there anything extraordinary in an Indian hermit passing some time, say three, four, five, or six years, in penance under a tree, living upon such scanty food as the neighbours thought fit to bring to him. The story of the single plum, the single grain of rice, and the absolute fast, must of course be relegated to the region of poetical hyperboles. It is doubtful whether the village maiden, Sujátá, was an historical personage, or merely the symbol of all those who charitably offered their doles to the fasting saint, who never begged for his meal; probably a symbol for the name appears to be a generic one, meaning the 'well-born,' or 'the good one;' and the Lalita Vistara, in one place, gives the names of twelve maidens (a) who used to give alms to the saint during his six years' meditations. Abstention from begging is a very effective method amidst unsophisticated villagers of bringing in regular supplies of food to a fasting hermit. The author of this essay well remembers a hermit who, five-and-thirty years ago, came to a mango tope near his residence in the suburbs of Calcutta and devoted a whole year to the performance of the most rigorous penances. The deluded man used to pass his winter nights seated in a tank with water up to his neck. During summer, for two or three hours every day, he hung himself by his feet from the branch of a tree and kept a burning fire below, his companion keeping him swinging to prevent the fire from scorching him. During rainy weather he used to sit in an open place, so that he may be thoroughly drenched. During the whole of the period neither the hermit nor his disciple ever went out to beg, but they got their food regularly supplied them by the people who lived around them. Nor is this a solitary instance. It is a time-honored custom in this country; and there is, therefore, nothing extraordinary in a hermit having done the like in India two thousand and four hundred years ago.

The transition from the penance to a different mode of living is also not uncommon, and the resolution to preach a new doctrine may be believed in without any stretch of imagination, if we will only reject as fabulous all the supernatural occurrences, the decorations of the road to the Bodhimaṇḍa, the warfare with the Evil One and his host, the divine visitations and exhortations, and the celestial

(a) Their names were (1) Balá, (2) Dáriká, (3) Balaguptá, (4) Priyá, (5) Supriyá, (6) Vyayasená, (7) Atimukta-kamalá, (8) Sundarí, (9) Kumbhakárí, (10) Uluvilliká, (11) Jeṭiliká, (12) Sujátá. In words the number is said to be ten.—*Lalita Vistara*, p. 331.

rejoicings which have been engrafted on them. In short, a petty prince, tired of home, betakes to the life of a religious pupil, then passes some time, the exact period being immaterial, though the period assigned is not long, in penance in a retired village, and then assumes the rôle of the teacher of a new doctrine, and this is the sum total of the historical Buddha as he now "stands before us as one of the few great leaders of humanity, who seem endowed with every virtue and free from every fault."(a)

The legends are due partly to poetical embellishments, partly to allegories, and partly to deliberate ingraftation of ancient stories on the original simple stem, to heighten its importance. The additions were not all made at one time, but at different times, and under different circumstances. Nevertheless they are all of very ancient date. Hiouen Thsang knew them all in the middle of the seventh century; Fa Hian, in the beginning of the fifth century, referred to several of them; and they occur in the Chinese life of Buddha, which dates from the first century. Even before the commencement of the Christian era we have some of them represented in frescoes and sculpture. They existed when the church split into Northern and Southern Buddhism within two hundred years of the saint's death, and the Lalita Vistara, which dates from the third century before Christ, gives them all in full detail.

The story of the assault of Mára on the saint is obviously an allegory, intended to illustrate the influence which the sensuous desires exert to subvert the moral instincts of man, or the struggle which the intellectually-disposed must undergo in order to overcome all the cravings of their passions and rise above all carnality. It is the counterpart of the Vedic allegory of the wars of the gods and the demons, the moral and religious faculties and the lust of the flesh. It occurs in some form or other in all the leading systems of religion. It was evidently current at an early period in the history of Buddha, as it occurs in the Gáthá portion of the Lalita Vistara. Perhaps it was originally accepted as an allegory and no more; but, as usual in such cases, the allegory passed into the concrete, and the faithful accepted it as true history. The change took place long before the commencement of the Christian era, as in the Ajantá caves we have a fresco painting, which is most probably about 2,000 years old, in which the story is fully delineated. (See Plate II.) The saint is represented seated on a throne under a tree, with Mára

(a) 'Amberley's Analysis of Religious Belief,' Vol. I, p. 219.

to his right brandishing a big sword, and a host of imps and hobgoblins fiercely attacking him from all sides. The daughters of Mára are represented standing in front of the throne. The monster forms shown in the picture are not numerous, nor always in keeping with the Lalita Vistara description, but there is no doubt of the whole being a pictorial representation of the story. The ideas are in some respects contemptible, and the attempt on the part of one of the monsters to frighten the saint by showing the white of his eyes by turning the eyelid is peculiarly puerile. Time and, possibly, inimical hands have very much injured the fresco, and large portions of it have been obliterated. But such as the picture is it is interesting as affording a tangible evidence of the antiquity of the story.

It is obvious that the story of the warfare between good and evil was borrowed by the Buddhists from the Hindus, for in its essential elements it is nothing but what suggested the wars of the Devas and the Asuras. In its modified form, as given in the Buddhist books, it occurs in the later works on Yoga and in the Tantras. Seated on a corpse in a cremation ground at midnight when a person is engaged in the performance of the demoniacal rite called *Sava-sádhana* for the acquirement of supernatural powers, he is, it is said, assailed by aerial spirits, which come to him in the forms of tigers, serpents, and hideous monsters, and frighten him in every possible way; and should he stand firm against them and give no attention to their doings and sayings, he is sure to accomplish his objects: otherwise he fails. In other forms of Yoga the same causes of interruptions are also apprehended. But in the last transition the story has lost its allegorical character. It is no longer Mára that assails, but demi-gods, instigated by Indra, who wish to put to test the fixity of purpose of the person engaged in the performance of a Yoga, and the name given to it is *Vibhisiká*, or 'frightening.'

Sanskrit Buddhist literature does not afford us any clue to the exact spots where the different events described in the above narrative took place. Fa Hian gives the bearings and distances of some of the places; but his account of Buddha Gayá is exceedingly brief, and in some instances manifestly inaccurate. Hiouen Thsang, however, makes some amends for the shortcomings of his predecessor. His itinerary is written in considerable detail, and, but for the absence of measured distances in some cases, would have left nothing to be desired, except plates. The bearings he gives are generally correct. He notices, too, several incidents in the life of the saint which find no place in the narrative of the Lalita Vistara. They have thus the disadvantage of being less authentic, but they are mostly founded on the Avadánas and other scriptural texts of his creed. Besides, whether authentic or not, they are so intimately associated with the history of Buddhism, and once figured so prominently in connection with the monumental remains of Buddha Gayá, that they cannot be overlooked without sacrificing, at least to a certain extent, the interest of the remains now extant, and of the history of the place, which forms the theme of this essay.

Leaving the southern boundary of Gayá, the first object of antiquity which Hiouen Thsang met with was a stúpa erected to the honour of the birth-place of Káśyapa. This stood to the south-east of the hill of Gayá, *i.e.* the Brahmayoni hill, and close by the Nairanjaná river. To the south of it, opposite the Prágbodhi hill, now called Mórá, there were two others at a place where Gayá Káśyapa and Nadí Káśyapa had performed a sacrifice (*yajña*) when they were Hindus.

Crossing the river at this place, the pilgrim came to the Prágbodhi hill, and there he noticed certain monuments which do not come within the scope of this essay. Travelling thence from 40 to 50 *li* (about 8 miles) to the south-west, he arrived at the foot of the Tree of Knowledge. The tree was surrounded by a substantial brick wall, very difficult of access. The area enclosed was oblong; the length stretching from the east to the west, and the breadth from the north to the south. The principal entrance to this enclosure, comprising a circuit of 500 paces, or 1,250 feet, *i.e.* about 350 by 275 feet, was from the east, facing the river. The southern gate had near it a large basin of water, covered with flowers. The western gate was particularly strong and difficult of access, and the north one communicated with a large convent. "Over every part of the ground surrounded by the wall there were sacred monuments of all kinds,—either stúpas (tumuli) or viháras (temples). Kings, ministers, and great personages from all parts of the Jambudvípa, who had respectfully received the doctrine which had been bequeathed by Buddha, had constructed them to preserve his memory" (p. 460). Their number was immense, and the pilgrim felt it too difficult to describe them. He accordingly remarked:—'*Dans l'intérieur des murs de l'arbre de l'intelligence, les monuments sacrés se touchent les uns les autres; il serait très-difficile de les citer tous*" (p. 477). Outside of this enciente, within a circuit of ten *li*, or nearly two miles round the Tree of Knowledge, the sacred monuments were also so numerous that he could not cite them all:—"*A environ dix li au midi de l'arbre de l'intelligence, les monuments sacrés sont tellement nombreux, qu'il serait difficile de les citer tous*" (p. 492). He has nevertheless noticed a great number, most probably all the more important ones, and I shall here attempt a synopsis of his narrative, illustrating it with a rough sketch (Plate III), showing the probable sites of the monuments seen by the pilgrim. The numbers given in the text correspond with those on the sketch.

Passing over his account of the Bodhi-tree (No. 1) and the Great Temple (No. 2) to the east of it, to be noticed in a subsequent chapter, the first monument he describes was a convent (No. 3). It was situated to the north of the tree, and there Buddha used to promenade for exercise. It was a massive structure of brick (p. 470), and to the north of that spot there was placed, in the centre of a stately temple (No. 4), a large flag of stone and an image of Buddha with his eyes uplifted, to commemorate that part of his career in which he, for seven days, watched the Tree of Knowledge without turning his eyes for a single instant. At a short distance to the west of the tree there was a large temple with an image of Buddha in brass, covered with the rarest and most precious ornaments (No. 5). The saint was represented standing and looking towards the east. Under the statue there was a flag of blue-coloured stone with wonderful veins and of extraordinary character. When the Bodhisattva was about to attain his perfection, the god Brahmá had built for him a magnificent palace with seven precious materials, and Indra built a seat with similar materials, and this stone was a relic of those structures; the pilgrim adding with characteristic *naïveté*, "during the immense interval which separates us from the saint, the precious stones have changed into ordinary stones" (p. 472).

At a short distance to the south of the tree there was a stúpa 100 feet high, which had been built by King Aśoka (No. 6). To the north-east of it there was another (No. 7), which marked the spot where the Bodhisattva had obtained from a grass-cutter some grass for his seat on the Bodhimaṇḍa (p. 472). It was in the neighbourhood of this spot that Bodhisattva beheld some blue birds (*nílakaṇṭha*) and a herd of deer, which presaged the success of his undertaking. (*a*)

(*a*) The *nílakaṇṭha* is to this day held by the Hindus to be a bird of good omen, and on the last day of the Dúrgá-pújá one is generally let loose to fly away as an auspicious sign. The deer is not so held by the Hindus, but it has been always a favourite in hermitages. The presence of the figure of deer on the throne of Buddha is generally explained as indicative of good luck.

To the east of the tree, close by the highway, there was a stúpa (No. 8), which marked the spot whence Mára twice assailed the great saint: once tempting him with the offer of universal sovereignty, and at another time deputing his daughters to display their charms to seduce the saint, for which fault they were metamorphosed into old hags. (a)

In the centre of a vihára (No. 6) situated to the north-west of the tree there was a statue of Káśyapa Buddha. As the saint was renowned for his divine powers and sanctity, there was always a great enthusiasm. It is said, in the words of the ancients, that if a man, animated by sincere faith, walks seven times round this statue, he obtains, wherever he may be born, the knowledge of his anterior existences (p. 473).

To the north-west of the last there were two houses built of bricks (No. 10). One was dedicated to the goddess of the earth for her appearance before the saint when Mára was overcome, and the other built by the people to commemorate that act of virtue (p. 474). At a short distance to the north-west of the wall round the tree there was a stúpa (No. 10), called the 'Saffron Stúpa' (*Kumkuma stúpa*). It was about 40 feet high, and had been dedicated by a merchant who had been saved from the perils of the sea by devotion to Buddha (p. 474).

At the south-east angle of the wall, near an Indian fig-tree (*nyagrodha*), there was a stúpa (No. 11), and by its side a vihára containing an image of Buddha in the act of receiving the request of Brahmá to turn the wheel of the law. When Buddha had obtained the sacred grass for his seat on the Bodhimaṇḍa, he walked to the four corners, and the great earth quaked; but when he took his seat under the tree every thing became quiescent. At each of the four corners of the enciente, within the surrounding wall, there was a large stúpa (No. 12); and these marked the spots to which he had walked on each side (p. 477).

To the south-west, beyond the circuit of the wall, there was an old house belonging to the two(b) peasant girls who had given a dish of frumenty to the saint (No. 13). Near by, where they had dressed the dish, there was another stúpa (No. 14); and there was a third (No. 15) where the saint received the dish of rice-milk (p. 477).

Beyond the southern gate there was a large tank, about 700 paces, 1,850 feet in circuit (No. 16). Its water was pure and clear like a mirror, and dragons

(a) See note, p. 36.
(b) See note, p. 49.

(crocodiles ?) and fishes lived in it. It had been excavated by two Bráhman brothers by order of the god Mahesvara (p. 477).

Further on there was another tank (No. 17), and it was the one which Indra had excavated with his hands for the saint to wash his clothes and bathe in. To the west of this tank there was a large stone (No. 18), which Indra had brought from the Snowy Mountain for the saint to spread his clothes upon to dry (p. 478).

Near by the last there is a stúpa where Buddha dried his clothes (No. 19). The remains of this stúpa now form a rubbish mound, which in the revenue survey map is called an 'old site.'

Further on, to the south, near a wood (No. 21), there is a stúpa (No. 20) where he received the clothes from the hands of a poor old woman (a) (p. 478). The wood still exists.

To the east of the tank excavated by Indra, the Lord of the gods, in the midst of a wood, there was a tank (No. 22), belonging to the King of Dragons, Muchilinda. Its water is of a bluish-black colour, and of a sweet agreeable taste. On the west of this tank there is a small vihára, where the saint remained in meditation for seven days after obtaining the perfect knowledge (p. 478).

On the east of this ancient tank there was the dwelling of the dragon (No. 23). The place is now called Muchárim, evidently a corruption of Muchilinda.

In the midst of a wood, to the east of the tank of Muchilinda, there is a vihára with a statue of Buddha, represented as very thin and emaciated (No. 24). Close by this there is a spot, about 70 paces long, where the saint used to promenade for exercise (p. 479).

To the south and north (*sic* in text) of the last there is a pipal-tree (No. 25), where the saint performed his six years' austerities along with his five companions (the name of one of them was Ajñàta Kaundinya). The oil from the fruit of this tree, mixed with offerings to the statues, cures diverse maladies. Close by this tree there was a stúpa raised by the five companions (p. 479).

To the south-east of the last there was a stúpa on a spot from which the saint went to the river for his bath (No. 26).

(a) The Lalita Vistara replaces the woman by a corpse.' See p. 29. One of the Avádanas supports the statement of Hiouen Thsang.

Near by this place there is a stúpa (No. 27), where a householder gave the saint some meal and parched grain, and further on another, (No. 28) where two merchants presented to the saint some parched grain and meal (a). They were passing by the forest, and, being apprised by the spirit of the forest that the Master of the Age was immersed in meditation for 49 days without food, came forward and offered the food, which was graciously accepted. By the side of this place, where the merchants offered the meal, there is a stúpa. This is the spot where the four kings of the sky gave alms-bowls to Buddha. When the revered of the age was offered the meal, he asked in what he was to receive it. At this moment the four kings of the sky came from the four sides of the world, bringing each a golden vase, which they offered him. The revered of the age remained silent, and expressed no wish to receive them. He thought within himself, since I have quitted my home it is not proper that I should use such vases. The four kings of the sky put aside the golden vases and offered those of silver. They then offered vases of rock-crystal, of lapis-lazuli, of cornelian, of amber, of ruby, &c. When the revered of the age would not look at them, nor receive any of them, these kings returned to their palaces, and each brought a vase of stone. These vases were of a violet colour and transparent. The kings submitted their new offerings to the Buddha. As the revered of the age had refused the former vases, he accepted the latter (p. 481. c.f.).

Close by the side of the place where the four kings of the sky had offered the vases, there is a stúpa (No. 29). It was at this place that the Buddha had explained the law to his mother.

By the side of the last, on the bank of a dry tank, there is a stúpa (No. 30). It marks the spot where Buddha displayed some wonderful miracles and converted many persons.

By the side of the last there was another, which commemorated the conversion of Uruvilvá Káśyapa and his two brothers along with a thousand disciples (No. 31). At this time five hundred disciples of Uruvilvá Káśyapa felt a desire to receive the law, and thereupon the Lord pronounced the memorable admonition,—"Cast away your vestments of deer skin and give up all your utensils of fire-worship." Thereupon all the Bráhmans saluted the lord with great respect, and cast into the waters of the Nairanjaná all their objects of worship. Nadí Káśyapa and his

(a) Honey and sugar, according to the Lalita Vistara. See p. 46.

disciples, seeing the sacrificial vases floating on the water, and the conduct of his eldest brother, likewise cast their robes and assumed the monastic ochre-colour. Gayá Káśyapa followed the example of his elder, and accepted the new faith in the company of his two hundred disciples (p. 483).

To the north-west of the last there is a stúpa (No. 32). This marks the spot where the Tathágata overcame the fire-dragon. When the sage was about to convert the three brothers and cause the destruction of the sacrificial articles, he stopped at the house of the dragon, which began, a minute after, to vomit forth volumes of flame and smoke. The sage absorbed himself in a fit of *samádhi*, and the house was enveloped in fire. The Bráhmans dreaded much that he would perish in the conflagration, and raised deep lamentations of pity. Uruvilvá Káśyapa thus addressed his disciples:—"What you have seen is certainly not the work of an incendiary: I am sure it is the Śramaṇa, who is conquering the fire-dragon" (p. 484).

The sage locked the fire-dragon in his alms-bowl, and on the following morning preached to, and converted, the disciples of the heretics (p. 485).

On the side of the last was a stúpa (No. 33), where five hundred Pratyeka Buddhas had obtained *nirváṇa*.

To the south of the tank of Muchilinda there is a stúpa (No. 34), which marks the place where the saint, after converting the Káśyapa brothers, was covered by volumes of cloud and rain. Káśyapa, fearing that the honourable of the age would be carried away by an inundation, procured a boat for his rescue. The honourable of the age, however, accepted not the succour, but walked on the water as on *terra firma*. While he was walking in the middle of the current, the waters separated wide apart, and gave him way. Káśyapa bore testimony to this miracle (p. 485).

Two or three *li* beyond the eastern gate of the enclosure one sees the house of the blind dragon (No. 35). This dragon, having accumulated in himself the evil deeds of his former existences, was made blind by way of punishment. Tathágata, having quitted the Prágbodhi Hill, when proceeding to the Tree of Intelligence, passed by this house. The eyes of the dragon were then completely closed to the impression of light. When the dragon saw the sage passing by, he said:—"O thou of boundless humanity, you are about to obtain the fullness of knowledge. It is now for a long time that my eyes have been plunged in darkness. Of the Buddhas who have appeared on earth, my eyes have suddenly fallen on some. During the Kalpa of the Sages, when three Buddhas will have appeared on earth,

I shall have already obtained my day. Man of boundless humanity! since you have arrived here my eyes have suddenly been opened: it is hence that I have perceived your approach. You will soon be a Buddha" (p. 486). This story does not occur in the Lalita Vistara, nor is there any mention in it of Buddha's having gone to the Prágbodhi Hill after his hexannual penance.

On the side of the eastern gate of the enclosure, where the king of the demons essayed to frighten the Bodhisattva, there is a stúpa (No. 36). In connection with it the Chinese pilgrim gives a brief account of the circumstances noticed above.

On a side, at a short distance, there are two stúpas: one built by Śakra Devendra (No. 37), and the other by Brahmá (No. 38).

Beyond the western gate of the enclosure there was a convent, called Mahábodhi Sanghárâma (No. 39). It had been built by the first sovereign of the kingdom of Ceylon. This edifice had six halls, belvederes, and three-storeyed pavilions, and a surrounding wall 34 feet high. It was constructed with admirable art, and decorated with marvellous pictures. The image of Buddha in it was cast in gold and silver, and all its ornaments were covered with precious stones. The stupas within the enclosure were of grand proportions, and richly decorated. They held the relics of Buddha. Some held his bones, which were thick as the joints of the hand. They were lustrous, of a pure white colour, and completely transparent. The relics of his flesh are as big pearls, and of a pinkish-blue colour. Every year, on the day of the full-moon, when the Tathágata had performed divine prodigies, these relics are shown to the multitude. Sometimes they appear in great brilliance, and sometimes buried in masses of flowers. The monks of this convent, who number below a thousand, study the doctrine of the school of the Árya-sthaviras, which belongs to the school of the Great Translation. They observe with great respect the rules of discipline, and are noted for the purity of their conduct. In days of yore the kingdom of Ceylon, which lies in the middle of the sea, had a king who had sincere faith in the law of Buddha; and this faith was natural in him. He had a younger brother, who quitted the family. Burning with love for the monuments sacred to Buddha, he afterwards came to the shores of India and lodged in the convents; but over the earth he had travelled he found nothing wrong except in a frontier country. At last he revisited his native country, and, through his intercession, the king caused the convent to be built.

CHAPTER III.

ARCHITECTURAL REMAINS.

ARCHITECTURAL REMAINS AT BUDDHA GAYÁ—RUINS OF OLD TEMPLES—MOUND FORMED BY THEM—TEMPLE OF TÁRÁ DEVÍ—TEMPLE OF VÁGÍŚVARÍ DEVÍ—CONDITION OF MOUND IN 1861—EXCAVATION BY MAJOR MEAD—GROUND-PLANS BY GENERAL CUNNINGHAM—DEMOLITIONS BY THE BURMESE EMBASSY IN 1877—NEW BOUNDARY WALL, ITS DECORATIONS AND GATEWAYS—LEVEL OF THE COURT-YARD—A SMALL TEMPLE—THE VIHÁRA OF CONTEMPLATION—SEVERAL MASONRY TOMBS—SAMÁDHS—AŚOKA'S RAILING—GRANITE PLINTH—EXTENT OF AŚOKA'S RAILING—AREA WITHIN THE RAILING—CELLS ON THE EAST SIDE—GREAT TEMPLE—ITS CONSTRUCTION—ITS SOUTHERN FAÇADE—ITS PINNACLE—ITS NORTHERN, WESTERN, AND EASTERN FAÇADES—SANCTUM AND ITS PRESIDING DIVINITY—SECOND-STOREY ROOM—THIRD-STOREY ROOM—THE TERRACE, SOUTH SIDE—THE TERRACE, NORTH SIDE—THE TERRACE, EAST SIDE—PORCH—PAVILION—CORNER PAVILIONS—THE TERRACE ON THE WEST SIDE—BODHI TREE—ITS PLATFORM—ITS HISTORY—BUDDHAPAD—ARCHED CORRIDOR—MATERIALS OF BUILDING, BRICKS, CLAY CEMENT, LIME CEMENT, WOOD, STONE, METAL—STYLE OF BUILDING—THE ARCHES—THEIR NUMBER—OPINIONS REGARDING THEIR AGE—ART DISPLAYED IN THE BUILDING OF THE TEMPLE—BUDDHOKAR TÁL.

Of the several monuments noticed at the close of the last chapter, there is only one now extant to attest to the accuracy of Hiouen Thsang's statements. It is a large brick-built temple, standing at the north-east corner of the village of Mastipur Táráḍí, close by the boundary line between that village and Buddha Gayá. When seen by Hiouen Thsang it was surrounded by an enclosing wall, and had several temples, stúpas, and monasteries about it. How many of the latter were *in situ* in the year 1305 A.C., when a Burmese Embassy visited the place, we know not; but at the beginning of this century Buchanan-Hamilton found them all reduced to amorphous heaps, except the one under notice, which I shall call the Great Temple. It was then in a dilapidated, ruinous condition, uncared for and deserted. The ruins around this Great Temple, in the time of Buchanan-Hamilton, formed a high uneven terrace or mound, covering an area of 800 × 480 feet.

Mound.

Formerly this mound was continuous with, and formed a part of, the large mound noticed in Chapter I (p. 2); but having since been cut across by the village road to Kohlurá, it has been completely detached from it. Its unevenness is due partly to hollows marking the sites of the court-yards of ancient monasteries and temples, and partly to trenches cut for excavating bricks from old foundations. On the west and the south sides parts of it have been levelled and brought under cultivation. On the east, at one time the mound abutted on the trunk road to Calcutta; but parts of it have latterly been cleared for building sites, and its boundary line has been thrown back about a hundred feet to the west. A narrow path along its middle marked the site of the road which led to the court-yard of the Great Temple. The road was originally covered by a vaulted roof extending as far as the bank of the Liláján, but only a few feet of it, at the western end, was *in situ* at the beginning of this century. The court-yard was open only in front of the temple, and covered a small area having a stone pavilion in the centre, and four small tombs. Thus the mound was uninterrupted all round, and enclosed a patch of low land of the form of the letter T, the upright stem of which was represented by the road, and the top line by the court-yard.

Tárá Deví's Temple.

When the mound was first brought to this condition is not known, but at the beginning of the last century it was very much in the same state in which it was found by Buchanan-Hamilton; for it was about that time that one of the abbots of the monastery cleared a portion of the north-east corner of it for a cemetery, and appropriated to Hindu usage an ancient temple standing right on the mound. This temple is situated close to the Great Temple, and in style is a miniature representation of it. It has been built with bricks of the same size and make as we find in the Great Temple, and cemented with clay. Originally it was, I think, two-storeyed, of which the lower storey lies buried in the mound; but I did not excavate round the base of it to ascertain the fact. The portion now visible measures 36 feet 5 inches in height on a base of 15 feet 9 inches by 15 feet 3 inches. The chamber inside is 5 feet 8 inches by 5 feet 10 inches by 11 feet 2 inches, having a vaulted roofing formed of a pointed Gothic arch. It was probably plastered in the same way as the Great Temple; if so, the plastering has since entirely peeled off. It was not provided with a porch. Its presiding divinity is Tárá Deví, but "the image which has been selected," says Buchanan-Hamilton, "in place of having the form of Tárá, one of the most hideous of the female destructive powers, represents a mild-looking prince standing on a throne supported by seven Buddhas."(*a*) The image was evidently dug out of the mound, and is that of Padmapáṇi, one of the principal Bodhisattvas, holding in his left hand a lotus-stalk with a fully blown lotus on its top, and having a rampant lion by his side. The figures on the throne are not of Buddhas, nor of supporters of the throne, but of pious ascetics. (Plate XX, Fig. 1.) The appearance, style, and make of the temple, leave no doubt in my mind of its having been built at an early age, and being one of the several minor temples noticed by Hiouen Thsang. The Mahants of the last century erected several buildings, but they never attempted anything like the reproduction of the old style; and, judging from what they have left behind, were not capable of doing any work of the kind. The temple stood there deserted, forsaken, and dilapidated, and they appropriated it to their own use by giving it and its presiding image new names. In doing so they did not even take the trouble to change the image, or bring to light the inhumed portion of the temple by removing the rubbish around its base. It should be added, however, that one of the Tántric divinities of the Buddhists is named Tárá, and there is nothing to show that the temple was not originally designed for that divinity. In either case it affords a curious instance of confounding of the sexes. But human credulity in religious matters is so overpowering that it is enough to blindfold people's eyes even to the extent of rendering them unfit to mark the differences between male and female figures. In the two Gayás I have met with at least a dozen instances of this kind.

Vágíśvarí Deví's Temple.

In front of the last, and at a distance of about 150 feet, there is a second temple, also built by a Mahant, but of a very modest character, comprising two square chambers, the front one of which never had a roof, and neither any plastering, except on the cornice of the inner chamber. The presiding divinity of the sanctum is known by the name of Vágíśvarí Deví, the goddess of speech; but, as in the last case, "the image placed in it was dug from the ruins, and in its new name no attention has been paid to its sex, as it represents an armed male" (*b*). The figure is that of Vajrapáṇi, seated on a throne; he has one foot bent across on the seat, and the other

(*a*) 'Transactions, Royal Asiatic Society,' I, p. 45. In the 'Tantra-sára' the goddess is described as "a short, blue-complexioned, fierce-looking female, with long matted hair, standing on a corpse with the right foot put forward on the chest, laughing loudly, and holding a broad sword, a lotus, a platter containing human gore, and a sheaf of wheat. She is surrounded by serpents, and is ready to destroy the three worlds." The form of Tárá is but slightly different from that of Káli.

(*b*) Ibid, loc. cit.

hanging down and resting on a full-blown lotus. The right hand of the figure holds an uplifted sword, and the left a lotus-stalk. On the head of the figure there was a small image of Buddha, but it has been broken off. On each side of the figure there is, on the background, a miniature Chaitya. (Plate XXXII, fig. 2.) The front room contains in its centre a circular slab of chlorite 5 feet 9 inches in diameter and 6 inches in thickness, carved in a complicated mystic pattern. (Plate XLIII, fig. 4.) It will be described in detail further on.

The north-east, the south, and the west sides of the mound were studded with huts; but the north side was perfectly unoccupied. The enclosure round the building was found by General Cunningham, when he visited the place in 1861-62, to be very much in that state, as shown on the ground-plan attached to his first report, and reproduced on a reduced scale on Plate IV, except the pillars and the plinth, which were then not visible.

Major Mead's excavations.

In 1864 Major Mead was employed by Government, on the recommendation of General Cunningham, to carry on excavations round the temple, and then the plinth and the pillars were first brought to light. The results arrived at by Major Mead have been thus summarised by him: "On the north and west fronts I found that the external walls of the platform were modern, and apparently not founded on the original solid ground, but in the mud soil which has accumulated.

"In front of the temple I found that the court-yard was paved with a granite floor 34 feet in width, and the whole length of the (eastern) front of the temple, which terminates under a cut-stone moulded plinth, which no doubt carried some sort of ornamental fence dividing off this inner court from the exterior (see basalt plinth in the accompanying plan, Plate IV, plan No. 1. (The 34 feet must be measured from the doorway of the entrance hall B, as the width of pavement from the actual outer walls of N.N. is only 17 feet from the basalt plinth. The granite pavement also extends beyond this plinth as far as the brick archway attributed to Amara Siñha Sauvira.)

"The eastern external trench running in front of this archway from south to north yielded a considerable quantity of masonry *in situ*, and large numbers of handsomely-carved model stúpas, of which some hundreds of specimens have been disinterred by our excavations. I consequently enlarged the trench here to above 20 feet in width, and endeavoured to trace these walls, which turned out to be the lower portions of four small single cell temples or shrines, the upper portions of which are gone. In one of the most complete, the stone door-frame of which still stands, we found in place, and on its original pedestal, a statue of Buddha in the usual seated position (perfect, except the head, which is broken off and missing) of rather more than life-size. On the pedestal of this figure, and on the base of the statue, are two lines of inscription in good order. * * Here we found a bronze bell of nearly hemispherical shape, about 10 inches in diameter, and part of some bronze ornament, representing, I fancy, the head of a peacock.

"Of the four internal trenches, that along the southern face of the temple has been excavated. It has exposed the southern basement of the temple, which is singularly perfect and handsome, although entirely in plaster. * * Here we obtained the corroded remains of two or three small bronze trumpets, * * and about 28 feet from the south-west corner of the temple this trench disclosed a broken pillar and rail of what in your instructions you term the Bhuddhist railing.

"On seeing this I decided * * to take the internal western trench along the line of this railing, and doing so, I found the railing still all along in place, except that every post had been broken off just above the insertion of the lowest rail, save only the two at an opening in the middle opposite the holy peepul tree. The two pillars standing are nearly perfect, with carving on two adjacent sides in view of the usual mortice holes"(a).

Cunningham's plans.

I visited the place, on the invitation of Major Mead, at the close of 1863, and during the few hours I was at the place I prepared a rough ground-plan which appeared in the journal of the Asiatic Society of Bengal(b). It was, however, not so full as those which have been prepared by General Cunningham, particularly the one made after a second visit to the place in 1871, and with Major Mead's working plans before him(c). Both his plans I reproduce for the sake of easy reference and comparison. (Plate IV, plans Nos. 1 & 2.) The General's first plan was, I presume, produced after the completion of Major Mead's excavations, *i.e.* four years after the

(a) Apud Cunningham's Archæological Survey Report, III, pp. 87-88.
(b) Vol. XXXIII, p. 173.
(c) Arch. Surv. Report for 1871-72, plate XXV.

General's report was written and published in the journal of the Asiatic Society of Bengal, as otherwise the indications of the sites of the pillars and the plinth become inexplicable. The second is defective, as it omits the ancient archway and the modern samádhs which existed in 1861, and still exist, and could not have disappeared in 1871. It is erroneous, too, as it represents at the south-east corner of the temple a flight of steps which did not exist at the time, and never could have existed. I examined the place very carefully, but could find no trace whatever of the ground before the wall of the terrace ever having borne the end of a staircase. The wall itself, though decayed, is still in such a state of preservation as to leave no doubt in one's mind about its age. It is decorated with plinth mouldings, niches flanked with attached columns, and a frieze formed of garlands pendant from lion-heads, which are the continuations and exact counterparts of similar ornaments on the south side. The plastering on the ornaments bore unmistakeable marks of having been repaired as often as the other parts, and therefore must be of the same age with the rest of the building. I peeled off the plaster in several places, and pulled out some of the bricks of the wall, but could nowhere see any sign of the wall ever having been perforated for the admission of a flight of steps. It is impossible to believe that after the removal of the steps the wall was repaired and restored to its original condition, and the gradual degeneracy of the ornaments produced by repeated coats of plaster was imitated at the time of closing the perforation; and it would be vain to speculate on what existed before the terrace as it now stands was built. General Cunningham does not represent the stairs in his first plan, but has in its place the broken stump of a wall, which I have no reason to believe ever existed; certainly there was no trace of it when I visited the place in 1863, and again in September last. I fancy the stairs on the left side have been drawn to preserve the relative symmetry of the front. Unquestionably ancient Indian builders were very particular in this respect; but as the stairs on the right side did not form an element in the original plan of the builder of the terrace, its counterpart on the left was not at all needed. Looking to its style,—so modern and so unlike everything else about the temple,—the presumption is that the flight of steps on the right side was built either by the Burmese Embassy of the 14th century, or in the last century by one of the Mahants of the Maṭh, to provide an easy passage for the Hindu pilgrims wishing to visit the Bodhi tree, without subjecting them to enter the porch of a heterodox shrine, and not by the architect of the temple. The builder of the new stairs did not at all trouble himself about symmetry and style, and the assumption of a stairs on æsthetic grounds appears to me, therefore, to be uncalled for and inadmissible. At the spot where General Cunningham located the end of the stairs there is a figure of Padmapáṇi, placed under the shelter of a plum-tree growing on the ruined wall. The modern name of this figure is Sávitrí Deví, the wife of the sun-god. (Plate XXXII, fig. 3.) It affords another instance of the confounding of the sexes. The present abbot of the Monastery has laid the foundation of a small temple over this figure.

The outer wall, marked W., on the north side, is said by General Cunningham to be a modern addition, built right against the old wall. This remark, however, is only partially correct. The plinth and the foundations are old, and only the superstructure is new. The angles in the walls shown at the south-west and the north-west corners of the temple are a little out of scale. The breadth of the platform on the west side was the same as on the north and the south sides. This has been shown by the dotted line put by me on the plan, all beyond that line being modern.

Changes produced by recent Burmese excavations.

With the few exceptions above noted, General Cunningham's plans are fair representations of the condition of the ground round the Great Temple as seen in 1861, 1863, and 1871. Most of the salient points in the plans were, however, missing when I visited the place in September last. Certain Burmese gentlemen, deputed by His Majesty the King of Burmah, arrived at Buddha Gayá at the beginning of 1877, and with the sanction of the Mahant, who is the present owner of the Great Temple and the surrounding ground, carried on demolitions and excavations round the temple which in a manner swept away most of the old land-marks. The remains of the vaulted gateway in front of the temple had been completely demolished, and the place cleared out and levelled. The stone pavilion over the Buddhapad had been dismantled, and its materials cast aside on a rubbish mound at a distance. The granite plinth beside it had been removed. The sites of the chambers brought to light by Major Mead had been cleared out. The drain pipe and gargoyle which marked the level of the granite pavement had been destroyed. The foundations of the old buildings noticed by Hiouen Thsang around the Great Temple had been excavated for bricks, and filled up with rubbish. The revetment wall round the sacred Bodhi tree had been rebuilt on a different foundation on the west. The plaster ornaments on the interior facing of the sanctuary had been knocked off and covered with a coat of plain stucco, and an area of 250 feet by 230 feet levelled and surrounded by a new wall. It is much to be regretted that the attention of the authorities was not drawn to the subject when the Burmese gentlemen first came to the place, and no means were devised to regulate and control their action. Had this been done, advantage might have been taken of their excavations to trace and identify most of those temples, topes, and other structures mentioned in Buddhist writings and in the travels of the Chinese pilgrim, and thereby to throw much new light on the history of Buddhism and of Buddha. This opportunity has now been lost. The Burmese gentlemen were doubtless very pious and enthusiastic in the cause of their religion, but they were working on no systematic or traditional plan. They were ignorant of the true history of their faith, and perfectly innocent of all knowledge of architecture and the requirements of archæology and history; and the mischief they have done by their misdirected zeal has been serious.

Additions and alterations made by the Burmese embassy.

The appearance of the place, as seen by me in September last, is shown in Plate V. The parts shaded by wavy lines were still covered by rubbish heaps, which had not then been touched by the Burmese gentlemen. Within these surrounding heaps of rubbish is shown the enclosing wall (*a a*) built by them. It measures internally 236 feet from east to west, and 218 feet 6 inches from the north to the south. It is four feet three inches in thickness, and seven feet six inches in height. At the middle of each side there is a gateway, 10 feet 10 inches in breadth, flanked by pillars five feet square (Plate XVII): at the corners there are also similar pillars. The outer face of the wall is perfectly plain, but on the sides facing the Great Temple on the east, the north-east, and the south-east, a row of niches have been made for the reception of the sculptures which had been exhumed from the mounds. On the south-west, the west, and the north-west sides, no niches have been attempted; but fragments of carved stones, mostly friezes formed of four or five tiers of miniature figures of Buddha, have been built in in a line along the whole length. The total number of niches exceeds a hundred, the niches in front being the largest, so made to contain several large figures. The figures are more or less mutilated, but in some cases attempts have been made to restore stucco-made heads and hands and feet on stone torsos. The additions are frightfully ugly, and utterly incongruous. In front of the pillars of the eastern gate on the inside some alto-relievo statues have been placed on slightly raised platforms.

The gateways on the north, the west, and the south sides open right against rubbish mounds; but that on the east side has a cleared broad roadway leading to the trunk road to Calcutta: it has also been provided with a pair of heavy sâl-wood doors.

Present court-yard of the temple.

The rubbish heaps on the area enclosed within these walls have been partly removed and partly spread out so as to raise the level of the ground by several feet. The drain-pipe and gargoyle, which were noticed by me in 1863, showed exactly the slope and level of the court-yard in front of the Great Temple; but as they have been removed, and the position of the granite pavement over them considerably altered, it is only by secondary evidence that the original level of the court-yard can now be determined. This evidence, however, is not unsatisfactory. None will question the fact that when the Great Temple was built its floor stood above the level of the court-yard. The reverse, however, now appears to be the case. The granite pavement, as now set, stands four feet seven inches above the level of the pavement of the temple, and steps have been provided for easy descent from the court-yard into the sanctuary. This would show that the level of the court-yard has been raised at least four feet six inches, and that without providing for the difference which must have existed between the level of the temple-floor and that of the court-yard. Ordinarily the difference between the floor of a temple and the terraced court-yard around it is not great; and if we take it to have been one foot in the case of the Great Temple, its court-yard must originally have stood five feet six inches below its present level. And this is exactly what is indicated by the evidence of the plinth of the temple and of some of the pillars, still *in situ*, of a stone railing which surrounded it. At first sight the plinth of the south side of the temple appears to be completely above ground as it now stands; but on digging by its side I came to a series of longitudinal plain mouldings carrying the plinth down to four feet below the level of the ground; and the gound there was nearly a foot below the level of the present granite pavement. This would indicate a rise of five feet above the old level of the court-yard. Again, in carrying on excavations on the south side along the line where the stone railing originally stood, I came upon five pillars *in situ* bearing in position, in one instance, the two lower bars, and in two others the lowest bar, of the railing; and the bases of the pillars were five feet three inches below the newly made ground, *i.e.* six feet three inches below the pavement. On the west side I found two pillars *in situ*, and their bases were five feet five inches below the ground-level. On the north side the rail-posts, which were disenterred by Major Mead and left in position, were five feet six inches below the level of the ground on that side. These posts are no longer traceable, but the plinth of the Great Temple is on this site buried as deep as on the opposite side, showing clearly that the ground has been raised over five feet six inches. The slight differences noticed above on the different sides are due to inequalities of the ground-level, and to the measurements having been made from the nearest ground-level, and not with reference to any fixed datum.

The area enclosed within the new walls is about two-thirds of the space which formed the enciente of the enclosure described by Hiouen Thsang (*ante*, p. 52), and must include the sites of several of the temples and stúpas noticed by him. As those structures had either crumbled down by gradual decay, or been knocked down by inimical hands, producing the heaps of rubbish which have now been partly removed and partly levelled, their foundations must have been *in situ;* and had proper care been taken during the progress of the excavations, it would have been easy to determine their exact sites. But the opportunity has been lost. The foundations have been dug out for bricks, and all traces of the ancient buildings have been swept away, except of three.

A small temple.

The first of the three exceptions is a small temple on the right hand side of the northern gate, close by the wall. Its spire alone had fallen down, but the rest, when seen by me, was entire, standing buried in rubbish. Its chamber was a square of 3½ feet, with walls four feet thick. The floor of the chamber was five feet above the present ground-level, and this fact induced me to believe that it was built on made earth at a comparatively late date; but the bricks used are of the old type, large and flat, with well-smoothed edges and sides, very like modern one-foot tiles. The cement used in building this temple, as in other ancient and mediæval buildings of this place, is clay, but the bricks being ground down and smoothed to fit on each other very accurately, very little of it was needed, and the layers of it, as we now see them, are extremely thin. When first brought to light, the chamber of the temple contained several carved stones heaped together, none *in situ*, showing that it had been forsaken as a place of worship before it was buried under rubbish.

Vihára of Contemplation.

To the south-west of this temple, at a distance of about 30 feet, there is a stylobate about 60 feet long, running from east to west. At first sight I mistook it for a foundation, as its upper surface was flush with the ground; but on digging by its side I found the southern or outer face of it was moulded into longitudinal bands to the depth of five feet, showing clearly that the original level of the ground here, as everywhere round the Great Temple, was over five feet lower. The mouldings were bold and well developed with plaster. The northern or inner face of the stylobate was, as was to be expected, plain and unplastered. On the top of this wall I found the bases of four large columns. Two of these had only the base-tile or plinth and the torus, one only the base-tile, and the last a portion only of the base-tile. The tiles were squares of four feet six inches a side, and six inches deep, and the torus with two fillets 10 inches deep and four feet in diameter. All these members were made of stone ashlars, fixed with lime cement and iron clamps. On the top of one of the bases there were stone ashlars of the first layer of a column. The diameter of this layer was three feet and eight inches; and with a height of eight diameters, the column must have measured twenty nine feet four inches. The intercolumnar space was six feet. Between the last two bases there was space enough to show that there must have been two more to form a hexastyle colonnaded verandah. The columns would at first sight appear to have formed the southern façade of a magnificent chaultry, such as are now so often seen, though with pillars of other designs, in Southern India, and where the Scriptures are expounded to large and devout congregations. The foundations, however, of three sides of this structure, and probably of a portion of the length of the side brought to light, having been dug out, and the whole ground being newly-laid rubbish, I could not ascertain its exact size, nor make out whether it was a chaultry with all its sides colonnaded, or only a verandah in front of a Vihára. The site it occupies is the same as that on which, at the time of Hiouen Thsang, stood a Vihára, whence Buddha, immediately after attaining perfection, is said to have continued to look at the Tree of Knowledge for seven days. It may very reasonably be inferred, therefore, that the columns belonged to that Vihára, and formed its southern verandah. Anyhow, the building was an ancient one, and of considerable importance; though of course not of the time of Buddha.

To the west of the last, I came upon the foundations of two walls running from north to south, but I could not ascertain what was the character of the superstructure which they sustained.

Tombs.

To the east of the plinth aforesaid the Burmese workmen brought to light three solid masonry mounds with rounded tops, and a small door-like framing on one side. The frames were 15×12 inches, and the mounds themselves four feet in height, with a diameter of five feet. These are evidently tombs over the graves of some saintly personages whose names have been lost in oblivion by the lapse of time.

Samádhs.

The space from the last of the tombs to the wall on the east has been so thoroughly ploughed up for bricks, that no trace of any ancient building can be found in it. This remark also applies to the whole of the area on the south and the west sides of the Great Temple. But close by the eastern gate there is, on the right hand side, a peculiarly ugly-looking chamber with four sloping roofs, and a high plinth, built about the end of the last century, over the mortal remains of the third and the fourth Mahants of the monastery. In the centre of the chamber there is a lingam, which is daily worshipped by one of the Sannyásis of the maṭh. The building looks like the first attempt to immitate in brick and mortar an ordinary Indian four-roofed hut, and if the principle laid down by Mr. Fergusson about calculating the period of transition from woodwork to masonry could be brought to bear on this case, the conclusion would be that the mason's art must have been introduced into Buddha Gayá in the middle of the last century.

Nearly opposite to the last monument there are, on the left hand side of the gateway, three small buildings in a line (Plate VI); two of these with sloping roofs are the counterparts of the last, but with very low plinths. The central one is flat-roofed, and has in front of it a verandah supported on nine four-sided carved pillars of stone. The westernmost building is the samádh of Mahádeva, the second, and the next that of Chaitan, the third, mahant. The last is called Pancha Páṇḍu, or the temple of the five Páṇḍava brothers. It contains a standing female figure holding a lotus stalk; six seated figures of Buddha in meditation, with one hand resting on the lap and the other stretched on the knee; and three standing figures of the same personage—all ranged against the wall. This building measures 15×15 feet, the other two 15×14 feet each. None of these has any architectural pretension or historical value; but the pillars inserted in the verandah of the second were originally the uprights of a stone railing set up by the Emperor Aśoka round a temple, or a stúpa, which he had built on the spot on which stands the Great Temple.

Stone-railing—its site.

The stone rail posts first noticed by General Cunningham (*a*), and subsequently traced *in situ* by Major Mead (p. 63) have been either removed or buried under rubbish. But from the few still in position, though under cover, and the ample details preserved by General Cunningham, it is not difficult to trace the position they occupied round the Great Temple. On the north and the south they stood at a distance of 19 feet six inches from the base of the terrace of the temple. On the west their distance from the new revetment wall lately built by the Burmese gentlemen is 10 feet six inches. On the east no trace of a railing has yet been found; but there is no reason to doubt that there was one, which probably stood at the edge of the granite pavement in front of the Great Temple, that is, at a distance of about 40 feet, or close by the east of the modern Pancha Páṇḍu temple. In lieu of it, between the first and the second samádhs, Major Mead found a massive plinth of basalt which stretched right across from the north to the south railing (p. 62); but General Cunningham very correctly thinks that "it must have been added many centuries afterwards, as the granite floor on which it stood was just two feet above the level of the granite floor of the temple, and of the brick floor of the plinth of the surrounding railing." (*b*) This basalt plinth was probably the remains of a stone wall set up by Purṇabrahma, king of Magadha, soon after the destruction of the Bodhi tree by Śaśánka. It has since been removed, and the granite pavement raised to a height of four feet six inches above the level

(*a*) Arch. Surv. Report, I, p. 1.
(*b*) Ibid, Vol. III, p. 90.

of the floor of the temple. On plate V the site which the railing had occupied has been indicated by dotted lines, and that of the basalt plinth by detached lines.

Stone-railing—its size.

The railing was of the usual Bhuddhist type, formed of a series of quadrangular pillars, ranged on a moulded plinth, and bearing three lines of elliptical bars, and a heavy coping. Some of the rail-posts and rails were of granite, others of sandstone; but they were all of the same pattern, and carved and decorated in the same style. "On the sandstone rails," says General Cunningham, "as indeed might be expected, the workmanship is smoother, and the details of the lotus flowers more minute, than on the granite rails. The length of the sandstone rails, 2 feet 10 inches, is also greater than that of the granite rails, which are only 2 feet 7 inches long. As granite is a stronger material than sandstone, the granite rails ought to have been longer than the others. * * * The pillars vary from 11¾ to 14 inches in breadth, and as the rails also vary in length, there is a considerable variation in the intervals, as for instance, 2 feet 5 inches, 2 feet 7½ inches, 2 feet 9½ inches, 2 feet 10 inches, 2 feet 11½ inches, and 3 feet 2 inches" (*a*). General Cunningham accounts for these differences by saying, "perhaps the difference is simply due to the different donors; one gave his order to some local masons for granite pillars, another gave his order to the masons of a different sandstone quarry, where the lengths of the measures may have been slightly different, although the names were the same." (*a*) This is, however, not in keeping with the conclusion he has elsewhere come to, that the rails were erected by the Emperor Aśoka. I think this conclusion to be the right one; and if so, there could not have been many donors to give orders to different shops. Besides, the difference is not confined to posts and rails of different materials; it is observable in different pieces of the same material; one sandstone bar, now in the Indian Museum, measuring 3′ 4″ in length, and another 3′. The obvious inference would be that, under the circumstances, the difference is due to the workmen employed by the Emperor not having been very particular about the size. Indian workmen are even now very indifferent in this respect, and it is not too much to suppose that they were equally, if not more so, two thousand years ago.

(*a*) Arch. Surv. Report, Vol. III, pp. 89-90.

Rail-posts—their number and character.

The length of the rails and the breadth of the posts being different, it is impossible to calculate the exact number of rail-posts which originally existed round the Great Temple. At present there are 33 pillars attached to the verandah of the Mahant's residence in the maṭh; nine in the verandah of the second samádh; four *in situ* buried on the south side of the Great Temple; two on the west side, two on the north, and fragments of three or four lying on the rubbish mound round the temple, making a total of 52 or 53. These, however, would not nearly suffice for a complete railing round the Great Temple. General Cunningham says:—"Taking the distance of the two western pillars from the wall of the terrace as the correct line of the western railing, and that of the south-east pillars as the correct line of the southern railing, I calculate that there were 37 pillars on each of the north and the south faces, with an outside length of 145 feet, and 12 pillars on each half of the western side between the corner pillar and the middle opening. This will give an outside breadth of 108 feet, with a total of 94 pillars, of which I have myself seen 43. But if, as we may reasonably suppose, there was a similar railing and opening on the eastern side, the number of pillars would be increased to 118, and the whole circuit of the railing outside would have been 506 feet" (*a*).

These results do not quite accord with what I have arrived at. The datum on the south side is unquestionable, so is that on the west side. There is no reason to suppose that the distance of the railing from the temple on the north side was otherwise than what it is on the south side; and on the east the margin of the granite pavement may be fairly accepted as the site of the rail on that side. Now, the temple with its terrace measures 75 feet 8 inches from south to north, and the distance from the base of the terrace to the plinth of the railing being 19 feet 6 inches, the total length of the railing required from north to south would be 114 feet 8 inches, inside measurement, or 117 feet outside measurement. The present length of the terrace from east to west is 105 feet 8 inches, and the two rail posts *in situ* on the west side are 10 feet 6 inches distant from it. On the east side it extended to between 38 and 40 feet from the base of the porch. The total length therefore would be 105 feet 8 inches × 10 feet 6 inches × 38 = 154 feet.

(*a*) Arch. Surv. Report, Vol. III, p. 90.

This would give a circuit of 537 feet 4 inches instead of 506 feet. Now, if the average length of rails be accepted at 2 feet 10 inches, and the average breadth of the posts at one foot, it would require 41 pillars to complete the length and 27 pillars to complete the breadth, allowing the corner pillars of the length to supply the place of those of the breadth. This would give a total of 136 pillars. Out of this, however, we must deduct some pillars for passages. It is unquestionable that there was a large opening or passage on the east side; and, judging from the character and disposition of Buddhist rails in other parts of India, it would not be unreasonable to suppose that there were similar passages on the other sides. Hiouen Thsang does not describe the railing in detail; but he says the outer wall had a gateway in the middle of each of its four sides, facing the cardinal points; and the presumption is strong that there were corresponding passages across the railing. Omitting two pillars for each of these passages, or an opening of over 10 feet, the total would be 128. On the other hand, I suspect, from a circumstance mentioned by General Cunningham, that there were subsidiary lines projecting from the main lines, and forming small enclosures either on the outside or on the inside.

At the south-west corner General Cunningham found "one pillar beyond the line of junction of the basalt plinth which runs from south to north. This one pillar, however, was a *corner* one, as it has socket-holes for rails on three sides. The fourth side to the east is occupied with a sculpture in high relief of two females, one holding to a tree with the left arm and left leg, and the other seated on the ground and apparently supporting the right foot of the first. Both figures are clad from the waist to the knees in finely creased drapery, over which is seen the well known bead-girdle" (*a*). I have not been able to trace this stone, but the description given of it fails to convince me that it was a *corner* post. I cannot make out how there can be socket-holes on three sides of a corner post. In a middle rail-post the socket holes are on opposite sides, and in a corner one on two adjoining sides; and the moment we put a rail-bar opposite to either of the socketed sides of a corner post, it ceases to be a terminal, and becomes a medial, one. And to account for the socket holes in the pillar under notice, I believe that there was a distinct set of pillars at some distance with similar sockets, and that rails projected

(*a*) Arch. Surv. Report, Vol. III, p. 89.

from these and formed a subsidiary enclosure. The space on the east side was wide, and had ample room for a subsidiary enclosure of the kind.

There are two pillars, each of which has mortices on two adjoining sides, and they were unquestionably taken from the corners of the railing. They show the corner pillars did not differ much in size and character from the medial ones. Whether pillars on the sides of the passages were uniform with the rest, or of a larger size and more elaborate workmanship, I cannot say, as I have seen no pillar with socket holes on one side only. At Bhilsá, Amarávatí, Baráhat, and elsewhere, it was usual to have highly-carved magnificent structures over the gateways, and, by a parity of reasoning, we should expect something like them at Buddha Gayá; but if such things ever existed there, they are no longer traceable.

The area between these railings and the Great Temple was originally left perfectly clear for the faithful to walk about freely, and to perform that all-important act of Buddhist worship, circumambulation from the right side, without which due respect to sacred objects could not be duly evinced; and even now the only structures within the area are the mean-looking, barn-like samádhs described above. The area was originally paved with bricks on the south, the west, and the north sides, and with flags of granite on the east. The brick flooring is now buried five feet deep under rubbish. The pavement on the east was first raised to a height of two feet above the level of the pavement of the temple, and this was probably done at the time when the temple was repaired by the Burmese in the 14th century. It has now been raised two feet six inches more.

Cells.

On the eastern edge of the granite pavement there was at one time a line of small cells—little square chambers—with perfectly plain walls, several of which were brought to light by Major Mead, and four of them were shown by me in the plan published by me in 1864 (a). They were probably intended for the dwelling of monks, when the larger monasteries in the neighbourhood had fallen into ruin; they were so plain that they could not have been meant for temples. They could not have existed when the railing on the east side was *in situ*. One of the chambers contained a large figure of Buddha with an inscription in the Gupta character, a copy of which was taken by me. The figure is missing now. It must have been transferred to the

(a) Journal, Asiatic Society, XXXIII.

cell from one of the larger temples when that structure was destroyed. It is not at all likely that so large a statue was originally designed for so mean-looking a cell.

I now come to the central Great Temple. Hiouen Thsang describes it thus:—

Great Temple. Hiouen Thsang's description.

"To the east of the tree of knowledge there is a Vihára from 160 to 170 feet in height. Its base is about 20 paces on each side. It is built of bluish bricks plastered with chunam. It represents niches disposed in tiers, which contain each a statuette of Buddha in gold. The four sides of the walls are covered with admirable sculptures, in some places by chaplets of pearls, and in some places by images of Rishis. It is surmounted on the top by an amalaka of gilt copper. On the east side was afterwards constructed a pavilion of two storeys, the roofs of which are sloping and ranged in three tiers. The beams and the columns, the doors and the windows, are ornamented with carvings in silver and gold, and set with pearls and precious stones. The deep chambers and the mysterious halls communicate with each other and with others by three doors. On the left and the right sides of the outer gateway there are two large niches. That on the left contains a statue of Avalokiteśvara Bodhisattva, and that on the right that of Maitreya Bodhisattva. These statues are cast in silver, and are nearly ten feet in height" (a).

The temple may be described under four heads, viz. first, the temple proper; second, the terrace round it; third, the porch; and fourth, the Bodhi tree on the terrace.

The Temple proper.

The Temple proper is nearly a square in the ground-plan, measuring, according to General Cunningham, 48 feet 8 inches by 47 feet 3 inches, enclosing a chamber which was originally a cube of about 22 feet. Its present length from the pavement to the highest point in the ceiling is 22 feet 1 inch; but having been built on two sides the floor now measures 20 feet 7 inches by 13 feet. The length of the room is cut off to the extent of 5 feet 9 inches by a stone platform, leaving a length of 14 feet 10 inches for the area in front of it. The measuring tape, tested by a good plotting scale which I had with me, appeared correct, and yet repeated measurements showed the results to be different from what General Cunningham had arrived at. His measurements are, length 20 feet 3 inches, breadth 12 feet 8 inches, distance from front wall to platform 4 feet. These differences are, I believe, due to the Burmese gentlemen having

(a) 'Memoires sur les Contrées occidentales,' Vol. I, p. 461.

peeled off the old plastering, which was thick and set off with niches on the walls, and a check pattern decoration under the ceiling, and substituted a thin coat of chunam plaster. My measurements give to the walls a thickness of 14 feet.

The body of Indian temples is usually a cube, and the spire rises from 1½ to 2½ times the side of the cube; but in this instance the height of the body is about one-fourth less than its length, and over it the spire rises to nearly four times the height, making a total height of 160 feet, or with the pinnacle over it, now lost, but seen by Hiouen Thsang, 170 feet.

The doorway of this temple is placed on the east side and measures 6′ 4″ in breadth, forming, with the depth of the wall, a vestibule 6′ 4″ by 13′ 4.″ The door-frame is formed of stone bars of a reddish grey colour, and over it there is a cross bar of grey-coloured stone forming a strong hyperthereon (Plate XVI). Then follows a blocking course of considerable thickness, and the space over it was left open, the sides first rising upright, but at a greater distance from each other than the width of the doorway, and then approaching each other so as to form a triangular slit of large dimensions. The opening was produced by the gradual corbelling of the walls from the two sides, which gave to the sides the appearance of reversed flights of steps, each step being three bricks deep. The two sides met at the top in a point (Plate XV). This shows the outline of the true Indian horizontal arch to perfection. It is said that this space was left open for the purpose of allowing the light at dawn to fall on the presiding divinity of the temple. "This feature of the eastern face of the building," says General Cunningham, "would have been purposeless if it had not been intended to throw the sun's light to the sanctum of the temple over the roof porch, and thus to illuminate every morning the figure which was the great object of worship. The same arrangement was adopted in the great Chaitya caves of Central and Western India, and it is difficult to see what other purpose this tall rent in the face of the building could probably have served" (a). How far this is true I know not, but the orientalisation of Indian temple-doorways is generally ascribed to this object. It was likewise the case with the Druids, and the remains of their sacred structures in Europe show that they invariably had their principal entrances on the east side. This was also the case in ancient Greece, for, with the

---

(a) Arch. Surv. Report, III, p. 83.

exception of the temple of Apollo Epicurius of Phigalia in Arcadia, all her principal fanes stood with their porticoes facing the east. ' There is reason therefore to believe that the arrangement was so made that the ray of light which fell on a particular spot indicated the time of the day with great precision. I do not remember to have read in any Buddhist writing any explanation of the object of placing the door of a temple on the east side, and in small temples I find convenience regulates the position of the doorway; but in all the principal temples, both of the Hindus and the Buddhists, the doorway invariably occurs on the east side. The triangular opening over the doorway is in masonry monuments exceedingly rare. The only instance, besides that of Buddha Gayá, that has come to my notice is the Temple of Konch, 14 miles to the south-west of Gayá. In Martin's 'Eastern India' there is a woodcut of a native drawing of this temple, and Mr. Peppe has thus described it in the Journal of the Asiatic Society:—

"Passing through the village proper you come to the temple mentioned by Buchanan, and of which a drawing is given in the first volume of 'Martin's India.' Photograph No. 28 (Plate XII) is a view of the front of the building from the east, with the opening above the entrance leading into the upper chamber. Photograph No. 29 is a view from the south-west. The accompanying ground-plan will give the reader some idea of its structure, and the section (woodcut No. 1)(a) will show the superstructure with the arched lower chamber and the interior recess over the entrance, which resembles that in the Bodh Gayá temple. Nothing but mud has been used to cement the bricks, but the latter have been so well prepared that they fit together most accurately. There would seem to have been a coating of plaster on the outside, but this has nearly entirely disappeared. A porch had been

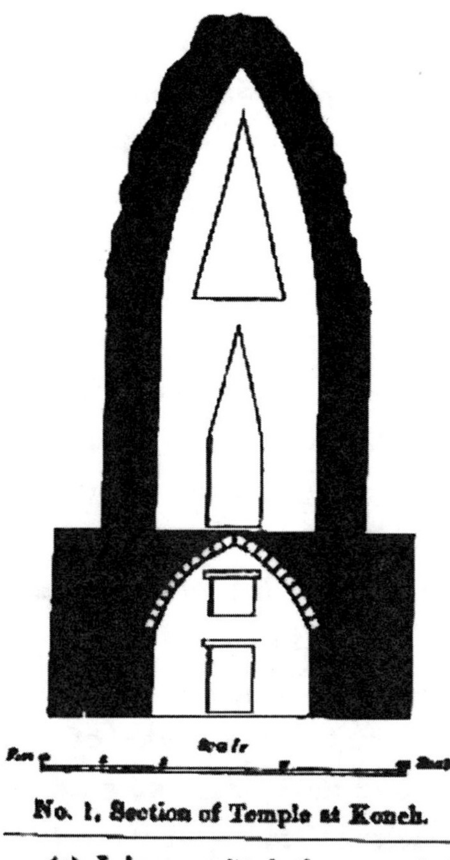

No. 1. Section of Temple at Konch.

(a) I have omitted the ground-plan as of no interest in connection with the question at issue. The section as shown in the woodcut is so far inaccurate as it does not show the corbelling on the sloping sides. The photograph (Plate XVIII) supplies the omission.

added with an arched roof, but it has fallen in. The only arch in the original building is that of the lower chamber, which is pointed" (*a*).

As the temple affords a very striking illustration of the peculiar feature under notice, I have reproduced a photograph of it from an original in the library of the Asiatic Society (Plate XVIII). But for the details on the shaft, which are different, it would well pass for a sketch of the great temple of Buddha Gayá. Indeed, the similitude is so close, that I was at first induced to believe the one to be a copy of the other, and the terrace round the Buddha Gayá fane to be an afterthought; but on cutting through the roof of the terrace on the south side I found the body of the terrace to be of solid brickwork, which bonded with the body of the temple. This could not have been the case had the terrace been added some time after the completion of the temple. The outer surface of the body of the temple would have in that case also shown traces of some ornamentation in keeping with what occurs on the shaft of it. Nothing of the kind was, however, seen. Seeing, besides, that the terrace and the body of the temple were built in one piece at Nálandá, which General Cunningham takes to be the model of the Buddha Gayá temple, I have had to give up my idea.

The Southern Façade.

The southern façade of the Great Temple is now in a fair state of preservation. The present condition of its shaft is shown in the annexed photograph (Plate VII), and the whole of the front, including the basement storey, has been reproduced in the restored drawing [Plate VIII(*b*)]. The surface of the shaft is broken by five broad bands running up the whole height, and of these the central one is the broadest. The bands are so arranged and diversified as not to obtrude on the eye. At the same time, by their perpendicular style, they so direct the attention of the observer as optically to add greatly to the height of the building. Horizontally the bands are divided into niches, and each line of niches has the appearance of a distinct storey, and of such storeys there are altogether eight. The storeys gradually recede inward as they rise, each forming a distinct stage; but the mouldings have been so arranged that instead of a succession of angles the outline appears

(*a*) Journal, Asiatic Society, Vol. XXXV, Part I, p. 64.

(*b*) There is a mistake in this plate; the number of storeys above the terrace should be eight, as in the photograph, and not nine.

unbroken and slightly arched, though such is not really the case. This is effected by the use, at the corner of every storey, of a ribbed figure which covers the receding angle, and adds greatly to the beauty of the structure.

The central niche of the first storey above the terrace is the largest and most fully developed. It is formed of two side-pilasters surmounted by a rich architrave and a peculiar pediment, which, in its highly-developed florid form on the Orissa temples, I have described as a coat-of-arms. It is formed of an oblong block with the two sides scalloped, and bearing on the top two bars so as to form two steps on each side. The centre of the pediment has a circular cutting within which is placed a lotus flower made of plaster. The pilasters are crowned with the ribbed domal capitals so well known in ancient Indian buildings under the name of *amla sild* or emblic myrobalan, having a torus below and a tulip-shaped ribbed dome over it. The last member bears on it a miniature representation of the pediment above noticed. The entablature is formed of a series of four small niches, standing on a plain horizontal moulding. Within the niche thus formed there is a second of the same pattern, but without the peculiar top-ornament. Its architrave is a plain projecting slab, edged with what in European architecture is called the echinus ornament. The lower part of the niche is widened by a projecting ledge with a lotus-bud bracket underneath, and on it is a seated figure of Buddha engaged in meditation. The bands next to the central one have the lower part shaped like plinths, and on them there is on, each side, a counterpart of the inner niche of the central one. The outer band is not pierced with a niche, but left entire in the form of a stout pilaster to give firmness and solidity to the structure. The recesses between the bands are also moulded into the form of niches, but their tops are modelled into trefoil arches, and their sides are finished with a plain band instead of pilasters. The niches on the right side of the central band have seated figures of Buddha as in the central one; but those on the left have standing figures. Originally all these figures were gilt; but they are so decayed that no trace of gilding can now be found on them. In the second storey the central niche is to a great extent covered by the pediment of the lower storey, but its upper part is fully developed. The side niches are counterparts of what occur in the first storey. The place of the outer pilaster is partially filled with the ribbed ornament described above. The upper storeys are all repetitions of the second, except that the niches are alternately left vacant, or filled with trees, bouquets, and other floral devices. The ornaments and mouldings are more or less dilapidated, as shown in the annexed photograph (Plate VII), but in the restored view (Plate VIII) they have been fully shown.

Pinnacle.

The upper edge of the shaft is finished with a series of four gradually receding horizontal plain mouldings, terminating in a flat roof. From the centre of the roof rises the pinnacle, of which the cylindrical neck alone is entire, the rest being more or less dilapidated. It comprised, besides the gullet, a series of circular mouldings, a dome shaped like a ribbed melon, another series of flat mouldings, and a cylindrical core supporting a tee-shaped crown or kalasa. Hiouen Thsang says the ribbed dome was encased in copper and gilt; and the kalasa over it must have been of the same material; but it is lost. The shape of the last I have, in the restored plate, copied from similar structures so abundantly to be seen in the model chaityas, of which thousands are now lying about all along from Gayá to Buddha Gayá. Of course, I cannot positively affirm that this was the exact shape of the original kalasa; but knowing that it is a conventional ornament, and that the chaityas are only miniature representations of larger originals, I venture to think that I have made a fair guess. It may be that I am mistaken in this assumption; but I cannot suggest anything which could even have the voucher of the miniatures. Mr. Fergusson says that the number of rings on the kalasa never did exceed nine; but I have deposited in the Indian Museum specimens in which 11 to 14 such rings may be counted. In the smallest chaityas the number is five. The number was evidently regulated by the size of the structure.

Northern and Western Façades.

Rigidly scrupulous about respective symmetry, Indian artists never allowed any deviation to take place in the ornamentation of the opposite sides of a building, and it is to be presumed, therefore, that the northern façade of the temple was an exact counterpart of its southern front, and from what remains of it the presumption is to a great extent verified. The same was also the case with the western front. Large portions of brick-work on those sides have, however, peeled off, and are completely destroyed, and it is difficult to support the presumption regarding all the details. The destruction appears to have been caused by bringing small guns to bear on those sides, and it is not unlikely that some Moslem fanatics attacked the temple from the north-west corner, placing their guns on the high mound or *garh* on that side. I was at one time disposed to believe that the destruction was caused by exposure for centuries to rain driven by nor'-westers, but on inquiry I found that nor'-westers are not common in this part of the country, and the prevailing directions of the wind are east and west.

Eastern Façade.

The general scheme of ornamentation on the east side was the same as on the south façade, but the triangular opening on that side prevented the carrying out of the plan in its entirety. The opening was afterwards filled up with a plain wall having two doorways placed one above the other. To the depth of several feet above the stone architrave the wall is solid, and then comes the first doorway, and over it, at a small height, the second. The doorways had pointed gothic arches over them, but the upper arch has since fallen. The lower one with that of the vaults beyond it will be seen in the annexed photographs (plates XV, XVI, and XVII). The arches must have been built at the time when the chamber of the temple was narrowed by building walls on the north and the south sides, and spanning them over with a vaulted roof. That the vaulted roof was no part of the original design none will question. General Cunningham, after studying the subject very carefully, says, "the thinness of the back wall, compared with the extreme thickness of the two side walls, has always been a puzzle to me. If this was the original construction, I should expect to find some passage in the side walls which once led to the upper-rooms. There is a difference of four feet in the thickness of the back and side walls, which would be more than was necessary for a staircase. In the Great Temple at Nálandá, which, as the Chinese pilgrim informs us, resembled that near the Bodhi tree, the inner-room is 21 feet square, and all the walls are of the same thickness of 21 feet. I am therefore inclined to think that the original cell of the Buddha Gayá temple was nearly square, and that all the walls were of the same thickness, and I would account for the present difference of 20 feet in length by 13 feet in breadth by supposing that, when the vaulted roof was added to the chamber, a new wall, 3½ feet thick, was built against the north and the south sides to carry the vault"(a). Nor is the close resemblance of the Great Temple with that of Nálandá the only argument in support of the view that originally the chamber of the former was a square, or very nearly a

(a) Arch. Surv. Report, Vol. III, p. 84.

perfect square. Of the many thousands of temples, Buddhist, Hindu, and Jain, which exist in India and have existed for centuries past, there is not one which has departed from the rule which requires the chamber to be a square. The peculiar character of these structures, square in outline, more or less a cube in body, and closed in by a gradually projecting series of ledges or corbelling on the four sides, rising into a tall spire, always suggests a square chamber, and anything but a square would disturb its symmetry. It is the simplest and most easily worked out, and there is no reason to suppose that any other was attempted in the present case. It is true that no excavation has been made into the side walls to show whether or not there is any break of continuity between the supposed new and the old walls, but the fact is evident from the circumstance of the third storey chamber being a square room, 20 feet a side.

The vaulted roof is of the simplest gothic pattern, being segments of circles drawn on a radius equal to the distance between the two walls, or the space spanned over, the point of decussation of the segments forming the crown. The arch is simple, too, as no attempt has been made to form a groined vault.

The piers designed for the support of the arches stand right against the corbelled edges of the tringular opening, but do not bond with them. Nor are they of the same thickness as the original wall. In 1863, when the upper arches had partly fallen, they had broken just where an over-weighted arch would break, namely, where the line of resistance cuts the intrados. In 1877 the side pier of those arches had also fallen completely, and thereby the corbelled edges of the triangular slit were exposed, and they bore no mark whatever of their ever having had any bonded connection with the piers. (See Plate XV.) Their edges are now as entire as they were when first built. The corbelled projection occurs after every three courses of bricks. In the semi-circular arches in the staircase they and the piers on which they rest being of the same age, this distinction is not apparent.

The Sanctum and its presiding divinity.

The chamber, as already stated, has a black basalt throne on the off side. It is of simple construction, and is set off in the front with a series of seven niches. (Plate XII A.) On this throne there was originally an image of Buddha in gold, but on the very first decline of Buddhism the rapacity of rival sectaries soon took it away; and in the fifth or the sixth century it was replaced by a black basalt one, which was seen by the Chinese pilgrim in the middle of the seventh century. About it he relates a curious story, of which the following is an abstract by General Cunningham :—

" About the beginning of the seventh century, the King Śaśánka, after destroying the Bodhi tree, directed one of his ministers to remove the statue of Buddha, and to put a statue of Mahádeva in its place. The minister, who was a Buddhist, was puzzled what to do. 'If,' said he, 'I destroy the statue of Buddha, I shall entail misery upon myself for countless ages; and if I disobey the King's order, I shall be killed with my whole family.' He employed a trusty servant, who built a brick wall before the statue of Buddha, and in front set up an image of the god Maheśvara. When the King heard that his orders had been carried out, he was instantly seized with fright, his whole body broke out into tremor, his skin peeled off, and he died on the spot. The minister then ordered the wall to be removed at once. Now, a glance at the plan of the temple will show that by building a brick wall in front of the pedestal the room would have been nearly square, while the back wall towards the west would have been increased to little more than the thickness of the side walls on the north and south" (a).

How far this story has any substratum of truth it would be hazardous to determine with certainty; but it suggests the idea that some Śivite Hindus wished to appropriate the temple to their use, and as it is absolutely necessary that the chamber of Mahádeva should be a square, converted it to that shape by the simplest expedient at command, and that subsequently, when it reverted to the Buddhists, the latter removed the partition and restored the chamber to its former shape.

In the eighth or the ninth century the last image was evidently lost, and in its place was set up a black stone image, which I believe was removed by one of the Mahants of the maṭh when he again consecrated a lingam in the middle of the sanctuary. The image was not destroyed, but removed to a small temple within the enclosure of the maṭh, where it still exists. A representation of this image is given on plate XI; its details will be fully noticed in the next chapter. There is an inscription on its base which records the name of the person who dedicated it. The lingam established in the centre of the square area in front of the throne is not an ordinary figure of the kind, but a big votive stúpa, which has been made to do duty for it. It is still worshipped by the Mahant of the maṭh. The pavement round this lingam,

(a) Arch. Surv. Report, Vol. III, p. 83.

and also those in the porch and the court-yard, are scratched with inscriptions and the images of devotees who visited the place in the 13th and the 14th centuries.

The Burmese ambassadors of 1831 placed on the throne a gilt stucco image, which I saw in 1863, and that has now been replaced by another of the same description by the Burmese gentlemen who visited the place last year. The new image is hideously ugly.

Second-storey Room.

The vaulted roof of the first storey is levelled on the top, and made the floor of a second-storey room, which, like the first, is oblong and covered by a vaulted roof, its length being 21 feet 6 inches. The walls of this chamber are plastered, and it has a throne on the off side, which is an exact counterpart of the stone pedestal in the first-storey room, only instead of stone it is made of brick and mortar. There was unquestionably a highly prized statue on it, for it was the *sanctum sanctorum*, to which only the select few who feed the priests heavily were allowed to enter. This *imperium in imperio* is common in every part of the earth where priestcraft prevails, and could not have been unknown among the Buddhists.

Third-storey Room.

The second vaulting, like the first, is level on top and made the floor of a third-storey room, accessible by the upper door-way in the triangular slit. The walls of this room are formed by the sloping sides of the spire, and, having never been plastered, clearly show the manner in which the spire was gradually narrowed to end in a small opening. The room is a square of 19 feet, the reduction from the original measure of 22 feet of the first storey being caused by the gradual narrowing of the spire. The top of this room narrows to a square of eight feet, which is closed in by a flat roof supported on six wooden beams; and this is the only place where wood has been used in this temple. Perhaps the difficulty of raising large stone flags to a height of 160 feet suggested this expedient. The beams are very thick, and, being very closely ranged, are fully equal to the weight of the metal pinnacle which once surmounted it, as also of its brick core which still exists.

The Terrace on the south side.

The terrace round the temple was originally over 25 feet 6 inches high from the pavement of the temple, and 14 feet broad all round; but, for reasons to be noticed lower down, it is now two feet higher on the north and the west sides than what it is on the south side. The south-side terrace still retains its original character. It was built along with the walls of the temple, and forms an integral part of it. The whole of it lay buried under rubbish till 1863, when Major Mead cut a trench and brought it to light. Its plinth still lies burried to the depth of five feet. The plinth is formed of a thick tile bearing an equally thick quirked ovolo surmounted by a series of flat mouldings, of which the upper three bands are now above ground. At first sight these last appear to be complete by themselves, and to form the plinth, but by running a trench along the line of the wall I found they were only the topmost ornaments of a larger and more comprehensive series. (See plates VIII and XLIX, H.) On the base-mouldings are placed a series of fifteen niches, each of which once held a seated figure made of stucco and gilt. The practice of gilding statues was common in ancient times, and is even now universally followed by the Burmese. Over the niches there is a thick architrave, and then comes a frieze formed of lions' heads holding garlands of beads, very much like similar ornaments in Roman architecture. Over the frieze is a moulded cornice formed of a caveto lined with lotus petals and capped by a tile. The cornice is surmounted by a line of little pilasters shaped like sand glasses, and over it there is a second series of niches with trefoiled arches. The last series has the appearance of the early English parapet as seen on Salisbury Cathedral. The cornice is on top rounded off, as shown in the annexed woodcut (No. 2), as also in plate XLIX H. The ornaments are very much decayed and in a ruinous state, but their characters are unmistakeable. To prove this I have to appeal to the photograph (Plate IX) showing three of the niches as they appear on the building, and to one of the niches restored by me (plate X). The brick mouldings are generally entire, and there is enough of plaster on them to show what the details on them originally were. The plastering shows that the mouldings had undergone at least three successive repairs before they were buried by the fall of the edifices which surrounded the Great Temple. The repairers were in every case less efficient than those who built the temple. In the course of these repairs most of the finer stucco mouldings, particularly on the bases and capitals of pilasters, have been covered over—fine, bold, clear

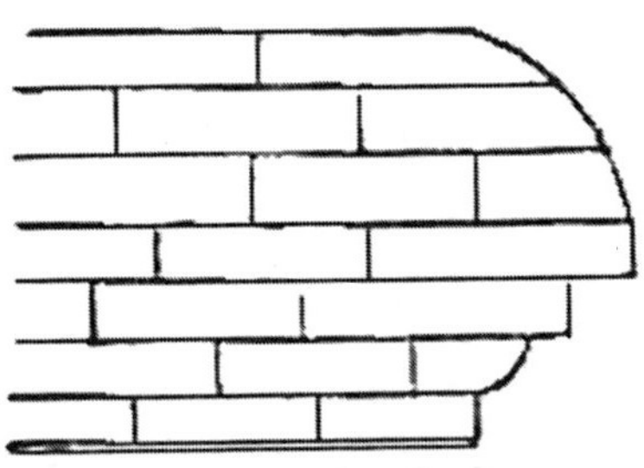

No. 2, Cornice of Terrace.

scrolls and forms, which, with the first touch of the repairer, became coarse and rude, and subsequently entirely hidden, changing well-formed, ribbed melon capitals into mis-shapened round balls, and floral bases into plain toruses;—but by peeling off the outer layers I have always found enough of the original moulding *in situ* to produce faithful representations. This peculiarity of the repairs has been also noticed in the Nálandá temple by Mr. Broadley, and General Cunningham has shown them in his plate XXXI, figs. 1 to 6. On plate XLIX I have figured some of the ornaments, representing their successive deteriorations.

The Terrace on the north side.

The terrace on the north side was originally the exact counterpart of that on the south side, but the wall had been, either by gradual decay or by inimical hands, injured, and had to be renewed. The renewal was affected by men who had not the slightest regard for the requirements of æsthetics, and accordingly they built a plain wall which bore no resemblance to the wall of the south side. General Cunningham is of opinion that the new wall was built in front of the old one; but such was not the case. The renewal was confined to the upper portion, and the old plinth and foundation remain intact. In one place towards the south-west corner one-half of an old niche still remains *in situ*; and such being the case, the projecting angle shewn at A in the General's ground-plan (Plate IV, Plan No. 1) must be accepted as inaccurate. The counterpart of the angle on the opposite side never did exist.

The Terrace on the east side.

The terrace on the east side was originally of the same character as on the other sides, having the same height and ornamentation; but it was open in the middle, forming a porch, with, probably, a flat roof, as at Konch. The niches on the left of the porch are still extant, but the wall on the right hand side is partly under cover of a layer of rubbish, and partly of a later date, and no niche is seen there.

Porch and Pavilion.

It would seem that when the vaults were built inside the temple the porch was also modified. The flat roof was removed; piers were built on the two sides of the doorway to widen the area of the porch; a vaulted roof erected over it; and thereupon a pavilion. In the restored plate of the east side (Plate XIX) I have represented this pavilion, although there is at present no such structure there.

" That this porch was built some time after the temple is," says General Cunningham, "confirmed by the difference in the size of the bricks used in the temple itself and in the additions to the eastern face. In the walls of the temple six courses of bricks average from 17¾ to 18 inches in height, while six courses of the eastern rooms average only from 15 to 15¾ inches. There is a consequent dislocation between the old and new walls; but this is not at first sight apparent, as the old walls have been faced with new bricks to a depth of more than one foot, which do not break joint with bricks of the old walls.' (a) The pavilion, however, was noticed by Hiouen Thsang in the middle of the seventh century, and at the beginning of this century Dr. Buchanan-Hamilton "met with several people in the vicinity who remembered the pavilion standing, and had frequently been in the chambers upstairs from the terrace leading to the uppermost." (b)

The remains of its side walls are also still extant, as will be seen by reference to the projection on the right hand side of the shaft on Plate VII. General Cunningham has noticed them, and says that in building them "no attempt has been made to bond the old and the new work together, and the hand can be inserted in many places between the plastered face of the old walls and the bricks of the later walls. Indeed, the old niches as well as the mouldings of the eastern face can be seen behind these later walls." (c) They show that from the roof of the terrace to the cornice the height of the pavilion was 20 feet. The details on the side walls are obvious, and in the drawing I have simply prolonged them over the whole length of the porch to cover it, and reproduced one of the same pattern in front. The general design of these new portions is the same as that of the old walls: it includes four tiers of niches one above the other; but the decorations are not so. The floral bands which run between the tiers are new; nothing like them occurs in any other part of the building. Specimens of these are shown on plate XLIX. The cornice is plain, as shown on the margin. (Woodcut No. 3.) Hiouen Thsang mentions that the pavilion had

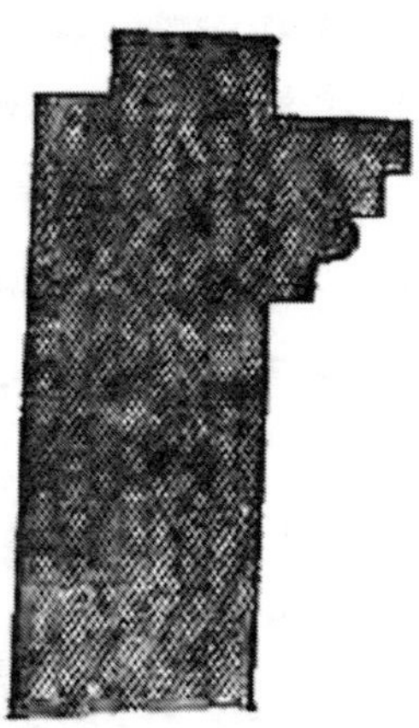

No. 3, Cornice of Pavilion.

(a) Arch. Surv. Report, III, p. 82.
(b) Martin's 'Eastern India,' Vol. I., p. 76.
(c) Arch. Surv. Report, III, p. 82.

three doors, two on the terrace and one leading to the sanctuary of the upper storey. It is doubtful, therefore, if there ever was an opening on the east side. But without such an opening there would be a dead wall over the hyperthyrion of the main entrance, and this no native builder would think of. I believe, therefore, that there was an opening, and as it was of the character of a window, it did not form a part of the three doors noticed by the Chinese traveller.

The roof of this pavilion Hiouen Thsang describes thus:—"Du côté de l'est, on a construit, à la suite, un pavillon à deux étages, dont les toits saillants s'élèvent sur trois rangs." (*a*) General Cunningham translates this passage into—"On the east side there was afterwards added a pavilion of two storeys, with projecting roofs, which rose in three tiers." (*b*) The words used clearly show that the pavilion itself was two-storeyed, and not the whole structure. Altogether there were three storeys, of which the first formed the approach to the first storey, the second to the second storey, and the third to the third storey of the temple. The third-storey room of the pavilion was a mere attic formed by the sloping roof of the building, and leading to the adjoining room, which was a repository of valuables, like the opisthodomus in Greek temples, and access to it was had when necessary, and that very rarely, by a ladder placed on the floor of the second-storey room of the porch. When Dr. Buchanan-Hamilton visited the place, the third-storey room of the temple was quite empty; but he supposed that it was "the place where treasure was deposited;" and he was of opinion that it was reached "by a stair from the terrace." (*c*) In Orissan temples the upper rooms are reached by stairs or vises placed inside the side walls. Adverting to the sloping roof of the pavilion General Cunningham says:—"The 'three tiers of roofs' which the pilgrim mentions I take to have been, 1*st*, a roof over the entrance portico of the lower storey; 2*nd*, a roof over the entrance room of the second storey; and 3*rd*, a roof over the portico of the third storey just above the top of the overlaping arch." (*d*) This explanation, however, is inexplicable. In a three-storeyed building one would expect the topmost cover to form the roof, and the opposite sides of the other two

(*a*) Julien's 'Memoires sur les Contrées occidentales,' I, p. 465.
(*b*) Arch. Surv. Report, III, p. 91.
(*c*) 'Transactions of the Royal Asiatic Society,' I, p. 48.
(*d*) Arch. Surv. Report, III, p. 96.

layers to form floors and ceilings; they are never in ordinary language called "three roofs rising in three tiers." What word the Chinese pilgrim has used in his journal I know not; but neither the French "rang," nor its equivalent, the English "tier," can idiomatically be used to indicate the succession of roofs on the three successive storeys of a building. To urge otherwise would be to say that every three-storeyed house has roofs 'in three tiers,' which would be absurd. I feel pretty certain, therefore, that the General is mistaken, and that the pilgrim referred to the topmost roof only, and that was formed in three tiers or layers, as the roofs of Chinese and Tibetan temples usually are, and such as are to be seen on some ancient Hindu structures, most prominently on the Dancing-hall of the Great Tower of Bhuvaneśvara. And as the outlines of such a roof are distinctly traceable on the shaft of the Buddha Gayá temple, just where the roof came in contact with it, and on which it left its marks when it fell down, there is no room for doubt on the question. The marks show that the first two roofs were concave on the outside, and the topmost one undulating like a cyma, and that it joined the temple by a gable end. I cannot positively say whether the free end to the east terminated in a gable, or by a sloping side. Gables, however, are not common in Indian temple architecture, and I am disposed to think, therefore, that the features of the side roof were reproduced in front, and accordingly I have represented it as such in the restored drawing. (Plate XIX.) The little finials or acrotarias at the edges and the pinnacle on the top of the roof are purely Indian, and such as one may *à priori* expect to find there; but they fell down centuries ago. I could find only the fragment of a finial, which I have copied.

The roof immediately over the porch was formed of a pointed radiating arch built of dressed bricks, having one end broader than the other, to provide for the difference in the span of the extrados and the intrados, and very neatly and closely put together. But the voussoirs, placed edge to edge, cut off by cross bricks, and cemented with clay, could not but produce a very weak form of arch. The second-storey room was covered by a vault of exactly the same kind. Portions of this vault are still *in situ*, and may be distinctly seen in the annexed photograph. (Plate XVI.) The top of the second vault formed the floor of the attic, the sloping roof of which rose sufficiently high to take in the door of the third-storey room of the temple, and thus it served the purpose of a porch to it.

Corner Pavilions.

Entering the porch there is on either hand a flight of steps, covered by a semicircular vaulted roof, and leading to the terrace round the temple. Round the upper end of this flight, at the south-east corner, there are remains of walls which formed a pavilion over the stairs. Knowing well how scrupulous old Indian artists were about respective symmetry, or the reproduction of the features of one side of a building on the other, I am certain that a similar one also existed at the north-east corner; but this corner having been rebuilt, no trace of it could be found. The pavilion was a necessity to protect the stairs, and to prevent the rain-water from flowing into the porch. Whether, for the sake of symmetry, similar pavilions were erected on the other two corners, I could not ascertain, as those corners had been rebuilt and renewed long ago, and no trace of their original forms have been left behind. The remains of the pavilion at the south-east corner consist only of a few inches of the base of the surrounding walls, and it is impossible to make out what the pavilions were like in their entirety. Seeing, however, that the same ordonnance reigns throughout the whole building, and knowing that Indian architects were particularly mindful of the laws of uniformity, I have, in restoring the pavilions, adopted the same order of decoration which obtains in the other parts of the building. Some cover must have existed over the upper ends of the staircases to protect the kutcha-built walls of the temple from being injured by rain-water, and its floor from being inundated, and the pavilions I have designed are in perfect keeping with the order of the temple. That similar structures existed I have no reason to doubt, but for the present they are authorized by nothing more trustworthy than a few inches of the bases of the old walls of a pavilion of some kind.

Terrace on the west side.

There is every reason to believe that the terrace on the west side corresponded with those on the north and the south sides; but the greater part of its wall has long since disappeared, and its original situation can now only be inferred from a small portion of the upper part of it at the south-west corner, which, I noticed, was in all its details the continuation of the southern wall. The situation I calculate was just 14 feet from the base of the temple and close by the east of the Bodhi tree. (See dotted line on the plan, Plate V.) But as the platform round the base of the tree was gradually raised, it encroached on the wall, and at last a revetment had to be built to protect the platform, and this produced a projection from the terrace 20 × 24 feet. This projection is well shown in General Cunningham's plan. (Plate IV, Plan I, A.) The revetment, however, gradually bulged out from the pressure of the growing roots of the tree, and in 1863 the northern part of it had been completely knocked down, exposing the rubbish mound inside, and showing clearly that this portion was not a continuation of the terrace of the north and the south sides, which are solid brick-work. The Burmese repairers have since prolonged the north and the south walls of the terrace, and run a new wall within ten feet six inches of the line of the old railing on the west side, thereby completely destroying the original appearance of the place. The new walls are perfectly plain, and plastered with chunam.

The Bodhi tree—its platform.

The Bodhi tree is the most sacred object of worship at Buddha Gayá. It was under its friendly shelter that Śákya obtained the perfection of wisdom, and it is therefore looked upon with the highest veneration. It is said by the Hindus to have been planted by Brahmá himself; but the Buddhists attribute it to one Dugdhakáminí, a king of Ceylon. The name is in the feminine gender, and means a "milk-maid," and this would suggest the idea of its being somehow related to the maiden Sujátá, who gave a dish of rice-milk to the saint. It must have originally stood on a level with the ground. When it grew big and umbrageous, the inhabitants of the village, most probably, made a platform by throwing some earth round it, and, possibly, though not very probably, protected it by a masonry revetment and a concrete floor. The height of this platform could not have been more than a foot and a half. It formed a convenient place of resort for the people, who assembled there to enjoy the cool of the evening, and to converse on the topics of the day. Hermits, who visited the village from time to time, generally selected this platform for their short sojourn, and paṇḍits thence delivered their sermons and religious and moral lectures to devout congregations. Thus in course of time the place was associated with religious teaching, and looked upon as one of some sanctity. Such has been the history of many a sacred tree in India, and hundreds of such trees may even now be seen in different parts of the country. That such was also the history of the Bodhi tree none will, I fancy, question. It was just the place suited to serve as a tabernacle for one like Buddha when he proposed to preach a new religion, or exhibit to the people the glory of the meditations which he wished to perform; and once sanctified by the presence of one who rose to great eminence as a teacher, the tree could not but be looked upon with the highest veneration (*a*). It then, I believe, first received the name of *Boddhi-maṇḍa*, or the "throne of wisdom." Pious people could not but associate the wisdom of the preacher with the place where that wisdom was first manifested, and soon covered the earthen floor (if it was earthen, and not of concrete) of the platform, the original *Boddhi-maṇḍa*, with a layer of substantial concrete. After this, the new roots which shot out from the trunk, not finding ready access to the ground, spread on the concrete, and fresh mould had to be thrown on them for their protection. This addition soon became unsightly, and a new platform had to be built on the old one, so as to raise its height by a foot to a foot and a half. This process repeated from time to time, gradually raised the platform till it was flush with the level of the terrace, and the tree in a manner rose with the rise of the ground-level, till it came up to the height of the terrace. When this was effected there was no room left to keep the platform distinct from the terrace, and then it was that the projection shown in General Cunningham's plan was built, and the platform converted into an integral part of the terrace. Nor did the necessity for supplying fresh mould cease at this stage. The growth of new roots above ground continued, and, to a certain extent, was promoted by the daily watering of the base of the trunk by the faithful, and some contrivance had to be made both for protecting the fresh mould put on the roots, and for preventing the water from spreading over the platform, and a circular masonry ring round the trunk was what appeared the most convenient. In 1809 Buchanan-Hamilton noticed a succession of five such rings, forming a pyramid of as many steps. In 1863 the roots had grown above the topmost of these steps, and last year, when a new tree had to be planted in the site of the old one, it was found expedient to build a cylindrical structure on the top of the pyramid for its reception.

In 1863, when the north side of the revetment had fallen, twelve layers of the platform came to view, and my attention was called to them by Major Mead.

(*a*) General Cunningham and others describe this tree as the one under which Śâkya performed his six years' penance; but such is not the case. It was here that he obtained the *Bodhi* (knowledge) after he found out the futility of the six years' penance, which he had performed under another tree at some distance to the south-east of it. See *ante*, page 55.

Last year, when the greater part of the revetment on the west side had been pulled down, and a new one was being built, I noticed a succession of four of them. Each layer of earth was from 14 to 17 inches thick, and the concrete over it an inch and a half, covered with a thin layer of chunam. The terrace is now 24 feet above the level of the original ground, and so there must be altogether a series of 16 platforms. The five steps together measure 7 feet 6 inches, and the new cylinder over it 3 feet 6 inches. These measurements give a total height of 35 feet above the original ground-level, and the tree has accordingly been gradually raised to that height.

Had the same tree existed all along on the spot, and the additions to the platform been made at fixed periods, the different layers of concrete and steps would indicate each a period of about 80 years, and we would have a fair index to the age of the platform. But the tree passed through many vicissitudes; it was cut down at least thrice, and renewed several times; and as the plan of renewing the tree was evidently not by cutting down the old one and planting a new one in its place, but by dropping a seedling into an axilla or into a decayed spot of the old tree, so as to lead to the supposition that it was only a new shoot of the parent stem and not a stranger brought from a distance, it was found necessary to cover up the stem of the old one, to prevent the imposition from being discovered, and the rise of the platform was quite irregular. It is impossible, therefore, to base any chronological argument on the data furnished by the layers. They are enough, however, to vouch for the great antiquity of the place.

When Hiouen Thsang visited the place in 637 A.C., the platform was quite distinct from the terrace, and bore on it a stone seat, which he thus describes:—"Just in the middle of the walls which surround the tree of knowledge there stood the diamond throne (*vajrásana*). It had been constructed in ancient times at the commencement of the 'Kalpa of the sages' (*Bhadra-kalpa*). It was erected at the same time as the vast earth, and it was supported on the centre of three thousand grand *chiliocosms*. At the bottom it descended to the extremity of the golden wheel; in height it attained the limits of the earth. It was made of diamonds, and was nearly a hundred feet in circumference. A thousand Buddhas of the Kalpa of the sages (*Bhadra-kalpa*) seated on it performed the meditation called the 'ecstacy of the diamond.' It is on that account called the 'diamond throne,' and as at this place the holy knowledge was seen face to face, they have named it the 'verandah of knowledge' (*bodhi-maṇḍa*). When the vast earth is agitated and trembling, this spot remains at rest and immovable. It is hence that when the *Joa-lai* (*Tathágata*) was on the point of attaining Buddhahood, he walked the earth to the four angles (of the monument). All the regions trembled, but when afterwards he arrived at this spot, the ground rested calm and immovable. Since the world has entered the last kalpa, the right law has become gradually enfeebled, sand and earth have covered the whole of the diamond throne, and it is no longer possible to see it. After the Nirváṇa of Buddha, the kings of all countries, having learnt by tradition the dimensions of the diamond throne which had been indicated by the Buddhas, marked the limits to the south and to the north by two statues of the Avalokiteśvara Bodhisattva, which are seated on the east side" (*a*). It is generally supposed that the stone here referred to is the same which is now lying in the temple of Vágíśvarí Deví.

Of the history of the tree the pilgrim gives the following account:—

Bodhi tree—its history.

"The tree of knowledge (Bodhidruma) which stood at this place over the diamond throne is a pipolo (Pippala, *Ficus religiosa*). At the time when Buddha lived on the earth, this tree had attained the height of many hundred feet. Although it had been cut down many times, it was still 40 to 50 feet high. Since Buddha obtained complete knowledge (*Samyak sambodhi*) while seated under this tree, it is called *Bodhi*. Its trunk is of a yellowish white colour, and its branches and leaves are blackish green. In winter and in summer its leaves fell not, but remained fresh and lustrous, without undergoing any change. But when the day of Tathágata's Nirváṇa arrived, they all fell, and little by little the tree again attained its former condition. On that day the kings of all countries, the clergy, and the laity of distant places, came unasked, by thousands and dozens of thousands, and watered the tree with odorous essences and perfumed milk. Then a harmonious music was heard around it, and fragrant candles and torches adorned with flowers surpassing the light of day were ranged around it; the whole world took part in the offerings.

"After the Nirváṇa of Tathágata, the king Aśoka (*Wou-yeou*) succeeded to the throne. As he had faith in false doctrines, he destroyed the vestiges left by

(*a*) 'Memoires sur les Contrées occidentales,' I. p. 460.

Buddha. He started at the time, at the head of a large army, to cut down the tree. The roots, the trunk, the branches, and the leaves, were cut and divided into small particles, and then at a distance of some tens of paces to the west side were piled a heap of the *débris*. He ordered a Bráhman adorer of fire to burn them as a sacrifice to his god. Before the flame and the fumes had dissipated, there was seen in the middle of the burning pile two trees issuing forth with leaves rich and verdant. The king, Aśoka, who had seen the tree of knowledge reduced to cinders, was struck by this miracle, and repented of his crime. He watered the roots which had remained unburnt with perfumed milk, and next morning, at the first hour of the day, the tree was restored to its former state. At the sight of this miracle the king was filled to overflowing with joy and goodness, and himself made offerings. In his delight he forgot to return home. The queen, who had just before given her faith to heretic doctrines, secretly sent men, who, after midnight, cut down the tree for a second time. In the morning, when the king, Aśoka, came to offer his adorations to the tree, he found that there was nothing of it left but the trunk, and was struck with a profound grief. He prayed with sincere fervour, sprinkled the root with perfumed milk, and in less than a day found the tree resuscitated. The king, imbued with respect and admiration, surrounded the tree with a stone wall about ten feet high. This enclosure exists to this day. In later times the king, Śaśánka, who was attached to heretic doctrines, impelled by base envy, reviled the law of Buddha and destroyed the convents. He cut down the tree of knowledge and dug out the earth to the bottom where water circulates, but without being able to exterminate the deepest roots. Then he set fire to the ground and steeped the earth with sugarcane juice and sugar to entirely destroy and prevent the fibres from germinating again. Some months after the news of this occurrence reached the ears of Púrṇabrahma, king of Magadha and the last descendant of the king Aśoka. At this news he said with a sigh, 'Alas! the sun of intelligence had set since many centuries; there remained only the tree of Buddha, and behold they have again cut it down; and men shall see it no more." After saying these words he started at the head of his men, threw himself on the ground, overpowered by transports of grief. The sight was sorely painful. He watered the tree with the milk of many thousands of kine, and in course of one night the tree was reproduced entire. Its height was 10 feet. Apprehending that it might be cut again, he surrounded it with a stone wall 24 feet high. It is thus that in the present day the tree of knowledge is protected by a stone wall which exceeds 20 feet."(a)

The story about the first destruction of the tree by Aśoka does not occur in the Buddhist Sanskrit biography of that emperor, but that of the second is thus given in the *Aśoka Avadána*:—

"Pavishya-rakshitá, *alias* Tishya-rakshitá, the chief queen of Aśoka, finding that her husband devoted whatever precious objects he got, whether flowers, fruits, metals, jewels, or money, to the decoration of the Bodhi tree, and neglected every thing else, felt greatly aggrieved. 'I cannot,' she thought, 'maintain my dignity as the chief queen so long as she (the tree), my enemy, remains the favourite of my husband. I should therefore diligently try to destroy that rival. What is the good of existence if I cannot destroy my enemy?' Having thus made up her mind, that mistress of the harem sent for Mátangí, and thus addressed her with earnestness:—'Mátangí, you know the tree to which the king sends with zeal whatever precious objects he gets. Can you destroy that Bodhi, my rival? If you can, I shall give you a profusion of wealth. Listen to me, and destroy the Bodhi tree. I shall bear you in mind with great regard, and give you whatever you wish.' Mátangí responded by saying 'Yes I can,' and proceeded to the Bodhi tree. She encircled the tree with some thread, and repeated over it, with due ceremony, an incantation calculated to destroy it. The tree was struck by the fire of the incantation; it became leafless, and its branches began to wither. The people were struck with wonder at the sudden drying of the tree, and speculated about its cause. The officers of the king heard the news, and, seeing what had happened, quickly repaired to the king, and after due prostration announced—'Oh, great king, the Bodhi tree, seated under whose shade Tathágata obtained the difficultly-attainable universal knowledge and became an all-knowing Buddha, is dying.' The king, on hearing this, fell senseless on the ground, and, after having been revived by the sprinkling of water on his face, thus cried in grief:—'Seeing that the root of the noble tree is destroyed, I know that my fate is adverse. When the lordly tree is dying, I know my breath is near at end.' Mourning thus the king constantly thought of the tree, and felt greatly puzzled why it should have dried up. Seeing her husband thus overpowered by grief and distraction, Tishya-rakshitá addressed

(a) 'Memoires sur les Contrées occidentales,' Vol. I, pp. 461 *et seq.*

him, saying :—'Lord, what is it that has caused you pain? What have you to fear? Tell it to me, O great king, if you reckon me dear to you.' Hearing this from his wife the king sighed repeatedly, and then said :—'My dear, you have heard that the Bodhi tree is dying, and grief for it has made my heart inconsolable.' The beloved Tishya-rakshitá, on hearing her husband's words, looked up to him, and thus tried to console him :—'Dear husband, grieve not even if the Bodhi does not live; here I am, thy beloved and beloving. Cast aside the poison of grief from your heart, and enjoy with me the pleasures of the world.' The words of his wife did not please him; he knew the tree was dying, and said :—'That tree which the great saint (Munîndra) called his own, even that is dying, and I cannot overcome the grief of losing it.' The Queen was brought to her senses by these words; she was overcome by remorse, and, sighing deeply, reflected thus :—'Alas! what grievous sin have I committed! What can I do now to do away with this distress! How inconsiderately have I sinned against myself and my husband! I shall certainly be doomed to grievous suffering in hell in return for this. When and how shall I obtain redemption from this dreadful crime! Abiding in hell I shall have to endure eternal misery. What shall I do now, and whose assistance shall I seek? Alas! who can save me, the great sinner! who can support me!' Thus oppressed by remorse Tishya-rakshitá sent for Mátangí and secretly told her :—'Mátangí, do you restore the Bodhi tree, the asylum of Sujáta, to its former condition, with all its green leaves.' Thus commanded by the queen, the vile hag replied, saying :—'Madam, if there be any remnant of life in it, I can easily restore the big tree to its former condition.' Having said this, and taking a profusion of wealth from the queen, that Chaṇḍála woman repaired to the Bodhi tree, and, untwining the thread, recited the incantation for restoring life. Then she dug round the roots of the tree daily, and watered them with a thousand pitchers of milk. Thereby the tree gradually thrived, and was soon covered by green leaves." (a)

(a) I quote the whole of the text for those who may be interested in it :—

यथाऽशोको नरेन्द्रोऽसावुपयुक्तविवेदन: । सर्वत्रापि नरत् कृपात् प्रतिदायाभवत्तदा ॥
यदेव भगवान् बुद्धो बोधिप्राप्तोऽभवज्जिन: । इति बोधौ विशेषेण प्रसादितोऽभवत्तदा ॥
तानि रत्नवस्तूनि वस्त्राण्याभरणानि च । सुवर्णादिरत्नानि वस्तूनि विविधानि च ॥
तानि सर्वाणि वस्तूनि बोधौ बोधाय निर्ददौ । सदर्श प्रेमभावेन बोधिवृक्षे सदा रत: ॥
दृष्ट्वा तत्पतेस्तत्र भार्यातिष्यरक्षिता प्रिया । पारिष्यरक्षिताख्या सा मत्सरेण व्यचिन्तयत् ॥

Of the destruction of the tree by Śaśánka I have met with no account in the Sanskrit Buddhist manuscripts collected by Mr. Hodgson in Nepal. General Cunningham calculates the date of the destruction to be A.C. 610.

At the beginning of this century Buchanan-Hamilton found the tree "in full vigour," and thought that it could not then "in all probability have exceeded 100 years in age."(a) In 1861 General Cunningham said—"The celebrated Bodhi tree still exists, but is very much decayed; one large stem, with three branches to the westward, is still green, but the other branches are barkless and rotten. The green branch perhaps belongs to some younger tree, as there are numerous stems of apparently different trees clustered together."(b) In 1863 the tree appeared to me to be "decayed and dying," and "scarce two hundred years old." The trunk was then leaning towards the west, and bore two green branches and the stumps of three or four dead ones. (See Plate VII.) In 1876 the tree was dead and knocked down by a storm, and its place has now been filled by a seedling about three feet high.

On the steps of the pyramidal basement of the tree there are, on the north side, the images of four Hindu divinities—(1) a Mahádeva with four arms, holding a pitcher, an alms-bowl, a rosary, and a lotus. The right lower hand of the figure shows a lotus mark on the palm, and on each side of the figure there is a female attendant; (2) a figure of Vishṇu of the usual style, with a male and a female

(a) Martin's 'Eastern India,' Vol. I, p. 78.
(b) Arch. Surv. Report, Vol. I, p. 5.

कथं राजा मया सार्द्धं रतिमेवानुभुञ्जते । प्रधानरत्नं मनुते बोधावप्रेममुदा ॥
तदहं किं करिष्यामि यतोऽसौ बोधकारिता । इत्थं प्रधानरत्नमिति सा मनसा समाप्यते ॥
रतिकामेच्छ किं सौख्यं यतो नाथो विरज्यते । यथा स्मरामि विषयैः कर्म्मलोके [illegible] ॥
यावत् सा विद्यतेऽत्रैव सा बधूरे नृपप्रिया । तावन्मे सौख्यता नास्ति यतो नाथो न [illegible] ॥
किं नाम यदि भुञ्जामि रतिका न [illegible] । [illegible] किं मम ॥
नाम [illegible] सुखं नास्ति [illegible] सौख्यञ्च किं रतिः । [illegible] किं [illegible] एवं [illegible] ॥
नैव [illegible] यावत् [illegible] यावत् सा विद्यते [illegible] : [illegible] ॥
यदहं [illegible] मां [illegible] । [illegible] किं जीवितं सुखं ॥
इति विचिन्त्य सा राज्ञी [illegible] । [illegible] ॥
[illegible] बोधिवृक्षोऽन्तरान् । [illegible] ॥
[illegible] बोधिं [illegible] । यदि [illegible] ॥
इति [illegible] बोधिं [illegible] । [illegible] ॥
इति [illegible] । [illegible] बोधि[illegible] ॥
[illegible] बोधिं [illegible] । [illegible] ॥

attendant; (3) Hara and Párvatí, the latter seated on the lap of her lord, and having her hands on his neck: her lord has one hand on her breast and the other on her chin. On the pedestal of this figure there is a Burmese inscription of a modern date; (4) Gaṇeśa. On the east side there are images of Padmapáṇi and of a demon.

Buddhapad.

The only other building at Buddha Gayá which demands notice, the only one of stone which was *in situ* till the beginning of last year, is the Buddhapad. It stood between the Pancha Páṇḍu temple and the grave of the second Mahant, right opposite the Great Temple. It was an open pavilion, formed of four monolithic pillars, bearing massive architraves, and a roof constructed in the usual style of four triangular diagonal slabs surmounted by a crowning-piece. It was improvised with stones which originally belonged to other temples, for they bear sculptures on the built and inner faces; two of the architraves were formed of fragments of the Aśoka rail-posts. The pavilion was erected some time after Hiouen Thsang's visit, for that traveller does not notice it; and the object of the erection was to provide a covering for a hemispherical block of granite, bearing the carvings of two human feet. The carvings are said to be impressions of Buddha's feet, and bear certain marks or symbols, which, however, are not characteristic of a Buddha. On the side of the hemispherical block there is a Sanskrit inscription, dated, which

---

तत: स बोधिसत्त्वोऽपि तत्कलाविधिविद्दित: । विभव: शाक्यमाचार्य: ममेव शासनेऽहं ॥
एवं तं सुविर्तं दृष्ट्वा सर्वंलोकाय विस्मिता: । चाहं बोधिसत्त्व: [illegible] कथमिति यथारवत् ॥
तदा राजजना: श्रुत्वा दृष्ट्वा चेमं विस्मोचितं । [illegible] राज्ञोऽग्रे प्रचलेनं न्यवेदयन् ॥
तत्रोपविश्य तथागतेन [illegible] यथावत् । सर्वं श्रुत्वा बोधिसत्त्व नरेन्द्र बोधिसत्त्वोऽसौ विमलं प्रयाति ॥
निर्वेदितं तैरिति भूपति: स कुमैव भूमौ न्यपतद्विचेता: । ततश्चिरात् संज्ञां निपीय [illegible] चैवं प्रवदन्नुवाच ॥
दृष्टं कृतं मा [illegible] कामादि दृष्टोऽस्य सदा [illegible] : । [illegible] चैव मते यथार्थं वाचा: [illegible] ॥
एवं स विलपमाना कुद्ध: भूमैव सं सद । कथं मया [illegible] इति विलापपुरोऽभवत् ॥
एवं विलापविह्वलाक्षं तत्रोपपरिवेदितं । [illegible] सा विलापचित्तामवदत् ॥
[illegible] किं कातरो दुःखं कृतवापि सर्वं तव । [illegible] भवतोऽर्थं यदि पिता ॥
इति मात्रोदितं श्रुत्वा स राजा नि:श्वस्य च । तां मात्रां सुचिरं दृष्ट्वा पुन एवमभाषत ॥
[illegible] मत्पुत्रेण [illegible] हृदये [illegible] ॥
इति [illegible] : श्रुत्वा सा विलापचित्ता प्रिया । [illegible] बोधिसत्त्वं यथाभवत् ॥
भो: [illegible] : शोकं यदि बोधिनं विद्यते । चर्यं ते [illegible] ॥
तस्मात् [illegible] परित्यज्य तत्रोऽभिविभ्रमात्मनि । किं [illegible] श्रुत्वा [illegible] तथा चर ॥
इति मात्रोदितं श्रुत्वा [illegible] बोधिं [illegible] । तं दृष्ट्वा स [illegible] दृष्टो भवेति मन्यते ॥

assigns it to Vishṇu. The inscription and the symbols will be noticed in detail further on. The pavilion was pulled down by the Burmese repairers in the middle of last year, to clear out the space in front of the Great Temple, and in September last I saw the hemispherical block lying in front of the Páncha Páṇḍu Temple (see left side of Plate VI), and the materials of the pavilion lying on a rubbish mound at some distance to the south-east of the temple enclosure.

Arched Corridor.

In front of the pavilion there formerly stood the arched gateway, but in 1863 I took no measurement of it, and now it is entirely gone. It is said that it was only the western end of a covered passage which extended from the temple court-yard to the bank of the river Nairanjaná, and had been so constructed to enable a princess, some say the daughter of Amara Siñha Sauvira, to perform her daily ablutions in the river, and then to enter the temple without being seen by the common people in the way. Her house having been on the mound, now called Garh, she had easy access to it from the temple. The story is fabulous, and calls for no remark, though there is no antecedent improbability in it.

Materials of building—Bricks.

In a district so abounding in hills as Gayá, and having inexhaustible supplies of building stones of a good quality, it is remarkable that so little of stone was there used in architecture in ancient times. The Great Temple and its appurtenances were built entirely

---

सोऽपश्य विषमं वात वन्धोक पैथं सा च मे । इति मर्त्योदितं श्रुत्वा सा राज्ञी परितोषिता ॥
पश्चात्तापाभितप्ता वचस्तेषं अभिमतत् । का दैवं मानवं कर्म यच्छ्रोऽपि कारितं ॥
मयाऽत्र किं तु कर्म्मणमत्वा मापतुम्बे । का पापमतमोऽपि जानित च्छमयोरपि ॥
अयं राजा महादुःखं ओष्टुं याजामि मारके । एवमपायैरुत्पतोऽरे: परितोषो कदा मम ॥
दुःखानि हि चिरं भुक्ता बधियं मरको यदा । तदत्र किं करिष्यामि याचामि शरणं कुरु ॥
यो मे सदा बहुवर्णा को दर्शनात्पाधिर्वि । इति चिन्ताभितप्ता या सिक्तरथिता सदा ॥
कारुण्य मात्र मात्रजी रहस्येकमागत । मातजि मं पुनर्येऽपि ह्यं तं तुमवातवं ॥
यथापुरायं संहृतं तथा कुरु करिष्यदे । इति राज्ञा समादिष्टं श्रुत्वा सा कुमारी सदा ॥
तां शिवरचितां राज्ञी पुनरेवमभाषत । अहो भाग्यानसेवोऽपि यदि तत्र नकुमरो ॥
यथा पुरायं संहृतं तथा कर्त्तुं हि समूर्था । इत्युक्त्वा सा च मयादी तथा राज्ञा सर्व तत्र ॥
परित्यक्त प्रचला महोदिष्टवाभिनंदा भरत् । तत्र दृष्ट्वा च सा हृयं ममवृक्षं समन्वत: ॥
सत्यातप्त पुनरेवं जलस्य मामवाचर्म । समसाकं सरोजैरपे: परिवम समाकृम: ॥
क्षीरकुम्भसहस्रैश्च दिने दिनेऽभ्यषावयत् । ततः क्रमात्स्वो वृक्ष: परिवृद्धो दिने दिने ॥
यथा पुरायं संहूतपत्वा पादपरिष्कृत: ।

of bricks; and the extensive mounds on all sides of it and the foundations under them show that brick was the material principally used in architecture. Doubtless plinths, pillars, and other articles of stone have been met with, but they bear no relation to the extent to which bricks were used. The bricks of the most ancient parts of the Great Temple measure 19 × 13 × 2:—

The following are the dimensions of ten other bricks measured by me:—

(1) 15' × 5' 0' × 0' 5' × 2' 7".	(6) 16' × 10' 0" × 2' 3".
(2) 14' × 10' 5" × 2' 6".	(7) 15' × 10' 0" × 2' 3".
(3) 16' × 10' 5" × 2' 6".	(8) 16' × 9' 8" × 2' 7".
(4) 16' × 11' 0" × 2' 6.	(9) 15' × 9' 8" × 2' 7".
(5) 14' × 11' 0" × 2' 6".	(10) 14' × 9' 0" × 2' 0".

Others are of smaller size, but none under 15 × 9 inches. They appear to have been very carefully made with well-puddled clay, having no grits or clots, and so planed and smoothed as to sit very closely on each other. The older bricks have the peculiar bluish tinge noticed by Hiouen Thsang. The bricks used in the arches were cut into the shape of voussoirs, after having been burnt, but they are not all of the same size. Generally speaking they measure 16 inches on the top, which is slightly arched, and 14 at the bottom, the sides being 10 to 11 inches. The keystones are triangular.

Cement.

The cement used in building is a finely-puddled, tenacious bluish clay, and only a thin layer of it was required, as the bricks, having well-dressed, smooth surfaces, sat on each other firmly enough without requiring the intervention of any cement. At first sight the bricks appear to be in direct contact with each other, and no part of the cement is visible or exposed in such a way as to be able to absorb moisture freely. Thus the sparing use of the clay has been of great value in preserving the buildings for a long time. Even in the construction of the arches nothing but clay has been used by way of cement. On roofs and floors a compost of brick-dust and kankar lime was the mortar used, and a variety of it with a larger proportion of lime was used for plastering, and for the formation of mouldings and other ornaments. This shows that the builders were not only perfectly familiar with the properties of lime mortar, but they used it very extensively. The supply of kankar was abundant everywhere, from Behar to Agra. It occurred often on the very surface of the earth, and could be, as it is now, collected by a mere scratching of the soil. Nor was fuel scarce; and the art of burning the kankar involves very little knowledge or tact; and yet, curiously enough, the builders never thought of lime-mortar in building radiating arches. The only way to account for this strange neglect of such a valuable material would be to attribute it to the inexorable dominion which custom exercises in this country. We learn from ancient texts that clay was the only cement used in the construction of altars in Vedic times, and that custom was handed down from generation to generation, and none ventured to do otherwise. Arrian, on the authority of Megasthenes, informs us that at the close of the fourth century B.C. "those cities in India which stood on commanding situations and lofty eminences were built of brick and mud" (a), and the practice seems to have been continued for a considerable length of time after that period. This would prove, too, that the art of building was indigenous, and not, as supposed by some, introduced by foreign architects.

Wood-work.

The only wood-work in the Great Temple is the framing of the roof of the third-storey room, but it is placed at so great a height that I could not come sufficiently near it to examine its character. Doors, too, were no doubt made of wood; but there is none existing now of any ancient date.

Stone.

Stone occurs in the door-frames, floors, and steps. The two door-frames of the Great Temple are of sandstone. The steps in the two staircases are of granite; so are the flags with which the temple and the court-yard are paved. The railings round the temple were partly of sandstone and partly of granite; and basalt, chlorite, and potstone occur in different forms as bases, plinths, model-stúpas, statues, and other sculpture.

Metal.

At Buddha Gayá there is no counterpart of the large iron beams and rafters so abundant in mediæval Orissan architecture, and the only use made of that metal was in the formation of clamps for tying stoneworks together. Gold was used for gilding statues, and copper for the pinnacles of temples; but of the last two no specimen has been met with by me: Major Mead found only a brass peacock and a bell. Hiouen Thsang makes mention of brazen statues; but none has been seen of late.

(a) McCrindle's 'Megasthenes and Arrian,' p. 68.

Style of building.

In the style of building there is nothing peculiar that calls for any notice. As elsewhere in India in former times, so here, the bricks were ranged isodomically as stretchers and bonders promiscuously in every course, and not in alternate courses, as is sometimes the case in Europe.

Arches—their construction.

But in the construction of the arches the plan followed was peculiar. The arches were formed exactly as a radiating arch should be, of voussoirs made of bricks with their sides so cut that each is thicker at the outside than at the inside of the arch, tilting inward and downward further than the course next below it till the two sides, rising together, met and received the keystone. The two extreme voussoirs rest on the abutments, and the intermediate ones are held together in their position by their mutual pressure, by the resistance of the keystone, and by the force of gravity drawing the voussoirs straight downwards while they stand in a slanting position. Instead, however, of ranging the bricks lengthwise across the arch, *i.e.* as bonders and stretchers touching each other by their flat sides, as is the case now, they were placed so as to have their longest sides resting edge to edge, in a line with the arch. The keystone, a triangular brick, was put on one side of the crown. And as only entire bricks were used, there was no bonding, each series forming a distinct line of its own, as shown in the woodcut No. 3. "In this construction," General Cunningham justly observes, "the strain is thrown on the narrow edges of the bricks instead of on their broad faces, and it is therefore weak. But it is still so greatly superior in strength to the overlapping Indian arch that it is difficult to conceive how any builder who had a knowledge of even this weaker kind of radiating arch should have deliberately discarded it in the greatest opening of a brick building, where its use would have been eminently judicious"(a). This arrangement was, however, obviously adopted with a view to simulate the appearance of stone voussoirs, which expose to the sight the broadest face, and that the thickness of a brick could not produce. This fact is worthy of special note,

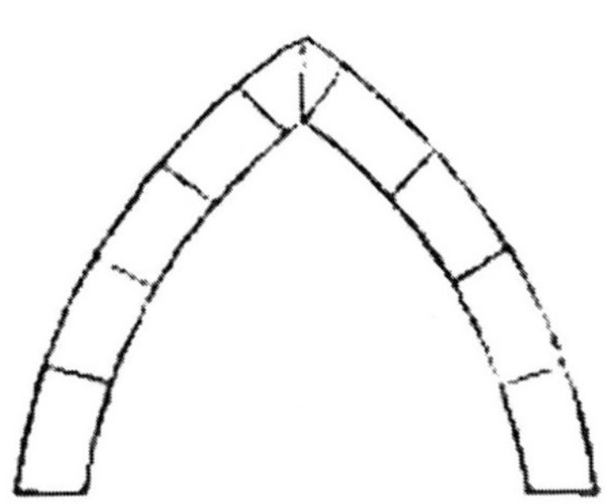

No. 3, Arch over Doorway.

(a) Arch. Surv. Report, Vol. III, p. 84.

as it shows that the arches were copies of stone originals, and such originals were known to the people.

This arrangement, however, was confined to the arches over the doorways. In the vaults, after every brick placed lengthwise, two bricks were put crosswise (woodcut No. 4), so no mechanical advantage was derived by the interlacing produced by bonding, and the clay used as cement being utterly worthless as a binding material, the bricks remained *in situ* solely by their lateral pressure and the resistance of the keystones. In the annexed woodcut (No. 4) is shown the appearance of the arch from the front as also from below. The voussoirs are all of entire bricks, and there is no bonding; but the cross bricks are bonded. The latter were evidently intended to strengthen the arch, by throwing the resistance on the narrow sides of the bricks. This arrangement, however, has not been adopted in the vault of the Konch Temple (see woodcut No. 1, p. 78), where the simple plan shown in woodcut No. 3 was preferred.

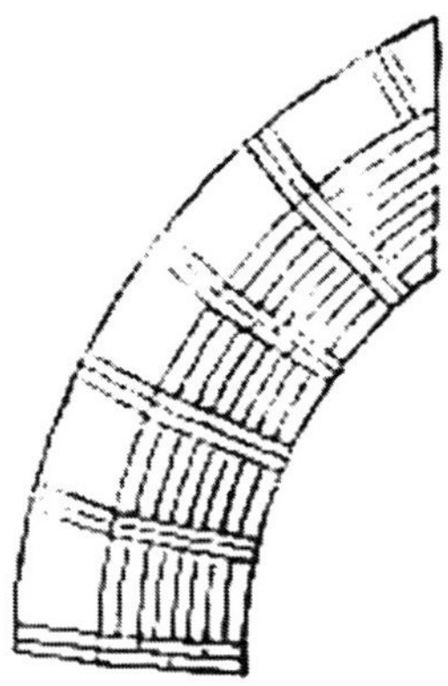

No. 4, Section of a Vault.

The form of the arch also differed. In the larger vaults and arches the form adopted was the pointed equilateral, formed by the decussation of arcs drawn on the radius of the span; but in the smaller vaults and arches the semicircular plan was preferred.

Arches—their number.

Altogether there were, in 1871, seventeen arches, viz. 1st and 2nd, the vaults over the porch; 3rd, the vault over the vestibule leading to the first-storey chamber; 4th, the vault over the chamber; 5th, the arch over the door of the second-storey room; 6th, the vault over the vestibule of that chamber; 7th, the vault over the chamber; 8th, the arch over the door of the third-storey room; 9th, the vault over the vestibule of that room; 10th and 11th, arches over the doorways of the two staircases in the porch; 12th and 13th, the sloping vaults over the staircases; 14th and 15th, arches over the doorways at the first landing of the stairs; 16th, the vault in the temple of Tárá Deví; 17th, the vault over the corridor, which extended from the front of the granite pavement to the bank of the Nairanjaná. Of these the 8th, the 9th, and the 17th, are now not in existence. The 10th, 11th, 12th, 13th, 14th, and 15th, are semicircular, and the rest pointed.

Arches—the author's first notice.

I was the first to bring to the notice of the public, in 1864 (*a*), some of these arches, forming so remarkable a feature of Buddha Gayá architecture. In my paper on the subject I said—"Such a structure in an Indian building more than two thousand years old struck me as a remarkable proof of the Hindus having had a knowledge of the principle of the arch at a very early period, though the credit of it has been denied them by all our Anglo-Indian antiquaries. Fergusson, in his 'Hand-book of Architecture,' concedes to the Jains a knowledge of the horizontal or projecting arch, but, adverting to the radiating or true arch, says (Vol. I., p. 78): 'In the first place no tope shows internally the smallest trace of a chamber so constructed (*i.e.* with a true dome); nor do any of the adjacent buildings incline to such a mode of construction, which must have ere now been detected had it ever existed.' Elsewhere he observes (p. 224): 'The Indian architects have fallen into the other extreme, refusing to use the arch under any circumstances, and preferring the smallest dimensions and the most crowded interiors, rather than adopt what they considered so destructive an expedient.' Adverting to the Kutub, he says, 'all the openings possess pointed arches, which the Hindus never used' (p. 418). Again, 'the Hindus, however, up to this time (*i.e.* of the Paṭhâns) had never built arches; nor indeed did they for centuries afterwards' (p. 424). These remarks do not, it is true, directly mean that the Indians *had no knowledge* of the arch, but they imply it. Elphinstone is more positive. In his remarks on Hindu bridges he says, 'nor does it appear that the early Hindus knew the arch, or could construct vaults or domes, otherwise than by layers of stone, projecting beyond those beneath, as in the treasury of Atreus of

(*a*) In using these words, it is the farthest from my wish to imply that none had seen the arches before me. The temple had been seen before me by thousands, including several distinguished antiquarians, and it was impossible for them, having eyes, not to see the arches so prominently exposed in front of the temple; but none had described them in print for the information of those who had not seen them, and I was the first to do so. This explanation will, I hope, satisfy my friend General Cunningham, who in a foot-note to his second report on Buddha Gayá (p. 65) complains by saying: "I may note here that Baboo Rajendra Lal makes a mistake when he supposes that the arches of the Buddha Gayá temple escaped my notice. I made a large drawing of them in December 1861, which is now before me, and I consulted Colonel Yule in the same month as to whether they were of Burmese origin." I could not have had the most distant thought of denying that he had seen the arches, or made drawings, or consulted Colonel Yule about them, for I knew nothing about those facts. All that I knew was that in his first report of 1861, which was before me, he had not adverted to them at all, and so I felt safe in asserting that I was the first to describe them. After the publication of my paper in 1864, the learned author devoted to them, in 1871, several pages in his second report.

Mycenæ' ('History of India,' p. 163). Depending on the testimony of these distinguished antiquarians, one may very reasonably assign to the Buddha Gayá temple a much later age than it claims; but the fact of its having been visited by Fa Hian, and, subsequently, by Hiouen Thsang long before the advent of the Muhammadans in this country, inevitably leads to the inference of its having existed at a pre-Muhammadan era; while the position the arches occupy is so natural and integral that it leaves no room for the hypothesis that they were subsequent additions. I brought the fact to the notice of Captain Mead, who had kindly undertaken to shew the ruins to me, and he readily acknowledged that the builders of the temple, whoever they were, certainly knew the art of constructing an arch, and the one before us was a very good specimen of it." (a)

Mr. Horne's opinion.

The late Mr. Horne visited Buddha Gayá in 1864, and published a note on the arches (in all 9—3 semicircular and 6 pointed) which he supposed were additions made in A.D. 500 to the shell of the building. He said, "the junction of the inserted work with the original is clear everywhere. The floor of the upper chamber comes through the wall of the building, *i.e.* the beaten puddled floor-line shows a white line most plain in the photograph. At the sides, too, the insertion is most plain. The use of the different-sized bricks in the different arches, whereas those in the body of the building are all the same, would indicate their having been built at a different date, which most probably was long subsequent." (b) Mr. Horne was mistaken about the floor-line; it does not anywhere permeate the wall. The "white line" is visible neither on the original nor on the photographs, and I have before me more than a dozen photographs taken by different persons and at different times.

General Cunningham's opinion.

In a private note to A. Grote, Esq., then President of the Asiatic Society of Bengal, Major-General Cunningham about that time expressed an opinion that the arches were modern additions, put in by the Burmese repairers of the temple in the 14th century. This, however, he has since been satisfied, was wrong, and he now thinks the arches to have existed from before the time of Hiouen Thsang.

(a) Journal, Asiatic Society, Vol. XXXIII, f. p. 175.
(b) Proceedings, Asiatic Society, Bengal, 1865, p. 108.

Mr. Peppe's opinion.

In the middle of 1865 Mr. Peppe, of the Opium Department, visited Buddha Gayá and prepared a series of excellent photographs of the ancient remains in the place. His attention was naturally drawn to the discussions which had taken place at the meetings of the Asiatic Society, and he made special investigation on the subject. The conclusions he arrived at after a careful examination of the place were thus summarised by him:—

First—"that the lower chamber, with its arched roof, is of the same age as the lower part of the temple;

Second—"that the middle chamber with its arches is of the same age as the main building;

Third—"that the porch was built at a later period;

Fourth—"that some considerable time after the temple and porch had been built the whole was replastered, with the exception of the outer wall of the terrace. Why this was not plastered it is difficult to say, most probably on account of the ornamentation; nor was it even then covered by the accumulation of rubbish?" (a)

Mr. Fergusson's opinion.

Subsequently Mr. Fergusson, in two letters to A. Grote, Esq., expressed his opinion that the arches were modern, and must have been inserted by the Burmese repairers in the beginning of the 14th century. He said: "Since I last wrote you, I have looked carefully into the evidence about the age of the tower at Buddha Gayá, and see no reason to doubt the evidence of the inscription given (Journal, Asiatic Society, Bengal, Vol. III, p. 214) that the building *we now see* was erected in the first year of the 14th century. From its architecture, as shewn in the photograph you have sent me, I would have been inclined to make it even more modern; and the evidence of the "arches," as explained by Mr. Horne, is to my mind quite conclusive that it was erected long after the Muhammadan conquest. Had it been built by true Hindus they would not have been found there even then; but the Burmese never hated the arch so cordially as the true Hindu. My impression of its history would be that in Asoka's time, or between that and the Christian era, the Bo Tree was surrounded by a rail of the Sanchi type. At some subsequent period a

(a) Proceedings, Asiatic Society, Bengal, 1865, p. 153.

"stupa" was erected, probably of a tower form, it may be by Amara, and the *lehras* may be of his time; but I feel nearly quite certain that the arches were inserted and the tower took its present form in the beginning of the 14th century."(*a*) This opinion has since been repeated in the learned author's 'History of Indian and Eastern Architecture' (p. 70), where he says: "The changes in detail, as well as the introduction of vaulted arches in the interior, I fancy, must belong to the Burmese restoration in the beginning of the 14th century." Elsewhere (p. 210) he adds: "We cannot assert with absolute certainty that the Bhuddhists never employed a true arch; this at least is certain, that no structural example has yet been found in India, and that all the arches or circular forms found in the caves are, without one single exception, copies of wooden form, and nowhere even simulate stone construction. With the Hindus and Jains the case is different: they use stone arches and stone domes, which are not copied from wooden forms at all, but these are invarialby horizontal arches, never formed or intended to be formed with radiating voussoirs." Again, and more emphatically (p. 120)—"The presence of the woodwork is an additional proof, if any were wanted, that there were no arches of construction in any of the Buddhist buildings. There never were, nor are, any in any Indian building anterior to the Muhammadan conquest, and very few indeed in any Hindu building afterwards."

Arches—Issues.

I pass over the positive argument that all the arches and circular forms found in the caves are "without a single exception" copies of wooden forms as untenable in the face of the Sonabhaṇdár cave, which is of exactly the pointed gothic form of the vaults, and which, according to General Cunningham, dates from the 5th century before Christ (*b*). It is not necessary also to notice the fallacy involved in the assertion embodied in the last extract, for the question at issue is exactly what the author accepts as a premiss. It is founded upon a foregone conclusion, and therefore evinces a want of critical caution. The questions raised in the discussions at the Asiatic Society were, *first*, the age of the temple; *second*, the age of the arches, *i.e.* whether they were contemporaneous with the shell of the temple or subsequent

(*a*) Proceedings, Asiatic Society, Bengal, 1866, p. 133.
(*b*) Arch. Surv. Report, III, p. 85.

insertions; *third*, the knowledge and use of the radiating arch by the people of India before they came into contact with the Muhammadans. (a)

Conclusions arrived at on the subject.

As regards the first, the position adopted by me in 1864, that the temple which we now see is the same which Aśoka built, is untenable; General Cunningham has, in his second report, already proved the temple to be of a subsequent date.

The second issue must also go against me, as far as the contemporaneity of the arches with the temple is concerned. The two are not of the same age. From the description given above it is obvious that the arches were inserted some time after the completion of the temple. When this was done it is impossible to determine with any precision in the present state of our knowledge on the subject. This much, however, is clear, that the arches existed long before the advent of Hiouen Thsang in India. That keen observer and faithful chronicler has given us a description of the temple, which applies most accurately to the structure now existing; and at his time, in 637 A.C., the temple had the identical two-storeyed porch whose remains are still extant, and as the upper walls of that porch rest on the spring of the vaulted roof of the first storey, it is impossible to deny that it existed at his time. And if that existed, we cannot deny the existence at the time of the vault over the first and the second storey chambers, as also those in the doorways. Regarding the latter

(a) At a meeting of the Asiatic Society of Bengal held in December last, Mr. H. F. Blanford, Meteorological Reporter to the Government of India, commenting on some remarks made by me on the occasion, expressed an opinion to the effect that the structures under notice "were not true arches;" but as no such issue has been raised by experienced engineers and architects like General Cunningham and Mr. Fergusson, I need not notice it. The description and illustrations above given will, I feel certain, convince all professional men that the opinion is not tenable. Sir Edward Clive Bayley, at the same meeting, remarked that "the arches may be described not as arches, but as structures showing progress towards the discovery of the true arch," and compared the arches to "well cylinders." Neither of the speakers defined what a true arch was, and it would take me too much out of my theme to discuss the bearings of the evolution theory of the last speaker. As an illustration of the arrangement of the bricks in the simpler arches, his comparison, however, is not inapt, and General Cunningham used it in his second report. A circular arch is necessarily a half cylinder, the junctures of each added course of bricks or stones lying in the plane of the axis of the cylinder cutting its surface. Mechanically, however, it is not at all correct. In the true arch the ends alone rest on the imposts, even as a beam spanning the breadth of a room rests on the side walls, and the body hangs on the air, supporting itself and the weight that is put upon it by the lateral pressure of its constituent bricks or voussoirs; whereas in the well cylinders the whole structure lies flat on the ground below it, and every brick has a support under it, requiring no imposts, and supporting no weight. It might be said that the lateral pressure of the surrounding earth represents the weight in a well cylinder; and if we assume the cylinder to be formed of two semicircles, the two ends of one of which rest on the corresponding ends of the other, we have the imposts; but it rests flat on the ground, and its shape is purely accidental. In square wells we have straight, and not curved, revetment walls, and the cardinal mechanical principle of the arch, its supporting itself by its two ends only, is wanting.

General Cunningham says:—"To the third period of the temple's history I would ascribe the addition of the two-storeyed pavilion to the eastern face, which, as we know from Hiouen Thsang's description, must have been built some time before A.D. 637. I infer also from the story of Śaśánka's minister placing a lamp in the *inner chamber* of the temple before the figure of Mahádeva *on account of the darkness*, that the front pavilion and all the vaults and arches had already been added before A.D. 590 or 600, say about 500 A.D." (*a*)

It might be urged that the fact of the existence of a porch like that which the Chinese pilgrim saw is no proof that it is the same with what we now have. The Burmese of the 14th century might have renewed it on the old plan, substituting a vaulted for a flat roofing for the first storey of the porch. Such a statement, however, in the *first* place, would be a mere assertion based on no proof whatever; *secondly*, the proofs to the contrary are too overwhelming to be gainsaid. The small portions now existing of the walls of the upper storey of the porch show clearly that they had been subjected to at least two thorough repairs before the front of the structure fell. The mouldings are completely daubed over by whitewash as they appear at first sight, leaving only a faint and smudgy outline of their details here and there; but, as I have already said, on peeling off the upper coat of whitewash, we come to the details developed in a rude, clumsy, coarse way; and then, on peeling off another coat, they appear sharp and fine as they were first made; and these coatings would be quite unaccountable if we assume the original to be dated in the beginning of the 14th century. The Buddhists had forsaken the place long before. If any faith is to be reposed on the inscription translated by Wilkins, the place had become a "wild forest," "infested by lions and tigers" in the 10th century, and there was none in India who would care to repair the edifice after the Burmese repairs. We have nothing definite to show the extent of the repairs in the 14th century. General Cunningham takes it to have been "extensive, including a complete coat of plaster, which has lasted very fairly until the present day." If we may judge of the past from the present,—of what they did in the 14th from what they have done in the 19th century during the past year,—the extent must have been exceedingly limited; a few stoppages of leaks and restorations of a moulding or a cornice here or there, and a coat of whitewash over the whole, would complete the sum total of their

(*a*) Arch. Surv. Report, Vol. III, p. 100.

work. As already shown, they also renewed the wall of the terrace on the north side, completed the projection on the west, and built the stairs at the north-east corner; and, in doing so, they resorted to the simplest expedients possible, making the walls perfectly plain, and building them with lime-mortar, such as was then in common use, leaving the surrounding ground perfectly uncleared and untouched. A new porch in the old style with a vaulted roofing could not have by any means entered their plan.

It is morally certain that the Burmese officers who came to repair the temple were not themselves architects, nor did they bring any bricklayers and masons with them. They came with money, as did their successors last year, and employed the masons of Gayá to carry out their orders. The masons of Gayá at the time were mostly, if not all, Hindus, who depended on their own knowledge of architecture, and did not borrow anything from the Burmese. They had unquestionably seen Muhammadan architects building arches, and if they had copied them they would have produced the true Saracenic foiled arch, with bricks placed crosswise, and cemented with lime-mortar. There is not a single Muhammadan arch, and very few buildings of that race of the 12th or the 13th century in the country, in which clay cement was used, and there is no reason to suppose that the Hindu builders, in imitating a Muhammadan arch, changed the order of building and resorted to a cement which was utterly worthless for the purpose. There was no want of kankar-lime in the country, and no builder with a head on his neck, after once seeing a modern arch, would fail to perceive its great superiority over the style of building we find at Buddha Gayá. An unbonded line of brick voussoirs cannot, in strength and durability, for a moment compare with bonded cross-bricks cemented with lime-mortar; and there was no engineering reason to set aside the one in favour of the other. It would be running against all reason and consistency to suppose that the Hindu architects employed by the Burmese Embassy in the 14th century did, even after having seen and learnt the value of the Muhammadan arch, originate a plan of their own, or, in the attempt to copy, reproduce a different structure. A copy doubtless is generally inferior to its original; but we should look to the inferiority in construction and execution, and not in the general principles and materials, unless it can be shown that the principles could not be easily worked out and the materials were inaccessible, or very difficultly accessible. In the present instance such was not the case. It was as easy to range bricks crosswise as lengthwise, and kankar lime and pounded bricks could not have been wanting, or dear. I have no hesitation, therefore, in subscribing to the opinion of General Cunningham, that the vaults existed before the time of Hiouen Thsang's visit. Moreover, if we should, even against the reasons above urged, admit that the Burmese did build the vaults and the arches at Buddha Gayá, how should we account for their counterparts in the Konch Temple? The Burmese never went to it. It was built by the Buddhists, and was a Buddhist shrine for centuries before the Hindus appropriated it to their own use and converted it into a Śivite sanctuary. The Hindu sculptures still existing in it clearly demonstrate that the appropriation took place many centuries ago; and whether we believe that the vault and the arches to have been there when the appropriation took place, or that they were introduced soon after, the fact would remain that they had been built by the people of this country, on models which cannot be attributed to Moslem archetypes.

The third question is entirely governed by the second; and if the decision regarding the latter be that the vaults and the arches existed before the time of Hiouen Thsang, the conclusion must follow that the Buddhists, as also the Hindus, who were of the same nationality, the same race, and the same castes, with their schismatic atheistic brethren, knew the art of building radiating arches, and did build them, though but rarely. The saying current among them, that "an arch never sleeps," which has been quoted by Mr. Fergusson, is a proof positive that they knew the radiating arch well and avoided employing it, "because of its *vis viva*, which is always tending to thrust its haunches outward, and the necessity it involved of very heavy abutments to overcome its destructive tendency." A saying like this could never have got currency had the people not known the object which gave rise to it.

The art displayed in the building.

The art displayed in the building of the temple is worthy of a passing note. The first essential element in a good building, according to the highest authorities on the subject, the Greek architects, is *taxis*, or order, "the proper arrangement of parts before putting them together;" and in this respect there is very little wanting in the temple under notice. Its parts are arranged with a degree of taste that speaks highly of the culture of the architect and his thorough knowledge of the details of his profession. There is nothing discordant, nothing extraneous, nothing incongruous, in the different members which enter in its composition. The design is doubtless conventional, but therein we have what Ruskin fancifully calls "the lamps of obedience and memory" fully illustrated, and it was by no means ill adapted for the purpose for which the building was intended. The second essential according to them was *symmetria*, or proportion in size; and the relative proportions between the terrace, the body, the spine, and the pinnacle of the Buddha Gayá fane, are such as it would not be easy to disturb without serious injury to the harmonious blending of its parts. They are the results of protracted study and consummate experience, governed by no mean conception of the cardinal elements of architectural beauty. The third essential is *eurithema*, or "harmony in number, in the adjustment of the parts both in their separate dimensions and in their interlocking junctures," and here again the architect of the Buddha Gayá temple has no reason to be afraid of any serious adverse criticism. The general design; the niches, their size, their symmetrical disposition on the two sides of a central band; their gradual diminution as they rise; the provision made to hide ugly angles at the corners of the different storeys; the disposition of the upright bands; the effect of those bands in adding to the apparent height of the structure; the dexterity displayed in producing a curved outline out of a zig-zag one;—are elements in the composition of the structure which speak highly in his favour. The fourth essential, or *diathesis*, refers to the "composition of the different parts of an extended edifice as a whole," or composite buildings, and cannot be brought to bear on a solitary temple. The last is *oikonomia*, or "the securing of the useful ends for which a building was erected," and in this respect, again, very little can be said against the architect. The purpose of the Buddha Gayá temple was the location of a statue in such a position as to inspire the highest amount of reverence and awe, and for that purpose it was admirable. Its dimensions of eighty feet by seventy-five feet, with a height of one hundred and seventy feet to the top of the pinnacle, were such as to produce an impression of the highest grandeur and sublimity, undisturbed by any obtrusive subdivision of parts. Whether viewed from a small or a great distance, there is nothing to divert the spectator's contemplation from the majesty of mass and outline, which forms the peculiar characteristic of the temple. Its "power," to use again the fanciful language of Ruskin, "in the display of its massiveness as an element of architectural effect" is all but perfect. There have been, and there are, larger and more pretentious edifices in India and other parts of the earth; they were, and they are, grander, handsomer, and nobler buildings, richer by far in style, material, and finish than the Buddha Gayá temple; but, viewed by itself, the last wants but little to serve the economy for which it was intended. It is a work in which both the science and the art of architecture were brought into play, and is not the result of untutored labour of a rude and uncultured people.

Buddhokar Tál.

The only other monument to which I wish to call the attention of the reader at this place is the tank to the south of the Great Temple. It should have been noticed in Chapter I, but was by an oversight omitted. It is called *Buddhokar Tál*, or 'Buddha's Tank,' and measures about 504 feet by 425 feet. Originally it was perfectly rectangular; but in course of time its sides have broken down and fallen into its bed, and its outline is now become very irregular. Referring to it, Hiouen Thsang says:—"En dehors de la porte méridionale des murs de l'arbre de l'intelligence, il y a un grand étang, qui a environ sept cents pas de circuit, et dont les eaux sont pures et claires comme un miroir; des dragons et des poissons y font leur demeure. Il a été creusé per deux Brahmanes, qui étaint frères, d'apres les ordres du dieu *Ta-tseu-thsaï* (Maheśvara Deva)." (*a*) General Cunningham is of opinion that this tank is the same with the one in which the dragon Muchilinda resided, and that the description is "so striking that it was seen at once by the members of the Burmese Embassy." (*b*) This identification, however, is not correct. The pilgrim, as shown above (p. 55), places the Muchilinda tank at a considerable distance to the south-east of this tank, and the two are quite distinct. The error has evidently arisen from the use of the word "dragon" by the pilgrim; but by it he simply means that there were crocodiles in the tank, as there now are. It is said that one of the Bráhman brothers built the Great Temple, and the other caused the tank to be excavated. There is no reason to doubt, however, that the tank was excavated to afford the earth required for the making of bricks for the Great Temple. I have seen no large ancient Hindu fane where there is not a tank adjoining, and where its presence was not due to this cause; and the same may with equal propriety be predicated of Buddhist shrines. The large

(*a*) 'Memoires sur les Contrées occidentales,' Vol. I, p. 477.

(*b*) Arch. Surv. Report, Vol. I, p. 11.

tank close to the Vihára at Sultánganj, the tanks near the Chaubárá Tilá, the Chaurási Tilá, the Kankálí Tilá, and other Buddhist mounds in the suburbs of Mathurá, the splendid sheet of water close by the Great Temple of Nálandá, the Markaṭa Hrada at Vaisalí, the large tank to the east of the Sárnáth tower, and the tanks at Sánchí and other places, clearly show that they supplied the earth with which bricks were made for the large monuments adjoining them. No one would for a moment think of bringing bricks from a great distance when they could be very economically and conveniently made where they were wanted, and where the result would be a tank, which none could object to. But at the same time it must be admitted that a tank of pure water is a very useful appurtenance to a temple. Both Hindu and Buddhist ceremonials require frequent bathing and ablutions and lustrations. No Hindu rite can be celebrated without a plentiful supply of water, and both Hindu and Buddhist ascetics and priests who dwell in the neighbourhood of temples require water daily for drinking, cooking, and the cleansing of their rooms. And those who go to the expense of building a large temple do not grudge the expense of so necessary an adjunct. Hence it is that tanks are met with not only near brick-built temples and viháras, but also in the neighbourhood of stone edifices and caves and rocky eminences, wherever Buddhist monks took up their abode. Such artificial reservoirs of water were absolutely necessary where no natural supply was ready at hand, and they were never omitted.

CHAPTER IV.

SCULPTURES.

PRIMITIVE BUDDHISM OPPOSED TO SCULPTURAL REPRESENTATIONS OF RELIGIOUS OBJECTS—BELIEF IN GODS—BEGINNING OF SCULPTURAL REPRESENTATIONS—BURIAL AND CREMATION—TUMULI OVER GRAVES—NAMES OF THE TUMULI—CENOTAPHS OR VOTIVE STÚPAS—THEIR SIZE, ORNAMENTATION AND VARIETIES—FOOTPRINTS—CONSPICUOUS MARKS ON SOLES—WHEEL OF LAW—VOTIVE TEMPLES—IMAGES OF BUDDHA HOW INTRODUCED—BUDDHA IN MEDITATION—BUDDHA IN ECSTACY—BUDDHA AS TEACHER—BUDDHA AS AN ITINERANT HERMIT—BUDDHA DYING—BODHISATTVAS—MINOR DIVINITIES—MÁYÁ DEVÍ—DEMONIAC FIGURES—HERMITS AND DEVOTEES—HINDU DIVINITIES—ARCHITECTURAL STONES—BASES, PILLARS, COLUMNS, CAPITALS, DOOR-FRAMES—VAJRÁSANA—AŚOKA'S RAILINGS—THEIR DIFFERENCES IN DIFFERENT PARTS OF INDIA—THEORIES REGARDING THEIR ORIGIN—WOODEN-MODEL THEORY NOT TENABLE—REASONS THEREOF—ORNAMENTS ON RAIL BARS—ORNAMENTS ON COPINGS—ORNAMENTS ON MEDIAL AND TERMINAL PILLARS—THE SO-CALLED HELIOS—CHARACTER OF THE SCULPTURES—SUPPOSED GREEK ORIGIN OF INDIAN SCULPTURE—ORIGIN OF INDIAN SCULPTURE—SUPPOSED FOREIGN CHARACTER OF SOME CARVINGS—TRUE TEST OF RELATION AS MODELS AND COPIES.

In a system of religion like Buddhism, founded on atheism or self-assertion, divinities must be unknown. Where nothing beyond the human soul was recognized as existent, gods could find no place. The cardinal point in theology is the existence of a divine soul which animates the creation and governs it according to its own supreme will; but where the existence of that soul was denied, there was nothing left to mark the distinction between the adored and the adorer. The belief that the phenomenal world was a mere illusion, the result of ignorance, was incompatible with any theory of adoration. Where the evil was of one's own creation,—where one's own passions and earthly cares forged the chain,—no supernatural powers of imaginary gods were needed to subdue them and free the soul from the bondage of flesh. But a system of negations and abstractions could not long continue to inspire enthusiasm, nor keep firm hold on the minds of the masses. The negative, therefore, soon passed into the positive, and the abstract into the concrete. Buddha himself took the place of the supreme divinity, and Bodhisattvas rose in plenty to be ministered to, and worshipped, by the gods of the Hindus.

Belief in gods.

When this change first took place is not known. It would seem that when Buddhism was first promulgated, the feeling of revulsion against the supremacy of the Hindu gods was strong, and it was entirely repudiated. But the gods themselves were never openly declared as mere creatures of fancy. They were denied all divine attributes, and relegated to a subordinate position; they were declared to be subject to the failings and the common doom of created beings; they needed, as much as man, the means of salvation: but they were accepted as beings of a superior order, possessing many supernatural powers. They ceased to be gods, but they lived as angels. It is probable that Buddha himself took the Hindu gods to be mere myths; but there is nothing in the Buddhist scriptures to show that he did so, and his disciples maintained the contrary everywhere. Brahmá and Indra and Śiva were not non-existent, but only the servants and adorers of those who had risen above the control of their carnal wants, and, in the fullness of their wisdom, learnt the true nature of creation. This belief opened the way for visible representations, and in time images became an integral part of Buddhist worship.

Burial and cremation.

The first impulse in this direction was probably given immediately after the death of Buddha. It was but natural that the disciples and followers of the saint should have looked upon his relics with the highest veneration, and treasured them with the utmost care. We may not believe in the truth of the story which describes the division of the mortal remains of Buddha into ten shares, and the assignment of most of them to the leading sovereigns of India at the time; but there is nothing positively incredible in the fact of certain kings, believers in the truth of the doctrine preached by Buddha, showing their respect to the teacher, and raising monuments on his relics. The earliest mode of disposing of the dead in India was burial. In the Rig Veda there is a hymn which describes burial (*a*), and it had from an unknown, but very remote, period served as the burial service or the mantra to be repeated on the dead just before inhumation. After a time burial was replaced by cremation, and this is fully described in the Bráhmaṇa of the Black

(*a*) *Vide passim* Dr. Roth's essay 'Die Todtenbestattung bei den Brahmanen,' and Grimm's essay on the 'Burning of the Dead,' in the 'Zeitschrift' of the German Oriental Society, and Whitney's paper on burial in the time of the Rig Veda in his 'Oriental and Linguistic Studies.'

Yajur Veda (*a*), which dates from before the eighth century B.C. This change, however, was not complete. It brought in cremation as a preliminary to burial. The body was first burnt, and the rite of sepulture was then administered to the burnt remains, and a tumulus was raised thereon, while the service or *mantra* remained the same. We know not what rules Buddha himself laid down during his long ministry of forty-four years for the disposal of the dead, but many of his disciples and followers must have died during his life-time, and some form of ceremony must have been designed for them; and if we may judge from the account preserved of the funeral of the saint himself, it must have been very closely like what prevailed among the Hindus. His body was first burnt, and the burnt remains were next buried, exactly in the same way in which, according to the Rámáyaṇa, the mortal remains of Ráma were disposed of by the Hindu king Bharata (*b*). The grave, then, or, what is the same thing, the tumulus erected over the ashes, was the tangible evidence of the defunct saint, and those who had adored the living preacher naturally transferred their adorations to the tumulus over his ashes, as the highest object of veneration. Thus the tumulus or grave became the first tangible object of adoration among the Buddhists, and relics, real or pretended, were widely circulated, and the faithful everywhere raised tumuli over them. These were, therefore, the most ancient religious and sacred objects whose representation engaged the attention of the Buddhists.

Memorial tombs and cenotaphs.

Originally the grave was called *dehagopa*, or repository of the body, whence the modern *dagoba*. It was also named *chaitya*, which in Sanskrit means a "tomb," or an "*altar*;" and *stúpa* or "mound." Nor was the tumulus confined to Buddha himself. Every one of his followers had the right to a tomb, and had a few basketsful of earth thrown on their last resting-place. But the more influential among them

(*a*) See my essay on 'Funerals in Ancient India' in the Journal of the Asiatic Society of Bengal, and in the Introduction to my edition of the 'Taittiríya Áraṇyaka.'

(*b*) See Griffith's Rámáyaṇa, Vol. I. The ancient Greek funeral did not differ much from the Hindu ceremony. (Guhl and Koner's 'Life of the Greeks and Romans.') The Yajur Veda prescribes that a bit of gold should be put on the palm of the dead before cremation, and the practice is followed to this day by every Hindu, the tongue being preferred as the place of deposit; but I have nowhere seen any reason or object assigned for this practice. Among the ancient Greeks the same practice obtained, and an obolus, being the ferriage (ναυλον δανάκη) for Charon, was put into the mouth of the corpse: and the *Preta pinda* of the Hindus had its counterpart in the *cœna feralis*, "the cake for the ghost," of the Romans.

got magnificent tombs erected over their graves. As they were all, without exception, houseless hermits, the cost of their burials was defrayed by householders and moneyed men; and in time the dedication of a tumulus came to be looked upon as an important and highly meritorious act of religion on the part of the laity. Sacred relics could not always be had, and so they had to be dispensed with; but cenotaphs could be always raised, and for purposes of religion they were as useful as tombs, and whoever could afford it erected one for the spiritual good of himself and his ancestors. Such dedications were always sources of profit to the clergy; and from the real tumulus they devised the model, whereby not only the rich, but every member of the community, however poor, could secure to himself and his ancestors the merit of dedicating a stúpa. Similarly, Hindu pilgrims in the present day, when they cannot afford to dedicate a temple to Śiva at Benares, satisfy their religious longings by dedicating a miniature. In the same way the high merit of bestowing a horse to a Muhammadan saint or *pír* is secured by the people of this country by little fictile images of that animal, thousands of which may be seen on the platform of every *pírasthán*, and under many a sacred banian-tree in India. The offering is made by all classes of the people, both Hindus and Muhammadans, and the occasions are various. Once I heard a respectable Bráhman lady promise to present six horses to the *dargah* of Mánik Pír, a local saint, on her husband recovering from a slight hurt he had received. I was surprised, and asked if she intended to keep her promise, seeing that the hurt under any circumstance would be cured in less than a week. "Certainly," said she, "why should you doubt my honesty?"

"Why," replied I, "the cost of the commonest pony would be more than 40 rupees. Would you give away 240 rupees to the saint for a hurt which will be cured in three or four days without any medicine?"

"Dear me," returned she, "how green you must be! Who ever gave a live horse to a *dargah*? I mean clay images, and they cost half a pice each."

Vows of the kind are frequently made by poor women for the safe delivery of kine and goats, and in such cases a quantity of milk is also given.

The dedication of stúpas was held most meritorious when made within the precincts of an old and renowned sacred fane, whose reflected sanctity could fall on the models; and hence it is that they are met with in large numbers round the most ancient topes. At Sárnáth, near Benares, fictile models, about three inches in height, have been met with by thousands. Sir Bartle Frere once showed me some which he had brought from Bráhmanábád, in Cutch. At Sánchí, Mathurá, and elsewhere, they have also been found in great numbers. Some of these were so ingeniously made as to include within their substance the Buddhist creed, or a miniature figure of Buddha, or both, stamped with a seal. A cheaper form of this is a small tile, stamped with the figure of one or more *chaityas*, with the Buddhist creed at bottom. This probably did not cost more than a pice, but its dedication cost more; and it formed a small but perennial source of gain to the clergy. Those who could afford to pay more preferred a stone-model to one of baked clay, and that, too, is pretty common.

Votive stúpas.

At Buddha Gáyá I met with no clay models of stúpas, but of stone representations of various forms and sizes hundreds were met with everywhere. Thousands of them have been taken away from this place to all parts of Gayá, and thousands more may be recovered by digging into the large and extensive mounds which surround the great temple. From the small area which has been levelled by the Burmese gentlemen upwards of two thousand such models have been recovered. Out of these I saw, in a godown adjoining the dwelling of the Burmese, about five hundred small ones, evidently picked out with a view to be carried to Burmah. Near the temple of Tárá Deví there are several hundreds lying in heaps, and other heaps exist on other parts of the mounds. A few have been built into the walls, and a great number have been taken away. Compared to images of Buddha, these model stúpas are considerably more numerous; and I infer from this that the merit of dedicating stúpas was evidently held to be greater than that of dedicating the former. It should be added, however, that the models have generally, but not invariably, the figures of the four Dhyáni Buddhas carved on their four sides, so that the models secured the merit of dedicating both images and stúpas, whereas the images could have the merit only of one kind of offering.

Stúpas—their size and make.

In size the model stúpas vary from three inches to nearly three feet, and in their execution and ornamentation fancy and ingenuity were allowed wide play. The oldest stúpas were hemispherical in shape (*a*), either perfect hemispheres or two-thirds sections of

(*a*) Cunningham's 'Bhilsa Topes,' p 169.

spheres, and devoid of all ornaments. This shape was the most perfect representation of the tumulus, which, whether originally made so or not, always assumes, after a few years' rain and decay, the form of a hemispherical mound: it is at the same time the most lasting which human art can devise. It represents, too, a water-bubble, which admirably typifies the evanescent character of all worldly objects, and therefore is the most appropriate emblem of departed life. A dozen models of this shape have lately been dug out, and they measure about two feet in diameter and 12 to 14 inches in height, their substance being granite. (Plate XLI, fig. 1.) They are unquestionably the oldest relics of their kind. The first idea of ornament for these was a pinnacle or *kalasa*. Four scrolls on the sides were next thought of (fig. 2), and they were soon replaced by niches. Mouldings round the base followed, and the base was gradually so altered and increased as to produce a plinth, which latterly took a square form. The plinth, too, gradually increased in height till the whole assumed the shape of a column ending in a hemisphere. The shaft in such cases was set off with an ornamental band round the middle. These gradual changes are not only perceptible in the models, but also in large monuments. The oldest monuments known, such as those of Sánchí and Baráhat, are nearly hemispherical, and the latest, those of Sáranáth and Affghanistan, columnar (*a*); and these facts afford a ready means of judging of the age of a monument.

Dr. Buchanan-Hamilton aptly compares the shape of the ordinary votive stúpa to that of a "bee-hive," but he mistakes the square mortice, designed to receive the tenon of the pinnacle on the top, to be "a hole for the burning of incense." (*b*) In some cases the outline of the body was so curved as to produce the shape of a bell. The niches on the four sides of the stúpas usually contain images of the four Dhyáni Buddhas, but in the earliest specimens they are left empty. In some modern ones I have, on the other hand, seen female figures in the attitude of dancing. (Plate XXIII, fig. 4.) In some specimens the whole of the shaft is covered over with miniature figures of Buddha, ranged in four, five, or six tiers. (Plate XLII, fig. 1). A few, very few, have the creed *Ye dharmá hetu*, &c., and also the name of the donor, engraved on the base.

(*a*) Cunningham's 'Bhilsa Topes,' p. 169.
(*b*) Martin's 'Eastern India,' Vol. I, p. 75.

The ordinary pinnacle or *kalasa* for the votive stúpa is a long tapering structure, formed of a series of rings, the number of the rings ranging from five to seventeen, according to the size of the stúpa (a). The rings were afterwards replaced by wedge-shaped projections, each set off with four triangular finials. Ordinarily the pinnacle rises from the top of the hemisphere without the intervention of any basement, but in rich specimens a square base with simple mouldings is supplied. The mortice hole on the top of these bases shows that the stúpas always had a pinnacle, though from its peculiar shape that structure was the first to break, and few are found entire. Judging, however, from some specimens of votive stúpas carved on rail-posts at Sánchí, Baráhat, and Buddha Gayá, I am of opinion that in early times the square basement on the top often served the purpose of the pinnacle, and nothing was added to the top of it; sometimes it was set off with a pear-shaped ornament. In such cases two flags were occasionally tied to the two sides of the basement. (Plate XXXV, fig. 3.)

In the accompanying plates I have produced representations of some of the leading forms of the votive stúpa.

Figure 1, plate XLI, shows the oldest hemispherical form. It is of granite, and has no ornament whatever.

Figure 2 is the first remove from it, the height being slightly greater than the half-diameter. The scroll work shown on it is sometimes present and sometimes wanting.

Figure 3 is of the same shape as the last, but provided with a plinth formed of two flat bands.

In figure 4 the bands of the plinth are more numerous, and the shaft is longer.

Figure 5 is a variety of the last. In all these the mortice hole occurs on the top for the reception of the kalasa, but none was found *in situ*.

In figure 6 there is a circular base, a base moulding, and a pinnacle formed of four gradually-receding tiles placed on a neck and a rounded kalasa.

Figure 7 is bell-shaped on a circular base, and has a simple finial.

In plate XLII, fig. 1, besides the base mouldings, there are several mouldings round the shaft.

(a) See the crown on Plate VIII.

In fig. 4 over the base mouldings there are four niches on the four sides, each having the figure of a Dhyání Buddha seated in it. The niches are flanked with pilasters and surmounted by foiled arches.

Fig. 5 is a variety of the last, but it has eight niches with a flat, instead of an arched, top, surmounted alternately by a miniature stúpa and a Buddhist pediment, similar to what occurs on the Great Temple.

Fig. 6 differs from the preceding in having four niches, of which one is very sumptuous and the others simple. The niches have no images.

Fig. 3 is a circular shaft surrounded by six tiers of miniature images of Buddha.

Figs. 1, 3, 4, and 5, have mortices for kalasas.

Fig. 2 is *sui generis*; it is mounted on a cubic base, and its niches have no images.

In figures 4 and 5, plate XXXIV, the mouldings on the middle of the shaft are replaced by bands, one formed of a series of mouldings, and the other of the Buddhist rail pattern. The top of figure 4 occurs frequently in carvings on rail-posts, but I have not seen it in solid relief.

In figures 1 and 3 of plate XXXV I give two other varieties of the same kind, the last having the flags.

Foot-prints.

Next to chaityas, the most important object of worship was the impression of Buddha's feet. In fact it was the first to come into vogue after relics, when the religion recognized no worship, and only veneration was shown to the relics of the great reformer. In later days, however, when the images of the last Buddha became popular, the feet, which constituted only a part thereof, fell to the background. But they were never altogether given up, and in all Buddhist countries carvings of Buddha's feet are held in great veneration. In many temples they occupy the most prominent place; and when the Hindus got hold of Gayá, the popular feeling in favour of the most sacred foot-print there was so high, that, unable to set it aside, the Bráhmaṇs recognized it, under the name of Vishṇu's feet, as the most sacred object of worship at that place; and thousands of Hindu pilgrims from the most distant parts of India to this day visit and worship it every year for the salvation of their ancestors. Indeed, to the Vaishṇavas the temple of Vishṇupad, at Gayá, is one of the most holy in all India, and most of the later Śástras earnestly enjoin that no one should fail, at least once in his life-time, to visit the thrice-holy spot. According to one of the Smṛitis, the wish for numerous progeny is commended on the ground that out of the many one son might visit Gayá, and, by performing a *śráddha* on the foot-mark, rescue his father from the horrors of hell (*a*). The stone is a large block of granite, with an uneven top. The frequent washings which it daily undergoes have worn out the peculiar sectarial marks from which its character could be made out, and even the outlines of the feet are all but perfectly imperceptible. It is impossible, therefore, from any evidence on it, to determine to which sect it originally belonged; but the history of the conversion of Gayá to Hinduism, as given in chapter I, leaves no doubt in my mind that it was originally a Buddhist emblem. In General Cunningham's first report a drawing has been given of the most important foot-print at Buddha Gayá, which was preserved in the centre of the pavilion noticed in the last chapter (p. 100). It bears a Sanskrit inscription, which is dated 1230 of the Śaka era = 1153 A.C. The sectarial marks on it comprise, on the right foot, a discus, an umbrella, a flag, a conch-shell, a pitcher, a fish, an elephant-goad, an arc, and a lotus-bud; and on the left foot the same, except the discus, which is replaced by a wheel. (Plate XLIII, fig. 1.) These marks do not correspond with any Vaishṇava description of Vishṇu's feet, nor with any Buddhist account of Buddha's foot-mark that I have seen. Nor do they conform to any known canons of palmistry, Hindu or Buddhist, regarding auspicious marks on the sole of the foot.

The Lalita Vistara (Chapter 7), in giving an account of the peculiar marks on, and the character of, Śákya's feet, says—"He has expanded hands and feet, soft fresh hands and feet, swift and agile hands and feet (like those of a snake-catcher), with long and slender fingers and toes. On the soles of the feet of the imperial prince (Mahárája Kumára) Sarvárthasiddha are two white wheels, beautifully coloured, bright and refulgent, and having a thousand spokes, a nave, and an axle-hole." Such wheels, we look for in vain on the stone under notice. Again, in the Indian Museum at Calcutta there is a large flag of white marble bearing the figure of a human foot surrounded by two dragons. It was brought from a temple in Burma, where it used to be worshipped as a representation of Buddha's foot. It is seven feet six inches long by three feet six inches

(*a*) एष्टव्या बहवः पुत्रा यद्येकोऽपि गयां व्रजेत् । यजेत वा अश्वमेधेन नीलं वा वृषमुत्सृजेत् ॥

in breadth, and has on it a great number of mystical marks. On the centre of each toe there is a figure of a conch-shell and a concentric line under it. A conch occurs also at the heel. On the centre of the sole there is a circular figure, with innumerable radii, standing evidently for the wheel; the radii are intersected with three concentric lines producing one hundred and eight compartments bearing representations of temples, houses, forests, rivers, men in different attitudes, birds and beasts of various kinds—mostly imaginary,—leaves and flowers, magical figures, and other objects unintelligible to me. But the counterparts of these objects do not appear in the foot-marks at Buddha Gayá. Its prevailing emblems are more Hindu than Buddhistical. The lotus, the *svastika*, the fish, and the discus, are identically what have been assigned to Vishṇu's feet in the Bráhmaṇical śástras. Thus in the Skanda Puráṇa, I find, the marks on Vishṇu's feet are enumerated at 19, including (1) a crescent, (2) a water-pot, (3) a triangle, (4) a bow, (5) the sky, (6) the foot-mark of cattle, (7) a fish, (8) a conch-shell, (9) an octagon, (10) a svastika, (11) an umbrella, (12) a discus, (13) a grain of barley, (14) an elephant-goad (*ankus*), (15) a flag, (16) a thunderbolt, (17) a *jambu* fruit, (18) an upright line, and (19) a lotus; of these the first nine belong to the left, and the rest to the right foot. (*a*) Viśvanátha Chakravartí, in his notes on the Bhágavata Puráṇa (10th Book), has given the marks appropriate to the feet of Ráddhá, which include (1) an umbrella, (2) a wheel, (3) a flag, (4) a creeper, (5) a flower, (6) a bracelet, (7) a lotus, (8) a perpendicular line, (9) an elephant-goad (*ankus*), (10) a crescent, (11) a grain of barley, (12) a javelin, (13) a club, (14) a car, (15) an altar, (16) an earring, (17) a fish, (18) a hill, (19) a conch-shell. The first eleven of these belong to the left, and the rest to the right, foot. (*b*) The scholiast has pointed out at length the different places which these marks should occupy, and the objects they subserve at those places. His opinion has been questioned, and Vaishṇava writers of eminence have distributed these marks in very different ways. None has, however, to my knowledge, given them as we find them at Buddha Gayá.

(*a*) चन्द्रार्द्धं कलस त्रिकोणधनुषी खं गोष्पदं प्रोष्ठिकां । शङ्खं सव्यपदेऽथ दक्षिणपदे कोणाष्टकं स्वस्तिकं ।
छत्रं चक्रयवाङ्कुशध्वजपविः जम्बूर्द्ध्वरेखाम्बुजं । बिभ्राणं हरिमूनविंशतिमहालक्ष्माचिंताङ्घ्रिं भजे ॥

(*b*) छत्रारिध्वजवल्लिपुष्पवलयान् पद्मोर्द्ध्वरेखाङ्कुशं । अर्द्धेन्दुञ्च यवञ्च वाम चरणे शक्तिं गदां स्यन्दनं ।
वेदीकुण्डलमत्स्यपर्वतदरं जानाति सव्ये पदे । तां राधां चिरमूनविंशतिमहालक्ष्मार्चिताङ्घ्रिं भजे ॥

On the whole the marks on the Buddhapad bear a closer resemblance to Hindu than to Buddhist religion, and I am disposed to accept the authority of the inscription, and to believe that the stone, though popularly called the foot of Buddha (Buddhapad), was put up by the Hindus to convert the place to Hindu worship. I am the more induced to this conclusion as some blocks have lately been excavated by the Burmese which bear very different marks. Four of these have been brought to Calcutta, and on one of them there is a wheel in the centre, above it a female in a dancing attitude holding the musical instrument called *vína*, and having a lotus by her side, and below it, near the heel, a bedstead. On each of the toes there is a conch-shell on a stand. (Plate XLIII, fig. 7.) Fig. 3 on that plate has the wheel with a conch-shell mounted on a tripod on one side, and a water-vessel with a spout [*gáḍu*] mounted on an hour-glass-shaped stand on the other. Above the wheel occurs a crown with a female attendant on one side holding a *chámar*, and a male figure on the other. Near the heel, instead of the bedstead, there is a star with curved rays. Fig. 6 has the wheel, a temple, a human figure playing on a flute, a staff mounted on a pitcher and bearing three flags and a pennon, and near the heel a mountain and three cranes. Fig. 5 has the wheel, the bedstead, the conch-shell mounted on a tripod stand, a lotus bud, and a female with the lower limbs of a bird. Thus, with the exception of the wheel, the emblems are not fixed, and no satisfactory conclusion can be drawn from them. It is especially worthy of note that the wheel which the Lalita Vistara describes as a characteristic mark, and which is present on all the four authentic stones, is shown at a wrong place, and that on one foot on the Buddhapad.

The Wheel of Law.

Next to the foot-print the Wheel of Law, Dharma-chakra, was the most ancient emblem of Buddhism. Perhaps it was even older than the foot-print, for when the idea of symbolism was first conceived the wheel, as the emblem of religion, was first taken up for lithic representation. It occurs profusely at Sánchi, Baráhat, Mathurá, and Amarávatí, both in bas-relief and in the solid form on the tops of gateways and other places. It occurs also as the principal object of adoration in many of the Buddhist caves of India. At Buddha Gayá I have seen no solid specimen, but among the bas-reliefs on the railing there is a specimen mounted on a stand surrounded by a Buddhist railing and placed in the centre of a temple. (Plate XXXV, fig. 2.)

Votive Temples.

Recognizing no gods, the primitive Buddhists did not feel the necessity for temples, and erected none. A room reserved for sermons and prayers was all that was needed, and it was called *Sangha-griha*, or the "room for the congregation," *i.e.* the place of prayer—a church or chapel. The first religious emblem for it was the chaitya, or the chaitya surmounted by the wheel of law; and when the wheel became popular, a separate abode for it, where there was no chapel, was felt a necessity, and this gave rise to the temple. In later works the religious merit of dedicating temples is largely extolled, and when temples became common the craving for such merit gave rise to miniatures, in the same way in which the tumulus merged into the votive stúpa. But the votive temple never attained the same popularity as the stúpa. In the midst of two to three thousand stúpas at Buddha Gayá I found only four miniature temples, one of which I have deposited in the Indian Museum. When complete it was probably two feet six inches high; but the portion found by me comprised only the body, and a representation of it has been given in plate XXVII, fig. 4. The stúpas probably served the purposes of both the temple and the chaitya, and as the former was more troublesome to make, and therefore more costly, it was not often resorted to.

Images of Buddha.

Next to the temple come the images of Buddha. If we may rely on the evidence of the great Tope of Baráhat, they must have come into vogue many centuries after the stúpa. That tope represents scores of scenes illustrating the history of Buddha's last, as well as of previous, life, but none in which an image of the saint is being worshipped. For purposes of adoration the Bodhi-tree, the Chaitya, and the Wheel of Law, were the only principal objects selected, and occasionally foot-prints, but we look in vain for statues of the saint. This would have never been the case had images of the saint been worshipped in the time of Aśoka. That Emperor would have never allowed so important an object to be neglected in his sculptures had it then attained the rank of one worthy of being worshipped. On the Buddha Gayá rails there is also the same entire absence of the image of the saint as an object of adoration. A century later in the Sánchi bas-reliefs we notice the same absence of statues of Buddha; but in Mathurá, two centuries afterwards, they are largely met with, and this I look upon as all but conclusive evidence against the use of statues as objects of worship for the first four or five centuries after the Nirváṇa of the great reformer. He fought most strenuously against ritualistic ceremony in general and idol worship in particular, and his teaching was respected for a long time before it was set aside. The Tree of Knowledge was the first to claim respect. It had been the means of bestowing the perfection of wisdom on the saint, and all who aspired to that wisdom naturally looked upon it with respectful solicitude. After the death of the teacher the grave or chaitya was associated with it, the one as the receptacle of him who had acquired perfect knowledge, and the other as the source of that knowledge. The worship or adoration paid to these was confined, probably, to prostration before, and ambulation round, them, and the offering of a few flowers for their decoration. These were the ways in which respect had been shown to the teacher himself, and in his absence they were rendered to his emblems. The pictorial representations of scenes from the life of the saint were intended solely as ready means of impressing on the minds of the masses the history of his life, and the moral maxims which they inculcated, and not to require any adoration. In fact they were purely ornamental; they were never adored; and, from the positions they occupied in the buildings, they could not be used as objects of worship. Images intended for worship would imply temples and sanctuaries, but down to the time of Aśoka temples were never thought of, and idols for worship could not have existed. The word *vihára*, so often used in later works for a temple, originally meant only a convent, a place where the homeless hermits of the sect could find a shelter during disease and decripitude, and also from the inclemencies of the Indian rainy weather, when travelling was prohibited; and the use of the word is therefore not a safe proof. The evidence of the earlier texts of the Buddhists is particularly significant in this respect. The Lalita Vistara, while referring frequently to the worship of chaityas, nowhere alludes to images. In ancient Hindu writings the word chaitya is occasionally used for a "temple;" but the earlier Buddhists could not have used it in that sense, for they could not have ordained the worship of the temple leaving unnoticed the presiding divinity of the sanctuary.

The earliest samples of the statue occur in the monastery of Mathurá, and we may conclude, therefore, that the statue came into use after the date of the Bhilsá Tope of the second century before Christ, and a little before the Mathurá monastery of the first century after Christ.

When the statue was first introduced it was probably accepted as an ornament and decoration for the chapel or *Sanghagriha;* but such an object placed in a prominent position could not long remain without attracting marks of respect and adoration, and soon to occupy the same position which the images of Madonna do in Roman Catholic churches. That the worship paid to them was of a ritualistic kind I cannot say, for I have seen no work in the Sanskrit Buddhist literature of Nepal which supplies any set formula, such as the Smṛitis and the Tantras do for the worship of Hindu idols. This is the more remarkable as the Buddhist Tantras supply very detailed instructions regarding the mode in which certain Bodhisattvas, Ḍákinís, and fierce forms are to be worshipped, and also give the set form of mystic words and phrases in which that worship should be conducted. Relying on this fact, too, it may, I think, be safely asserted that statues of Buddha never rose to the same ritualistic importance during the prevalence of Buddhism in India that Hindu idols have done.

Varieties of Images.

The number of images of Buddha is not near so great as that of stúpas, but images were at one time quite abundant, and there is scarcely a part of Northern and Central India in which they are even now not to be met with, though Buddhism has there ceased to be a living religion for well nigh a thousand years. They may be described under five heads—1st, Buddha in meditation, (Dhyání Buddha); 2nd, Buddha in ecstacy (samádhi); 3rd, Buddha as a teacher; 4th, Buddha as a pilgrim; and 5th, Buddha on his death-bed. The first three are shown seated, the fourth standing, and the last in a reclining position.

Dhyání Buddha.

The first style is the most abundant; it varies in size from the colossal height of nearly 10 feet to two or three inches. It represents the saint seated cross-legged, with the left palm resting, ventor uppermost, on his lap, the right hand extended on the right leg or knee, and the eyes half-closed in meditation. The ears are long and pendulous, and the head is covered by buttons of curly hair, with a top-knot on the crown—never by straight, soft, flowing hair. The dress consists of a *dhuti* falling low on the leg, and collected in a ruffled mass (*konchá*) in front, and not unoften a *chádar* or hymation thrown athwart the chest, passing over the left shoulder. In all well-executed figures the sacred Bráhmanical chord is distinctly shown, extending athwart the chest from the left shoulder to the right side, as is usual all over India among the Bráhmaṇs of the present day. In the Yajur Veda mention is made of an ancient style (*Prâchînâvîti*), in which the chord flowed from the right shoulder to the left side; but of this I have seen no example, nor of the old style of wearing it over both shoulders as a garland. This is a remarkable peculiarity, as it not only shows the old styles to have been common in remote antiquity, but that the Buddhists of India never gave up their caste symbols. The top-knot is sometimes covered by a richly-decorated high crown or cap, and in such cases a rich jewelled necklace is also added. (Plate XXV, figs. 2 to 5.) No other ornament of any kind was ever assigned to this class of figures. The seat is a full-blown lotus, or lotus-petals carved on the rim of a chair or stool. In the larger specimens the panelling under the chair bears images of deer, elephants, lions, and devotees. The image is generally in 'complete relief' as understood by sculptures, *i.e.* fully one half in relief, but in some cases fully three-fourths and even more of the depth is shown. A few, very few, are perfectly detached, without any framing behind. Inscriptions on these statues are not common; but when they do occur, they are seen on the base of the stool or chair, or on the circular space behind and around the head. They comprise the Buddhist creed *Ye dharmá hetu*, &c., with occasionally the name of the dedicator, and the object and the date of dedication. The stone back is formed into a circular ornament representing either a framing for the back of the throne, or a nimbus, and on it occurs a Buddha in ecstacy. On each side there is an attendant in a standing position, and a stúpa over him. In a few specimens the stúpa is replaced by miniature figures of Buddha (generally four) in other attitudes, and on the top, over the head, either the crown of a tree, or, rarely, an umbrella, and still more rarely a human figure reclining on one side, and representing the death-scene of the saint. Attendants on the lying figure, and angels in a flying position, advancing to present garlands to the saint, are also seen. Dr. Buchanan-Hamilton noticed a group of this kind; but, mistaking the sex of the reclining figure, he remarked: "It seems to me to represent a prince who has lost his wife, and she is represented lying over his head and attended by two mourners." (*a*) The history of Buddhism is too well known in the present day to leave any doubt as to what it represents. The accessories are entirely optional, and a good deal dependent on the size of the principal statue and the space

(*a*) Martin's 'Eastern India,' Vol. I, p. 74.

available on the background. Generally speaking, the stúpas are rarely omitted. The relief of the sculptures varies from one-fourth to three-fourths of the depth.

One of the oldest figures of this kind I have seen was found in one of the smaller chambers brought to light by Major Mead in 1863. It was of blue basalt, and perfect in all its details, except the head, which was mutilated. It bore an inscription in the Gupta character, and must have been of the fourth if not the third century. The figure was missing when I last visited Buddha Gayá in 1877. Adverting to the basalt plinth, General Cunningham says: "As far as my experience goes, it must be as late as 800 or 900 A.D., as I have not seen any work in either blue or black basalt that could be referred to an earlier date." (a) If this remark should include statuary work, the figure under notice would falsify it. For certain there is no instance of the Gupta character having been used on works of so late an age as the 8th or the 9th century. Ordinarily, however, the character used in these inscriptions is the Kuṭila of the tenth century, more or less antiquated, rarely the Gupta: the oldest, therefore, cannot be earlier than the third century.

Figure of Buddha in the Maṭh.

The most perfect figure of the Dhyání Buddha I have seen is now kept in a small temple in the monastery, where there are two other figures of different kinds. It is made of black basalt, well polished, and generally well executed. (Plate XI.) Its measurements are—

	Feet.	Inches.
Height	5	5
Across the shoulders	3	0
Arm	2	3
Forearm	1	8
Hand, from wrist to tip of middle finger	1	4
Thigh	2	6
Leg	2	8
Foot	1	4
From top-knot to navel	4	4

These measurements show that the figure in a standing position would have the height of nine feet four inches, reckoning the height at seven times the foot. This would also be the height if the lengths of the body and of the lower limbs be totalled. The fathom, however, is not in keeping with this reckoning. The total of the chest, arms, forearms, and hands would give thirteen feet six inches. This is evidently due to the belief that Buddha, like other great men, had very long arms. (b)

(a) Arch. Surv. Report, Vol. III, p. 90.

(b) See my 'Antiquities of Orissa,' Vol. I, p. 63.

The figure is seated, not on the conventional lotus, but on a large pedestal of basalt, having a rich moulding in front. Below the moulding the front is divided into five panels, of which the two outer ones have a lion each, the next two an elephant each, and the central one, which is slightly projecting, a female figure. On the lower edge of the pedestal there is an inscription in an ancient form of the Kuṭila character, which gives the name of its dedicator.

The size, material, and the details on the pedestal of this statue, are so closely similar to those of the throne in the first-storey chamber of the Great Temple, that one would be disposed to think that it once occupied that throne; but there is nothing positive to support this conjecture. The details are conventional, and the material is common to a great number of statues in the place.

The attitude of this figure is typical, and obtains wherever Buddhism prevails. In bas-relief it has been noticed in thousands of instances, and it is no less common in the round. In the Pancha Paṇḍu temple there is a perfect specimen of this style of statue, and I have copied it on plate XX, fig. 2. It represents the saint seated on a throne supported by two lions and three human beings. The seat is a double lotus, and the back-framing is surmounted by two acrotarias and a circular glory capped with two leaves. The circle is intended to represent an ornament of the throne, and not a halo. The figures on the sides of the image represent two standing Buddhas, two seated ditto lecturing, and two attendants. One of the standing Buddhas has a disciple, a boy, by his side. The compartment on the right side of the throne has a devotee seated, and its corresponding one on the left a standing human figure, and another throwing himself into a well. Elsewhere the last figure is unmistakably that of a monkey, and there is a legend which says that a monkey in that way evinced its devotion. On the top the reclining figure is that of Buddha dying.

Buddha in ecstacy.

The next most common attitude is that of ecstacy or *samádhi*. It differs from the last in having both the hands resting on the lap, one supinate palm resting on the other, either in a prostrate or a supinate position. When both the palms are supinate, a round object is sometimes placed on the upper one, but what that object is—a flower, a pitcher, or a sacred figure—I cannot make out: it looks like a pitcher. The accessories to this statue are the same as those of the last, except that I have not noticed any crown on its head.

In a figure seen at Sherghâṭi by the late Major Kittoe the object on the hand was distinctly a hemispherical vessel, very like the earthen cooking pot called *málsá*, often used by Hindu devotees to burn incense in. I have several times seen ladies of high rank placing, in redemption of a vow for the cure of a son from a severe attack of illness, such a vessel full of live coals either on the palms, placed on the lap, or on the crown of the head, and burn incense therein. I am not aware of any story associating such a form of penance with Buddha; but as the figures unquestionably are of a comparatively late date, it is not at all unlikely that some schismatics have tried to heighten his glory by making Buddha undergo the penance.

Fig. 2 of plate XXIII offers a good illustration of this style of Buddha. It has been taken from one of the images stuck on the new enclosing wall lately built by the Burmese repairers. The figure has an ornament round the neck—a very unbecoming decoration for one who has entirely renounced the world, and is immersed in the ecstacy of the deepest meditation.

Buddha as a Teacher.

The third attitude is that of discussion. Seated on a throne, Buddha is represented explaining some abstruse question of metaphysics, and closing a discourse with a clinching argument, which is expressed by the clinching of one fore-finger against another. Sometimes the fingers are held apart as in the act of unravelling a knotty point; at others the left hand is raised as in the act of blessing or encouraging, and the right rests on the thigh. In a variety of this, rather rare, the figure is not seated cross-legged, but has one leg bent along the line of the seat, and the other hanging down, and resting on a footstool formed of an expanded lotus on a stalk. In a few specimens both the legs are let down and placed on a footstool; such figures have generally more ornaments on them than those which represent the saint as engaged in penance.

Of this attitude fig. 2 of plate XIII affords a good illustration. It has been copied from a statuette fixed by the side of the gateway of the monastery.

Buddha as a pilgrim.

In standing figures both feet rest flat on the lotus, which has no chair or stool under it. The left hand either holds the hymation, which gracefully covers the greater part of the figure, or has the palm raised to show the mark of a lotus on its centre, or it is raised as in the act of blessing. The right hand hangs by the side, but when the left holds the hymation the right palm is gently raised to show the lotus-mark. In seated figures this mark is also shown on the soles of the feet, as it has been held to be the special characteristic of Buddha. The background bears stúpas and attendants on the sides, but no other figure of Buddha himself. I have seen no standing figures without a back framing. The position of the feet is such as would be consistent only with perfect repose; but the theory is that Buddha is represented as going about in his rambles, and, meeting some disciple, stopping short to receive the homage of the party and to bless him, the raised hand being an indication of blessing.

The annexed plates afford several illustrations of this form. Fig. 3 of plate XXI represents the saint proceeding on a journey, having an umbrella held over him by a crowned attendant, and a disciple carrying his alms-bowl. It occurs in one of the niches of the new wall. Plate XXX represents the saint with the attendants, but without the umbrella. Fig. 1 of plate XXIII has the saint only without any following. In plate XXXII, fig. 1, we have an elaborate piece of workmanship. It represents the saint fully draped and crowned, standing in front of a throne with a high and rich back-frame. His right hand, showing the lotus mark, rests on an expanded lotus; the left holds a lotus bud. He has earrings and ornaments round the neck. On the sides of the principal figure are shown eight small images of the saint, in meditation, in ecstacy, as a lecturer, and as an itinerant hermit; on the top occurs the death-scene. The stone was found by Buchanan-Hamilton in the cemetery.

Death-scene of Buddha.

The death-scene of Buddha is shown by itself in a single specimen, now built into the surrounding wall of the court-yard on the west side. It is of small size, about 14 inches long, made of basalt, and by no means of good workmanship. The subject, however, was a favourite one with early Buddhist artists, and occurs repeatedly on the tops of seated figures of the Dhyání Buddha. In the first and the second centuries of the Christian era the artists of Mathurá often represented it in high relief, along with the birth and other scenes. Two of these are now deposited in the Indian Museum, Calcutta, and an outline drawing of one of these occurs in the learned M. Foucaux's translation of the Tibetan version of the Lalita Vistara. Of other scenes from the life of the saint, with which we are familiar from the sculptures of Baráhat, Bhilsá, Mathurá, and Amarávatí, there are no representations now available at Buddha Gayá. If they ever existed, they have long since disappeared.

Bodhisattvas.

Of Bodhisattvas images are not rare; but the only two Bodhisattvas represented are (1) Padmapáṇi and (2) Vajrapáṇi. The attitude assigned to the former varies greatly. He is sometimes shown as standing, at others seated, in either case holding by the left hand a stalk bearing a full-blown lotus, and carrying on the head, in front of the top-knot or crown, a small image of Amitábha, a Buddha of a former age, and said to be his father. In seated figures the left leg sometimes hangs down and rests on a lotus. Sometimes both the legs are let down. This saint is also represented with four, six, or eight arms,—generally four; and images of this description have been mistaken by the Hindus for those of Vishṇu, and worshipped accordingly.

In fig. 1, plate XIII, we have him seated in a very undignified style. He is decorated with a crown, a necklet, armlets, bracelets, and anklets, and shows the divine mark of the lotus on the palms of both his hands. Without this mark I would have taken the image for that of a hermit. In plate XX, fig. 1, he is shown standing on a lotus-throne, and holding the stalk of a lotus. This figure is now worshipped as the goddess Tárá Deví in the temple of that name. In fig. 1, plate XXI, he occurs in the form of a four-armed figure seated on a lotus and engaged in explaining a knotty question. In plate XXIII, fig. 3, he appears standing on a lotus and holding a lotus flower in each hand. By his side is buckled a broad sword. He has shoes on his feet; ornaments round the waist, wrists, arms, and neck; a crown on the head; and flowing locks. The figure is now standing by the side of the eastern gateway of the temple. The original of plate XXVIII is now deposited in the Indian Museum. It is of a martial character like the last, but much more sumptuously ornamented. Instead, however, of shoes it has the feminine anklet. The cloth shown on the body is of a striped and spotted pattern. Fig. 3 of plate XXXII is also of a rich pattern. It is now kept leaning against the wall of the terrace to the left of the entrance to the Great Temple, and, in this position, is worshipped by the Hindus under the impression of its being a representation of the goddess Sávitrí. Fig. 6 of plate XXIII gives another illustration of this saint; but in this instance he holds a lotus in one hand, while the other, clenched, rests on the left thigh. The pose is that of a man in an uneasy condition, and not in calm repose, such as a person in a state of meditation is expected to be.

Of Vajrapáṇi, 'the wielder of the thunderbolt,' a Bodhisattva of a very fierce nature, I have seen an only specimen: it is kept in the temple of Vágíśvarí Deví, and worshipped as a representation of that Hindu goddess. (Plate XXXII, fig. 2).

Máyá Deví.

Figures of Máyá Deví, the mother Buddha, are by no means common, but at one time they were not wanting. Major Kittoe, in 1847, recovered several of very large sizes. One of them, now in the Indian Museum, measures over six feet. In the Pancha Páṇḍava temple there are two of a medium size, most richly executed. The illustration given in plate XXIX has been copied from the former. Its character is unmistakable from the figure of the chaitya shown on the right side of the top-framing. A counterpart of this is shown in plate XXVI, figure 3; and fig. 1 of that plate gives another illustration of a female figure, which I believe is intended for the mother of Buddha. It is nearly as richly ornamented as the last, but it has no attendants. Ordinarily the lady is represented as standing by the side of a sál tree, and supporting herself by holding one of its branches. This was the position in which she is related to have given birth to Buddha in the Lumbiní garden. She is also represented as lying on a couch while under the travails of confinement. But of these two forms I have seen no specimen at Buddha Gayá.

Demons.

In the later Tántric systems of Buddhism superhuman beings, some male, others female, of a malignant nature and fierce character, also found cognizance as objects of worship; and the Tibetan pantheon includes a whole host of them. In the 'Tathágata Guhyaka,' which forms one of the nine most sacred texts of Nepalese Buddhism, several such divinities have been described under the name of Ḍákinís. The Hindus recognise them as imps, attendants on the goddess Kálí. To judge from the sculptures now met with at Buddha Gayá, it would seem that these systems never got into any wide currency at that place. It was, however, not altogether unknown. Among the remains dug out by the Burmese gentlemen there are four small images of females, with fierce-looking faces and large tusks, engaged in the horrible task of ripping open, with their nails, the bowels of human beings. They bear no inscriptions, and to judge from their make they must be of a comparatively recent date, probably made to order of some Nepalese, or Tibetan, pilgrims, who thought fit to dedicate them at the holy shrine. There are a few other female figures, but of a benign aspect, whose identity I could not make out.

In the compound of the monastery there is a piece of sculpture which represents a female standing on a car drawn by ten horses. The lady has six arms, and between her feet is shown a small figure—that of the charioteer. (Plate XXXI, fig. 2.)

Another lady, a Buddhist unmistakably from the chaitya over her head, has eighteen arms, holding various kinds of weapons. She is seated on a lotus throne, and from the position of her two foremost hands appears to be engaged in solving some knotty question of religion. This sculpture is stuck on the side of the gateway to the monastery. (Plate XXXI, fig. 3.) A representation of this lady, but with only two arms, occurs on plate XX, fig. 2. She is seated on a lotus throne, and is engaged in explaining some difficult question or other.

A female seated on a lotus with a child on her lap, and having over her head a hood formed of a seven-headed cobra, belongs to this class. The lady is intended to represent a Nágakanyá. (Plate XXI, fig. 2.)

Devotees.

Although Buddhism was founded on the assumption that the human soul can be raised to the rank of the deity by a long course of penance and righteousness, and many disciples of Buddha were raised to the rank of great saints, it would seem that no attempt was ever made to raise them to the rank of a Buddha or to worship their images. Of devotees of lower grade statuary representations were rarely made. Amidst 2,500 carvings of various kinds, I noticed only a few. Among these are three figures of devotees, females, in alto-rilievo, in a kneeling position with folded hands. These were evidently intended only to serve as ornaments beside a large figure of Buddha. They seem to be of Burmese origin. (Plate XXIII, fig. 5.) Plate XXIV shows a hermit seated at his ease and examining his waist-band. By his side there is an alms-bowl full of fruits, and two pious ladies are come to present him a panful of milk and some other articles of food. Figures of this kind are rare.

In a place so thoroughly heterodox as Buddha Gayá it is not to be expected that there should be any images of Hindu divinities. The place was never thoroughly converted to Hindu usage, and none thought of dedicating Hindu images there. But as later Buddhism recognised several of the Hindu divinities as subservient to it, it is not remarkable that there are a few images which may be called Hindu or quasi-Hindu. A remarkable one is that of the goddess of the earth, Prithiví Deví. She is shown standing on a tortoise, the emblem of the earth, and has an umbrella over her head. By her side stands an attendant (plate XX, fig. 4). The goddess is recognized by the Buddhists, and described to have paid a visit to Buddha during his meditations (*ante*, p. 36); she can scarcely therefore be called a Hindu goddess. The character of the next is more marked. In the small unconsecrated temple in the east of the monastery, close by the figure of Buddha noted above (p. 132, plate XI), there is a monster figure with six heads and six arms, two of which are broken. It holds an uplifted sword, a staff, and a lasso: it is dressed in a tiger skin, and is shown dancing on a bull. The figure is apparently that of a Bhairava, a class of demoniacal attendants of Mahádeva. (Plate XXX, fig. 4.) A counterpart of this is seen in fig. 2, plate XXVI. In it the figure has four heads and eight arms, and, instead of standing on a bull, has under its feet a man and a woman. In one of its hands the figure holds a closed umbrella. It is a curious article, and I have nowhere else seen a counterpart of it. Another figure of a Hindu character is that of a female with four hands, mounted on a flying human being, who has wings instead of arms. The rider I take to be Lakshmí, wife of Vishṇu, and the vehicle, the Garuḍa of that divinity. (Plate XIII, fig. 3.) Another occurs in the courtyard of the monastery. It represents a female standing on a car drawn by seven horses. Between her legs is seated the charioteer. I fancy it is intended for Sávitrí Deví, who has apparently seized an opportunity to have a drive in the chariot of her husband, the sun-god Súrya.

Hindu Divinities.

The great temple, as described in a preceding chapter, is of brick, and all its different members, decorations, and ornaments, except the jambs and the pavement, are made partly of that material and partly of mortar and stucco. The jambs are of rusty brown sandstone, relieved in the front by three lines of plain longitudinal moulding of very much the same pattern, both in the inner and the outer gates. (See Plates XVI and XVII.) The jambs of the outer gate are supposed by General Cunningham to be of a later date than those of the inner one, as they had been most likely set up when the two-storeyed porch was built. The architrave over the inner

Architectural Ornaments.

doorway is of dressed granite, but devoid of ornaments; the pavement was originally of plain flags of granite, but some pilgrims in the 14th, 15th, and the 16th centuries carved in outline their own effigies, and added short Sanskrit inscriptions to record their visit. General Cunningham has given a plate of these carvings, which for ready reference I copy from his first report. (Plate LI.) Some of the minor temples and other buildings, the ruins of which I dug into, were also made of the same materials. The columns of the verandah noticed above (p. 69) were, however, as already stated, built of stone ashlars with lime cement; and, to judge from the many fragments of sculptures now scattered all about the place, it would seem that several of the minor temples, or their appurtenances which surrounded the great fane, were built either entirely of, or in good part with, stone. Monolithic columns of six to eight feet in height, and of rich designs, have been met with, and bases for these, of equally elaborate designs, as also architraves and lintels, are also abundant. Some of these are lying on the ground; others have been used in the building of the Mahant's private dwelling. One set of ten bases have been built into the new enclosing wall of the court-yard; others have been carried away by the people of the neighbourhood. Fragments of mouldings, friezes, architraves, and other architectural stones, are to be met with in almost every part, stuck in the mud walls of huts over an area of five miles round the sacred spot (Dr. Buchanan-Hamilton noticed them scattered from eight to ten coss round the country); and these incontestably prove the former existence of a considerable number of stone temples or other stone buildings in the neighbourhood of the great one. But the clearances which have lately been made have swept away all traces of their original sites. Possibly in the mounds now existing outside the new boundary wall, if dug into, traces might be brought to light of some of their sites; but I could find none.

Bases of Pillars.

Of the architectural stones already brought to light, some bases of pillars appear remarkable. They are of different sizes and make; some designed for square pillars from 14 to 20 inches a side, others for columns of 10 to 16 inches in diameter. In their ornamentation the cyma, the torus, the fillet, and the tile, are the principal mouldings used, and these have been combined in a variety of ways. The rich ones have niches with human figures. In some sumptuous specimens the niche has been replaced by human figures ranged in tiers. The following are some of the leading varieties.

Plate XXII, figure 2, is of the simplest form, and designed for a column. It has a set of threefold mouldings over the plinth, then a neck, and then a double set of mouldings.

Plate XXII, figure 2, was intended for a square pillar. It has a projection on each side, bearing a niche and an image of Buddha.

Plate XXII, fig. 3, is a variety of the last. Its niche is smaller, but it has on the torus an ornamental design.

Plate XXII, fig. 4, is very much like the last in its lower part, but above the torus it has two niches and two sets of mouldings, each formed of a tile, a cyma, and two fillets.

Plate XXVII, fig. 2, has the niche replaced by a lancet-head ornament, and the topmost line of mouldings supported by a series of dentils.

Plate XXVII, fig. 1, is an imitation of the body of a temple. It has a threefold projection on each side, each having a rectangular niche flanked by pilasters and containing an image seated on a lotus. The central image, is a male, and the side ones females. Altogether the base is a very sumptuous one, and the square pillar over it must have been an elaborate piece of work.

Plate XXVII, fig. 3, is *sui generis*. It has a threefold projection, like the last two; but its plinth, instead of being plain, is covered by a range of images of Buddha. The member placed immediately over it is sloping. On its centre there is a niche, and by its sides are rows of images. Above this member there is a niche, and then the member is repeated, but without the niche, the surface being covered by a line of nine images of Buddha.

Pillars.

Of the square pillars designed for these bases I have seen none; but, judging from brick pillars extant, I suppose they were square in the lowest portion (from one-fourth to one-third); then octagonal, so made by the canting of the angles; and then polygonal, produced by another series of canting. Sometimes the third section was either rounded, or allowed to remain square. Elsewhere alternate sections of square and rounded shafts are common, but I have no data to show that that style was used at Buddha Gayá.

Columns.

Of the column I met with only two specimens. One of these is now deposited in the Indian Museum. I give a drawing of it. (Plate XLVIII, fig. 2.) It measures 5 feet 9 inches in length and 13 inches in diameter at the lower end, the diameter of the upper end being

10 inches. It is of the rich Jain pattern, set off with broad bands of scroll work. It was evidently intended for the front part of a porch. Of the base and capital suited for this column I found no specimen. The material of the column is sandstone. The fluted column, so common in Káshmírí architecture, is to be seen only in bas-relief at Buddha Gayá.

Capitals.

For capital for square pillars the crucial bracket was the most common. Its upper edge was modelled into a simple moulding, and the ends of the cross-bars set off with scrolls like the ram's horn of European architecture; rarely by female figures. In a few I noticed lotus flowers. The remains of this member of pillars are rare, and those of columns have not at all been met with. It is to be presumed the latter were of the ribbed melon shape so common in the niches of the Great Temple.

Door-frames.

The door-frames are usually selected by Indian artists for the display of a considerable amount of ornament, and at Bhuvaneśvara, Puri, and elsewhere, they are generally very elaborately carved. It is to be presumed that at Buddha Gayá this was also sometimes the case; but the only two door-frames extant of the Great Temple are very simple. The lintel and the side-bars have plain mouldings on the outer surface. (Plates XVI and XVII.) In some minor temples the lintels were set off with richer carvings than what was shown on the side bars. A rich specimen of it is shown in Plate XLVIII, figure 3. Intended to be constantly trodden, the sill is a member of a door which is ill adapted for the display of ornament. A squared bar is the form most common and best adapted for it; but Indian architects revelled in ornaments, and no part of the building was thought too insignificant or commonplace for the display of art. It is not remarkable, therefore, that among the stones lately exhumed at Buddha Gayá there should be several specimens of sills sumptuously carved in floral devices. One of these is shown in plate XLVIII, fig. 4. It is five feet long, and made of black chlorite. The ordinary decoration for this member is a flat band on the outer surface. The top is invariably smooth.

Vajrásana.

Reference has already been made (p. 62) to the carved stone lying in the temple of Vágíśvarí Deví, which is supposed by some to be the same whereon seated Buddha acquired the perfection of knowledge. It is called the *vajrásana*, or the 'thunderbolt seat.'

It is a circular slab of chlorite 5 feet 9 inches in diameter and 6 inches in thickness. Its lower surface is rough and uneven, but the upper one was originally carefully polished and decorated with a curious design. Exposure to rain for centuries and rough usage have, however, obliterated the design in several places, and this the more readily as it was engraved in very faint lines: for a seat, deeper engraving would have made the stone uncomfortable.

The design on it is a complicated one. Roughly it may be described to comprise nine outer bands, covering about two-fifths of the surface, and within them a square pattern, the corners of which cut into the three inmost bands, and each side of which has an elaborate gateway, which cuts into the six inner bands; the centre of the square area enclosed by the pattern having a lotus. The outer band is formed of a series of leaves ranged in a slanting position. The second comprises a string of clawed forms, which have the conventional shape of the thunderbolt (*vajra*), whence the name of the stone. The third has a row of lotus petals; the fourth a trailing vine; the fifth lotus petals again; the sixth a line of Indian dumbbells or *mugdars* ranged in an upright position; the seventh looped garlands intervened by lion-heads; the eighth a series of alternate lozenges and thunderbolts; and the ninth a scroll. The square pattern is meant to be a wall; it has a line of pilasters ranged on lotus petals and capped by globular figures. The gateways are very complicated, and their design will be best understood by reference to the plate. (Plate XLIII, fig. 4.) What this design is intended to typify I cannot say; probably it is intended to represent some heavenly tope with its surrounding rails and enclosing walls.

From the narrative given in the second chapter (p. 32), it is evident that Buddha sat on a bundle of grass spread on the platform of the Bodhi-tree, and not on any throne; and the description of the *vajrásana* given by Hiouen Thsang (p. 94) is, on the face of it, legendary, and not at all in keeping with the stone which now passes under that name. Fa Hian notices a place, four *li* to the north of the Bodhi-tree, where he saw the tree under which, and the stone on which, seated Buddha ate some rice-milk. The stone he found to be about four feet square and two feet in height (*a*); and General Cunningham is disposed to think this to be the same stone. (*b*) Referring, then, to a blue stone with remarkable

(*a*) Beal's 'Buddhist Pilgrims,' p. 131.
(*b*) Arch. Surv. Report, Vol. I, p. 7.

veins which Hiouen Thsang saw, he says: "This simple stone I believe to be the same as that mentioned by Hiouen Thsang." The first supposition is not tenable, as Fa Hian's stone was a square one, and cannot be the same with the circular one under notice. The second is more consistent, as it refers to a stone given by Brahmá to Buddha. Obviously, however, the stone under notice was got up a lông time after the death of Buddha for purposes of priestcraft.

The stones above described, though few in number, are of much interest as specimens of art-design current on this side of India several centuries ago; but in the utter absence of dates they subserve very little historical purposes. None of them can be carried beyond the second century of the Christian era, and the latest come to the 15th century. The great bulk is probably due to the sixth, the seventh, the eighth, and the ninth centuries, when the glory of Buddha Gayá was for the last time revived with great *eclát.* The sculptures, however, are so thoroughly conventional, so got up by the rule of thumb, so monotonous in every respect, that they are utterly worthless for purposes of comparison.

Carvings on railings.

Very different is the case with the carvings on the Aśoka rails. Their date is unquestionable, their subjects are so diversified, their execution is so vigorous, they are so unmistakably life-like, though exceedingly coarse, that they cannot but engross the attention of the antiquarian in a variety of ways; and at the same time they serve to throw a mass of new light on one of the darkest periods of Indian history. Major Markham Kittoe, who first noticed the sculptures on the rails, and presented some drawings of them to the Asiatic Society, remarked: "I invite * * particular attention * * * to the drawings in which will be found the figure of a female with the head of a horse or an ass; another of a goat on a pedestal or altar; the water jars; the three figures, two female and one male; the lotus oft repeated; and again the couple caressing each other, beside whom water jars are placed; the centaurs or minotaurs, the winged oxen and horses, and the sphynxes,—all are objects at once curious and instructive."(a) The drawings referred to above were taken back by the donor for the purpose of making out a detailed descriptive account, and never after returned. General Cunningham, in 1861, prepared some very faithful and well-executed drawings of some of the bas-reliefs on the railings, and published them along with his first

(a) Journal, Asiatic Society, Vol. XVI, pt. I, p. 338.

report; (a) but he did not notice them in detail, contenting himself with the remark—"Some of the sculptured bas-reliefs in these pillars are highly interesting. They show the Buddhist belief of the donor in the veneration for solid towers and trees; they show the style of architecture in the representation of temples, (b) houses, gates, and city walls, and the costumes of the people in the dresses of the king, (b) and of other worshippers of each sex."(c) In his second report (d) the learned antiquarian has dwelt at greater length on the history and form of the rails, and noticed in detail a group which he takes to be of the sun-god, Helios, and the decorations of some of the coping stones of the railing. The late Mr. C. Horne published, in 1866, rough sketches of some of the bas-reliefs (e), but added no description to explain their character. I have deemed it proper therefore to copy all the bas-reliefs that are now available at Buddha Gayá, including those which have been already figured by General Cunningham and the late Mr. Horne, and to reproduce them in the annexed plates.

Their position.

In order fully to understand the character of these bas-reliefs, it is necessary to bear in mind the positions they occupy on the railings. As already described, the railing consists of a series of posts standing about three feet apart from each other, on a stone plinth, and having a coping on top and three rail bars morticed on their sides. (Plate XXXIII.) This is the typical form wherever the peculiar railing has been met with, and a very ancient specimen of it occurs among the bas-reliefs of Udayagiri; (f) but in its dimensions and ornamental details taste and fancy were allowed extensive play. In the earliest Sánchí tope all the stones, the posts, the bars, and the coping, were dressed, but left perfectly bare. (g) In No. 2 tope of that place the posts have each a circular disc on the centre, a half disc just under the coping, and another above the plinth; but the rail bars, the coping, and the plinth, are left bare. (h) At Buddha Gayá the circular discs are produced on the rail bars, and the coping has a running frieze. (See plate XXXIII.) The same arrangement occurs at Mathurá, but the discs are set

(a) Arch. Surv. Report, Vol. I, plates VIII to XI.
(b) I have nowhere noticed any temple strictly so called, nor any royal personage.
(c) Arch. Surv. Report, Vol. I, p. 10.
(d) Arch. Surv. Report, Vol. III, pp. 96f.
(e) Journal, Asiatic Society, Vol. XXXV.
(f) My 'Antiquities of Orissa,' II. plate XIV.
(g) Fergusson's 'Eastern Architecture,' p. 93.
(h) Idem, p. 93.

off with floral buds at the corners, some pillars having large human figures in high relief, and the frieze is surmounted by elaborate arched ornaments. (*a*) The Baráhat rails are of the same construction, but not quite so ornate. Round the Gautamiputra cave, at Nassik, the rails are brought so close to each other as to leave only a barely perceptible space between them; the semicircular discs are replaced by circular ones, and the coping is rich, but the plinth is bare. (*b*) At Amarávatí the discs are much larger, the friezes on the coping much more elaborate, and the plinth covered with a rich frieze formed of animals and floral devices. (*c*)

Theory of gradual improvement.

These differences in the ornamentation of rail-designs would at first sight suggest the idea that their progress was due to gradual development,—that the simplest were the oldest, and the most elaborate the latest. Unquestionably the latest, or those of Mathurá and Amarávatí, are the most ornate; but the rails at Sánchí are, according to General Cunningham, later than those of Baráhat, and the latter are far more elaborate and sumptuous than the former. Again, accepting the Baráhat and the Buddha Gayá rails to be due to Aśoka's munificence and earnest devotion to his newly accepted faith, they should be synchronous or all but synchronous; but the former are by far richer than those of the latter, and their differences cannot be reconciled on any chronological scale founded upon relative art-excellence, unless we set all other historical evidences aside; and to do so in the present state of our knowledge would be to shut the door against truth with a vengeance. The principle of gradual improvement is *à priori* so thoroughly established that it cannot be reasonably questioned; but it is hazardous to apply it to isolated cases. The data now available for such a purpose as regards the Buddhist rails are quite insufficient, and cannot be at all relied upon for the deduction of any general premises. One building of one age may be poorer than another of another and a later age; but it cannot be accepted as a proof positive of the former age having been lower in the scale of architectural art-excellence than the latter until it is proved that the former never had, and could not produce, anything better. If the principle be admitted without the rider, it would justify the

(*a*) Arch. Surv. Report, Plate VIII.

(*b*) Fergusson's 'Eastern Architecture,' p. 94.

(*c*) Idem, pp. 93–100, and 'Tree and Serpent worship,' p. 130. Mr. Fergusson invariably misspells the name of the place and makes it Amravati.

belief of the Nágás and the Duflás on the eastern frontier of Bengal, who see beer-bottles enough, but no Bohemian glass, that Europe produced only beer-bottles and nothing like Bohemian glass was known there. Even in the case of the railings, had the Baráhat ruins not been brought to our notice, we might have safely believed the Sánchí rails to be the oldest. The fact is, ornamentation is as much dependant upon wealth as on artistic ingenuity, and in the ratio in which wealth is withheld art must deteriorate. The man who proposes to spend a few thousands on a house cannot have as sumptuous and well decorated a house as he who sets down a million for the purpose, though both may live in the age of Praxiteles. Again, the capacity or taste of the individual architect engaged, and the honesty of the agent employed to superintend the disbursement of money, are important factors in the calculation of the result to be obtained; and these should never be lost sight of. These are doubtless trite axioms, unfit to be repeated, but in the domain of Indian archæology they have not always been borne in mind.

Wooden-model theory.

Mr. Fergusson believes the mechanical construction and ornamentation of the rails to afford positive evidence of the design having been taken from wooden models. He says, "the pillars, for instance, could not have been put up first and the rails added afterwards. They must have been inserted into the right or left hand posts, and supported while the next pillar was pushed laterally, so as to take their ends, and when the top rail was shut down the whole became morticed together as a piece of carpentry; but not as any stone-work was done either before or afterwards." (a) Adverting to the discs on the pillars, he adds: "In carpentry the circular ones would represent a great nail meant to keep the centre bar in its place, the half discs, top and bottom, metal plates to strengthen the junctions—and this it seems most probably may really have been the case." (b)

Its value.

In the history of human progress, wood-work must unquestionably have long preceded stone, and it would be an insult to the understanding of the reader gravely to formulate that man first put up wooden railings, and when he learnt to work on stone, prepared stone railings from his original wooden models. There can be no difference of opinion

(a) 'History of Eastern Architecture,' p. 93.
(b) Loc. cit.

anent such a theory; but as I gather from the author's writings, his object is to assert that the transition took place in the time of Aśoka, and not gradually in course of a long series of years, like the pile-huts of the lake inhabitants changing into Swiss villas. I cannot acquiesce in this view of the case, for I cannot help thinking the theory in this sense to be opposed to fact, and mischievous in its tendency. As regards masonry buildings generally, I have already elsewhere given reasons for not accepting the hypothesis of the learned author. (a) I shall therefore confine myself here to a statement of the arguments which might be urged against the hypothesis regarding the rails. The shape of the railing, whether in original or in effigy, as seen in the oldest monument extant, in the caves of Udayagiri, is quite unlike anything wooden that can be appealed to. In the wooden railing everything is light and airy. Even in the strongest fence the posts are comparatively thin, the coping slender, and the bars attenuated and set wide apart; whereas the bars, the pillars, and the coping of the stone railing, are as heavy and thick as possible, and the spaces between the bars reduced to a minimum. Had the latter been the result of the first attempt at copying the former, such would never have been the case. It is far more convenient to move about and work light, small pieces of stones than heavy ones; and there could be no mechanical difficulty in producing thin bars of stone,—at least those who chiselled the thick ones so neatly could not have found thin bars less easy of management. Doubtless, size for size, the commoner stones are more fragile than wood; but the object of the stone fence was not to keep out intruders bent upon using force, but to set up an ornamental appendage round a sacred spot. Looking to the height and the ladder-like construction of the stone railing, it is impossible to believe that any man having the use of his limbs at command could for a moment find any difficulty in scaling it, and against animals a much lighter structure would have amply sufficed to serve as an efficient protection; and the man who first copied the wooden fence in stone would not have so far departed from his model. The interval must have been long before the copyist could to such an extent neglect his model as to differ in every detail except the barest outline.

In the mechanical construction of the railing the difference is as remarkable. In wooden fences the rails are either four-sided bars or rounded bolts, never elliptical, the latter being weaker and much more difficult to work out. How is

(a) 'Antiquities of Orissa,' I, chapter I.

it that in the first attempt at copying the masons changed the easily-managed four-sided bars into the most difficult and troublesome form of the ellipse? The tenons and the mortices in wood are either four-sided or round, never, in any ordinary case, elliptical or lens-shaped; and yet in the stone railing they are invariably lens-shaped. These changes could not have taken place within the single reign of Aśoka; and yet if we are to believe Mr. Fergusson, the art of sculpture was first originated in his reign, and the rails and stone-houses were for the first time made in stone from wooden models, and as the rails were put up by Aśoka, the change was accomplished in fifteen to thirty years.

Admitting, however, for the sake of argument, what is otherwise quite inadmissible, that the beginning and progress of stone rail-making was accomplished in the single reign of Aśoka, it might be asked—how does this accord with the other theory of the learned author, in which he attributes the beginning of stone masonry and sculpture to the advent of Greek artists in India during Aśoka's reign? If accomplished artists came from Greece or Bactria, why did they begin by copying wooden models, and not introduce a completed art? Why should they have preferred lens-shaped tenons and mortices, which were not common in Greece or Bactria, to square and round ones, with which they were perfectly familiar? Doubtless the number of the artists who came from beyond India was not large, and they had to train up the natives of the country to practise the art; but in such a case the pupils, whatever they may do in original designs, should follow the mechanical details taught them by their foreign masters, and not devise indigenous methods of their own.

Mr. Fergusson is probably right in his supposition that in the construction of the railing one pillar was first set up and fixed in its position, the rails were then adjusted and supported, and the next pillar then pushed laterally and brought into position; the process being repeated till the whole line was completed. This would have been the simplest plan possible, and it was most likely the one that was followed. It might be supposed that all the pillars were first put up in large loose holes, one corner pillar then fixed, the bars belonging to it adjusted, and the next pillar then pushed laterally to receive the nearest tenons of the bars, and the pillar itself then fixed into its position, and the process repeated till the entire line was completed. In either case the pillars were first set up and the bars put in afterwards. The copings were of different lengths, some covering one compartment, some one and a half, others two; so they must have been put up after the pillars and bars had been fixed in their position. In so far there is doubtless much that would imply "pure carpentry;" but the work could not be done in any other way. If we assume that if the rails were not set up piecemeal they must have been left on the ground, the bars and the coping all fixed, and the whole structure, about a hundred feet or more long, twelve feet broad, and weighing two to three hundred tons, raised at once into position. Such a feat has never been attempted, and could never have been accomplished, by men destitute of the most powerful mechanical appliances. Even in a wooden fence such an attempt would imply the most consummate stupidity on the part of the artists. Nor could the true masonry pillar-and-lintel construction, where all the pillars are built first and the lintels laid upon them afterwards, be conveniently adopted in fixing rails into monolithic pillars. In masonry work, holes are kept on the sides of the pillars for the tenons of rail bars, and these holes are either twice the depth of the tenons, so that one end of a bar may be pushed in deep and the other end brought within the intercolumnar space to be slid into its corresponding hole; or one side of the hole is broken into or kept open, and after its corresponding tenon has been shoved in the side is built up. Neither of these plans could be adopted in the case of not-very-thick monolithic pillars without either disfiguring, or seriously weakening, them.

The nail-head and clamp argument is weak at best. It presupposes that in former times wooden railings were not, as in the present day, simply morticed, or morticed and then secured by wooden pegs cut flush on the outside so as to be imperceptible, but in the centre bars were strengthened by nails having heads about a foot in diameter, and clamped in at the four corners with iron plates having semicircular ends. This is simply gratuitous. There is no evidence extant which could prove this. It might be said that the nail-heads were small, but in copying them they have been enlarged. This is not what is usually done at the first attempt. A competent artist could have readily imitated a nail-head; it is scarcely conceivable that an incompetent person would in the first attempt to imitate a nail-head produce a well-developed lotus flower. It should be added that in the oldest rails of Sánchí there is no indication whatever of this feature of a wooden railing. Supposing that the artists were too inefficient to attempt the imitation in their first essay, one may ask if the hypothetical nail-head be the type of the lotus disc, how are we to justify its presence on the middle of the rail bars, where no nail-head could by any possibility find a place in a wooden model? In mediæval and modern Indian door-frames, both of wood and of stone, there are lotus discs at the four corners, and also on the middle of the bars, where no nail is ever required. In these cases, as also in that of the rail bars, we cannot but admit the purely ornamental character of the disc; and, if so, I see no reason why it should not be accounted for in the same way elsewhere.

Clamps at the corners of railing frames are quite exceptional in the present day, and to suppose them to have been common two thousand years ago, when iron was not so easily worked, or so abundant, as in our times, and that without an iota of evidence, is to assume a major which can serve only to mislead.

If one were to judge very carefully the design, construction, and finish of the different railings above referred to, the impression in his mind would be strong that the simplest Sánchí rail is as perfect in its design and finish as the more elaborate Mathurá work. It differs from the latter in not having the ornaments, and not in its artistic finish, and this shows that the design of the rail was current in the country long before the age of Aśoka. A small tree planted singly in an open place needs the protection of a fence round it, to save it from the attacks of cattle. No one in India neglects this necessary precautionary measure. When the Bodhi Tree was multiplied all over the country, such a fence was everywhere deemed essential, and from the necessary to the ornamental in connection with religion the transition was an easy one. We must look to the beginning of the rail to a few years after the death of Buddha, that is, some two centuries before, and not at the time of Aśoka.

Carvings on rails.

To turn now to the ornaments of the Buddha Gayá railings. As already stated (p. 72), the pillars are not all of the same material; some are of sandstone, others of granite; and it is doubtful if they were used promiscuously in the making of the same railing; most probably not, and the dates of the sculptures on them must, therefore, spread over at least two centuries. I am not in a position to mark the distinction, and must therefore notice the carvings on them all under one head.

Of the rail bars the number seen by me is small, and the bars are all of sandstone; but General Cunningham has noticed some of granite. Of copings the number is also limited, and they are all of sandstone. But the leading feature of their ornamentation is the same in all: the rail bars have a lotus disc on the opposite sides of its middle, and nothing more. (Plate XXXIII.) The lotus is formed generally of two consecutive rows of petals, with the thalamus or disc in the centre and a double-line border. The petals of the outer row are all well developed and laid side by side, and not overlapping each other, as is natural. In some instances, however, the overlapping is well shown. (Plate XXXVIII, fig. 6.) In others the petals, instead of issuing in straight lines from the centre, are whirled in a manner which is not natural. (Plate XLIV, fig. 2.) Between the points of the outer row of petals are shown the tops of other and outer whirls. The petals of the inner row are also laid side by side, but they are slender. The thalamus is distinct in some cases, showing the seed-holes (Plate XXXVIII, fig. 2); in others it is covered by small petals (Plate XXXVIII, figs. 5 and 2). The inner row of petals is sometimes replaced by a human head (Plate XLIV, figs. 2 and 3), and in another by a mermaid with her fishy tail curling round the thalamus. (Plate XXXVIII, fig. 2.) The mermaid or *Matsyanárí* is an object of popular belief common all over the Aryan world from a very ancient date, and is not unknown in Assyrian and old Persian sculpture. It is the counterpart of the semi-piscine Triton of Greece, and a close congener of the Nágakanyá or semi-ophide female of Orissan architecture. (*a*)

Carvings on copings.

The topmost bar forming the coping is square on three sides, and rounded on top; on the two opposite flat sides there are two slightly-raised fillets, within which is a running frieze of animals on one side and a floral device on the other. Of the former General Cunningham has figured and described four varieties, and of the latter also four. I have found seven of the former, including the four noticed by the General, and four of the latter, being those which the General has figured. Most of these stones have been brought and deposited in the Indian Museum, Calcutta. The floral designs are complicated but chaste, and remind one of the designs sometimes adopted in cast-iron works of the present day. (Plate XLVII.) The animal designs include on one stone a line of three winged Centaurs followed by three horses, all in a running posture. (Plate XLVI, fig. 1.) On another a series of bouquets, each formed of a lotus petal, with alternately two long or four short leaves rising on its sides and a

(*a*) My 'Antiquities of Orissa,' Vol. I, page 43; Fergusson's 'Tree and Serpent Worship,' p. 53.

loop on top, and having on each side a monster figure formed of the forepart of a Centaur and the hind of a fish's tail curled. (Plate XLVI, fig. 2.) The monsters with folded hands are paying their adoration to the bouquet. The stone seen has four such monster figures. The third stone has the top of a pillar supporting two leaves and a flower, and three dogs are running towards it in a line. (Plate XLVI, fig. 3.) The fourth stone has a human-headed winged bull or Minotaur, two winged horses, and two bulls, the last driven by a monster-looking pigmy. (Plate XLVI, fig. 4.) General Cunningham takes the last to be a monkey, but the face is very like that of a human being; and the dwarf was so great a favourite with ancient Indian artists, that I cannot help taking it as such. Below this frieze there is an inscription in the character No. 3 of Prinsep. The fifth stone has a procession of two heavy-looking animals crouching, two elephants crouching, a bull running, and a lion standing. (Plate XLVI, fig. 5.) The stone was found on the roof of the Buddhapad pavilion by General Cunningham, who takes the first two animals to be hippopotami. The hippopotamus is unknown in India in the present day; but Dr. Falconer and Sir Proby Cautley found fossil remains of that animal in the Sevalik hills, and the probability of its having been known to ancient Indians will be made apparent from the remarks which will occur lower down. The sixth comprises two winged goats followed successively by two rams, two bulls, and a winged horse. (Plate XXXIII.) General Cunningham takes the sheep to be a ram and a ewe, but both have long, curving horns. The seventh stone is the longest, being seven feet five inches, and must have covered full two compartments of the railing. General Cunningham describes it thus: "In this bas-relief the sculptor has given the run to his fancy, and exhibited a procession of sea-monsters by simply adding fish tails to the foreparts of well-known land animals. The elephants seem to me to be the most comical, although they are by nature half aquatic.' Below the procession there is a long inscription, which is unfortunately much injured in the middle. It is certainly a Buddhist record, as the words *Bhagavate Buddhâya* occur twice in the upper line, as well as the well-known term *vihâre* just before the second *Bhagavate*. On the back of this stone there is the flower pattern marked D."(a) (Plate XLVI, fig. 6.) As these stones were found in the rubbish mounds away from their original positions, it is impossible to determine whether the processions

(a) Arch. Surv. Report, Vol. III, p. 99.

were joined so as to make a continuous line, or broken into separate pieces by the intervention of pilasters, or by some other contrivance.

The pillars may be divided sculpturally into two classes—the medials and the terminals. The medials have their corners canted (Plate XXXIII), whereas the terminal ones retain their rectangular shape perfect (Plate XLVIII, fig. 1). The former are also less elaborately carved than the latter.

Carvings on pillars.

The medial pillars have the lotus disc on the centre, and a half section of it at the lower end, the cord of the section being seated on the plinth of the pillar. (Plate XLVIII, figs. 5, 6, and 7, plate XXXIII.) The central disc is commonly the lotus perfect, but in many instances the inner circle contains representations of various kinds. In one there is a lion with its tail uplifted (plate XXXIII); in another a crocodile (plate XLV, fig. 9); in a third a horse (plate XXXIII)); in a fourth a winged goat or deer (plate XLV, fig. 10); in a fifth a bull (fig. 11); in a sixth a Centaur (fig. 12); and in two others geese (plate XLIV, fig. 1; plate XLV, fig. 7). The Centaur is remarkable as calling to mind the Greek representations of this monster, to which it bears a close resemblance. The human head is very common, and several styles of it have been met with. The heads have generally heavy turbans (plate XXXIII, plate XLIV, figs. 2 and 3), but buttoned hair is not uncommon. In all these cases the space between the double line of the outer rim is filled with a row of beaded ornaments. In one instance a squatting human figure with a staff in hand forms the central ornament (plate XXXIII). Sometimes the lotus petals are minimised or entirely omitted, and the space within the beaded circle filled with grotesque lion-heads (plate XLV, fig. 5) or the petals changed to fanciful ornaments (plate XLIV, fig. 4). The grotesque head in fig. 5, plate XLV, is worthy of special note, as it is very like an ornament common in both Roman and Gothic architecture, and is now found in escutcheons of brass drawer-handles of Birmingham manufacture.

Bas-reliefs on medial pillars.

At the upper end the semi-circle is lengthened into a half transverse section of an oval figure, and the area within it is filled with a variety of designs. In one there is a boat in a lake full of lotus plants, the leaves and buds of which are well shown. (Plate XXXIV, fig. 1.) In the boat there are three persons, one standing near the helm, the second propelling the boat with a pole, and the third prostrating himself before something sacred at the prow. A scene somewhat like this occurs at Sánchí, but in that the sacred relic is shown prominently in the middle of the boat (a). We have next a woman with a horse's head leading by the hand a villager to the side of an old dilapidated wall. (Plate XXXIV, fig. 2.) In the Hindu Śástras mention is frequently made of a race of beings with human bodies and equine heads; they are called *Kinnaras*, and believed to be highly proficient in the art of music, on which account they are assigned the rank of heavenly choiristers or the musicians of Indra. They are also said to be attendants on Kuvera, the god of wealth. The female members of this race (Kinnarís) are supposed to be fond of human society. The Buddhists believed in the Kinnarís; and in the *Bodhi-sattwávadána-kalpalatá* there is a story which relates that Buddha in a former life had been born a Kinnarí. The following is an abstract of the story. 'Vidyádhara, a serpent-catcher, attempted to capture the king of serpents and drag him out from his abode by means of drugs and incantations. The king, greatly terrified, took shelter with a hunter, named Padmaka. This man killed Vidyádhara with poisoned arrows, and obtained from his protegé a charmed noose of wonderful power. On his death he bequeathed the noose to his son Utpala, who dwelt at Hastinápura, in the vicinity of Valkaláyana's hermitage. Once upon a time Utpala heard a charming song resounding in the air. Learning it was being sung by an exceedingly beautiful Kinnarí, he captured her by means of his noose. The Kinnarí, to regain her liberty, offered to give him her jewelled coronet, which lends the power of traversing the universe at pleasure. When the two were settling their bargain, in came Sudhana, a young prince of Hastiná, on a hunting excursion. Utpala gave him the jewel, and the Kinnarí married him, and the married couple proceeded to the palace.

'At this time there lived in the royal household two Bráhmans, Kapila and Pushkara, the former serving as priest to the king, the latter in the same capacity to the prince. They were vain of their learning, and always quarrelled with each other. One of the feudatories of the king rebelling, the king directed his son to lead an army against the unruly vassal. Sudhana left his wife with her jewel under the care of his mother. The king, after his son's departure, dreamt an inauspicious dream, and Kapila, his priest, advised him to offer a Kinnarí as a burnt

(a) Fergusson's 'Tree and Serpent Worship.'

offering to propitiate the enraged divinity who had caused the dream. Kapila was a shrewd man, who took this opportunity of humbling his rival, for he knew full well that the prince was sure to die if the Kinnarí be killed in a sacrifice. But he was disappointed. The queen privately warned her daughter-in-law, and sent her away with the jewel to Kinnarapura.

'The Kinnarí left a ring and some charmed butter with Valkaláyana, requesting him to hand the two things to Sudhana on his return.

'Sudhana returned victorious from the war. But his joy was damped by the loss of his wife. He determined to proceed to Kinnarapura, and immediately set forth in a northerly direction. On his way he obtained the ring and the butter from Valkaláyana, which helped him a great deal in overcoming the fatigues of his journey. He crossed the mountains Himálaya, Kulada, Ajapatha, Kámarúpa, Ekadhara, Vajraka, and Khadira, one after another, and encountered many adventures. Beyond mount Khadira he found two great mountains turning on a wheel, which made the road impassable. He destroyed the axle of the wheel, and fixed the mountains in their proper places. After this adventure he had to ford the Gúhá, Patangá, Rodiní, Hasiní, and several other furious mountain-streams before he reached Kinnarapura. There he met his wife, and the two wept tears of joy.' (a)

It is probable the bas-relief under notice is a pictorial illustration of a scene in the old story.

The next figure in the plate under notice (fig. 3) represents a domestic scene. A lady is seated on a bedstead, by the side of which there is a cane morá, or stool, holding her betel-boxes. By her side is seated a stranger who is making a request with folded hands; but the lady is dissatisfied with him, so with averted face, her right hand uplifted, she desires him to go away, and to avoid him falls back, and with her left hand leans on a maid who is standing beside her. From his dress and the gourd alms-bowl placed before him, the man would seem to be a hermit, who, having got admission to the house on the plea of soliciting alms, has attempted to abuse the confidence of the lady. In the Sanskrit Buddhist Avadánas there are several stories of this kind, but it is not possible to determine which of them the bas-relief is intended to reproduce. Figures 4 and 5 of plate XXXIV contain effigies of Chaityas which have already been noticed (p. 122). Figure 6 represents an enclosure with several

---

(a) My 'Sanskrit Buddhist Literature of Nepal,' p. 62.

Bodhi trees, surrounded by the typical Buddhist railings, and some vessels for watering the trees. Below this there is an inscription in the Láṭ character.

Figures 1 and 3 of plate XXXV have Chaityas, and these have been already noticed (p. 124). Figure 2 shows a doorway through which is seen a platform with its sides decorated with the device of a typical Buddhist railing, and having on the top of it a pedestal bearing the figure of a wheel. The doorway has the ancient Indian pointed arch on top, and round it a framing which terminates in a weather moulding supported on corbels. The door is evidently meant to belong to a temple which has the Wheel of the Law, and not an image of Buddha, for the object of worship. In figure 4 we have the Bodhi tree on a high pedestal, to which a devotee is paying his devotion, while an aerial spirit in the form of a human being with a peacock's tail and feet is approaching from a hill to offer a flower garland to the tree. The figure is the conventional one of a Garuḍa, and occurs often at Sánchí. According to the Buddhists there are eight classes of heavenly or aerial beings, among whom the Garuḍas stand sixth in rank (a). Figure 5 is a hermit's abode—a stone building, not a hut,—with the door surmounted by a semicircular arch, and a terrace in front. The hermit is seated cross-legged in front of his room under the shadow of a tree. The sides of the terrace are set off with the device of the Buddhist rail, and is high enough to require two steps to be easily accessible. On the side of the steps is seen the gourd alms-bowl of the hermit. The house is worthy of note, as showing that stone houses were common enough in the country, and even poor ascetics could afford to have them. Figure 6 is a Bodhi tree surrounded by the typical railing, and having on each side an umbrella planted on the ground, and having garlands hanging festooned from its sides. Similar garlands are seen hanging from the top by the sides of the upper part of the tree. The scene is repeatedly met with in the Buddhist sculptures of Sânchí, Baráhat, Mathurá, and Amarávatí.

In plate XXXVI, figure 1, we have the pavonian figure of Garuḍa, with the head and trunk of a human being and the feet and tail of a peacock, as in plate XXXV, figure 4, but without hands. The next figure (2) represents a familiar scene in India, a lady showing her little boy a juggler's goat standing on a pedestal. Figure 3 is a goose in a lotus pond. The animal is in the act of attacking some one who has

---

(a) According to the Lalita Vistara the eight, in the order of their ranks, are—(1) Devas, (2) Nágas, (3) Yakshas, (4) Gandharvas, (5) Asuras, (6) Garuḍas, (7) Kinnaras, (8) Mahoragas.

disturbed it. Its caudal appendage is a grotesque representation of a peacock's tail. Figure 4 is a bull with a bell tied to its neck, and the next an acrobat or juggler supporting himself on his hands, with his feet twisted round and placed on his head. The rays behind the head are meant for the folds of his gown. This acrobatic performance is common all over India in the present day, and no one who has seen the performances of the *nats* or *bájigars* of the country can be unacquainted with it. The bas-relief shows that the exhibition has been popular in this country for more than two thousand years. The last figure on the plate shows a domesticated deer, with a collar and a bell round her neck and a fawn by her side. The pose of the ears shows that the animal is not a goat.

In plate XXXVII the first figure exhibits an acrobatic performance, in which a man supports on the back of his raised thigh and leg a boy, while he supports himself on one foot. The next (2) has a covered vessel for its central figure, with a bird on each side having a curiously-curled tail, and four persons on the foreground, one of whom is a man of consequence, receiving the salutation of a bare-headed inferior in front of him. On plate XXXIII is shown a man lying on a wall or rock with his legs uplifted and holding a tuft of leaves. The position is the conventional one for flying, but the chest and the thighs are shown leaning on the wall. Figure 3 of plate XXXVII shows a crouching dog playing with a pup. The faces of the animals are of an equine character, but the long tails and crouching position induce me to think that dogs are meant. Figure 4 has a tree in the centre, and on each side a man seated on a chair and holding a flower with folded hands. The tree has not the conventional railing, nor is it of the shape usually given to the Bodhi Tree. Though their hands are folded, it is doubtful if the men are worshipping the tree, for in such a case they would not have taken their seats on chairs. Figure 5 is an elephant being tethered by a *máhut*; and the next the grotesque lionhead monster noticed above, but slightly different in detail.

In plate XXXVIII, figure 1 has the semi-pavonine human form shown in full face with the wings outstretched. Figure 3 is a peacock with the head of a horse, the tail curling round the body. Figure 4 shows the front of a house, with a central doorway of the old style, having an arched weather moulding, and the walls set off with pilasters. The balustrades round the roof are of the Buddhist rail pattern, and on the roof are three persons seated, enjoying the cool breeze of an evening. The make of the wall is not shown, but, looking to the make of the door and its similitude to the hermit's house, I take it to be of masonry,—the whole a pucka-built house with a flat roof, and not a hut or a wooden structure. Plate XXXIII shows an angel or Devaputra in a flying position, holding in his two hands a garland intended as an offering to some chaitya or Bodhi Tree. Figure 6 is a female hermit seated cross-legged, and holding a staff with a rectangular top. She is the counterpart of the Yoginí of the Hindu Tántric system.

Bas-reliefs on corner pillars.

Plate XLVIII, figure 1, shows a perfect corner pillar, having its two adjoining, and not the two opposite, sides carved, and the angles entire and not canted. The half-discs at the bases are the same as in the medial pillars, and have a ram's head carved in the triangular space between the two adjoining discs. The central discs are replaced by panels, of which the lower edge is bound by an effigy of the Buddhist railing, from which graceful festoons hang at the corners. Each side of the panel is chiselled into a fluted pilaster, which is so joined with the nearest pilaster of the adjoining side as to appear like a fluted square pillar. It has the typical ribbed domal form at the base and at the crown. Over the domal capital there is a couchant bull supporting an architrave formed of interlacing festoons, and thereupon a cornice. The centre of the panel is occupied by a couple of human-beings standing in an amatory mood. The space for the upper half disc is surrounded by a double line in the form of a semi-oval, and in the centre of it is a female standing in the midst of a lotus bush, and holding a lotus stalk in each hand. The form is of Rájalakshmí, a goddess whose effigy is common enough both in Hindu and Buddhist architectures. (a) The corner garlands are repeated, but with slight variations. In other pillars of this class the form of the middle and the upper panels differs, and the attitudes of the human figures are changed (plate XII, figs. 1 and 3). In one there is a single figure, a female holding a trident (plate XII, fig. 2).

Gate pillar.

The most remarkable pillar of this class was seen in the verandah of the monastery. It is so built in that only the front and portions of the two sides are visible; the back, built into the wall, being out of sight. On the left hand side the stone is not fully dressed, and the remains of three lens-shaped mortices are the only chiselled work visible on it. The

(a) 'Antiquities of Orissa.' Vol. II, p. 31.

right side is sculptured, but the details are partially covered by the wall in which it is built. Not having seen the side facing the wall, I cannot say whether it has sculptures or mortice holes. If there be sculptures on that side, the pillar was originally designed for flanking a gateway; but if there be mortices, it was a corner pillar. From the elaborate carvings on the front and the right side I am disposed to think it has carvings on the off side, and was intended for a gate-pillar. The details on the right side, as far as visible, comprise three panels, of which the uppermost is occupied by a man standing with folded hands to offer his adorations to some sacred object placed under an umbrella; but that object cannot be made out. The entablature below it shows crouching dwarfs supporting the cornice. The middle panel has a group of six persons, of whom those on the foreground are a woman and a boy. The persons are engaged in saluting a Bodhi Tree before them. Below this panel is shown a Buddhist railing. The lowest panel is broken, and what remains of it is very much defaced. The front of this pillar differs from that of other pillars in not having any plain space, the whole surface being divided into three panels. The lowest panel is flanked by pilasters of the same kind as those on the sides of the central panel of the last described pillar, only wanting the fluting and the railing below, and the festoons being of a different type. The middle panel has side pilasters of a different pattern, being sections of octagonal pillars in antis by themselves, and bearing no relation to the adjoining sides; they have bell-shaped capitals like those of the Aśoka láts, and crouching human beings like sphynxes over them. The sphynxes support an entablature, the frieze of which has three compartments, in each of which there is a crouching dwarf with uplifted hands, supporting the cornice. The lower edge of the panel has the Buddhist railing. The upper panel has also octagonal independent side pilasters, but their capitals are domal and not bell-shaped, and the sphynxes are replaced by crouching deer. The figure in the centre of the panel is a grand gateway, with a pointed weather moulding, over which there is a Buddhist railing, and thereupon a central large and two small side pavilions. The design is peculiarly Indian, and not to be met with out of this country.

The group of figures shown on the surface of the middle panel is by far the

Figure of so-called Apollo.

most important. It represents an Indian war-chariot drawn by four horses, two going to the left and two to the right. The horses have waving plumes on their heads. The driver is seen standing on the middle of the chariot. Behind him there is a nimbus formed by the back framing of the chariot, and over it an umbrella. Close by the driver there is on each side a female warrior shooting arrows at a person who is tumbling down in pain. This is the only instance in which the ancient Indian war-chariot is shown at Buddha Gayá. General Cunningham thus comments on the group:—"The subject is *Súrya*, or the sun driving a four-horsed chariot, with two attendant archers shooting his rays like arrows upon the earth. In this treatment I think that there is a decided evidence of Greek influence in the restricted number of *four* horses attached to the chariot; for the Indian Súrya, from the earliest times down to the present day, has always been represented as driving a chariot with *seven* horses. In the Rig Veda he drives "seven bay" or bright-backed steeds, and in all the Brahmanical sculptures that I have seen there are seven horses carved on the pedestal, which are being driven by Aruna, while two attendants on each side (? one on each side) shoot downwards the golden arrows of the solar rays. The chariot, however, is Indian, as may be seen by comparing it with the specimen given in figure 3 of plate XXVII, from the Sanchi Tope. But whence came the four horses? To this question I can only reply, "from the Greeks," and in proof of this opinion I have given in figure 2 of the same plate a sketch of the well-known classical representation of Phœbus Apollo in his chariot drawn by four horses. It is true that this composition is of later date than the age of Aśoka; but as both the chariot and horses are mentioned in the Homeric Hymn to Helios, they are much earlier than the time of Aśoka. That this particular treatment of the subject was familiar to the Eastern Greeks we learn from a recently discovered tetradrachma of Platon, on which Helios radiated is represented driving to the right in a chariot drawn by four horses. There was a famous temple of the sun at Taxila, of which place Aśoka had once been Governor during his father's lifetime. Here then the Indians might have seen the Greek representations of the sun god, which was afterwards carried to Palibothra by either pure Greek or half Greek sculptors." (a)

The premises from which these conclusions have been drawn are, however, not correct, and the conclusions are consequently wrong. On carefully examining the photograph annexed (Plate L) it will be seen that the group has nothing to do with the sun. The pose of the central figure is not like that of the Greek Apollo, but that of a

(a) Arch. Surv. Report, III, p. 97.

plain turbaned Indian charioteer, and the side figures are two Amazonian ladies, not males as delineated by General Cunningham (a), shooting at men, who are shown falling down in pain from the wounds they have received. In General Cunningham's drawing the nimbus has been converted into a second umbrella. It is really nothing more than the back framing of the chariot. But assuming the arrows to be emblematic of rays, it should be observed that the rays of the sun may be fiercely and intolerably hot, and as a matter of fact sun-strokes are common enough in India during the hot weather; but the rays are invariably described by poets as beneficent to mankind, and not causing men to tumbledown with uplifted hands, and holding their wounded sides in great pain. And the fact of the bas-relief having represented such wounded figures is quite enough to dissipate the solar theory. The number and position of the horses are doubtless similar, but, bearing in mind the fact that the chariot in Greece and in India was of the same shape, we may ask, could an artist, whether Greek or Indian, represent effectually horses in bas-relief in other than profile, or three-quarter view? A front view of a horse in bas-relief would show only the fore part, or must project considerably more than what any bas-relief would admit of; consequently the Greeks generally adopted the profile, or three-quarter view,—in the former case ranging their horses in a line, so as to show the side of one and parts of the heads and legs of the others, and in the latter case showing the front view of the chariot with half the number of horses running on one side and the other half on the other, an arrangement which militated against all laws of the resolution of forces, which could make the chariot move onwards. This unnatural and awkward position was necessary for the sake of art, and could not be avoided; and if we find a similar disposition under similar circumstances in India, we see no reason to assume that it must necessarily imply a borrowing or interchange of art. As a matter of fact, the Hindus ranged their horses, according to the exigency of their work, either in profile, as in most sculptures of the sun-god Sûrya, or some on one side and some on the other, as in fig. 2, plate XXXI. The last figure is worthy of particular attention, as it shows ten horses arranged in the same way as we see in the Apollo figure. The General's argument summarized runs thus:—the position of the horses in the Bhuddhist sculpture is the same as we find in the figure of Apollo, therefore it must have been

(a) Major Kittoe described the side figures to be "Amazonian ladies," Jour. As. Soc. XVI, pt. I.

copied from the latter. The figure in the chariot consequently is that of Apollo; and if Apollo has no umbrella over his head and the Indian figure has a double one, it is of no consequence. The horses have crests in the Indian and none in the Grecian specimen, but that is accidental. Apollo has no side figures, and to account for the said figures in the Indian scene we must assume them to be emblematic, and the bows and arrows they hold to be symbols of the golden rays of the sun, and the wounded persons falling down to be men suffering from sunstrokes. Inasmuch, however, as I have shown that the position of the horses do not imply borrowing, but is the natural result of art, the whole superstructure of assumptions built on it must tumble like a house of cards. It might be added that the gist of the argument depends on the similitude of the treatment; but the Greek specimen which is of any weight in the question is later than the Indian, and in the coin of Platon the horses are all on one side. Doubtless Homer alludes to Apollo, but that does not at all imply that in Homer's time Apollo was represented standing on a chariot having two horses running on one side and two others on another side. To assume it would be simply gratuitous, and even then the argument would not advance at all.

Quality of the sculptures.

Chronologically the sculptures may be ranged in two groups—1st those of a pre-Christian period, 2nd, those of dates subsequent to the commencement of the Christian era. The latter spread from the second to the ninth or the tenth century; but they are not dated, and it is exceedingly difficult, if not impossible, to range them into sub-groups; and in the absence of dates they are valueless for a history of the progress of art in this country. Generally speaking they are, in all the finer and larger specimens, well designed, laboriously chisselled, and carefully finished. The shape is becoming, the relative proportions are fair, the modelling is appropriate. The pose, too, is good, the repose becoming, and the expression of calm contemplation admirable. On the whole the larger figures of Buddha bespeak considerable tact and talent in the artists concerned. But they are thoroughly conventional, all done according to traditional custom and universally current rules, without the slightest regard to nature,—all copied from models, and not from living objects. The heads are oval because heads have been always made oval, and not because in nature they are so; the limbs taper because older figures had tapering limbs, and not because human limbs are usually tapering; the heads and limbs bear certain relations to each other because they have always done so in statuary, and not because in nature there are any such relations. It is probable that the artists had ruled frames such as are still current in Tibet, and used them in determining the sizes of the different parts of their statues. Every limb is plump and rounded, and no attempt is made to develop or indicate the outlines of the muscles and tendons. In this respect Bhuvaneśvara sculptures of the seventh century are far superior, though they, too, are to a certain extent conventional. It should be noticed, however, that at the latter place the artist had a wide range of subjects, and, in representing ordinary human beings in different attitudes and engaged in various occupations, was not so tied down by rules as at Buddha Gayá, where statues of Buddhas and gods were all he had to carve—at least the only kind of work that we have before us to judge of their capacity. In animal figures there is the same scarcity, and little can be said about them. But in carving flowers and conventional architectural ornaments the artists of Buddha Gayá had made sufficient advance to claim considerable credit.

In sculptures of the pre-Christian era, *i.e.* in the Aśoka rails, there is a coarseness and want of finish bordering on rudeness, but there is more life, more action, and greater freedom of execution than what we find in those of the post-Christian age. The subjects are well conceived and vigorously worked out, with a keen eye to nature and effect. But the specimens are few; they are of small size, and so much decayed by the wear and tear of the last two thousand years as to be ill able to afford very favourable evidence. On the whole, however, they are inferior to the sculptures of Sánchí and Baráhat. This is accountable on the supposition that the artists employed at Buddha Gayá were inferior to those of the other two places; and as probably only local artists were employed, the work turned out according to the capacity of the persons employed, and not owing to one being of a later cycle than the other. This inference of mine is opposed to the opinion of some distinguished antiquarians, and I put it forth with considerable diffidence, but I think there are many facts and arguments which go far to support it.

Origin of Indian sculpture. Mr. Fergusson's opinion.

Mr. Fergusson is clearly of opinion that the art of sculpture and also that of stone-building were first introduced into India long after the invasion of Alexander the Great. He says: "It may create a feeling of disappointment in some minds when they are told that there is no stone architecture in India older than two-and-a-half centuries before the Christian era; but, on the other hand, it adds immensely to the clearness of what follows to be able to assert that India owes the introduction of the use of stone for architectural purposes, as she does that of Buddhism as a state religion, to the great Aśoka, who reigned from B.C. 272 to 236"(*a*). Elsewhere he observes: "When we first meet the Buddhist style it is in its infancy—a wooden style painfully struggling into lithic forms." In one place he admits that "the Indian art in the mode of treatment is so original and so local that it is difficult to assign it any exact position in comparison with the arts of the western world. It certainly, as a sculptural art, is superior to that of Egypt, but is far inferior to the art as practised in Greece. The sculptures of Amravati are perhaps as near in scale of excellence to the contemporary art of the Roman Empire under Constantine as to any other that could be named, or rather they should be compared with the sculptures of the early Italian renaissance as it culminated in the hands of Ghiberti and before the true limits between the provinces of sculpture and painting were properly understood. The case is somewhat different as regards the sculptures of Sánchí. These are ruder, but more vigorous. If they want the elegance of design at Amravati, they make up for it by a distinctness and raciness of expression which is wanting in those more refined compositions. The truth seems to be that the Sanchi sculptures, like everything else there, betray the influence of the freedom derived from wood-carving, which, there can be little doubt, immediately preceded these examples and formed the school in which they were produced"(*b*). He is nevertheless of opinion that "there can now be very little, if any, doubt but that this school of Indian art owes its origin to the influence of the Greek kingdom of Bactria," *i.e.* that which is so local and so original that no comparison could be made of it with any art of the western world is a mere copy of the western art, and that which was immediately copied from local wood-carving was likewise at the same time a copy of Bactrian stone models. Again, "the knowledge that the architectural history of India commences B.C. 250, and that all the monuments now known to us are Buddhist for at least five or six centuries after that time, are cardinal facts

(*a*) Fergusson's Eastern Architecture, p. 47.
(*b*) Tree and Serpent Worship, p. 97.

that cannot be too strongly insisted upon by those who wish to clear away a great deal of what has hitherto tended to render the subject obscure and unintelligible" (a).

General Cunningham's opinion.

General Cunningham gives but a qualified and guarded assent to this opinion. He says: "I agree with Mr. Fergusson in thinking that the Indians in all probability derived the art of sculpture from the Greeks. In the Punjab this would have been introduced as early as 300 B.C., and in a few years it would have found its way to the great capital of Palibothra. I speak now only of the sculptor's art, not of the mason's trade, for I do not suppose that building with stone was unknown to the Indians at the time of Alexander's invasion. On the contrary, I will show, in another portion of this report, not only that stone buildings were in use before that time, but that some of these are still standing in the present day" (b). Adverting to the presence of mermaids in the Buddha Gayá sculptures, he adds: "Their first appearance in the sculpture of Aśoka's age is, in my opinion, a strong presumptive proof that the Indians derived the art of sculpture from the Greeks. It is a fact which receives fresh proofs every day that the art of sculpture, or certainly of good sculpture, appeared suddenly in India at the very time that the Greeks were masters of the Kabul valley; that it retained its superiority during the period of the half Greek rule of the Indo-Scythians; and that it deteriorated more and more the further it receded from the Greek age, until its degradation culminated in the wooden inanities and bestial obscenities of the Brahmanical temples." (c)

Contradictory statements.

As regards architecture we have thus what are insisted upon with great earnestness by Mr. Fergusson as "cardinal facts" never to be lost sight of summarily set aside by General Cunningham, whose high scholarship, thorough knowledge, personal experience of well-nigh half a century of almost every place of any archæological interest in India, and official position as adviser of the Government of India on matters antiquarian, claim high respect for his opinion. And with such a marked

---

(a) 'Tree and Serpent Worship,' p. 49.
(b) Arch. Surv. Report III, 97.
(c) Ibid, p. 100.

difference of opinion on so fundamental a question in Indian archæology among men who are the greatest experts in the matter, the public may well pause before accepting either the one set of opinions or the other. It might be added that, whatever may be the result of modern reasoning on the subject, there are facts noticed in Greek history which cannot be easily set aside, and they all unquestionably prove that architecture of a considerably advanced kind existed in India at the time of Alexander the Great, or well nigh three quarters of a century before the flourishing period of Aśoka's reign. Alexander found in India more than one city furnished with walls and gates (Rooke's Arrian, pages 51-77). These walls were of brick (pages 53—88), and strengthened at intervals by towers (pages 81—89). The city of Palibothra was found by Megasthenes "surrounded with a ditch which took up six acres of ground and was 30 cubits deep; and the walls were adorned with 570 towers and 64 gates" (page 222). (*a*) Arrian, in another place, quoting Megasthenes, says,—"The Indians allow no monuments to be raised in honor of the deceased, esteeming their good deeds sufficient to perpetuate their memory, for which reason they make odes and sing songs in praise of them. Their cities are so numerous as not to be easily reckoned. Those which are situate near the sea or any river are built with wood; for no buildings of brick would last long there, not only because of the violence of the rains, but also of the rivers which overflow their banks, and causes an annual inundation over all the flat country. But the cities which are seated on any eminence are frequently built with brick and mortar" (*b*).

(*a*) The wall was in existence when Hiouen Thsang visited Patna in the middle of the seventh century, and its remains are still in *situ*. "During the cold season of 1876, whilst digging a tank in Sheikh Mithia Ghari, a part of Patna almost equally distant from the *Chauk* (market-place) and the railway-station, the excavators, at a depth of some 12 or 15 feet below the swampy surface, discovered the remains of a long brick-wall running from north-west to south-east. How far this wall extended beyond the limits of the excavation—probably more than a hundred yards—it is impossible to say. Not far from the wall, almost parallel to it, was found a line of palisades. The strong timber of which it was composed inclined slightly towards the wall. In one place there appeared to have been some sort of outlet; for two wooden pillars, rising to a height of some 8 or 9 feet above what had evidently been the ancient level of the place, and between which no trace of palisades could be discovered, had all the appearance of door or gate posts. A number of walls and sinks were also found, their mouths being in each case indicated by heaps of fragments of broken mud vessels. From the best preserved specimens of these, it appeared that their shape must have differed from that of those now in use. One of the wells having been cleared out, it was found to yield capital drinking water, and among the rubbish taken out of it were discovered several iron spearheads, a fragment of a large vessel, &c.—McCrindle's 'Ancient India,' p. 118.

(*b*) Rooke's Arrian, Vol. II, p. 221.

My own opinion on the subject, and the arguments on which it is founded, I have already given at length in my 'Antiquities of Orissa' (a), and need not repeat them here, particularly as no serious attempt has yet been made to refute them. When Mr. Fergusson brought out, in 1876, his "History of Indian and Eastern Architecture," my book, published three years before, was evidently known to him; for, adverting to the form of the Indian spires, he, in one place, says:—"In his work on the antiquities of Orissa, Bábu Rájendralála Mitra suggests at page 31 something of this sort; but if his diagram were all that is to be depended upon in favour of the hypothesis, I would feel inclined to reject it." But he does not make any reference to my objections to his conjecture about the origin of Indian architecture. He has, however, made an important concession. While persisting in the statement that Indian architecture before the time of Aśoka was entirely of wood, he admits, "stone in those days seems to have been employed only for the foundations of buildings or in engineering works, such as city walls and gates, or bridges or embankments; all else, as will appear from the sequel, were framed in carpentry" (b). Some of his arguments I have already referred to in my remarks on the supposed wooden origin of the Buddhist rails. The others appear to be of no great weight, and need not detain me here. The admission that the Indians did employ stone in building foundations of houses and in city walls, gates, bridges, and embankments from long before Aśoka's time goes a great deal further than what its author wished it to go. It throws on the author the onus of proving that men who could, and did, build stone walls confined their talent to city walls and embankments, but could not, or did not, extend it to the superstructure of their houses; that having built a brick or stone foundation as high as the plinth, they encountered some obstacle, intellectual, material, or artistic, to push it higher, and bring it to the level of the ceiling until taught to surmount it by Greek adventurers or their half-caste descendants. The admission drives us to the inference that the men who, according to Megasthenes, had built walls 30 feet high round Palibothra could not feel the advantage of having a masonry wall for their king's residence for the protection of his treasury. Such an inference is unjust to a nation whose inventive and

Author's opinion regarding the origin of Indian architecture.

(a) Chapter I.
(b) History of Indian Architecture, p. 47.

intellectual faculties were second to those of no other race on earth, and which in the domain of philosophy attained an altitude which none has yet surpassed. The only proof the historian of architecture has yet attempted to adduce is the apparent wooden character of the stone work now extant. But in many instances, as in the nail-head developing into a lotus, the apparent similitude is more fanciful than real, and in others it is fully accounted for by that spirit of conservatism of the nation which led the good Abbe DuBois to describe the habits and customs of the Indians to be as indelible as the spots on the skin of the leopard. In art this spirit of conservatism, or mannerism, or survival of custom, is peculiarly inveterate, and crops up even in the European architecture of the present day, and should not be held at all remarkable in the architecture of India twenty centuries ago. The question at issue is, whether those peculiarities, which are taken to be indications of direct copying from wooden models, are really so, or simply mannerisms of ancient date?—and as yet nothing has been attempted to solve it. In history, as in other concerns of the world, it is infinitely better, in any given point regarding which sufficient data are wanting, to acknowledge the fact, than to conjure up hypotheses hedged in by flimsy pretences of "it seems," "it is probable," "it is very likely," which, when proceeding from men of high standing and undoubted talent, serve only to shroud the cause of truth in impermeable gloom. Ancient Indian history, from its hazy character, has suffered particularly from hasty generalizations and *ex cathedra* assertions, and we cannot be too careful in guarding it against them.

Origin of Indian sculpture.

The remarks made above with reference to Indian stone architecture apply equally to Indian sculpture, for the two are intimately connected, and cannot well be separated. Sculpture may or may not presuppose the existence of stone architecture. The one may, at least in some cases, be posterior to the other. But the desire of decorating houses leads to the elaboration of ornamental forms, and the progress of the two arts cannot be studied by looking upon them as independent of each other. And since Indian stone architecture is older than the age of Aśoka, sculpture must likewise be so, and the bas-reliefs of the Udayagiri caves, which I take to date from the middle of the fourth century before Christ (*a*), show that Indian

(*a*) 'Antiquities of Orissa,' II, p. 39.

plastic art is much older than Aśoka. And those bas-reliefs are even bolder, more natural, better executed, than any work of Aśoka's time. As, however, I have already discussed the subject at considerable length in my "Antiquities of Orissa" (a), and nothing has yet been urged to controvert the position there assumed by me, I need not dwell upon it further than to point out some of the subjects on the Aśoka rails which at first sight might suggest foreign ideas.

Supposed foreign character of some carvings.

The most important of these is the one which General Cunningham likens to Helios; and I have already, I think, satisfactorily shown that the conjecture on the subject is not tenable. Adverting to the figure of mermaids on one of the railings (page 152), the General says: "The original idea of these sea-monsters I believe to have been derived from the well-known Tritons, Hippocamps, and Capricorni of the Greeks." (b) The margin here given is wide, but the belief in the *Matsyanári*, or the semi-piscine maid, is old, and we have much older instances of it in ancient Assyrian sculpture. Inman, quoting Lucian, gives an account of the goddess Syria (Dea Syria), whose image Lucian saw in Phœnicia, and "which was a woman in the upper parts and from the body downwards a fish" (c). The same author informs us that "the name Oannes was given by Sanchoniathon and Berosus to an Assyrian deity, who was the teacher of mankind, and who was mystically united with the form of the sacred fish." The goddess Anna or Annes, too, had a piscine character; and in ancient times the fish was frequently associated with the idea of virginity. Among the Chinese, too, the belief in the mermaid has been of a very ancient date. It is futile, therefore, to urge that the idea of the figure *must* have come from Greek or half-Greek sculptors. By "half-Greek" I suppose General Cunningham means the descendants of Greek adventurers by native women. If so, I cannot conceive how such descendants, bred and brought up in Indian homes, could acquire the Greek art of sculpture and evince a higher proficiency in it than the natives. Certain it is that the descendants of Albuquerque and his followers did nothing of the kind; and even in the present day, with all the facilities of steam communication, the Eurasians, as a race, are not more distinguished in their taste for art than the natives.

(a) Vol. I, pp. 68, *et seq.*

(b) Arch. Survey Rep., Vol. III, p. 100.

(c) *Apud* 'Ancient Faiths embodied in Ancient Names,' II, p. 785.

The Centaurs and Menotaurs are more exclusively Greek than the mermaid, and the figure on one of the discs (plate XLV, fig. 12) certainly bears a very close similitude to the Thessalian monster. Doubtless the Greeks located the Centaurs in Thessaly, the people of which place were great experts in horsemanship, and, mounted on bare-backed horses, were given to hunting wild bulls and ferocious animals. The belief in it, however, has prevailed from a very remote period of antiquity. Hesiod tells us that the battle of the Centaurs and the Lapithæ was engraved on the shield of Hercules, and Valerius Flaccus describes it as having been painted on one of the Argonautic ships. It was also shown as an ornament on the cap of Ulysses, and there is every reason to suspect that even as the gods and goddesses, whom the Greeks located on Parnasus, had their origin much farther east, so must have had the Centaurs; and since the relation of the Greek mythology to the Indian is exceedingly close, and there is strong evidence to show that the similitude is due to the fact of the Aryans having had a common mythology, which the western branch carried with them to Greece and the southern to India, it is simply impossible to determine whether the Centaur came with the rest of the ancient Aryan mythology, or were brought by the Greeks or their half-caste descendants in the time of Aśoka. Besides, the conception of a human head on a horse's body is the counterpart of the human body with a horse's head; and as the latter has been the exclusive property of the Indians, in the Kinnaras, it is not at all necessary to assume a foreign origin for it, not to advert to the fact that those who could change the Centaur into half-Centaur and half-fish, or design the human-headed bird, would find little difficulty in originating the idea of a human head for the body of a horse or a bull.

The same may be said of the winged horse, the winged deer, and the winged bull. At Sánchí the winged lion is always shown in a flying attitude, carrying a rider on its back. In Assyria this was not the case, and, commenting on the fact, Mr. Fergusson says: "The representations at Sánchi are, of course, very much more modern than those in Assyria; but it is not clear that the Indian form may not be of an original stock as old or older than the Assyrian." The human-headed lion is the reverse of the lion-headed man, and those who designed the leocephalic Nrisiñha, the fourth incarnation of Vishṇu, could not be much troubled in the effort to originate the counterpart of it. The human-headed bulls and lions and the eagle-headed lions and men, as also the winged varieties of those animals, were, besides, familiar to the Assyrians long before the time of Aśoka. Mr. Layard is of opinion that "there can be little doubt that they were invested with a mythic or symbolical character, that they typified the Deity or some of his attributes, his omniscience, his ubiquity, and his might. Like the Egyptian sphynxes, they were probably introduced into the architecture of the people on account of their revered character." (a) And as the intercourse between the Indians and the Assyrians was free, it would be the merest assumption to say that they came for certain with the Greeks in the time of Aśoka: and accepting that assumption as a major, to draw our conclusions regarding other matters from it would for certain be highly illogical.

The next figure I shall refer to is the grotesque head of a lion described on page 154. But the lion has all along been an Indian animal and not a European one, and it would be absurd to suppose that it came to Buddha Gayá from Greece. It might be added that the head is very like that of the Egyptian god Typhon, figured by Wilkinson; and if there be any necessity for an archetype for the Buddha Gayá exemplar, it would afford a much more reasonable one than a Birmingham drawer-handle. It should, however, be accounted for in a very different way. Mr. Wright, in his "History of Caricature and Grotesque," very justly says that "a tendency to burlesque and caricature appears, indeed, to be a feeling deeply implanted in human nature, and it is one of the earliest talents displayed in a rude state of society. An appreciation of, and sensitiveness to, ridicule, and a love of that which is humorous, are found even among savages, and enter largely into their relations with their fellow men." It is not remarkable, therefore, that we should find it in ancient Indian human nature and its manifestation in ancient Indian art. Nor is their location round a sacred fane at all to be wondered at. "Caricature and burlesque," says the author just quoted, "are naturally intended to be heard and seen publicly, and would therefore be figured on such monuments as were most exposed to public gaze. Such was the case in the earlier periods of the middle ages, chiefly with ecclesiastical buildings, which explains how they became the grand receptacles of this class of art." Even in the illumination of sacred books they were not held inappropriate, and we find a number of them of a very ludicrous character in "Queen Mary's Psalter."

(a) Layard's 'Nineveh,' Atlas.

The only other figure which calls for notice is that of the hippopotamus. It is represented with a thick-set, heavy body on short, stout legs, like those of the rhinoceros, and a long head with wide, open, massive jaws having serrated teeth, like those of the crocodile, the muzzle ending in a short trunk, like that of the tapir. The tail is long and cord-like. The head, as seen in profile, may be taken for that of a badly-drawn crocodile, but the body is such as to preclude the inference of its being intended for that animal, particularly as the artist has elsewhere represented the crocodile in a different style. (Plate XLV, fig. 9.) Nor can the figure be taken for a grotesque representation, as the other animals on the frieze are not so, and this particular form appears repeatedly on the Baráhat rails, showing that it was the conventional form of some at-the-time well-known animal. General Cunningham takes it to be an effigy of the hippopotamus, but the profile is not that of a hippopotamus' head, and the most characteristic peculiarity of that animal—its tusks, whence its fossil congeners derived their sub-generic names of *Hexaprotodon* and *Tetraprotodon*—is wanting. The trunk, too, is inconsistent; the front view of the hippopotamus' head does not suggest anything of the kind, for the face is specially flat and chubby; nevertheless, the entire figure is strongly suggestive of the hippopotamus, the more so as it is contrasted with a fairly spirited figure of a couchant elephant by the same artist. Not wishing to rely on my own judgment in the case, I communicated a tracing of the figure to my learned friend, Mr. W. Theobald, of the Geological Survey of India, and the following is an extract from a letter I received from him on the subject. He says, "It might be urged that the whole figure is a grotesque idea of the brain, having no prototype in nature, and such might have been truly the case had the animal been adorned with wings or horns; but it is singular that the artist's idea should have fixed on the massive jaw and disproportioned head (the very points which distinguish the hippopotamus) of that animal: or some vague idea of it, perhaps, was present to his mind. The short trunk that is given to the animal may be an addition of an imaginative artist, or it may have originated in a misrepresentation of some sketch or drawing in which the great tubular nostrils of the 'river horse' may have been mistaken or transformed in the process of copying into a short trunk. On the whole I think the sketch strongly supports the view (first advanced by Falconer) that the hippopotamus was known to the early inhabitants of India."

Accepting, on these grounds, the opinion that the figure is a representation, however imperfect, of the hippopotamus, the question arises—was that animal known, either traditionally or by sight, to the people of this country, or was it brought from Africa bodily, or in a sketch or drawing? The idea of the Buddhists having brought a live hippopotamus from Africa two-and-twenty centuries ago may be disposed of as utterly untenable; but Mr. Theobald justly observes "that it was by no means improbable that the knowledge of the animal, of which your sketch is an attempted representation, was derived from the account of travellers who had seen the animal in Egypt or Abyssinia, and described it with tolerable fidelity on their return. When one remembers that within the present century artists have depicted or modelled the Indian elephant with tusks projecting upwards from the lower jaw, like a pig's, we must not be too critical respecting the short trunk given to the sketch of the 'river horse' by the artists of Buddha Gayá." Dr. Falconer repudiates the African idea. He says, "a quadruped, so remarkable for its size, form, and habits, must everywhere have forcibly impressed itself on the attention of mankind; and, struck with the close resemblance of the Nurbudda fossil buffalo to the existing species, the question arose with me—'May not this extinct hippopotamus have been a contemporary of man? and may not some reflection of its existence be detected in the extinct languages or of ancient traditions of India, as in the case of the gigantic tortoise?' Following up the inquiry I ascertained from the profound Sanskrit scholar, Rájá Rádhákánta Deva, that the hippopotamus of India is referred to under different Sanskrit names of great antiquity, significant of the 'jala-hasti' or 'water elephant,' in the 'Amarakosha' and the 'Sabdaratnávalí.' This view is confirmed by the opinion of two great Sanskrit scholars, Henry Colebrooke and H. H. Wilson. The former, in his annotations on the 'Amarakosha,' interprets the words 'Gráha' and 'Avahára' as meaning hippopotamus; and the latter not only follows this version, but gives two other words 'karí-yádas' and 'vidu,' which he supposes to signify the same animal. It is therefore in the highest degree probable that the ancient inhabitants of India were familiar with the hippopotamus as a living animal; and it is contrary to every probability that this knowledge of it was drawn from the African species imported from Egypt or Abyssinia." (a)

(a) Falconer's 'Memoirs,' Vol. II, p. 632.

This philological evidence, however, is not satisfactory, as, on a reference to several Sanskrit lexicons, I could not find sufficient authority to support the interpretation. My attention was drawn to the words by Mr. Theobald in 1874, and the following is the substance of the reply I sent him:—

'The *jalahasti* does not occur in the *Amarakosha*, but in some of its commentaries it is given as a synonym of *avahára*. In the *Nágánanda*, a Sanskrit Buddhist drama, *jala-kunjaras* are described as sporting in the waters of a river: *kunjara* is but another word for *hasti*. The counterpart of this occurs in the Rájataranginí, where *jala-gandhebha* is used for *jala-hasti*. Neither of these books, however, afford any clue to the nature of the animal they describe. The Sanskrit Dictionary of Böhtlingk and Roth gives 'wasser elephant' on the authority of Hemasuri, who says it is an elephant-like animal, which dwells in water (*jaleshu hastyákárát vá*). The *Amarakosha* takes the *gráha* and the *avahára* to be the same animal, which, according to one commentator, is the same with the shark, (*hángara, hángarákhye jala-jantau*); and according to another, a slender, long animal that frequents the confluence of large rivers with the sea (*samudra-mahánadyoh sangame latákára-jantu-viseshuh*). At least half-a-dozen others add to the above definition 'commonly known by the name 'hángara' (shark), but not applicable to crocodiles;' and I see no reason to differ from them. There is nothing in any Sanskrit work which can be accepted as a positive proof of the *jalahasti* being other than the *gráha*, and was used to indicate the hippopotamus. I must add, however, that Wilson, in his Sanskrit Dictionary, gives the word 'hippopotamus' against *avahára* with a mark of interrogation. He has not given the word *jalahasti*.

This opinion, however, is founded on mediæval and modern commentators, and is of no importance when opposed to the incontrovertible fact that fossil remains of the hippopotamus have been met with in the Sevalik Range and in the Jumna and the Náhan beds, and they prove that the animal did once exist in India. Doubtless the animals which occur in the miocene strata could not have been seen by man, but the same cannot be said of animals of the upper pliocene age; and Dr. Falconer justly says, 'After reflecting on the question during many years in its palæontological and ethnological bearings my leaning is to the view that the *Hippopotamus numadicus* was extinct in India long before the Aryan invasion, but that it was familiar to the earlier indigenous races." (*a*) He has, moreover, very ably shown that other animals of the same age are still remembered by the Hindus. He cites for example the *Colossochelys atlas*, or colossal tortoise, which fought with an elephant; and the *Ciconea gigantea*, which is the type of the bird-god Garuḍa. And if the memory of these long extinct animals have been preserved to our day, there is no *à priori* improbability of the memory of the hippopotamus being preserved. The artists drew it from the traditional account they had heard, and they could not therefore be exact in their delineation; and the commentators of a much later date could not but interpret the ancient words in a blundering and misleading way. Even in the case of the lion, which became extinct in Orissa only sixteen hundred years ago, the Orissan artists disfigured it with a long dog-like face, very unlike that of a lion; and in the case of an animal extinct several thousands of years ago, misconceptions could not but follow. (*b*)

True test of relation as models and copies.

In making these remarks it is the furthest from my wish to deny that some sculptures have been met with in the north-western frontier which are peculiarly Greek in their treatment. The Greeks did exercise supremacy in that part of the country for a long time, and could not but leave the impress of their art in some cases; but I cannot help denying that that impress has had anything to do with the origin, or the amelioration, of the Indian art. The designs for natural objects, for men, horses, trees, and flowers, must be alike everywhere, and it is the technical treatment of the subject that can determine the nationality of the artist; and in this technical treatment and of excellence which, though an unsafe guide, is of some consequence, we have not, in Indian works of art, the smallest trace which can recall to mind the character of Grecian art of the third century before Christ, of the time of Phidias and his successors. It is not a standing human figure with an extended hand, but a certain undefinable and inimitable grace and beauty and perfection which make the Apollo Belvedere; and as long as that grace and beauty

(*a*) Falconer's 'Memoirs,' Vol. II, p. 644.

(*b*) To those who are interested in the inquiry, Falconer's Essay on "Primeval Man and his Contemporaries," in his Memoirs, Vol. II, pp. 570f., Falconer and Cautley's papers on the *Colossochely's atlas* in the Proceedings of the Zoological Society of London, Part XII, 1844, and Theobald's remarks on Dr. Falconer's papers in the Records of the Geological Survey of India, Vol. VII, will afford much valuable information.

are wanting, it is idle to say that the sculptor of the Apollo was the introducer of his art in another country, simply because we have there a human figure with an extended hand before us. The illustration might appear too trite and self-evident to be worth recital, but it is not uncalled-for. In discussions regarding Indian art the principle involved in it has but too often been overlooked, and conclusions arrived at which are in no way justifiable on the premises given. A remarkable instance of this is afforded in the essay on *Kṛishṇa-janmáshṭamí* by the learned Professor Weber, than whom few are better familiar with the Indian classics, and whose opinions naturally command very high respect. Few scenes could be more natural or indigenous in every country than that of a woman nursing a child, and in delineating it in one country it is all but utterly impossible to design something which would not occur to other artists in other parts of the earth; and yet the existence in India of pictures representing Yaśodá giving breast to her foster-son Kṛishṇa has suggested to Dr. Weber the idea of their having been copied from Byzantine representations of Madonna and Child. Advancing from Byzantium to Egypt, he observes: "What further occurs to us here as specially worthy of attention among the representations lying before us is the striking similarity which they show to the Egyptian type, Isis nourishing Horus, particularly as regards the attitude and upper part of the group, in so special a degree that a closer reference is superfluous: a comparative glance at the two pictures suffices. The explanation of this would be easily found if Raoul Rochette's or Mrs. Jameson's opinion, that the type of Byzantine Madonnas rests upon this Egyptian group, could be clearly proved by Byzantine pictures of the kind. We should then have to consider these last as the medium which had served as a model for the Indian picture. That such a Byzantine Madonna type should still be preserved so faithfully in India, while to us it belonged as a type to a departed age, would not be surprising: in similar cases the same thing often appears in the travelling of ideas to foreign lands." (*a*)

Now, the similarity so strongly insisted upon by the learned Professor results, such as it is, from the fact of all the pictures representing each a woman giving suck to a child, which, being a natural act common to humanity, could not but be alike everywhere. The relation of original and copy in such a case can be inferred only by the details, the technical treatment, and general arrangement

(*a*) 'Indian Antiquary,' VI. p. 351.

and style of execution; and in all these respects the pictures are totally different. This will be apparent from the figures on plate XXXIX, which I have copied from the 'Indian Antiquary' for ready comparison.

The supposed Egyptian archetype (fig. 3) shows a female in profile seated on a high chair, holding up her breast with her right hand, and extending her left arm in almost a right angle from her body, and allowing the fore-arm to hang down straight and stiff and rest on the knee by the tip of the fingers. The child, though sucking, is a grown up one; it sits bolt upright on the thigh of the mother, holds the right hand of its mother by its right hand, and allows the left hand to hang by its side. There is no halo round the head of either the mother or the child. The group, as usual with ancient Egyptian figures, is as stiff as possible, and the dress, ornaments, and accessories, are purely Egyptian.

In the Byzantine Madonna (fig. 2) the figure is full-faced, and the child, much younger, is shown lying on the lap supported by both the hands of the mother, and holding the breast with both its hands. The head of the mother and also that of the child are encircled by double lines, meant for haloes. The pose, expression, dress, ornaments, and accessories, are entirely different, and as unlike the Egyptian model as they well could be.

The Indian Yaśodá(a) (fig. 1) is seated, profile, in the Indian style, on a *takhtaposh* or wooden divan; she has one thigh resting flat on the bedstead, and the other raised to form a support for her child, which she encircles by her left hand, while with her right she presses her breast to help the child in sucking. The child has its right hand resting on its knee, and the left stretched out to hold the other breast. Haloes formed of rays of light are shown round the heads of both. The pose, dress, and ornaments, are thoroughly Indian, the raised thigh especially so, and totally unlike the Byzantine.

Thus we are called upon to believe that a figure in profile seated on a chair and having no halo is the archetype of a full-faced one seated on a chair with a double line of halo round her head, and the latter the model of a figure in profile squatting on a bedstead and having rays of light round the head, the only character common

(a) Dr. Weber erroneously calls the mother Devakí, who never had an opportunity to perform the maternal duty of nursing her child. According to the Harivaṅśa and the Bhágavata Puráṇa, the child, as soon as born, was taken away from her prison abode and left with Yaśodá, who reared it up. Hindus in this country would never so grossly falsify the story as to make Devakí nurse her son.

to all the three being the nursing of a child by a woman. Had nursing been unknown in India and Byzantium, there would have been some justification in the assumption of its travelling from Egypt to Byzantium, and thence to India. But nursing being common to mankind the assumption can only be justified by the pose, details, and accessories being identical; but as these are different, the theory has not a leg to stand upon.

As the Indian picture is between two and three hundred years old, there is no *à priori* impossibility in its painter having seen a European picture of Madonna and Child, and the Byzantians had certainly seen Egyptian figures; but the question is, did either of the former copy the latter? and the fact of their being so unlike each other forces on me quite an opposite conclusion.

It might be added here that representations of a mother nursing a child is by no means confined to the nations named. The Assyrians and other ancient people revelled in the idea, and represented it to imply a variety of mystic doctrines. In India it is not limited to Yaśodá and Krishṇa, nor are they of modern date. At Puri there are eight alto-rilievo figures, each three feet high, representing eight different goddesses giving suck to their children. Some such figures at Bhuvaneśvara are twelve hundred years old, and others at Jájapur older still. Dr. Weber himself gives a remarkable example of this kind. In his figure 4 he has a picture representing Rati nursing her child Kámadeva, the Indian Cupid, and the character of the principal figures are well indicated in it by their being mounted on a parrot and surrounded by a fish-banner, flowery arrows, and a bowstring made of bees. The Nágakanyá figured on plate XXI is a fair representation of a *madonna lactans* at Buddha Gayá.

Adverting to two drawings published in my 'Antiquities of Orissa,' the learned Professor says: "looking at his plates, we have a distinct suggestion of Greek art; for example, in the two fountain nymphs in plate XVI, No. 46; while the Bayadere in plate XVIII, No. 59, from the temple of Bhuvaneśvara, middle of the seventh century (p. 31), seems to be resting her right hand on a dolphin, beside which a Cupid (?) is crouching, and might therefore very well be an imitation of some representation of Venus." (*a*) As regards the first picture, which is that of a pediment, I cannot conceive how the nymphs have been associated with

(*a*) The History of Indian Literature, p. 274.

a fountain. Their figures are remarkably well sculptured, and they are nudes; and in so far they may be called Greek or Roman or modern European. But the question at issue is are they really so? and the learned orientalist begs it by suggesting that they must be so, because they are nudes. Doubtless to Praxiteles belongs the honor and glory of introducing the idea of nudity in Greek art; but there is nothing to show that the idea could not spontaneously arise elsewhere. On the contrary, there is a much more potent incentive to the idea in men's sensuous desires than the example of the Greeks, and it would be as reasonable to suppose that Indian love songs must owe their origin to the odes of Sapho as to believe that the idea of nudity must presuppose a Greek paternity.

The second instance is even more unsatisfactory. In it there is a draped female, a dancing girl, with the right leg a little raised, and having the right hand stretched down and coquettishly taking up one end of her uḍhṇá or scarf which has fallen off her right shoulder, the other end being shown *in situ* on the left shoulder. The attitude is that of dancing, and no one, European or Indian, who has once seen a nautch can mistake it. The supposed 'dolphin' is the wavy fallen end of the cloth. In front of it there is a boy seated dog-like with his haunches raised and bearing a huge turban on his head, and that is Professer Weber's turbaned Cupid crouching on his haunches. The female may be likened to a Venus in the same way as every sparingly draped female in a dancing attitude may be so compared; but the attitude, unquestionably graceful as it is, has not an iota of peculiarity in it which could not be produced without imitating Greek art.

Those who can carve and develop the human form in stone can have no difficulty in producing a mother nursing a child, or a reclining nude female, or a dancing girl, from the living models around him; and a borrowing theory in such a case is the merest assumption: and however numerous such assumptions, the chain produced is not stronger than its weakest link. Like the novelist's chain of circumstantial evidence, conjured up to excite a thrilling interest in the reader, but destined to crumble down by the first touch of truth, such assumptions, founded on the merest coincidences, can result in no ultimate good. While the spell lasts they may amuse, but cannot edify; and as bearing upon sober facts they are false analogies, calculated to mislead unwary readers and to sap the foundations of true history.

CHAPTER V.

INSCRIPTIONS.

PAUCITY OF INSCRIPTIONS AT BUDDHA GAYÁ AND IN INDIA GENERALLY—ITS CAUSES—INSCRIPTIONS IN THE LÁṬ CHARACTER—INTERPRETATION OF THE WORD "DÁNA"—GUPTA INSCRIPTIONS ON COPINGS—GUPTA INSCRIPTION ON A STATUE—INSCRIPTION ON AN IMAGE OF A BULL—INSCRIPTION ON A SLAB IN THE INDIAN MUSEUM—KUṬILA INSCRIPTIONS ON STATUES—INSCRIPTION ON A SLAB OF SANDSTONE—INSCRIPTION ON THE BUDDHAPAD—WILKINS' INSCRIPTION—OLD BURMESE INSCRIPTION OF 1305—BURMESE INSCRIPTION IN THE BÁRADWÁRI TEMPLE—BURMESE INSCRIPTION ON A STÚPA—BURMESE INSCRIPTION ON A STATUETTE OF ŚIVA-PÁRVATÍ.

For a place of such remote antiquity as Buddha Gayá, which was the earliest seat of Buddhism, which has been held the most sacred on earth for nearly five and twenty centuries, which was enriched by the largest number of monuments ever dedicated in any Buddhist place of pilgrimage, the number of ancient inscriptions hitherto discovered there is exceedingly small. Of the thirty-nine monuments noticed by Hiouen Thsang there is not a single lapidary record extant; nor is there any of those which the pilgrim saw, but could not, on account of their number, describe in detail. And even of the few inscriptions that have been found by antiquarians, none belongs to any of the larger monuments, nor were they intended to record the erection or the dedication of those structures. On the whole, they are not only few in number, but of comparatively little interest.

Nor is this paucity of inscriptions confined to Buddha Gayá alone. It is equally observable in most other ancient seats of religion or of political greatness in India. Certain it is that as yet not a single stone has been met with which is a record of the dedication of any of the great stúpas of Sánchí, Baráhat, Mathurá, and Amarávatí. The larger ancient temples still extant, either Buddhist or Hindu, are equally deficient in this respect. Nor can this absence be always attributed to sectarian animosity; for that animosity, to be effectual, should have raised its hands against the structures themselves, and not against little slabs which recorded their dedication. Doubtless often were those hands so raised, and most ruthlessly too; but where the structure itself was spared, there is no reason to suppose that the inscribed stones were subjected to them. This paucity of inscriptions would suggest the idea that with the downfall of Buddhism and the destruction of its sacred fanes all records of its rise and progress were systematically destroyed, and every trace of its history was either swept away or so mystified as to be illegible; or it might be that the practice of putting up memorial stones on the face of religious edifices was not common: people who dedicated them depended upon the edifices themselves to perpetuate their fame, and sought not the secondary aid of inscribed tablets. The case was different with memorial pillars; their avowed object was to record noble deeds, and they could not well dispense with inscriptions. It was likewise different in regard to repairs, or to small or moderate gifts made in sacred places, as they generally comprised clothes, metal utensils, and cash, which soon disappeared, and the memory of them could only be preserved by records made in some prominent place or other in a sacred fane. But what with sectarian jealousy, iconoclastic zeal, the ruthless hand of time, and the utilitarian propensity of unthinking people, employing dressed slabs of inscriptions and fragments of inscribed columns to domestic use, sometimes converting them into curry-stones, or hatchet-grinders, or supports for door-hinges, or street-rollers, ancient lapidary records have rapidly disappeared; and the loss is irreparable.

The following is a summary of all the inscriptions that have hitherto been discovered at Buddha Gayá:—

Inscription on a rail pillar. No. 1.

The oldest inscription found at Buddha Gayá is a short record of three words in the *Láṭ* character, which was current in the second, the third, and the fourth centuries before Christ. It occurs on a rail pillar, just below the upper disc, on its front. (Plate XLVIII, fig. 1.) Major Markham Kittoe was the first to notice it (a), and his reading, which has since been confirmed by General Cunningham, is

Ayaye Kuragiye dánam.

The first word is an irregular form of the masculine dative singular of *idam*. The proper form is *asmai*—'to him.' It has been met with so frequently and

(a) Journal, Asiatic Society, Vol. XVI, Part I, p. 339.

explained so often that there can be no mistake about its import. The second word is also in the dative singular, though the form is irregular. It is either a proper name, or an epithet used for a proper name. Its radical form is *kuragi*, but we know of no Buddhist notability who had such a name. General Cunningham takes it to be an epithet formed of the word *kuḍa*, which, he says, means "boiled rice." This word does not occur in any Sanskrit dictionary. It is probable the General had in his mind the word *kuru*, which means boiled rice, and took the former to be a corruption of the latter. As in the old *Láṭ* character the vowel marks were never much cared for, we may, without any violence, assume the right reading to be *kuru*. The *gi* which follows must under this supposition be accepted as an abraided remnant of *gila*, 'the swallower,' from the root *gai*, 'to swallow.' The compound word would thus mean "the eater of boiled rice," referring to the dish of rice-milk which was given by the village maiden Sujátá to Buddha after his six years' penance. We must further assume that the epithet was given to Buddha, and was in such extensive use at one time as to pass for Buddha, though it is not to be met with in any Sanskrit-Buddhist text of Nepal. Anyhow, the meaning of the record can be either "gift to (the person named) Kurugi," or "gift to the eater of boiled rice."

The pronoun 'him,' being in the same case with *kurugi*, can only refer to it, and not to the object on which it is inscribed; consequently we have no information given as to the donor, nor of the nature of the article presented by him to the holy *kurugi*.

Inscription on a rail pillar. No. 2.

This, like the last, is in the ancient Láṭ character, and occurs on a rail pillar. It was first noticed by General Cunningham, who found it to comprise thirteen letters, of which the 5th, 6th, 8th, 9th, 10th, and 11th, were illegible. It runs thus—

Patihara - - ná - - - - dánam.

The case-mark being lost, it is difficult to say whether the first word stands for the donor or the donee. The last word, *dána*, 'gift,' leaves no doubt about the real character of the monument. It is a record of some gift to the temple or some person connected with it.

We are indebted to General Cunningham also for the third record. It, like the two preceding, is in the Láṭ character; but it occurs on the lower edge of a sandstone rail, and not on a pillar. It reads as follows:—

Inscription on a rail bar. No. 3.

Bodhirakshitasa Tabapanakasa dánam.

It may be rendered into "gift of Bodhirakshita of Tabapanaka." The use of the letter 'b' for 'p' is not extraordinary in the Láṭ character, and the last word may be read "Tapabanaka," or Ceylon; but if this be inadmissible, the word must be taken to be the name of some now-unknown place.

In none of these three records is the nature of the objects presented at all defined. But it is obvious, from the fact of there being more than one donor, each commemorating his gift in a separate record, inscribed apart from that of others, that none of them meant the entire railing. The question then arises—did each donor refer to the individual bar or pillar on which the record appears to be his gift? or to some gift made to the temple or to the Bodhi Tree unconnected with the railing? The subject is one of great importance as relating to the dates of many important ancient monuments of India, and a careful consideration of it is necessary. It attracted my attention in 1870, when, adverting to some donative inscriptions from Mathurá, I said:—'The inscriptions on the pillars are likewise records of gifts to the monastery, and in language, style, and grammar differ not in the least from similar records at Sánchí and other Buddhist sanctuaries. The shortest inscriptions of this class simply say—'The gift of so-and-so;' others add the purpose for which the gift is made, being the spiritual good of one's own self, or that of his parents, or of mankind at large, and the more elaborate include the date of the gift, the name of the monastery, and perhaps the name of the reigning sovereign. The nature of the gift is sometimes mentioned, but not often; and the question may be raised as to whether, in the case of inscriptions recording gifts (*dána*) without specifying their nature, they are to be taken as mere records of gifts, or of the gift of the objects on which they occur. General Cunningham is in favour of the latter branch of the alternative, and is of opinion that the things on which donative inscriptions occur are themselves the objects of those inscriptions. There is generally, however, no pronoun of any kind in such inscriptions to fix a meaning, and it often happens that a single bar of a railing records two or three or more gifts of different dates, each in the usual form of 'gift of so-and-so'—*amukasya dánam.* Of the two inscriptions given on plate V (No. V), that on the torus records the gift of some Dása, the son of Vasumihira, while the one on the plinth gives the name of Visvasika Vikramahára, son of Siñha. They cannot possibly be intended to record the gift of the pillar, but of some gift in money or other article to the shrine. Had the object been the joint gift of two or more persons, their names would have been given, not in separate inscriptions, but in one record, as is the case in many inscriptions which have come under notice. I am disposed to think, therefore, that the *dána* inscriptions were designed partly by wily, covetous priests, who, for a consideration, dispensed sanctity to ordinary mortal names by recording them on sacred edifices, and partly by a desire to buy celebrity or immortality at a cheap cost by having one's name recorded on buildings frequented by millions, and which were supposed to last to all but eternity—a counterpart of that feeling which makes the modern tourists scribble their names under the dome of St. Peter.'

This opinion apparently did not meet with the approval of General Cunningham, who, in accounting for the different sizes and materials of the pillars and bars of the Buddha Gayá railing, says " they must be due to the different donors, one giving his order to some local masons for granite pillars, another gave his order to the masons of a distant sandstone quarry." (*a*) Professor Dowson is more positive on the subject. Adverting to my remarks on the Mathurá inscriptions, he says :—" The Bábu, while stating the inscriptions on the pillars to be records of gifts, raises the question whether, in the case of inscriptions recording gifts (*dána*) without specifying their nature, they are to be taken as mere records of gifts, or of the gift of the objects on which they occur. He then notices the inscription No. 12, in which the inscription on the base says 'gift of so-and-so,' and that on the plinth 'gift of some one else.' A single railing bearing records of several gifts of different dates has never come under my notice; (*b*) but dealing

(*a*) Arch. Surv. Report, Vol. III p. 90.

(*b*) If we change the words 'a single railing' into 'a single bar,' the architraves and pillars of the Sánchi gates will afford several instances.—*See* Cunningham's 'Bhilsa Topes,' Chapter XVI.

with the inscriptions before us, there seems to be no reason why two persons, naturally or spiritually related might not agree to contribute separate parts of a column. The Bábu's reading of this short inscription is rather different from mine. I find that the two donors are connected by a common patronymic, Vasumihira. What can the words 'gift of,' inscribed upon a pillar or anything else, mean, unless it be that the object so inscribed is the thing given? If we find a stained window inscribed 'gift of,' do we understand that something else was given, not the window? It might have been convenient to make records of gifts on pillars, railings, or other conspicuous objects; but unless the object inscribed were the one presented, some mention would undoubtedly have been made of what the gift really was. The earliest researches of Prinsep showed the gift of a pillar to be a favourite act of Buddhist devotion, and two of these inscriptions (1 and 23) distinctly state the base of the pillar to have been the donation. The Bábu seems not to have been aware that the word *kumbha*, or *kumbhaka*, has 'base of pillar' among its other meanings; and so in inscription No. 1 he has read *kumbhaka* 25 (base of pillar 25) as *kumbhaka sanjna*, which he translates 'breath suspended,' and applies it as an epithet to the donor."(a)

As an *à priori* one, the argument of the learned Professor, though not logically perfect, is apparently a good one; but with every deference to the opinion of so thorough a scholar, I cannot help thinking that facts lean a great deal on the other side. There is nothing certainly in two persons "naturally or spiritually related" jointly dedicating a single object; and instances are not wanting in which two or more persons have done so. In No. 23 of Professor Dowson's Mathurá inscriptions several mendicants, some disciples of Súrya, some of Buddharakshita, and others of the sect of Prahánikas, all jointly make a gift. But in such cases the record is one, and in it the names of the donors are set forth in detail. There is no reason why, under such circumstances, there should be separate records in different languages and in different parts of the same article to express a joint donation, as in inscription No. 12, to which the learned gentleman refers. The article in question is a single block of sandstone of which the lower part 23″ × 23″ × 5″ forms the base-tile or plinth, and above it another five inches the torus, and thereupon two and a half inches of the

(a) Journal, Royal Asiatic Society, N. S., V, pp. 191-2.

lower end of a column which was 16 inches in diameter. Now the base-tile has one inscription, and the torus carved over it, but without being separate from it, has another. The whole block carved could not have cost more than a rupee; the base-tile, had it been separate, would be worth in the present day, when money is cheap, not more than threepence. Professor Dowson has not given a *fac-simile* of No. 12; but in the one published by me (which was prepared by General Cunningham) the letter [illegible] in the lower inscription has a mark under it (*a*), and the letter following is illegible, whereas in the upper one the letters are [illegible] and [illegible], showing that the patronymic in the former is different. It is true that in the old Láṭ character the vowel marks were frequently omitted, but no marks were put where none was wanted, and so, instead of Vasu, we should read Buddha or Buddhamihira, or something else. This, however, is immaterial, for I go further than the Professor in thinking that there is no necessity for any "natural or spiritual" relationship between two or more donors. Even as in the present day men of different castes and nationalities join in erecting a single monument, so did men in former times. Admitting, therefore, the Professor's reading to be correct, I cannot help asking—"did the donor of the plinth or base-tile record his contribution of threepence to the cost-price of the entire block, or the gift of the lower portion of it? If he did the latter he paid more for the record than for the gift. When a donor's name occurs on a stained window, it is usual, I admit, to accept the whole of the window to be the subject of the gift; but a similar record "to the memory of so-and-so" over the main entrance of a building or mausoleum applies to the whole structure, and not solely to the doorway. Remove the record to the inner wall of a public building or a church, it ceases to imply the church, or the wall, or even the slab on which it occurs, and means that the record itself is the memorial. The argument, therefore, is by no means conclusive.

(*a*) The readings given by Professor Dowson are not always borne out by the originals now in the Indian Museum, nor are the translations always warranted by the texts. A remarkable instance of this occurs in inscription No. 1, in which the *fac-simile* has *Sarvasatta hita sukham*. The reading given by the Professor is *Sarva hita sukham*, omitting the word *satta*, and the translation "May it be to the benefit, welfare, and happiness of all" invokes three blessings, whereas *hita* and *sukha* of the text can only imply two blessings: the third is evidently a flourish to round off the translation. This is, however, not the place to notice these readings, and I advert to one instance only to guard against too implicit a reliance on the interpretations.

Accepting, however, the sense in which the learned Professor has put forth the argument to be correct, we cannot apply it to the case under notice, for even as the window is an entity, so is the pillar; and as in the case of the window the inscription is not limited to the single mullion on which it is written, so in the case of the pillar we cannot limit it to the torus or the base-tile. Again, at Sánchí, there are inscriptions on the gateways which General Cunningham describes as the "later inscriptions." These occur along with old ones, and one of them is of the time of Śatakarṇi, whose reign extended from the year 19 to 37 of the Christian era. "It is carved on the bas-relief of a tope in the middle of the upper architrave of the south gateway."(a) Its difference in age from the others is nearly 300 years; and, if the opinion of the Professor be accepted, it must follow that either the bas-relief of the tope on the upper architrave, or the architrave itself, was made and put up about three centuries after the rest of the gateway had been erected. Several other bars have similar "later inscriptions;" and we must, in justice to the theory, believe that originally there were gaps in the construction of the gateway and in the railing which were filled up centuries afterwards. Such a conclusion would be simply absurd, and the only way to get over it is to believe that the later records refer to other gifts than those of the constituents of the gateway or of the railings. In the Baráhat railing, now in the Indian Museum, almost every pillar and every separate rail has the name of a donor, but the copings none; so we must, in obdience to the principle laid down by the learned Professor, believe that every single bar of the railing came from a separate donor, but the copings, though much more elaborately carved, and therefore more costly, came for nothing. Some of the rail bars which have no inscriptions would also be placed under the same predicament. At Buddha Gayá, out of 53 pillars seen, only one has a donative inscription, and of ten or twelve bars two have similar records, and we must assume that the inscribed ones are gifts of the persons named, and the rest have come from unknown individuals. If so, we must drop the conclusion arrived at by General Cunningham, that the Buddha Gayá railing is the same which the Emperor Aśoka put up. It cannot well be the gift of the king as also of the private donors at the same time. Then there is a coping at Buddha Gayá (now

---

(a) 'Bhilsa Topes,' p. 264.

in the Indian Museum) which has a long inscription in the Gupta character of the second or the third century of the Christian era, and in its case the inference would be justifiable that the railing at the place which it occupied had no coping for five centuries after the erection of the entire structure. It might be said that this was a renewal; but in the case of plinths and the architrave at Sánchí such an argument could not be sustained. At Mathurá the number of inscribed bases is large,—about one-half of the total number seen,—and the conclusion must be that either the bases were subscribed for at once and put up, and then the donors subscribed their names each on his respective donation, some failing to do so; or that the columns were set up at different times by different individuals, and they remained in their places till some one came forward and paid for the architraves and roofing and completed the structure. The latter course would suggest itself also in the cases of Sánchí and Buddha Gayá railings. At Sánchí General Cunningham has noticed no less than three hundred donative inscriptions, and we must suppose either that donations of single stones or parts of stones came from so many persons all at once, or that the pillars and the rails were put up from time to time as they came in till the whole was completed. I cannot accept either branch of the alternative as probable. Under such circumstances the uniformity of the design could never have been preserved; nor are large monuments costing thousands or lakhs of rupees erected in this way in any other part of the earth. Besides, if we accept the former course, we must reject the evidence of No. 1 of Professor Dowson's inscription, which says the donation was máde in the *vihára* of Huvishka, the Indoschythian king, and assume the *vihára* to have been the result of private subscriptions, of which the cost of the base-tile represented the donation of one, that of the torus above it of another, that of the column over it of another, and so on with every successive column, for the *vihára* could not exist without the stylobate, the bases, and the columns.

Even in the case of inscriptions specifying the natures of the donations, the evidence is not always conclusive. In the Queen's College at Benares every archway of the verandah has round it an inscription, stating that the arch was the gift of a particular individual. I quote at foot overleaf eight such inscriptions, (a) and in each case one or two doors are assigned to the donors. But it is well known that the persons named did not each defray the cost of an arch or two in the arcade round the building, but subscribed sums of money for the college premises. Major Kittoe, the architect, accepting the Sánchí and other records to be mere records of gifts, and not of the articles on which they occur, improved upon it and produced his inscriptions. In the olden days such falsification was probably not tolerated; but unless we accept the records to mean gifts only, and not of the objects on which they occur, we shall be driven to conclusions which would be obviously forced, and not unoften absurd.

I am disposed to think also that the positions which the inscriptions under notice occupy are not such as would be usually selected for the record of inscriptions intended for the memorial of large structures. The man who put up the Sánchí gateway would have selected the most prominent place on it to record the fact. He would never have selected a nook or a corner. But inasmuch as all the inscriptions hitherto found are of the nook-and-corner description, I do not believe that we have yet come to any such record, if it ever existed; and those we have come across are of the same character which belongs to mural tablets of the modern times. When a tablet is now put "to the memory of" so-and-so, it does not imply that the church or the hall in which it is put

---

(a) Inscriptions on the archways of the Queen's College building at Benares.

मालुमदार दाऊदपुर के राव श्रीपाल सिंह ने अपने कीर्ति के लिये दोद्वार रचवाये ॥

१

राजराज बाबू कुंवर वैजनाथ चौधार। रूपचन्द सिंह के नवम रचवाये दुद्वार ॥

२

राजा पटनीमल के पुत्र नारायण दास। रचवाये दुद्वार बहु अचल कीर्ति के आस ॥

३

श्री देवकीनन्दन ठाकुरजीको अमजी पूर्वपद प्रकार सदकुमो द्वारसिंह प्रम मन राव प्रसन्नोपकारीकरोवे।

४

श्रीमत् बाबू देवकीनन्दन घोष बहादुर। बाबू राम प्रसाद सिंह रचवाये बहु द्वार ॥ संवत १८०७ ॥

५

श्री बाबू जगन्नाथदास बड़े हाकिम सिद्धित, बजापुर जिन नाम जिन रचवाए द्वार दुइ ॥

६

कुंवर जानकिदास के श्री गिरिधरदास। रचवाए दुइ दुआर बर कुलि कुंवर के पास ॥

७

राजाउदयवंत सिंह के कुल कुल पति अधिकार। राजा रघुबरदयाल जन पाचि किए दुइ दुवार ॥

up has been built to the memory of the person, nor the slab of marble on which the record is made, it being necessitated by the nature of our plastered walls not being fitted for permanent records, but the writing itself which is inscribed on the slab, or on the stones of the building, where the building is of that material, serves the memorial. And what is true of the records of the present day there is no reason to suppose was otherwise in the days of Aśoka and his successors.

Inscription on a coping. No. 4.

The next inscription occurs on the lower edge of a coping stone, now preserved in the Indian Museum. (Plate LI, fig. 1.) The stone belonged to the Aśoka railing, but the record is of a much later date, as it is inscribed in an antiquated form of the Gupta character, and cannot be earlier than the second century of the Christian era. The stone is broken at the end, and it may be suspected that the record as we now have it is wanting in some letters at the beginning. Two letters in the middle and two or three at the end are illegible, and the meaning of the record cannot be fully made out; but from what remains its purport is obvious. It is, like that of the preceding three, the commemoration of a gift to the temple; but in this instance the nature of the gift is defined. The legible letters afford the following reading:—

दीपटंका कता येषां दान × × मुनिनाचार्य्ये

The first word appears like *dvípa*, but the scroll at the foot of the first letter seems to me to be a mere flourish, and the correct reading therefore should be *dípa*. Dvipa means an 'island,' which can have nothing to do with the gift; whereas dípa, 'a lamp,' was a very appropriate article for presentation to a temple. The second word is *tankám*, a 'takká' or rupee, which in ancient times in India was equal to a śatamána, or a silver-piece of a hundred ratis, or 175 grains. The next word is *kata*, an incorrect inscription for *krita*, 'done.' The fourth is clearly the possessive pronoun of *yat*, 'for whom.' The fifth is the well known word *dána*, 'a gift.' The missing letters with the next formed the name of the donor. We have next his title in the instrumental case *munina* 'by the muni' or sage. The next word, *áchárya*, or 'teacher,' was probably in the possessive case, and corresponded with the pronoun *yeshám*. The meaning of the whole would accordingly be "By the sage——a gift was made of money or *tanká* for a lamp for the teacher who—." The record is of no importance by itself, but the character shows that the rails were resorted to many centuries after their erection for the record of a gift, which bore no relation to them, and in so far supporting the position assumed by me with reference to the meaning of the word *dána* in the first three inscriptions.

Inscription on a coping. No. 5.

The fifth is also a record in the Gupta character. It occurs inscribed on the lower edge of a coping stone of the Aśoka railing. It comprises two lines, each about six feet long, and written in a neater and apparently later style (Plate LI, fig. 2); but it is full of lacunæ, and cannot be fully translated. As far as legible, I read it thus—

१। कारितो भगवचायतन बृहद्गर्भकुटी यं माद्‌यसैविकोर्ध्वा मगतैयंपुदेयक्षकुल चक्रिय। किम रेहमुट
माद्‌भगाद्वं मारकं भगवते बुद्धाय × × रद्दावेन युक्तद्दीपः × दारिक हिर यत्तो यवकवे
रद्‌मी मार्वा च मद्दयं दुग्धद्दीपैः शुभे मबद्दानेमापरेष कारितः विकारैपि भगवते रेत्यच
२। कृपर्ता वाचय मः छिकरो वकहक सं दं मं म प्रदेय च च मं पं
× × × × च × मवीद्रू माधुरं कालोयं मद्यं वर्ष्म या प्रहृतव × चतुमतपादितं मद्देमत् वर्म्मं यकवा बुद्धौ
प्रवेव कमारंबन

The purport of the inscription apparently is to record the dedication of a sum of money to defray the cost of keeping up a lamp fed with clarified butter burning as long as the moon and the stars last, to the honor of Bhagaván Buddha. The record is so corrupt that I cannot make out whether the word *vrihadgarbha-kúti*, 'the great chamber,' refers to the chamber of the Great Temple, or to that of a separate building; probably the former is meant.

Inscription on a statue. No. 6.

The next in the order of age is a record found on the base of a statue exhumed by Major Mead from one of the cells in front of the great temple (p. 132). The statue was of basalt, and in perfect order except the head, which had been mutilated. The statue is missing now, but I saw it in 1863, and took a *fac-simile* impression of the inscription, from which the reduced copy on plate LI (fig. 3) has been produced. The original is now deposited in the library of the Asiatic Society. A reading of the record was published by me in 1864, (*a*) but it was incorrect in two or three places. The following is my revised reading:—

रद्दर्माविनरचितं कर्मेभमाद्दुकक्लिने। भवबधरमहारविजनाराय घतये।
ड (छ) दाक्षा कारवामाय बोधिमावंरत्तीयति:। बो॑िव वे (वि) यो (यो) विधिवृगतो दृमवडविमाचक:।
भवमर्थविद्वुक्रमर्यं पियोर्दंमुजनक्ष च। दमोषाब्दाबदुयंमाभाङ्गमाथभिवाविवा॥ श्री॥

(*a*) Journal, Asiatic Society, Vol. XXXIII, p. 177.

Translation.—For the lord, who is merciful to all created beings, who is the destroyer of all the nine worldly passions, and is victorious over Mára, this most beautifully-executed statue is dedicated by the pure-minded Yati and follower of Buddha's road, who is renowned as Bodhisena, an inhabitant of Dattagallah, for the emancipation from wordly trammels of his parents and relations, as also of his teachers, inhabitants of *Khavágra*.

The spelling of the name is incorrect. The cerebral sibilant is intended either for ksh (क्ष) or the dental sibilant. In the former case the name should be *Bodhikshaṇa*, and in the latter *Bodhisena*. The subject of the record is of little value; but the fact of the record being inscribed in the Gupta character of the fourth century shows that the temple in which it originally existed was of considerable antiquity.

Inscription on a bull. No. 7.

I am not aware of any inscription of the sixth or the seventh century found at Buddha Gayá. There must have been several extant; but none has yet been met with. The one that I shall next notice is that of the eighth century. It occurs on the figure of bull-couchant, which was some time ago presented to the Asiatic Society of Bengal by A. Grote, Esq., then President of the Society. The figure is an alto-rilievo, and measures about 12 inches in height, the length from the croup to the end of the neck being sixteen inches: the head is mutilated. Around the back is a string of bells, and the neck is bedecked with a variety of beaded ornaments. The inscription occurs on the back of the animal, and is in the well-known Kuṭila character. It records that the bull was consecrated in the Samvat year 781 = A.C. 725 by Śrí Suphandi Bhaṭṭáraka, son of Bhimaka-ullá, for the purpose of securing progeny. The language is simple, but, owing to mutilations, two or three words are not legible. The second figure of the date is indistinct, and the word 'Samvat' has the final consonant wanting. The practice of dedicating bulls, either alive or in effigy, to secure progeny is common enough among the Hindus, but I am not aware of its having been observed also by the Buddhists. The fact of the bull coming from Buddha Gayá would suggest the idea that it was. The evidence, however, is not satisfactory, as there is nothing in the inscription to show that it is a Buddhist record. The following is a transcript of the record:—

स संव ७८१ वैशाख वदि ८ नवम वासर × × × सम भिमक उल्लाकुतेन श्री सुफन्दिभट्टारक च (?) च (?) न मवरा × × । अपत्यहेतोः वृषभमुरस्थापितमिति ।

A *fac-simile* of the record will be found annexed to my paper on this bull, published in the Journal of the Asiatic Society, Vol. XXX.

Inscription on a black stone slab. No. 8.

In his first report on the antiquities of Buddha Gayá General Cunningham adverted to an inscription on a slab of black stone which he had seen attached to the gate of the monastery, where it served the purpose of a fulcrum for the gate-hinge. At my request the late Mahant presented it to me through Major Mead, and I have since made it over to the Asiatic Society of Bengal. Adverting to it General Cunningham says:—"Brahman malignancy has sadly mutilated this inscription by boring two large round holes in the midst of the letters to serve as a socket for the lower pivot of one-half of the gate to work in."(a) These holes, the result, correctly speaking, of indifference or want of respect for archæology, and not of "malignancy," are shown in the annexed *fac-simile* (Plate XL); they cause only small breaks in six lines. The inscription comprises twenty lines of Kuṭila character, and records the dedication of a repository for aromatics and incense, or a well-scented temple for the service of Buddha. The word used to indicate the edifice is *gandha kúṭi*—a compound of *gandha*, 'scent' or 'aromatics,' and *kúṭi*, 'a house,' an uncommon compound and susceptible of different interpretations. The letter न्ध *ndha* is so unmistakably clear that I cannot accept the word to be *garbha-kúṭi*, a 'sanctum' or 'cella,' sometimes used in Buddhist writings for a temple. The compound letter, however, may be due to a mistake of the engraver. The dedicator was a king, named Tunga, grandson of Nanda, a Rahtor prince ("of the race of Ráshṭrakúṭa"), who once took or held the fort of Manipura, which is apparently the Sanskrit form of Mainpuri. The composer of the document was a Sinhalese mendicant of the name of Jana Bhikshu. The date given is the 5th of Śrávaṇa in the 15th year of the prince's reign. The subject of the record thus is of no interest, and the date being in the reign of an unknown prince, even if the "perfumed house" to which it refers had existed would have served to throw little light on the history of Buddha Gayá. From the form of the letters I infer the record to be of the 10th century.

(a) Arch. Surv. Report, III, p. 126.

The following are transcripts and translations of the document :—

Transcript in the Deva Nâgari character.

(१) नमो बुद्धाय । आसीद्[illegible]विजयी श्रीराष्ट्रकूट[illegible]श्रीमान् इति त्रिलोकविदित[illegible] ।
[illegible] प्रवर्तेन [illegible] [illegible] विख्याचित[illegible] प्रथवित् प्राज्ञो नरेन्द्र[illegible] ।

(२) यो [illegible]नरेन्द्र[illegible]सुरेन्द्र[illegible]गामी । [illegible] विजित्य वीर: [illegible] ।

(३) [illegible] श्रीमहा[illegible] च य: । तेनापि नरेन्द्रवंश[illegible]
[illegible] सूरिभि: ।

(४) य: [illegible] (?) [illegible] इति च [illegible] ।
[illegible] तीर्थान्यव: ।

(५) [illegible] : [illegible] । [illegible] : पूर्वेण [illegible]-
[illegible] ॥

(६) [illegible] । [illegible] ।

(७) [illegible] । [illegible] प्रतीगम[illegible] । [illegible] ।
[illegible] । [illegible] ॥

(८) [illegible] । [illegible]
[illegible] ।

(९) [illegible] । [illegible]-
इति च प्रथित: [illegible] ।

(१०) [illegible] । [illegible]
[illegible] × × × × [illegible] ।

(११) [illegible] । [illegible] ।
[illegible] ।

(१२) [illegible] । [illegible]-
[illegible] ॥

(१३) [illegible] × × [illegible] । [illegible]—[illegible]-
[illegible] ।

(१४) [illegible] । [illegible]
[illegible] ।

(१५) [illegible] । [illegible]—[illegible]-
[illegible] ।

(१६) [illegible] । [illegible]—॥

(१७) [illegible] । [illegible] ॥

(१८) [illegible]—[illegible] । [illegible]
[illegible] ॥ [illegible] १५ [illegible] । [illegible]
[illegible]

Translation.

Salutation to Buddha! There lived a king, known to the three worlds by the name of Nanda. He was a descendant of the auspicious Ráshṭrakúṭa race, a conqueror of many proud kings, and the foremost among the mighty. This learned son of a king was well known for his integrity, penance, goodness, purity, wisdom, and unbounded munificence to the indigent, in which he represented the tree of desire, *kalpa briksha.* With the swiftness of the swiftest of horses he once encountered a mad elephant careering in the street, and overcame it by the lash of his whip. Impelled by noble heroism he conquered unassailable forts of powerful kings with the righteous force of his beautiful long sword. For this reason even now learned men, who can excite constant horripilation by their thrilling descriptions, recite in royal courts the glory of the fort of Manipura. He was known as the Mahibhidáraka (or the sun-gem among kings) on account of his extraordinary and unparalleled valour. For his righteous behaviour he got the glorious epithet of *Gundaloka.*

In his last days he, like a Yogi, took refuge in a retired sanctuary (Tirtha) conformably to the established rule, and died singing hymns in praise of the high merits of Buddha, which are worth singing, and which on that occasion came forth from the bottom of his heart. He has a son, who is the conqueror of his enemies, and whose splendour shines forth on all sides. He gratifies those who seek his alms, as also those who take shelter under his feet, even as the sun does the lotus. He has imbibed the essence of virtue, wealth, and desire, and his lotus feet are always worshipped by Srí, the goddess of prosperity.

He is a lion among his elephantine enemies. His flag of fame is renowned in the three worlds. He is death itself when he is angry, a tree granting all requests when pleased, a lover of elegant arts, and conversant with their application. He is inaccessible, powerful, graceful in appearance, of a fair complexion, and glorious as the moon. He is as beautiful as a well-executed painting. His fame as a graceful rider of elephants has been noised abroad everywhere. He is also an accomplished horseman, and his fame as the noblest in noble deeds shines forth among kings.

His son is distinguished by a hundred noble deeds, beautiful as Cupid (Káma) with his emotions well under control. He is, to proud, hostile kings, as the raging fire is to wood, and is in every respect true to his name, Tunga (the high). He was even as the sun to the lotus of feminine countenance, and as the soothing-rayed moon to the lily of the mind of the scholar. He is well known in the world for his wisdom in the application of the Sástra, and for his earnestness to follow what is good, and to have always an eye to virtuous deeds.

He is pure, has sufficient knowledge of time, is thoroughly acquainted with the Sástra, and an adept in the art of elephant-training, subduing wild elephants huge as mountains, like so many deer. The swarms of humming-bees, which resort to the unceasingly-flowing fluid from the temple of these elephants, perform the part of the kettle-drum of his fame.

He surpasses the ocean in depth, the Munis in quietism, the sun in splendour, the moon in beauty, the lion in prowess, Vrihaspati in polity, Karṇa in charity, and the king of the foes of the Daityas (Indra) in dalliance. As regards the purity of diction in his conversation, he is above comparison.

He firmly supports the very foundation of virtue, which is the refuge of prosperity, and which takes away the influence of Kali, the present sinful age.

He obtained untarnished fame by reciting the unrivalled and noble hymns which lead to the path of heaven. He always performs praiseworthy and hospitable rites to the Yatis, by offering them unblemished food and drink, as Mahádeva performed when the great hill was stirred by Rávaṇa. Hence the king has become pure-minded * * * takes the dust of the feet of high Brámhaṇas on his head * * * has been enriched with the jewel of good qualities, conquered the dreadful foe, lust, passed the ocean of life, and become the sole friend of the three worlds.

His sun has risen, repelling the darkness of delusion (*moha*); he is the cloud to suppress the dust of war, a Garuḍa in the work of extirpating the serpent of *dvesha* (ill-feeling) * * * has the force of the thunderbolt, capable of rending mountains asunder.

He is, to the hostile, as fierce as a lion is to a herd of elephants. His mind is animated by the roaring of the lion of asceticism (*Vairágya siñha*, an alliteration on the name of Śákya Siñha, the greatest of ascetics).

He purifies the three worlds by establishing virtuous * * is the great ocean of excellent qualities.

This lofty perfumed house (*gandhakuti*) erected by him is like unto a flight of steps to heaven * * *

He, who has taken the best of those who are prosperous on account of wealth, * * * who is prudent, beautiful as the bright autumnal moon, devoid of pride, and having by his pleasing qualities done away with the presence of the conquerable * * *

May the Muni * * * who shows the way in which there is no fear be always present, granting the wished for success to the children of this king, who is averse to vice.

On the 5th of Śrávaṇa, in the year (Samvat) of his reign 15, by Śri Jana Bhikshu, a distinguished paṇḍit (or having the title of Paṇḍitaratna), born in the island of Siñhala.

Inscription on a statue. No. 9.

On the base of the statue figured on Plate XX (fig. 3) occurs an inscription which is of a slightly later date than the last. The following is General Cunningham's account of it: "A very poor copy of it, with a drawing of the statue of Buddha, will be found in Buchanan's 'Eastern India,' Vol. I, Plate X, fig. 6. He makes four lines of the inscription, but it really consists of only three lines, of which the first is very much broken. In the first line the words *mátá pitri* show that some gift is recorded in the usual form for the benefit of the donor's 'father and mother.' The second line reads as follows :—

Parama bhaṭṭáraka parama saugata śríman Mahipála Deva pravardhamána rájye • • *daśame samvatsare* • •

"In the 10th year of the prosperous and victorious reign of the paramount king, the eminent Buddhist, the fortunate Mahipála Deva." (a)

I have only to add to this that, though in the case of the ordinary *dána* inscriptions I take the gift to be something undefined and not the receptacle of the records (p. 184), in the present instance I feel certain that the dedication refers to the statue on which it occurs. A *fac-simile* of the record has been given on Plate XXXVII (fig. 5) of volume III of the Archæological Survey Report.

Inscription on a statue. No. 10.

Of the same age with the last is an inscription on the statue figured on Plate XI. It is inscribed in two lines, each six feet long, in the Kúṭila character of a late date. Owing to the roughness of the stone and several erosions, I have not been able to read it fully. It gives the creed *ye dharma hetu*, and a brief account of the donor, Púrṇabhadra, son of Samantasa, and his ancestors; and these are all that are legible. The base of the statue being broken by projections, the inscription occurs in fragments thus :—

१। मातकशैव हथकुल: पङ्कु: ।—
२। विख्या। घर: श्रीमान् मख सुत: श्रीचर्ं: —
२। जिंव जनती हरिवक प्रतापनेमतां वाता ।। तेन चम:

१। ये धर्मा हेतुप्रभवा हेतुस्तेषां तथागतः ह्यवदत् तेषाञ्च
यो निरोध एवंवादी महा—
२। श्रमण: ।
२। श्रीमामन्तभद्राजनचक्र। श्रीपूर्णभद्रनामा प्रतापेन
चन्द्र:कीर्त्ति: ।। हाच

१। सिन्धौ दाव × गजो नकहृमव:—
अरवर विच म
२। कुछपुरन्धी चतुरवकल × उन: पुत्र: श्री
कुर्वाणबद्दन: कृपा कृ
नर चढ़ु घाम म्नोधिवासुकन म

१। छ × विहो × × श्रीमान्
२। दिवोकम श्रीत: ।। श्रीकवि चन्द्रपूरे श्रेय
२। निखरवकजाम × सिंव चन्द्रवसहुल। सुविल: ।।

Inscription on a slab of sand-stone. No. 11.

The next inscription is at least a century and a half later. It was met with by Mr. W. Hawthorne on a slab of sandstone near the Mahá Bodhi Temple, and a *fac-simile* of it is said to have been taken by Mr. Buchanan-Hamilton and deposited in the East

(a) Arch. Surv. Report, III, p. 122.

India Company's museum, labelled 113. Mr. Hawthorne's *fac-simile* was communicated to James Prinsep, who published it in the fifth volume of the Journal of the Asiatic Society of Bengal (pp. 658f). The stone has since disappeared, and I could not trace it. I am obliged, therefore, to content myself by quoting the following from Prinsep's paper on it :—

"No. 2, then, is the only one of the series which requires further observation. From my acquired experience in such matters, there was little difficulty in transcribing the whole from the *fac-simile* (lithographed on a reduced scale in plate XXX) into the modern Nágari, nor in preparing a translation with the assistance of the Society's Pandit, and of Ratna Pála, whose acquaintance with the Buddhist tenets enabled him to correct the former in several doubtful readings.

"The character may be properly designated as the Gaur alphabet, the parent of the modern Bengali form. The specimen is chronologically valuable to the investigation of the gradual alterations it has undergone, because it contains a date, Samvat 73 or 74, of an era that has been the subject of some misapprehension. Mr. Colebrooke rectified Dr. Wilkins' mistake in supposing this Sambat could refer to the era of Vikramáditya, and assumed a position for it 1,000 years more modern in connection with the Gopála or Bhupála dynasty of Gaur. The document before us corroborates this view; but by the expression "after the expiration of the reign of Laxmana Sena" it would seem that the term Samvat applied generally to whatever epoch might be mentioned in the preceding sentence. Laxmana Sena, the son of Belál Sen, who built the city of Gaur, reigned in A.D. 1116–1123, so that the date of the inscription on this supposition would be A.D. 1197, only three years prior to the destruction of the monarchy by the Musalmans. The figures, however, are unfortunately doubtful, just where their identification is of the greatest consequence. The first might be read as the Nágari I, were not the numerals of the month so clearly of the Bengali form. If counted from the foundation of Gaur in 1066, the date would fall in 1140. Were there any possibility of assuming a starting-point on satisfactory data, the day of the week, Thursday, would afford a sure test of its being correctly fixed, by the calculation of the luni-solar period elapsed, but according to the formula in my calendric tables neither of the epochs above selected will bring about such a result.

"The following is the transcript of the *fac-simile* in modern Nágari. One letter after Namo-buddháya is illegible, and the next word is consequently doubtful: Anusvara is substituted for ङ :—

[illegible]
[illegible]
[illegible]
[illegible]
[illegible]
[illegible] सं ७४ वैशाख वदि १२ गुरौ ।

Translation.

"Salutation to Buddha.—May this votive aspiration of the devoted votary to Mahávira Svámi(a) (of him who is) in holiness like the blue-bee steeped in the honeyed lotus of the foot of a divine personage, and in might like the lion triumphant over the infuriate elephant, who reigns over the royal and puissant progeny of Hulkara Bhupála, named Krishṇa Nripati and Garuḍa-náráyaṇá his inveterate antagonists—who is himself the gracious father (protector) of tributary kings—who, adorned with such might and virtues, sways the imperial sceptre over 125,000 kingdoms, well peopled with mountaineer warriors, the king of kings, the auspicious and high in dignity Aśoka Chandra Deva—(of the aforesaid Raja's) younger brother, Dasaratha Kumára, supported and maintained through the lotus of his gracious feet, his dependent treasurer, a conscientious Bodhisatwa – the light of his tribe and family, by name Sahasrapada, son of the dignified Sri Chaṭa Brahma, and grandson of Rishi Brahma, may (this his holy act) united with the virtues of his teachers and guru, his mother and father, enable to attain the fruit of immortal wisdom, salvation from passions and delusions of sublunary existence, and absorption of his soul in the Supreme Being."

"Written after the conclusion of the reign of Srimat Laxmana Sena Deva, in the year '74, on Thursday, the 12th day of the dark half of the month of Vaiśákha."

"The inversion of the sentences, and the multitude of epithets applied to each party, make it difficult for an English reader to follow the sense through such a labyrinth. In a few words it prays that some good act (probably the building or endowment of a temple) may redound to the eternal welfare of one Sahasrapada, the treasurer of Dasaratha Kumára, the younger brother of Mahárája Aśoka Chandra Deva, the reigning prince of a dynasty that had supplanted by conquest some descendants of the Bhupála family (of Gaur doubtless) by name Krishṇa and Garuḍa-náráyan. All these names and persons, I believe, are new to history: at least I find no Asoka among the successors of Belal Sen. From his assumption of such a name it may be presumed that he was of the Buddhist faith, as the invocation shows to have been the case also with his officers of state."

The Aśoka Sena here referred to was an *alias* of the prince whom the Muhammadans have named Lakshamaṇiyá, the last prince of the Sena dynasty of Bengal. (b) He is well known to the people of this country, and his name is usually given in the Bengali Almanacs as that of a sovereign of Gaur. His grandfather, Lakshmaṇa Sena, established an era which is still current among the paṇḍits of

(a) Buddha, the transcendently victorious hero. The construction of the sentence, which it is endeavoured to follow closely, will be hardly intelligible without explaining that this first epithet belongs to Sahasrapada, whose name occurs lower down—J. P.

(b) See my paper on the Sena Rájás of Bengal, Journal, Asiatic Society, XXXIV.

Tirhut. It is indicated by the letters ल सं, which are abbreviations of the words Lakshmana Samvat. In the present year it numbers 770; its initial date must therefore correspond with A.C. 1108. The prince was a strict Hindu, but we have the evidence of the Dinájpur pillar to show that in those days a prince of one religion did not scruple to employ a minister of another sect.

Inscription on the Buddhapad. No. 12.

With reference to the next inscription I have to notice—that on the Buddhapad—I quote again General Cunningham. He says:—"This inscription is very indistinct, but it occupies so important a position on the east face of the Buddhapad itself that it is necessary to bring it to prominent notice. Luckily the date of *Sake* 1230 or A.D. 1308 is very distinct."(a) A reduced *fac-simile* of the record will be seen on plate XLIII, fig. 2, taken from General Cunningham's plate. As far as I can make out from a *fac-simile* brought by me, the letters are—[illegible] १२३० [illegible] [illegible] देउल।

This might be translated into "in the Śaka year of the moon, sun, fire and cypher, (in figures) 1230, the Aśoka temple of (him who is) tender of body as Cupid, knower of every thing, and omniscient." At first sight the temple here referred to would appear to be the pavilion put over the footmarks. If so, it is annoying that there should be no mention in it of the Buddhapad itself. It would suggest the idea that the Buddhapad existed from before 1230 Śaka, and that the pavilion over it was added on the date in question. The use of the word *Aśoka deüla*, however, induces me to think that the Great Temple is meant, and that the temple was at the time attributed to Aśoka.

The symbols on the feet are, however, all Hindu (p. 125), and I take the stone to have been put up by a Hindu to convert to Hindu usage the court-yard of the great temple, even as the terrace, including the sacred Bodhi tree, had long before been by the Gayá Máhátmya devoted to purposes of Hindu worship (*ante*, p. 18). We find a glimpse of this in the inscription which we shall notice next.

Wilkins' inscription. No. 13.

The first inscription from Buddha Gayá brought to the notice of European scholars was found by Mr. Wilmot in 1785. It was 'copied from a stone' and translated by the well-known Sanskrit scholar of the last century, Sir Charles Wilkins. The translation was

(a) Arch. Surv. Report. III, p. 128.

published without any note or comment in the first volume of the 'Asiatic Researches' (pp. 284f). In the absence of a *fac-simile* it is impossible to determine in what character the original was inscribed; and in the absence of a transcript in Devanágari we cannot, from the style of its language, guess its date. As published in the 'Asiatic Researches,' the translation runs thus:—

Translation of a Sanskrit Inscription, copied from a stone at Buddha Gayá, by Mr. Wilmot, 1785, translated by Sir Charles Wilkins.

In the midst of a wild and dreadful forest, flourishing with trees of sweet-scented flowers, and abounding in fruits and roots, infested with lions and tigers, destitute of human society, and frequented by the Moonees, resided Buddha, the author of happiness, and a portion of Nārāyăn. This deity Hărēē, who is the Lord Hărēēsa, the possessor of all, appeared in this ocean of natural beings at the close of the Dvapără and beginning of the Kălēē Yōōg: he who is omnipresent and everlastingly to be contemplated, the Supreme Being, the eternal one, the divinity worthy to be adored by the most praiseworthy of mankind, appeared here with a portion of his divine nature.

Once upon a time the illustrious Amără, renowned amongst men, coming here, discovered the place of the Supreme Being, Buddha, in the great forest. The wise Amără endeavoured to render the god Buddha propitious by superior service; and he remained in the forest for the space of twelve years, feeding upon roots and fruits, and sleeping upon the bare earth; and he performed the vow of a Moonee, and was without transgression. He performed acts of severe mortification, for he was a man of infinite resolution, with a compassionate heart. One night he had a vision and heard a voice saying "name whatever boon thou wantest." Amără Deva, having heard this, was astonished, and with due reverence replied, "first give me a visitation, and then grant me such a boon." He had another dream in the night, and the voice said "How can there be an apparition in the Kălēē Yōōg? The same reward may be obtained from the sight of an image, or from the worship of an image, as may be derived from the immediate visitation of a deity." Having heard this he caused an image of the Supreme Spirit Buddha to be made, and he worshipped it according to the law with perfumes, incenses, and the like; and he thus glorified the name of that Supreme Being, the incarnation of a portion of Vishnoo; "Reverence be unto thee in the form of Buddha! Reverence be unto the Lord of the earth! Reverence be unto thee, an incarnation of the Deity and the Eternal One! Reverence be unto thee, O god, in the form of the God of Mercy, the dispeller of pain and trouble, the Lord of all things, the Deity who overcometh the sins of the Kălēē Yōōg, the guardian of the universe, the emblem of mercy towards those who serve thee—om! the possessor of all things in vital form! Thou art Brahmá, Vishnoo, and Mahesă! Thou art lord of the universe! Thou art, under the proper form of all things movable and immovable, the possessor of the whole! and thus I adore thee. Reverence be unto the bestower of salvation, and Resheekesa, the ruler of the faculties! Reverence be unto thee, Kesävä, the destroyer of the evil spirit, Keeĕĕ! O Dămordără, show me favour! Thou art he who resteth upon the face of the milky ocean, and who lieth upon the serpent Sesă,; thou art Treevikrămă, who at three strides encompassed the earth. I adore thee, who art celebrated by a thousand names, and under various forms in the shape of Buddha, the God of Mercy! Be propitious, O most high God."

Having thus worshipped the guardian of mankind, he became like one of the just. He joyfully caused a holy temple to be built of a wonderful construction, and therein were set up the divine foot of Vishnŏŏ for ever purifier of the sins of mankind, the images of the Păndoos and of the descents of Vishnŏŏ, and in like manner of Brahmá and the rest of the divinities

This place is renowned, and it is celebrated by the name of Buddha Gayá. The forefathers of him who shall perform the ceremony of the srádha at this place shall obtain salvation. The great virtue of the srádha performed here is to be found in the book called Váyoopoorănă, an epitome of which hath by me been engraved upon stone.

Vikramáditya was certainly a king renowned in the world. So in his court there were nine learned men, celebrated under the epithet of the Navaratnănee, or nine jewels; one of whom was Amără Devă, who was the king's chief counsellor, a man of great genius and profound learning, and the greatest favourite of his prince. He it certainly was who built the holy temple which destroyeth sin in a place in Jamboodweep, where, the mind being steady, it obtains its wishes, and in a place where it may obtain salvation, reputation, and enjoyment, even in the country of Bhărătă and the province of Keekătă, where the place of Buddha, purifier of the sinful, is renowned. A crime of a hundredfold shall undoubtedly be expiated from a sight thereof, of a thousandfold from a touch thereof, of a hundred-thousandfold from worshipping thereof. But where is the use of saying so much of the great virtues of this place? even the hosts of heaven worship with joyful service both day and night.

That it may be known to learned men that he verily erected the house of Buddha, I have recorded, upon a stone, the authority of the place, as a self-evident testimony, on Friday, the fourth day of the new moon in the month of Mádhoo, when in the seventh or mansion of Gánisa, and in the year of the era of Vikramáditya 1005.

Dr. Buchanan-Hamilton visited Buddha Gayá in 1805, but could not trace the stone which contained the above inscription; and, judging from the character of the record, he came to the conclusion that it was a forgery. In his report of a survey of South Behar, he says—"I have no doubt * * * that this inscription is modern, and was composed by some person of the sect of Vishṇu, and has been erected to account for the continuance of the worship paid at this place to the *pippali tree*, which, in compliance with ancient superstition, has been ordered in the

Gayá Máhátmya. I presume that it is on some such authority as this that certain persons have imagined the followers of the Buddha to be a branch of the sect of Vishṇu. The inscription in question has probably been removed by the person who transmitted a copy to the 'Asiatic Researches,' as I met with none such." (*a*)

Adverting to the inscription in 1864, I remarked—'The writer of the record leaves his readers entirely in the dark as to who he was; he does not even deign to give his name, and he talks of things which happened a thousand years before him. Such testimony can have no claim to any confidence. The value of an inscription depends upon its authenticity and contemporaneousness—upon being a record of circumstances that happen in the time of the writer, who must be a trustworthy person. But here none of these conditions has been fulfilled. We have a tradition a thousand years old, if any such tradition then existed, served up by an anonymous writer on the alleged testimony of so unveracious a witness as the Váyu Puráṇa. (*b*) The tradition itself bears the stamp of fabrication on its very face. Buddha Gayá, whatever it was in the time of the writer, could not have been 'a dreadful forest,' 'infested by tigers, and destitute of human society,' in the first century before Christ, when Buddhism in India was in the zenith of its splendour, and when the place of Buddha's apotheosis was held the most sacred spot on earth. Nor could Amara Siñha, of the court of Vikrama, who was known to have been a staunch Buddhist and a clever scholar, (*c*) be so far forgetful of his religion as to glorify his god by calling him Hari, Vishṇu, Brahmá, the destroyer

---

(*a*) *Apud* 'Transactions, Royal Asiatic Society,' II, p. 43.

(*b*) There is nothing in the Puráṇa in question on the subject. The 'Gayá-Máhátmya,' a long extract from which has been given in Chapter I, does not by name refer to Buddha Gayá.

(*c*) General Cunningham calls Amárá a Bráhmana. But in the invocation at the beginning of his Dictionary the great lexicographer has given no reason to his readers to describe him as such. The invocation itself is as follows:—

यस्य ज्ञानदयासिन्धोरगाधस्यानघा गुणाः ।
सेव्यतामक्षयो धीराः स श्रिये चामृताय च ॥

"To him who is an ocean of wisdom and mercy, who is unfathomable, and whose attributes are immaculate—even to him, O intelligent men, offer ye your adorations for the sake of prosperity and immortality."

Here the deity invoked is not named; and the commentators, having tried to the utmost their ingenuity to apply the verse to most of the leading Hindu divinities, but finding it inapplicable, have one and all taken it to imply Buddha. Mallinátha, the most distinguished among the scholiasts, and the author of at least twenty different commentaries, explains the verse thus:—"O intelligent men, for the sake of 'prosperity,' *i. e.* wealth, of 'immortality' and salvation, adore Buddha, whose virtues, whose charities, whose forbearance, &c., &c." हे धीराः श्रिये धने चामृताय मोक्षाय च स बुद्धः सेव्यतां यस्य गुणाः दानशीलक्षमादय इत्यादि ।—Manuscript, Asiatic Society's Library, No. 188, p. 5.

of the demon Keshi, the deceitful Vámana who cheated the giant Bali of his dominion, or a little shepherd tied to a post with rope round his waist for stealing butter from the houses of his neighbours. Such stories belong exclusively to the Puráṇas, and can never be expected in a Buddhist writing. Then the Amara of Vikramáditya's court and author of the Dictionary was a Káyastha,(a) and his surname was Siñha. I have nowhere seen him addressed as a Deva, which title formerly belonged exclusively to Bráhmans and Kshatríyas, though of late years the rule has been considerably relaxed. The story of the dream is of course a fiction, and the statement of a temple built for Buddha having for its chief penates the image of Vishnu's feet, those of the five Páṇḍu brothers and of the several incarnations of Vishṇu, is equally so.'(b) I have seen no reason since to change this opinion. When writing the above I was under an impression that the forgery was of the date of the Buddhapad; that it had been composed with a view to give weight to the footprint which was set up under the pavilion built with the *debris* of the Aśoka railing. I am, however, now disposed to think that it is not even so old.

Its date, the era of Vikramáditya 1005 = to A.C. 949, would suggest the idea that the character used in it was the Kuṭila. If so, it is difficult to conceive how either Mr. Wilmot or Sir Charles Wilkins could read it, as the key to that alphabet had not then been discovered. It is obvious, therefore, that Mr. Wilmot must have seen an inscribed stone, which he requested a paṇḍit of the monastery

---

Raghunátha, another commentator of some eminence, says,—"O intelligent men, let that Buddha be adored,' that is by you. Here, though Buddha is not openly named, still it is evident from the epithets used that he is meant. This is called the rhetoric of *prasáda*. Thereof it has been said by Kaṇṭhábharaṇa, where the object is evident from the meaning, such a figure of speech is called *prasáda*, thus (the verse)—'Here rises the breaker of the sleep of the lotus,' without alluding to the dispersion of darkness or the assuaging of the sorrow of the Bráhmaṇí goose, evidently means the sun." यच वा हे धीराः स युष्मः सेव्यतां इत्यन्वयः [illegible] बुद्धो विशेषेण प्राक् नोक्तो इति प्रसादाख्यालङ्कारः। तदुक्तं कण्ठाभरणे। यत्र प्राकरणिक प्रसादः स्फुटः प्रतीयते इति। यथा, उदयत्ययं कमलनिद्राभञ्जनः [illegible]- [illegible] सूर्यः प्रसादादुपलभ्यते।—Asiatic Society's Manuscript, No. 443, p. 2

Náráyaṇa, another commentator, in the 'Padártha Kaumudí,' has reproduced the words quoted above without a remark. (Asiatic Society's Manuscript, No. 438, p. 1.) Ramánátha Chakravartí, after explaining the verse as applicable to Buddha, accounts for the name of Buddha not being openly given in the invocation notwithstanding the epithets used being peculiarly his, by saying—"that to conciliate those who are not Buddhist the name of Buddha has not been used." [illegible] न कृतं। (Asiatic Society's Manuscript, No. 443, p. 1, second series of pagination.) This remark has been quoted verbatim by Raghunátha Chakravartí in his commentary on the Amara Kosha. (Asiatic Society's Manuscript, No. 173, p. 1.)

(a) I have no better authority for saying this than the author of the *Káyastha Kaustubha*.

(b) Journal, Asiatic Society, XXXIII, pp. 183f.

to decipher for him, and that worthy, unable to do the needful, composed a rambling story of his own, in which he not only glorified his own religion, but worked into it references to all the leading remains of the place. the Buddhapad of the 14th century, and the Pancha Páṇḍu of the last century. The date he put in was hit upon at random. He had of course not read, and could not read, the inscription on the Buddhapad, and so he did not perceive the anachronism of referring in a document of 1005 Samvat a stone which was set up in 1230 Śaka = A.C. 1308, and he never thought that the style of the Pancha Páṇḍu temple and the sculptures deposited in it would bear any evidence against him. Hiouen Thsang has been at great pains to notice all the leading objects of adoration and respect which existed at Buddha Gayá in the middle of the 7th century; and in his account we find no notice of the footprint; and it is therefore not open to us to suppose that the Buddhapad existed in his time, and got its inscription afterwards. The stone which Mr. Wilmot referred to was probably the old Burmese one inscribed with the Burmese lapidary square character, which none there could read, and which, then lying in the compound of the great temple, must have attracted his attention, or the black stone one which was afterwards used for the support of the door-hinge. Nor is a literary imposition of the kind at all improbable. Within the last ten years I have had at least a dozen instances brought to my notice. While I am writing this I have before me an official letter, in which a paṇḍit is reported to have read the legend of an old Kanouj coin to be *Rámaráma*, of which not a syllable is to be found on the coin, the legend being *Srimad Gángeya Deva*. At the close of the last century such attempts to impose upon foreigners was greatly more common, and notable instances of it are offered by the forgeries committed by Colonel Wilford's paṇḍits.

Old Burmese inscription. No. 13.

On the east wall of the compound of the monastery there is a slab of greyish basalt, measuring 20 × 18 inches, and bearing an inscription in the Burmese lapidary character, called *Kyouktsa*, or stone-letters. These letters bear the same relation to the Burmese character in common use which the printed English does to the written English character, *i.e.* while the written form of Burmese is made up of fragments of circles variously combined, the lapidary form is made of straight lines and angles, or fragments of squares. This square form bears a close resemblance to the square Páli, and hence it has often been erroneously called Páli. Its language is Burmese of the Arakanese type. The record was first brought to public notice by James Prinsep, who published in his Journal a translation of it by Ratna Pála, a Ceylonese Páli scholar. A revised translation, prepared by Colonel Burney with the aid of Burmese Páli scholars, subsequently appeared in the 'Asiatic Researches' (vol. XX, pp. 164 *et seq.*). Commenting on the last General Cunningham says:—"The dates were read wrongly for the purpose of making the inscription tally with their own native history; for, as Colonel Burney confesses, 'if we take the two dates to be 667 and 668, the inscription cannot refer to any of the Kings of Pagán, as the capital was destroyed by the Chinese in the Burman year 646, or A.D. 1284.' Now, as the two dates of the inscription are beyond all doubt 667 and 668 (*a*), we must give up the attempt to connect the Burmese with the repair of the temple and accept the Raja of Arakan as the pious worshipper of Buddha. This is in accordance with the belief of the people of Rangoon, who told Colonel Burney that 'the form of many of the letters, as well as some of the idiomatic expressions, proved the inscription to have been put up by a native of Arakan.' This also is Sir Arthur Phayre's opinion, who says:—'The archetype of this inscription has evidently been written by an Arakanese, or the stone was engraved by an Arakanese workman, from a peculiarity in the spelling of certain words still prevailing among the Arakanese.' (Journal, Asiatic Society, 1844, p. 40). All these probabilities amount to certainty when we find that *Meng-di*, the Raja of Arakan at the date of the inscription, had entered into friendly relations with *Nga-pur-kheng* (Nasiruddin?) the Thu-ra-tan or Sultan of Bengal."(*b*) The accuracy of the translations have been questioned also with reference to some of the words used, particularly the word 'rebuilt,' which has suggested the idea of the present Great Temple being an erection of the 14th century. In order to test this I submitted the *fac-simile* I had brought with me to Mr. M. Hla Oung, an assistant in the Accountant General's Department, and a competent scholar, with a request to favour me with as literal a translaion of the text as he could prepare. His version,

(*a*) The second is actually 660, as read by Sir Arthur Phayre; but as the previous date is unquestionably 667, the second must necessarily be later. Now the figure 8 is a three-quarter circle, which a slip of the chisel or the lapse of time might easily have made into a complete circle or O.'—A. C.

(*b*) Arch. Surv. Report, Vol. III, pp. 102-103.

as well as those of his predecessors, along with Colonel Burney's transcript in modern Burmese, is printed below.

Colonel Burney's Burmese transcript.

ဘုရားသခင်သာသနာ ၂၁၈ လွန်လေပြီး သောအခါနှိက်။ဇမ္ဗူဒိပ်ကျွန်းကိုအစိုးရသောသီရိဓမ်မာသော
ကာသည့်သာမင်းကြီးစေတီရှစ်သောင်းလေးထောင်အရက်။နှိက်ဆွမ်း တော်ပုန်းပေးရာပါယာသဘတ်
ကိုအခါလေးမြင့်ပျက်၍ဖြင်သောသခင်ပင်သကျကြီး တလေသံထိုပြီတချက်ပျက်ခဲရကားသတိုမင်း
ပြုဆို့ထိုပြီတချတပျက်ခဲတုံရကား ဆင် ပြူ သခင်တရားမင်းကြီး၊ မိမိကိုယ်စား သရာသီရိဓမ္မရာဇ
ကုရုကိုစေသော်မူလတ်သောအခါ နှိက်ပါလက်သောတပည့်သားသီရိကဿပသည်၊လုပ်ဆောင်သည်
ညွှတ်၍ရှိလျှက်မလုပ်ရတဝ်ရကား။ဝရတသီသခင်ထေရ်ကိုခံဝန်ခံစေရကားပျူတသိန်းမင်းကျွ၍
လုပ်စေကာပျူသခင်ငယ်ကိုအမတ်ကြီးရထကိုအကျွင့်ပြုရကား။သက္ကရာဇ်၆၆၇ခု။ပြာသိုလဆန်း၁၀ရ
က်ငဲ့နေ့ပြုဘုံ၏။သက္ကရာဇ်၆၆၈။တန်ဆောင်မုန်းလဆန်း၈ရက်တနင်္ဂနွေနေ့ဥပသောတံခွန်ကုက္ကား
တံခွန်များ၊ကိုလည်ပူဇော်၏။ သင်ပုတ်တော်သီ။မိတောင်ကိုအကြိမ်များ၊ ခွာလျှင်ပူဇော်၏။သားသမီး
တုမှတ်၍သူငယ် ၂၁ ယောက်နှင့်ပန်၍၊ ပန်းခွက်၊ ပုဆိုးဆွဲ၊သောပဒေသာလည်ပူဇော်၏။အခါခပ်သိမ်လျှ
င်သင်ပုတ်ဝတ်မပြတ်တည်စိပ်သောကြောင်ကိုအကျွန်ုပ်ဘိုကိုယ်လေ၊ ဝယ်၍ လှူ၍ချစ်ဦပြုသော
ကောင်မှုကားနိဗ္ဗာန်ပစ္စည်အသံအပင့်ဖြစ်ချင်သတည်။အရိမေတ္တာဘုရား၊သခင်လက်ထက်လျှင်ရ
ဟန္တာဆုလိုသတည် ။ ။

Ratna Pála's translation.

"This is one of the 84,000 shrines erected by Sri Dharm Asoka, ruler of the world (Jambodwip), at the end of the 218th year of Buddha annihilation (B.C. 326) upon the holy spot in which Bhagaván (Buddha) tasted milk and honey (madhupáyasa). In lapse of time, having fallen into disrepair, it was rebuilt by a priest named Naikmahanta. Again, being ruined, it was restored by Raja Sado-mang. After a long interval it was once more demolished, when Raja Sempyu-sakhen-tara-mongi appointed his *guru* Sri-dhamma Raja-guna to superintend the building. He proceeded to the spot with his disciple, Sri Kásyapa, but they were unable to complete it, although aided in every way by the Raja. Afterwards Varadasi-naik-thera petitioned the Raja to undertake it, to which he readily assented, commissioning prince Pyutasing to the work, who again deputed the younger Pyusakheng, and his minister Ratha, to cross over and repair the sacred building. It was thus constructed a fourth time, and finished on Friday, the 10th day of *Pyadola*, in the Sakkaraj year 667 (A.D. 1305). On Sunday, the 8th of *Tachhaon-mungla*, 668 (A.D. 1306), it was consecrated with splendid ceremonies and offerings of food, perfumes, banners, and lamps, and púja of the famous ornamented tree called *calpa-vriksha*, and the poor (two ?) were treated with charity, as the Raja's own children? Thus was completed this meritorious act, which will produce eternal reward and virtuous fruits. May the founders endure in fame, enjoy the tranquillity of *Nirbhan*, and become *Arahanta* on the advent of Arya Maitri (the future Buddha)."(*a*)

Colonel Burney's translation. (*b*)

"(The temple of) Páyatha-bhat, place of (Gandama's) eating charitable offerings, (which was one) among the 84,000 temples of the great King named Theeri Dhamma Thauka, who ruled over Zaboodipa Island, subsequently to (the year) 218 of the lord god's religion, having been destroyed for a long time, the lord who repaired (it) was one Penthagoo-gyee. When afterwards (it was) again destroyed, King Thado built (it). When afterwards (it) was again destroyed, and the lord of the white elephant, the great king of righteousness, deputed (as) his representative the teacher Theeri Dhamma Pada Raja Goona, (he) was accompanied at the time by (his) disciple Theeri Kathaba. There was property to do (it), but (it) could not be done. Let the lord

Mr. M. Hla Oung's translation.

"Of the 84,000 shrines of the great king Dhamma Asoka, (*c*) who ruled over Zamboodwip Island, when 218 years had elapsed since the lord's religion came into existence, Payathabat, (*d*) a temple built on the spot where Buddha took a meal, having fallen into disrepair by lapse of time, a Penthagoogyee (*e*) repaired it. When it again fell into disrepair, king Thado (*f*) repaired it. When it again fell into disrepair, the lord of the white elephant and king of righteousness (*g*) sent, as his representative, his teacher Sri Dhamma Rajguna, who was accompanied by his disciple Kathaba Thera. Not being able to perform the work, although he had money to do it, the lord of the 100,000 Pyoos made a priest, (*h*) Wardathi, to undertake

(*a*) Journal, Asiatic Society, III, p. 214.

(*b*) Asiatic Researches, XX, pp. 164-5. The learned translator has attached to this version twenty-two elaborate and highly interesting notes, but I cannot make room for them here.

(*c*) This is, of course, Asoka of the Indian History, who, on his conversion to Buddhism, built 84,000 pagodas, 84,000 monasteries, and dug 84,000 tanks and wells. It is said that his sway extended to a portion of India extra Gangem.

(*d*) *Payathabat* (*lit.* milk-rice) is so named because Gandama took the milk and rice offering of a pious lady, Thoozata, on the spot.

(*e*) *Gyee* (*lit.* great) is applied to a person who is worthy of veneration. 'Penthagoo' is a common name for a pious layman who is zealous in the propagation of religion.

(*f*) *Thado* is a common title of the earlier kings of Pagán and Ava. It cannot be identified with any particular king of the Thado dynasty, as the Burmese history says nothing about the repair referred to here.

(*g*) After a deep consideration of all the facts, I have not the least doubt that this is no other than Aloungtsethoo of Pagán, who was an unusually enterprising king. Although the dates in the inscription may be interpreted as 667 or 467 equally with good reason, yet when we compare the history of Arakan with that of Pagán, and both of them with this inscription, no other conclusion can be arrived at than that Aloungtsethoo sent his teacher to repair the shrine, and when he could not do the work, the—

(*h*) then king of Arakan, Ming Lekyah, who might have been styled lord of the 100,000 Pyoos, because he regained his ancestral throne from usurpers through the assistance of 100,000 Pyoos and 100,000 Taliner, and who was equally a zealous Buddhist, undertook the work either of his own accord or at the request of priest Warada-thi fulfil his engagement, and let Pyoo-ta-theim-men (or chief of 100,000 Pyoos) assist, and have (it) done. Authority was given to Pyoo-thakennge and to the great officer Ratha, (and the temple) was rebuilt on Friday, the 10th day of the waning moon of Pyatho, in the year 467. On Sunday, the 8th day of the waxing moon Tazoun-mohun, in the year 468, worship was paid (to the temple) with various flags worthy to be presented. Worship was paid repeatedly with offerings of food and a thousand lights. Reward was prayed for with 21 young persons considered as our own sons and daughters, and worship was paid with a Padatha (tree), bearing flowers, cups, and clothes. In order that the duty of (making) religious offerings might continue without interruption throughout all times, purchase was made with the weight of our bodies, and bestowed (on the temple). May such good works become (our) aid (to obtain) the thing Neibban, and (we) desire the reward of becoming Rahandas (or inspired apostles) in the days of the lord god Arimadeya."

the work, and spared the lesser lord of the Pyoos (a) and prime minister, Ratha, for it. The work was commenced on Friday, the 10th of the waxing moon of the Pyatho month in the year 667, and on Sunday, the 8th of the waxing moon of Tazoungmon month in the year 668 offerings were made of pretty flags and kookahs. (b) Offerings of 1,000 thinboats (c) and 1,000 lights were repeatedly made. Offerings were also made of 21 lads (d) regarded as children of the bosom, and of a Padetha (e) tree suspended with gold and silver flowers, cups, and clothes. And in order that the meal offering (f) may be regularly observed, debtor slaves and cows were purchased and dedicated to the service. It is desired that this meritorious act may be an aid to the attainment of Nirvána, and of a reward of salvation at the time of Arimadeya Buddha."

Aloungtseethoo, in whose capital his father, Ming Beeloo, took refuge when driven from Arakan by a usurper, and whom he owed a debt of gratitude. Ming Lekyah sent—

(a) a priest, and the lesser lord of the Pyoos, who might have been either his brother or son, as well as his minister, Ratha, to repair the shrine. Hence the inscription in the Arakanese dialect, and not in the Burmese language proper.

(b) *Kookah* is a variety of religious paper streamers now in use in Burma.

(c) *Thinboat* is rice made into conical-shaped lumps, just like small pagodas.

(d) Offering of 21 lads is merely admission of them into the sacred Buddhist priesthood on probation. It is a great merit to dedicate one's own child to the service of Buddha's religion; and if other people's children are admitted, the man who causes the admission gets half the merits. It is now the usual practice in Burma to admit one's child, or, if there is no child, to get other people's children admitted into the Buddhist priesthood at great expense.

(e) *Padetha* is a tree-like structure of wood and bamboos, from the branches of which are suspended the articles offered to the priests, &c.

(f) It refers to the daily offering of eatables to pagodas and images, for the regular performance of which slaves are sometimes kept.

The dates as given in the inscription are, Mr. Oung informs me, susceptible of two readings—467 or 667 and 468 or 668, but the historical inductions of Colonel Burney, Sir Arthur Phayre, and General Cunningham leave no doubt in his mind that the alternative forms give the correct readings. The Báradwárí inscription noticed below gives, however, a new date. According to it the first date of the inscription under notice is 657. The figures are given in words as well as in figures, and there can be no mistake in the reading. The first two figures in square character are slightly different in their formation, and are, therefore, open to doubt, but neither of them bears any resemblance to what is known to have been the form of 5 in the old character. But probably those who read them in 1822 had good reasons to support their version of them.

There are, in a small temple in front of the Báradwárí in the monastery, three inscriptions, inscribed on a slab of marble mounted on two iron frames. The marble is of a bluish colour, and measures 4′ × 2′ 3″. The edges of the slab are bevelled on three sides, and left upright on the fourth side. From its make and modeled edges it is evident that the slab was intended for a chiffoneer, and must have been imported from Italy. On its front there are two inscriptions, the first in a corrupt form of the Pálí language, and the next in the Burmese. The former comprises fourteen lines in modern Nágarí, and the latter thirty-two lines in the rounded Burmese character. On the reverse there are thirty-nine lines of Burmese, but no Sanskrit. The two inscriptions on the front cover the whole surface, leaving a small margin all round. On the reverse the inscription terminates about four inches above the lower edge. The Nágarí record opens with two stanzas in corrupt Sanskrit, the rest of it being in Sanskrit words, spelt in the Pálí style, with case-marks some of which are Sanskrit, others Pálí. The work is evidently that of one who was no adept either in Sanskrit or in Pálí. Its subject-matter is the same as that of the Burmese record which follows it, and is with some difficulty intelligible to one familiar with the Sanskrit language. The Burmese is the modern vernacular of Ava. The Nágarí transcript given below has been prepared by me, and the Burmese transcription and translation by Mr. M. Hla Oung:—

The second Burmese inscription. No. 15.

Transcript of the Nágarí record.

१। [illegible]
[illegible]
[illegible]

२। द्विकायं वर्णिकाणं प्रवररालर्वमालुक्रमेण चतुविमानोग्रिवनंसको। सम्मासमीकाख्येकबुद्धाभिषयांसे। द्वाकराजेन
यमोचकासनंरा। भणितो धर्मसुवर्णकेतुधर्मधूतो। बुद्धादिरतनमये सतर्क धनिडं विहारीय च ×
रक्तदयो। सायाविवाधि। सरिरिस। परिमोन। चडेसन चैत्यादि मानामकारेय बन्धति माले

३। ति पूर्वेति चंकरोति। आरम्भमनोहरबिम्बुमधर्मसंघर्वविमानमधीदृशं मयावौविणि। चलिमसारेन युग्मयुगं
समधि × × × ×। संयति परिहुत्यति मलेरारम्भे अन्न। चमत्यहिके मते। मदुरतनकुमम्ं?।
धर्मविहने। स भारम्भः। पुरातनविम म × ×। माया देवी सुषोदनी। विमविमा × सदुक
चतु × च ×।

४। सं मद्दे तेन सुदेषिनो धर्मो संघो मासानुमापितो। दिकते हानिदोप। स बोधिमण्ड न दिकते। इति
चि पुरातनमारगनानुकूर्ष। चयं मशाधर्मराजमञ्चि करोसो विमयतो। परिसमन्तो शीतामलचन्द्र
मलराजनाथि मशाधर्मराजकाले। मसबरैरानतेषि वाविरेषि वातवेषि × औषि च।

५। मलबराजु। मशाबोधिमण्डे च मयानेरञ्जनायतीरे सुसमे भूमिभागे। समप्रतिष्ठमा प्रतिष्ठितभावं। चर्मसमक्ता-
प्रमाणेन इत्यनतविसाराद् वे प्रमेमावं। × आदी यानि करायं स्पष्टमस। सेयस। विहारं इतिच
महाशायाय अवलोकितआकारदया मानभावं। बोधिमण्डसंघरामभासमयान, परिभ्रमासोतोति।

६। म नाम सवस जम्बुद्वीपेश्वरमहाराजा कारयेनिवस विहारमानभावं। पूर्वं चतुमनसप्रमारमसकराजे सेतगजेन्द्र-
महाराजेन सं चैत्यमतिसंस्करिता धर्ममाणाय दिमम स्वामिभावं च कृता। मदेतत् वचनं चनेकतमागत-
वचनेन सं सन्दति वलेति। सभालं मदोहदेन मनुमोदयथि। मुक्तामुक्तं विदि

७। मा। चकाढकेन मनवना चर आनो महाबोधीपि विचंचवं। सविमानकाधि। सयायत कदोय विरोध
विवधिते पि। मदुरपानं संवस्मादिशमंकरच × सतो सयानुमानमुनामानायेन सद्धी पुमेषे। चदरात-
करोच मायविमारोसेय मधु प्रमानान्मयिति मानमधिकते। सम्मानिलकता।

८। मनं सुमवमहतोमं प्रदक्षिणावर्ताम्बुदपरिवारितो रवतवर्णमाणुकाधिकविवं। संरिसकनिस चले कुमिभाने।
बोधिसम्मसंघरासक मशाचमनदलत्र सकलसमलकरित सगुक्ता। माता यो × मधियन्नतिव पटिमारदेवा
महाबोधिविहुष: प्रतिमादि लक्षित् वनमानसमपले चव (च)।

९। म (स) देवि काले सबेपि चर्यसेषा सतत् सम्पुत्रा मातापायसकुमानपादकर्मविराकोटिवतलक्षणविमयता
ज्ञातसंधानं महाबलमारम मावेमा च।

१०। सातंचद्दाल सर्वदान कालवनि रचिद्द। न चाकि। समुहसे बस्ते सवसं सपुरिले। विमानसमेपि च ×
विसुमनो चमकपहेयो सुद्दीप × षो।

११। विवर्को साम संगति। वलं चतिवरिस जम्बुद्वीपरिस महाबोधिविहस रचतन विहिमा चजिमयारमायबंर।
सता चारि × चसमर्थिपिरिसकासोसो च × मधिसोचयेरा। सवार्थ अमितो महाबोधिकमि-
पूजंलु। सवा पूजेतुकामो। सिरियवरमुचमसराराजाधिराजाति। सममाताय श्रीप्रवरजमिक राजा
× × × सम

१२। वतो चलेमचेनि × प्रतिमारदक्षतदकुमदमुप्रमारममानसंघदममकराजमनाथिमपायवरराजा। पुरोहित महाराजिन्द
चयन् मशाधर्मराज मुहुमि× सं मूनिमन्दमारिकामत् सममपाराजामिवय वामरवरजानय। चमोकमत-
परिसनेपि सुद। द्विवयमवनिमलपयरहिताजमर्दे। रचनकाले

१३। क मशमाजमिसकराजे वानिकम समरदमातुलं। कविनिमरराजाकुदेन सु पार सलामसलममायेन सेनेसा निरियर
मशाराजिन्दारःता देवी मानिमाय चमपदेयिया सार्धे। महाबोधिविहुले पुदत प्रामं समनमहदेय।
दकिणोदकं यातनो। इदं महासुतिं नापिं सामा सचानं

१३। चि योर्वं रैय माणिक्य चितिवेदि। ष। ×। रव। पुष्प। पवोत। वचन। माशाकूर्वेदि कशावोदि
कपिपूर्वेदि। संघारैकमिकुंसम धजमवत्तावक्षं पि पृवत धनतमकादि। भामापीवृदीतावयवाम्रक
पाष्यकाद्दिम पि षत्रा अंपुष्पागमहादि। षघामेष्ठ रविषधि। मायत् षड्गावविहति।

१४। तथापि दवेसवरं। मिहत षघुमोदवति। इदममेकदेतिमपविषदनमज्रादामाभिमकाषकंरामोवर पुष्पदेवदारं।
मकाकेयवजमुसमाभेम पण्डितामम्बेम वर्णितं। इदं येवयरं पिटितामिम्मकामकंरावगुरुवामिवेम
पुरोहितेम मागरीवेषाय लिखितं। :॥१॥

As the above professes to be a translation of the Burmese version of which an English rendering is annexed, it is not necessary to give a translation of it here; but it contains a few words which are worthy of notice. The first is *chhadanta*, as applied to an elephant. The Burmese take it to mean a celestial elephant; but it means an elephant with six tusks—*chha* 'six' and *danta* 'tooth.' I am not aware of any species of elephant, living or fossil, which had so many tusks, and yet the manner in which it is named suggests the idea that it is, like the hippopotamus, the colossal tortoise, and the monster crane referred to above (p. 173), an instance in which the memory has been preserved by man of an animal that has become long since extinct. It can neither be a Mastodon nor an Elephas, for neither the Trilophodons and the Tetralophodons of the former, nor the Stegodons, the Luxodons, and the Enelephases of the latter genus included any animal with more than the normal two tusks. Mr. Baines, in his 'Explorations in South-West Africa' (p. 454), describes an elephant skull with nine tusks. He says:—"One of the most wonderful freaks of nature I have heard of is an elephant with nine tusks, shot about the year 1856 by this man (a native of Thatabili). It had on the right side five, and on the left four, all growing, as usual, out of the upper jaw. The pair occupying the usual place were of about thirty pounds weight each; just behind them were a pair somewhat larger, pointing downward and backward. Between these was another smaller pair, and before and behind them, in the right jaw, were two others; but in the left only one behind, all these being much smaller. I made two sketches, one of each side, in his presence; and there is no doubt of the fact, as Mr. Edwards, the partner of Chapman, bought six of the tusks: the head, unfortunately, was broken up."

I am not aware of any reason to doubt this statement; and it may be asked, is a similar abnormal animal of a former age the type of the animal referred to in the inscription? Such is, however, not likely the case, for natural monstrosities are never selected as types for celestial or adorable objects. It is more probable that we have in the word the name of the extinct hippopotamus, which had six long projecting horizontal incissor teeth. That animal was mistaken by the Hindus for an elephant, and its memory was carried to Burma. There was a hippopotamus in Burma, the Hexaprotodon Iravaticus, but the use of the Indian epithet *chhadanta* instead of the Burmese term for it would suggest the idea that the *H. Sivalensis* was the animal meant. The mistaking of a hippopotamus for an elephant in primitive times would by no means appear remarkable when in our own day we have the "sea-horse" and the "whale fish." But this is a mere conjecture, and the animal meant might have been the figment of a fancy.

The second is the word *áditya-kula*, or solar race, to which the Burmese sovereign lays claim to relationship. It makes him the descendant of an Indian prince; but the high renown of the solar line of kings was too widespread to be overlooked, and the desire of sharing a ray of the reflected glory of those sovereigns was too strong to be checked by any ethnic considerations. That the king should after that call himself a Kshatríya is not a matter of wonder. I am informed that the Burmese kings go further, and represent themselves to be of the Śákya tribe, the same in which Buddha was born, and marry their own sisters, even as the founder of the Śákya tribe is said to have done. Is it possible that herein we have the reminiscence of an Indian emigrant who carried Buddhism to Burma and became the founder of a dynasty, like unto Vijaya in Ceylon?

The next is the use of the word *śaka* for an era. The dates in three places are put both in figures and in words, and then the compound term Śakarája; thus, *Ŝhad-sata-sápta-pannase śakarája*, "in six hundred and fifty-seven of the royal era" or year. The era referred to is the current Burmese one, which was first established by the king Pup-pa-chav-ra-han in A.C. 639. It entered in the 1240th year in April last. An era called *Sasámvartha* is also named; it is in the Burmese called the era of religion, *i.e.* of Buddha's Nirváṇa. It reckoned 2365 on the 1183 of the Burmese era, or 1822 A.C. This makes the Nirváṇa to fall in the year 543 B.C.

The following is the Burmese text of the Páli version above given :—

နမော တဿ ဘဂဝတော အရဟတော သမ္မာသမ္ဗုဒ္ဓဿ ။ ။ဇယတု။ ။သဒ္ဓမ္မ။ခပ်သိမ်းကုန်သော။
သဗ္ဗ ဉေယျဓမ္မ။သဗ္ဗညု ဘုရားတို့သည်။ဗောဓိမူလ။မဟာဗောဓိပင်ရင်း၌ ။ဗုဒ္ဓိသုယသော ။ အောင်
မြင်တော်မူကုန်သကဲ့သို့။တထာ ။ ထိုအတူ ။အယံမဟီရာဇာပိ ။ ဤမင်းကြီး အသျှင်ဘုရားမင်း မြတ်သည်
လည်း ။ ဗောဓိပြသာဒတော ။ မဟာဗောဓိကို ကြည်ညိုတော်မူသောတန်ခိုးအားဖြင့် ။ ဇယတံ ။
ဇယတု ။ အောင်မြင်တော်မူစေသတည်း ။ ပဌမံ အဂ္ဂကါထာ ။ ။ဟိယျုဂ္ဂ ။တိရိကာသင့်မြတ်ငါ၏ ။
အနေကဒေသိတိ ။ဘုမ္မိတ်ဆဒ္ဒန္တဂဇရာဇသဝ္ဒါသိ ။ ဆင်ပြောင်မျိုး ရှင်ဆဒ္ဒန်ဆင်မင်း သခင်ဖြစ်တော်မူသော ။
အသံမဟာဓမ္မရာဇာ ။ဤတရားမင်းမြတ်သည် ။ အနေကာနေကာနံ ။ အများမကကုန်သော ။ အသဒိသကုလ
သမ္ဘူတာနံ ။ အသဒိသ ဘင်မင်းမျိုး၌ဖြစ်ကုန်သော ။ ခတ္တိယာနံ ။ တရားစောင့်ကုန်သော ။
သမြတ်ဓိဒ္ဓိဟာနံ ။ သမ္မာဒိဋ္ဌိဖြစ်ကုန်သော ။ ဝိဘုဝိတာ ။ မဟာအသျှပါယျအာဝီမဟာဓမ္မရာဇာ ။ ခမ
ည်းတော်ဘိုးတော်ဘေးတော်တော်အစရှိသောမင်းတရားကြီးတို့၏ ။ ဗြိုဟ်ရာဇဝံသတ္တော ကြွင်းမ
န်းမြတ်သောရာဇဝင်အစဉ်အဆက်အားဖြင့် ။ အဿမ္ဘိုဠ္ဌံ ဆွေကြီးသဝံသအား ။ ဆသမ္ဘန္တိ ခတ္တိယဝံသ
စ်ဖြစ်တော်မူ၏ ။ သဒ္ဓါဝလေါန္နနကဒဿာဂတော ဒိဝါဘာ ။ သဒ္ဓါသီလအစရှိသောကျေးဇူးသောဂု
ဏ်ကျေးဇူးအပေါင်း၏တည်ရာဖြစ်တော်မူ၏ ။ ဒါနဝ တကော် ။ လှူဒါန်းပေးကမ်းစွန့်ကြဲ ခြင်းတို့၌ ပို
က် ။ အသင့်သာယမာနသော ။ မရောင့်ရဲ နှိုင်းသောနှလုံးရှိတော်မူ၏ ။ ဓမ္မိကော ။ တရားဆိုစောင့်တော်
မူ၏ ။ ဓမ္မဂုရု ။ တရားကိုအလေးအမြတ်ပြုတော်မူ၏ ။ ဓမ္မိကကတု ။ တရားလျှင်မှန်ကင်းရှိတော်မူ၏ ။
ဓမ္မဂေဟာ ။ တရားလျှင်တံခွန်ရှိတော်မူ၏ ။ ဗုဒ္ဓါဒိရတနတ္တယ ။ ဘုရားစသော ရတနာသုံးပါး၌ ပို က် ။
ဗလဝ ။ အပြိသဒ္ဓေတံ ။ မပြတ် ။ နိစ္စပါလာပဟာရ ဂုဏ်ဒသော ။ ကြိုင်းညွတ်ရှိုင်းငြမ်း သောနှလုံးရှိ
တော်မူ၏ ။ နိုနိုပိသ္မိ ။ အထူးထူး အပြားပြားကုန်သော ။ ဥ ဂီရိကပရိဘောဂဥဒ္ဓိဏကဓေတွာနိဘာ
ဓိရိ ကာဓောဘိ ။ ပရိဘောဂဓေတီ ။ ဥဒ္ဒိဿကဓေတီသို့ကို ။ နာနာ မြကာရေန ။ အထူးထူးအပြားပြားအား
ဖြင့်၊ ဝန္ဒတိ ။ ရှိ ခိုးတော်မူ၏ ။ မာနေတိ ။ မြတ်နိုး တော်မူ၏ ။ မူဇေတိ ။ ပူဇော်တော်မူ၏ ။ သက္ကရေ
ာတိ ။ အရိုအသေပြုတော်မူ၏ ။ မာရဇ္ဇယာဂ္ဂဇပိဋ္ဌသနသဗ္ဗ ဓမ္မ ဗိဇနုဂဥ္ဇာနုဘူတံ ။ ယောင်ငါးပါးကို
အောင်မြင်ရာ ။ ကိလေသာအပေါင်းကိုဖျက်ဆီးရာ ။ တရားခပ်သိမ်းကိုသိမြင်ရာဖြစ်သော ။ မဟာဗော
ဓိပ္ပမဟာဗောဓိကိုလည်း ။ အဘိပြသာဒေန ။ အလွန် ကြည်ညိုတော်မူသဖြင့် ။ ပုနပ္ပုနံ ။ အဖန်တလဲလဲ ။
မနသိကာရတိ ။ နှလုံးသွင်းတော်မူ၏ ပိမံ သတိ ။ ချစ်ခင်းတော်မူ၏ ။ ပရိပိုဘေတိ ။ မေ မြန်း တော်မူ၏
။ ။ဟိဒိဒုဿာဒရမိ ။ ဘိုးစကားကိုချဲ့ပြီးအဲ့ ။ ကာဠလ ။ ကာလိယုဂ်၏ ။ အာဤသိ တော ။ အစမှ ။ ငဆိရော နှစ်

သည်။ဗုဒ္ဓသတ်ပဉ္စနွိကော။၂၅ရ၀ဘိုး။ဂဒေါ။ဆုံလတ်သော်။မမြဲပါ။တရားအပေါင်းတို့ကိုသိတော်မူသော။ဂေါတမဘုရား။ဂေါတမမည်တော်မူသောဘုရားသည်၆ ၀။စင်စင်။ဗဟုဝ း။ဖြစ်တော်မူလပြီ။ ။မာယာဒေဝီ။မာယာမိဘုရားတွင်ထွေးမြင်သော။သုဓောဒန။ သုဒ္ဓေါဒနမင်း၏သားဖြစ်သောဘုရားသည်။ကပိလဝတ္ထု၌။ ကပိလဝတ်အမည်ရှိသော။ပူရာ။ပြည်မှ။နိက္ခမိထွား။တောထွက်တော်မူ၏။အဇ္ဈတ္တမူလေ။ညောင်ဗုဒ္ဓိဗောပင်ရင်း၌ရိုက်။အမြတ်ပန်။အမြိုက်နိဗ္ဗာန်ကို။အဇုတ္တ။သိတော်မူလေပြီ။ ။ဧတန။ထိုသဗ္ဗညုဘုရားသည်။ သုဒေသိတော။ ကောင်းစွာဟောတော်မူသော။ဓမ္မံ၁၀။တရားတော်သည်လည်းကောင်းအသျှ။ထိုသဗ္ဗညုဘုရား၏။အနုသာသိတော။ဆုံးမတော်မူခဲ့သော။သံဃောတ၀။သံဃာတော်သည်လည်းကောင်း။ဒါနိ။ယခုအခါ။ လောကမှိထေါကန္နိက်။မိဇ္ဈတော။တင်ရှား၏။အသျှ။ ထိုသဗ္ဗညုဘုရား၏။ပူရာဏာတန္တ္က၁ဂတန္ဒ္ဓပံ။ ပူရာဏ်ကျမ်းဂန်လါသည်နှင့်လျော်စွာ။အယံမဟာဓမ္မရာဇာ။ဤ တရားမင်းမြတ်သည်။မနုသီကာရာဇင်္ဂြော။ရှလုံးသွင်းတော်မူလျက်။ဗိမင်္ဂြော။ရုံစမ်းတော်မူသည်ဖြစ်၍။ပရိပုစ္ဆင်္ဂြော။ မေးမြန်းတော်မူသည်ရှိသော်ပိတာမဟသေန္တ္ကဂအရာအဿာမိမဟာဓမ္မရာဇကာလေ။ ဘိုးတော်သခင်မင်း သခင်မင်းတရားကြီးလက်ထက်တော်၌ကို။မဇ္ဈိမဒေသင်္ဂတပါ။မဇ္ဈိမဒေသသို့သွားကုန်လာရောက်ကုန်သော။ဝါနီဇေဟိစ။ကုန်သည်ဘို့သည်လည်းကောင်း။ဖြပဗ္ဗဇိတာဟိစ။ပုဏ္ဏားတို့သည်လည်းကောင်း။ယောဂီဟိစ။ယောဂီတို့သည်လည်းကောင်း။ယထာဒိဋ္ဌံ။မြင်ခဲ့တိုင်း။ပြောဘ္ဗံ။ပြောဆိုကြသော။မဂဓရာဇ ။မဂဓရာဇ်တိုင်း၌ရိုက်။ဂယာသီသဂါမြဒေဝ။ဂယာသီသအရပ်၌ကို။နေရဉ္ဇရာနဒီ။နေရဉ္ဇရာမည်သော။နဒျာ။မြစ်၏တီရ။ကမ်းနား၌ကိုသုသာနေ။ ကောင်းစွာညီညွတ်သော ။ ဘူမိဘာဂေ။ မြေအဘို့၌ကို။နဝပြတိဘုတ္တာ ။ တောအိုးသစ်ပင်ဖြစ်၍။ဖြတိုင္ဂတဘာဝံစ။တည်သောအဖြစ်ကိုလည်းကောင်း။အဇ္ဈိဂ္ဂသာခါပြမာဏော။ပင်စည်ထက်ဝက်ကိုင်း မတက်ဝက်အဝိုင်းအချည်အား ဖြင့်။ဟဋ္ဌဂတဗိဿာ ရုမ္မေဘဘဝံစ။ အတောင်တရာမြင့်သောအဖြစ်ကိုလည်းကောင်း။ သိကာဒီပါဘိဟာရဇ္ဈ။ဘိန်း ချိုး ကျွန်သို့ခေါင်ဆုံသော၌။ဖြပေဏကာလေ။ယူသောအခါ၌ကို။ယထာဝမိဠ္ဍါနံ။ဘုရားအမိန့်တော်အားလျော်စွာ။ဒေကွိဏမဟာသာခါယ။လက်ယာကိုင်းမှတွင်။သွယောမေ၀။အလိုလိုပင်လျှင်။ဆိန္နာကာရဒိဇ္ဇမာနဘာဝံစ။ ပြတ်ရလေသောအခြင်းအရာထင်ရှားရှိသောအဖြစ်ကိုလည်းကောင်း။ဓောမိမဟာဗိဿာသံခါတဝ ဖြာသာနှဋ္ဌာနေ။ဓောမိမဟာမိုင်ဟုဆိုအပ်သော။ဝဇီရာသနပလ္လင်ရာ၌ရိုက်။ထင်ရှိမြှောသောကောနှုဘ ။ သိမြို့မြှော်သောကမည်သော။ သကာလဇမြို့ ဒီပေပိရမဟာဇရာဇ္ဈိဇမြို့ ဒီပါကျွန်ထုံးကိုအစိုးရသောမင်းကြီးသည်။ဇူတစေတီယသ၁ျ။ပြုလုပ်ခဲ့သောစေတီ၏။ မိဇ္ဈမာနဘာဝံစ။ တင်ရှားရှိ

သောအဖြစ်ကိုလည်းကောင်း။ ပုဗ္ဗေ။ ရှေးသောအခါ၌ခတသတ်ပဏ္ဏာသကရာဇေ။ သက္ကရာဇ်၆၅ရခု နှိက်။ ဝေဠိတာဒေဏ္ဍမဟာထေရာဝ။ ဆင်ဖြူရှင်မင်းကြီးသည်။ တံတေဇျ။ ထိုဘီရိမ္မာသောကမင်း တည်ခဲ့သောစေတီကို။ အဘိသံခရိတွာ။ တပန်ပြင်ဆင်ပြန်၍မရမွှသောသာရ။ မြန်မာဘာသာဖြင့်။ သေ လက္ခာရဋ္ဌပိတဘာဝံစ။ မဟာဒေဝမိနှိက်။ ကျော်စွာဘာဝံသောအဖြစ်ကိုလည်းကောင်း။ ဂြုတွာ။ ကြား ရ၍။ ဂေဟံ ဒါဒေကာ န။ ဂ်ဂါဒေဝ နှင့်။ ယမုနာဒေဒ။ ယမုနာရေသည်။ သံသရွတ်ယတော။ ရေစုန့်သကဲ့သို့။ သသမ္ဘာယတော။ ညီညွတ်သကဲ့သို့။ တဒေတတ်ဝဝန်။ ထိုသို့ပြောဆိုသောစကားသည်။ အနေကာထ ကြိဒ္ဓာတဝခုန။ များစွာသောကျမ်းဂန်လါသောစကားနှင့်။ သံသရွတ်။ ရေစုန့်၏။ သမ္ဘေဒ။ ညီညွတ် ၏။ ဒွေဘီ။ ဤသို့။ ယုတ္တာယုတ္တံ။ သင့်မသင့်ကို။ ဗိစာရေတွာ။ ဆင်ခြင်တော်မူ၍။ ဂဇ။ ထိုသို့ပြောဆို သောဒုဉ္ဇာင်ဗုဒ္ဓဟောသည်။ အဝဇ္ဇမေဝ။ မချွတ်မလွဲပင်လျှင်။ ဘဂဝတော။ သဗ္ဗညုသုရားနှင့်။ သဟာဝ တော။ ဟာက္ကဘွားဘက်ဖြစ်သော။ မဟာဗောဓိထိ။ မဟာဗောဓိပင်တည်းဟူ။ နိစ္ဆယံ။ ယုံမှါးမဲ့။ သန္နိဋ္ဌါ နံ။ သံနိဋ္ဌာန်ချခြင်းကို။ အကာသိ။ ပြုတော်မူ၏။ ။ ဟိပါကဒုကာရောမိ။ ထိုးစကားကိုထင်စွာပြပြီ အုံ။ ယာဝတာဇဋ္ဌာနုဗိဌေဇနိယာပိတော။ သိခဲ့ထိုင်းသောအရပ်အသုးတို့ဖြင့်မှတ်အပ်သော။ မနုဇျ။ လူတို့နှင့်။ ဘကျွတြဲဝဏ္ဏာဗိကမ္မာ ကရဏာဝုန္နတော။ လယ် ယာစသောအမှုထုပ်ရာအရပ်တက်ယ တာ နှ ကြွမအစည်အထိုင်း။ ဥန္နတုန္နဘာဝေန။ တစတစမိုမြင့်သောအဖြစ် ဖြင့် ဇနဗိဗ္ဗေဇွဲဆျ တောင်မြင့်သော။ ခဇင္ဋိရာဇကေရိပမာဏြိဗိဌ္ဌာဒေ။ ဘဂမင်းပယ်စာ းအပြန်ကျယ်သော။ ကေဇမ ဂြုပြမာဏာနုမ္ဗိသံမှတ်ဆိတ်မှုပမာဏာလည်းရှိကုန်သော။ ထိဏာဒနံ။ မျက်တို့၏။ အဗိရုဠှ။ မဂပါက် မဒေုံချဖြစ်သော။ သမန္တာ။ တက်ခန်းကျင်မှ။ ထိဏာလတာဂဆိရုဇ္ဇဝန်ပြတိနံ။ မြက် နွယ်ချုံ သင်ပ င်ဃယ်။ သစ်ပင်ကြီးဘို့၏။ ပြဒက္ခိဏာဝဋ္ဋ ဘတိမုခပရိဝါတော။ လက်ယာရစ်ရှေ့ရှုမှလျက်။ ခြံရံအပ် သော။ ရဇတာဝဋ္ဋဝါလုဏာပိပြကိဏ္ဏော။ ငွေစကြာဘက်အဆင်ရှိ သေးသဲတို့ဖြင့်ပြိုးပြွမ်းရှိသော ဘေရိတလပိဝ။ စည်မျက်နှာကဲ့သို့။ သမညီညွတ်သော။ ဘူမိဘာဂေ။ မြေအဘို့နှိက်။ ဗောဓိမဏ္ဍသ ဘဲဝသျှ။ ဗောဓိမဏ္ဍိုင်ဟုဆိုအပ်သော။ ဝဇိရာသနပလ္လင်္ကဿ။ ဝဇိရာသနပလ္လင်၏။ အပရာယဒိသာဖစ ကပိဝ။ တဘဲပျဉ်ကဲ့သို့။ ခန္ဓ။ ပင်စည်သည်။ ဟုတွာ။ ဖြစ်၍။ မကိုးပြမိဝ။ မြတ်စိုး ကဲ့သို့။ သာခါမဏ္ဍော ဟိ။ အခက်အရွက်တို့ဖြင့်။ ပဋိမဏ္ဍိတော။ ရိ းကာ၍။ မဟာဗောဓိ။ မဟာဗောဓိပင်သည်။ ပြုတိဋ္ဌိတ တည်၏။ ။ တဿို့ပန ဝဇိရာသနပလ္လင်္က။ ထိုဝဇိရာသနပလ္လင်နှိက်ကားအနုမကြေပြိကာလေ။ အစမထ င်သင်သာရကာလအတွင်းလည်း။ အသင်ချုပ္ပါ။ မရေတွက်နှိုင်သော။ သဗ္ဗေ ဗိ။ အလုံးစုံလည်းဖြစ်ကုန် သော။ သဗ္ဗညုဗုဒ္ဓါ။ သဗ္ဗညုဘုရားတို့သည်။ အသဏာပြာဏာစဝဒုက္ခတ္ထာခုပါဒက်။ အသဏာပါဏာဝဒု

ဣဿရျာန်လျှင်အားဖြင့်ရှိသော။ဆတြွ၀ကောဏ္ဍိဂတသဟာသာဝိပဿနာဉာဏသင်္ကြတ်။ တုနုဥသန်းဖြ ဘိန်းသော။ဝိပဿနာဉာဏ်ဟုဆိုအပ်သော။မဟာဝဇိရဉာဏံ။ မဟာဝဇိရဉာဏ်ကို။ဘာဝေတွာ။ ပွါးစေ၍။ အဂ္ဂမဂ်ပဒဋ္ဌာနံသဗ္ဗညုတဉာဏံ။အရဟတ္တမဂ်လျှင်နိုးစွာသောအကြောင်းရှိသော။သဗ္ဗ ညုတဉာဏ်ကို။ပဋိလဘိ။ ရတော်မူကုန်၏။ တတာပဲ။ တတာဝေ။ ထိုသို့သဗ္ဗညုတဉာဏ် ကို။ရတော်မူခြင်းဖြစ်သောကြောင့်သာလျှင်။သော။သိဝဇိရသနပလ္လင်သည်။ကသေ့သကောင်ပဟာ၁တ္တ။ ကမ္ဘာတည်သသော်။ပြဘမ်သဘာဝဟိတော။ရှေးဦးစွာတည်သော။ကသည့်ဝိန်ရှုဂန္ထ၀။ကမ္ဘာပျက်လ သော်လည်း။ပဋ္ဋိဝိန်ရှုဂန္ထ။ရေနဲ့ဆုံးမှပျက်သော။အစလပဒေဝါ။မတုန်မလှုပ်ကြံ့ကြံ့တည်တံ့သော အရပ်ဖြစ်သော။ဤထုဝိသာရေ။၂သိန်းလေးသောင်းသောမြေကြီး၏အနှစ်ဖြစ်သော။ဗောဓိမဏ္ဍ နာမ။မဟာဗောဓိမဏ္ဍပိုင်မည်သည်။သာသထိ။၏။ ။ဧဝံ။ မျှသို့။အတိဂ္ဂရိယမဇ္ဈိရိယံ။ အလွန်အံ့ ဩဘွယ်အဖန်တလဲလဲအံ့ဩဘွယ်ရှိသော။ မဟာဗောဓိဉ္ဇိကွဲ။ မဟာဗောဓိပင်ကို။ ဧကံသတော စင်စစ်အားဖြင့်။ပိဒိတွာ။သိတော်မူ၍။ အဘိပြသာဒမာနသော။ အလွန်ကြည်ညိုသောနှလုံးရှိတော်မူ ရကား။ကာသိကံစကြဝတ္တိ။ကာသိက်စကြာဝတေးမင်းသည်။ သီရိဓမ္မာသောကော။သီရိဓမ္မာသောကမ င်းသည်။ပသေနဒီကောသလော။ ပသေနဒီကောသလမင်းသည်။ မရှုပ္ပဘုတ်သော။ ဒေဝါနံပိယတိ သာမင်းသည်။မဟာဗောဓိ။မဟာဗောဓိကို။အဘိပူဇေသုံ့ဝတော။ရွှေရှုပူဇော်ကုန်သကဲ့သို့။တတာ။ ထိုအတူ။ ပူဇယကာမော။ ပူဇော်တော်မူလိုသည်ဖြစ်၍။ သီရိပဝရသုဓမ္မမဟာရာဇာဓိရာဇာထိ။ သီရိပဝရသုဓမ္မမဟာရာဇာဓိရာဇာဟူသော။ မူလာဘာသာယ။ မူလာဘာသာဖြင့်။ ဗြိမြိဝရမ္မိကရာ ဇာရာဇာနာမလဍ္ဍနော။ ကြက်သရေရှိသောမြတ်သောတရားစောင့်သောမင်းတို့အားထိုက်တန်သော နာမံဝံဆိပ်ရှိတော်မူသော။ အနေကဒိဝိတိဘပြပဟိ။ ဆင်ဖြူများ ရှင်ဖြစ်တော်မူသော။ သရေဒကုမု ဒကုန္ဒုရုရူ။ ပြဘာသမာနဝဏ္ဏ။ ဆဒ္ဒန္တဂဇရာဇသဒိသံ။ တန်ဆောင်မုန်လဆန်းကပ်ပွင့်သောကုမုဒ္ဒရာ ကြာ ဖြူသင်းခွေပန်း တန်ဆောင်မုန်းလပြည့်လရောင်နှင့်။တူသောအဆင်းရှိသောဆဒ္ဒန်ဆင်မင်း သခင်လ ည်းဖြစ်တော်မူသော။ မဟာသမ္မဂရာဇာ။တရားမင်း မြတ်သည်။ မဟာရေဗျိဥ္ဇအဂ္ဂမဟာဓမ္မရာဇဂုရုဘိ ဓါနံ။ မဟာရေဗျိဥ္ဇအဂ္ဂမဟာဓမ္မဂုရု။ ဘွဲ့ရသော။ ဂုရောဟိတံစ။ ဂုရောဟိတ်ကိုလည်း မဟာရာဇာဓိ ဂုပသာရေသုရနှာက်။မဟာမင်းတွဲသာသေရွှေဘွဲ့ရသော။ဘုပိန္နဘွဲ့အာဒိကာဝေ။ မြေနှန်းဝန်အမ တ်ကိုလည်းကောင်း။ အနေကာဒိတပရိဇနေ့ပဟိ။ အရေမကာသောအချင်းအရင်ထိုနှင့်။သဟ။ထက္ကူ။ နှိ သဟာသာကြီးတောပဥဂန္ဓီသာသာသန၀ဂ္ဂ။သာသာနာတော်၂၃၆၅နှစ်။ ဧကေသဟာသောကာဇ တကြောဥ္တိ သကရာဇ။သက္ကရာဇ်တထောင်ရှစ်ဂဥ္ဓ။ကတ္တိကမာသ။သဒ္ဒရဋ္ဌတုယံ။ တန်ဆောင်မုန်လဆန်းတရက်။

သွဒိဒီဘရဘွဂ်ဒေဿကါနူသာရဇလဒဏ္ဍလဇမဿဂ်နှ ။ လက်နက်နိုင်ငံတော်ဖြစ်ဂသာရေနိုင်အရင်ကို
အစည်ရှိဿသာ။ရေကြောင်းကြည်းကြောင်ခရိုပြင်။ပေသေဝွာ။ဆော့ခန့်တော်မူ၍။ သိရိပဝရမဟာရော
ဖိန္ဒာရဘနာဒေဝိနာမိဏာယ ။ သိရိပဝရမဟာရာဇူနာ္ဒာရတနာဒေဝိ ။ ပဌမမြား ဘွဲ့နာမံတော်ရှိသော ။
အဂ္ဂမဟေသီရော။ဒိဘုရားမြတ်နှင့်။ သဒ္ဒိ ။ တကွ ။ ။မဟာဗောဓိမူလေမဟာဗောဓိပင်ရင်းနိုက်။ဗုဒ္ဓိ
ဃ္ဃပြတ်။ဘုရားအဖြစ်သို့ရောက်တော်မူသော။ဘဂဝန္တံ။မြတ်စွာဘုရားကို။ဥဒ္ဒိဿ။ရည်မှတ်၍ ။ ဧကတ္တိင
ဏာဒကံ။ အလှူရေစက်ကို။ ပါတေတွာ ။ သွန်း ချတော်မူလျက် ။ ဇမ္ဗုမဟာပဌ္ဌဝိ ။ ဇမ္ဗုမဟာပန္
မြေကြီးကို။သာက္ခိံကတွာ။သက်သေပြုတော်မူ၍ဝသ်မဟာဂလပျံ ပင်။အဘိုးများစွာတိုက်ကုန်သောဖ
ဒေသဏ္ဍာရောပျမာဏ်ကိုဂိမိခဲ ကြပင်။ရွှေငွေပတ္တမြားတို့ဖြင့်ဆင်းကြယ်ကုန်သော။ လာဇာခံကြ။ ဝိ
ဇပြဒ္ဓါဘာဘလခ မာဠုဒရေငွေပင်။ပေါ် ပေါ် တီးတခွန်တန်ဆောင်ထိုင်မြွတာ။ပန်းကုံးပန်းခိုင်တိုင်တို့
ဖြင့်။မဟာဗောဓိမဟာဇေတာဓိကို။ အဘိပူဇာသိ။ရှေး ရှုပူဇော်တော်မူပြီးသော။ရောဘဒိမ္ဗိ ဂုလာတွဂဏော
ထာရဏာဏ္ဍိမ္ဗိ။သင်္ဘသရေဘဲခြာစာနိုက်။နှစ်မွန်မြေးပါးလေသောသဂ္ဂတ္ထဝါအပေါင်းတို့ကယ်ဆယ်ခြင်း
အကျိုးငှါလည်မှဒီဃပဌွနံ။ ဘုရားဖြစ်လိုသောဆုပန်ခြင်ကို။ အကာသိ။ ပြုတော်မူပြီ။ မဟာဓေဝိတုပိ
တာမဟာအဿုကာပါယျအဝိနံ။မယ်တော်။ခမည်းတော်။ဘိုးတော်။ဘွားတော် ။ ဘေးတော်။ဘီတော်။အ
စရှိကုန်သော။သတ္တာနမ္ပိ။ သဂ္ဂဝါ ပေါင်းတို့အား လည်း ။ ပုည္ဇအဘ်ကုသိုလ်အဘို့ကို ။ အဒါသိ။ပေး
ဝေတော်မူပြီ။ ။နေ ရူ။မြင်းမိုရ်တောင်မင်းသည် ။ ရပိ။နေမင်းသည်။သသိ။လမင်းသည်။ယသဝတ်
ကွ သာဝ။ကမ္ဘာကုန်သည်တိုင်အောင်ပင်လျှင် ။ တိဋ္ဌတိယသတာ။တည်သိသကဲ့ဘို့။ တထာ ။ ထိုအတူ။
ရှုနံသေလက္ခရံ ။ ရှုကောင်း မှုတော်ကျောက်စာသည်။ ယာဝကပ္ပ ယာဝ ။ ကမ္ဘာကုန်သည်ကိုင်အောင်
ပင်လျှင် ။ အနူမောဒယာ။ သာဓုဂမ်ဂါခေါ်စေခြင်ငှါတိဋ္ဌတံ။တည်ပါစေ။ ထည်ပါစေသတည်း။ ။ရှုနံ
အာနုကဒ္ဓတိအပြတ်သေဒ္ဒ ဘ္ဘဏအရာအသွဲသမိမဟာဓမိ ရာဇဂြိုပုည္ဇသေလက္ခရံ ။ ဤသည်ဆင်ဖြူများ ရှင်
ဆဒ္ဒန်ဆင်မင် း သခင်မင် း ဘုရား ကြီး ဘုရား၏။ကောင်းမှုတော်ကျောက်စာကို။ မဟာဓမ္မရာဇာကြိမ္
နာဿမ ။ မဟာဓမ္မရာဇာ အမည်ရသော။ ပဏ္ဍိတာမစ္စေန ။ သုခမိန်အမတ်သည်။ ဇနိုဝါ။ ဘွဲ့စီရေး
ထားအပ်ပြီ။ ။အာဒိစ္စာဝပရိဌိဝိ ငေ့တ္တာ။ အရွှေနော ဂတဇသာဘနုဘဲ။ ဝရစတ္တ ။ ဇနဝိဂုဏ်။ ဇကာဒေဝ။ ဝယ
ကိဿရော။ ။အာဒိစ္စာ။ နေမင်း သည်။ အရွှေနော ။ ပိဋိ၏။ ဇတဇသော ။ တဆောင်မကာဘုန်းတေဇဖြင့်။
နုဘာ။ တောက်ကင်သို့။ အဘုဒ္ဓုတက်လတ်၏။ပရိဌိ ငေ့တ္တာဝ။ပတ်ပတ်လေးကျွန်းအရပ်ဝန်းသို့။ဖယ
ကိဿရော။ ပါးတွေ့ဆယ်ပါး။ မာန်အပြား ကိုးအောင်ခြင်ငှါ။ ဖွမ်းနိုင်တော်မူသော ။ ဝေဿဝိနော။ အကြင်မ
သုံးသုရှင်သည်ဇနဗုဒ္ဓိ။ ဝေနေယကြာ။ သတ္တဝါကို။ အတ္တဟိနော။ ကိုယ်တော်၏ ။ တေဇသော။တန်ခိုးဖြ

င်။ဗောဓိယာဉ်တော်။ပွင့်စလျက်။ဝရေဇ္ဇံ။ဇိဒသနာမြတ်စကားရဟတ်ကို။ ပရိသတ်တော်။ပတ်ပတ်လည်ခြံစ
တော်မူပြီ။သဘာဇိနော။သိုသုံး လူရှင်သည်။ဓမ္မရေစာသ။ ငါတို့ရွှေနန်းသခင်။ မင်းတရားအား။ဇာင်။
ဂေါင်မြင်ခြင်းကို။ဒေဘု။ပေးတော်မူစေသတည်။ ။အာဗိဒ္ဓော။ နေမင်းသည်။အဂ္ဂနော်။ဒိဓိ၏။
တေဇသာ။တန်းခိုးဖြင့်။နဘံ။ကောင်းကင်သို့အ ဖျက်၍ယျတက်လတ်၍။ ပရိသတ်တော်။ပတ်ပတ်လှည့်
တွန်း၊အရောင်ဝန်းကဲ့သို့။အယက်ရော။ရန်အပေါင်းကို။အောင်မြင်ခြင်းငါပြခွမ်းတော်မူနိုင်သော။
ဂေါဓမ္မရေစာ။အကြင်ငါသို့။ ရွှေနန်းသခင်။ ဘုရားရှင်သည်။ဇနုဋ္ဌဇံထိုင်းနိုင်ငံသူရှင်လူအပေါ
င်းကို။အဘိဘွာ။ကိုယ်တော်၏။ တေဇသာ။တန်းခိုးတော်ဖြင့်။ဝိဒေဓမဏ္ဍော။ ကွပ်ဘုမိလျက်။ ဝရေ
ဇ္ဇံ။ဓမ္မစက်အာဏာစက်၂ပါးကို။ပရိသတ်တော်။ပတ်ပတ်လည်ဇစတော်မူပြီ။သောဓမ္မရေစာ။ ထိုတရား
မင်ကြီးသည်။မဟာဇနသ။လူအပေါင်းအား။ဇယံ။အောင်မြင်ခြင်းကို။ဒေတု။ပေးတော်မူစေသတ
ည်။ ။နမောဘဂဝတောအရဟတောသမ္မာသမ္ဗုဒ္ဓဿ။ ။သင်ချလေးကိန်း။ထိန်းကမ္ဘာ
မ။ဘာဝိဝဋ္ဋ။ သံသာရန္တိက်။ဒါနစသောပါရမီအပြားတရားအပေါင်းတို့၏။ကွတ်တိပ်ရွှေမှော်။ ဥကို
င်ဆောင်သော။ဘာတမည်တင်။ သုံးလုချစ်သျင်ဘုရားရှင်သည်။ ။သာရမဏ္ဍကမ္ဘာလွှန်လေခါ
န္တိက်။ဒိပင်္ကရာ။ဗိရိယသမိကတွန်းကျူးပြလျက်။ နိယတဗျာဒိတ်။ဘိသိတ်ထားတင်။ ပန်ဆင်တော်
မူသည်မှစ၍။ဇုဋ္ဌိပုညဥ်ပါပြငါးရပ်။ဆဲ့တကာပ်ထက်။ ကောဋ္ဌာဥကသသာ။အစဥ်အဆုံးနှစ်ကျိတ်
သုံးထိ။ပြီလုံးထိပ်တက်ရွှေခွန်းတော်ဖြွက်ဆင့်ကဲ ချက်ပြီ။မဟာဗောဓိမဏ္ဍာဝိုင်ဒေဝ်။ အန်အပ်သော
ကိလေသာမှိရကား။သစ္စာလေးပါး။ တရားမုံရင့်ပွင့်တော်မူလတ်သည်ရှိသော်။ထိုလသမ္မာဒီ။ပညာ
ဘိညည်။ ပါးခြည်နက်ကိဗိမ္မပ္ပဋ္ဌိမဟာကရုဏာဟူသောအမြစ်အပင်ခက်ရှင်ဘုရားပွင့်။ မှည့်ရင့်နိုင်
ပြီး၊အမြိုက်သီးတို့ဖြင့်။သတ္တဝါသာဂရဝေနေယျထို့အား။ တရား မြိုက်ဆေးတိုက်ကျွေးတော်မူ
လျက်။ပင်ကြီးညွန့်ဟုန်။ ချမ်းရိပ်မြို့နိက်။ဒိဋ္ဌိကိန်းကြ။ ကျွတ်ပွဲမှုသတည်း။ ။ဘုရားကိုယ်ထ
င်မမြင်ရထိုက်။ မကျွတ်ထိုက်သောအကြိုက်တို၏။ သတ္တဝါတို့အခါ း နေ့ဝတ်စည်လါသာသ
နာန္တိက်။ဖိုလ်မက်တင်မေး။ ထိုက်ကုန်သေးဟု။ စလယ်ဆုမ်းဖျား။ သုံးပါးဒေသနာဝေ့တော်သာ
ဖြင့်။ကရုဏာ ရှင်ပြီး။ ဘဝက်ခုံးဆောင်။မိုးလုံးသီတင်ပိုက်ခဲ့ကျင်တည်း။ ။ရွှေခွန်းတော်
မြွက်။မှါတော်ချက်နှင့်။စည်ဆက်ခင်ကာ။သဒ္ဓရေခတ္တရာ။ပုဂံ။ မြင်စိုင်။စကိုင်း။ ပင်းယ။ဇေတနာ
ပူရ။ ရတနာသိင်္ဃ။ အမရပူရပြည်မရွှေထောင်။ ထိုင်အောင်တလျှော်။ ထော်သည်မိ း ကဲ့သို့
ဖြစ်ဥ် ၊သုနာပရန္တ။ ထိုင်းမတ်ပ်ဦး။ ဟံ့ခဲ့ဘုရားသော။ ခန့်စာူးကျောင်းနုံ့ပျံ့လတ်ရကား။ နမ္မဒါ
မြစ်ထိပ်နှစ်ထပ်နိုပ်လျက်စက်ရိပ်ခပ်တပ်။ရှင်တော်ကွင်၍ ရတနာသုံးဦး။ မျိုးလူရာဂိက်။ဇမ္ဗူဒီ

ပါသောင်းကိုက်။ ငြိးမွမ်းထိုက်သော ဤ ဂြိုဟ်ပြည်ကြီးနှိက်။ ။ကုန်းဘောင်နဂရဇေယသုမ္ဘိ၊ အေ
ဝင်ဇာတိဘက်။ ကြိဘဝနဒနနတ်နာတအာဒိကဖြစ်၍၊ ဧမြန္တိက်ဘဝါးနှင်းသွခႏႈကွဲဇာဂိုင်း။ ဟာဝိုင်း
ဗိုးဝင်း။ ချဲတွင်အာစက်ဆောင်းလက်ဝရဇ်နဲ့။ မိုးရွှေးထိနဲ့သောဘောအတော်မင်းတြားကြီး၏။ ရွှေနန်းခွယ်
နတ်။ မြစ်တော်မြတ်တမူလည်း ဖြစ်တော်မူသောသော။ ။ကုသဝတီပြည်။ မဟာသုဒဿနဘေ းဝ
လင်းဇာနဲ့သို့။ ဥပက္ခာညာဏ်ပေါ်ထွရာနဲ့ဖြင့်။ မြန်မြန်ပွါးမှု။ တရားရှုသောအခွန်ဆင်မင်းသခ
င်။ သိရိပဝရတိလောကပဏ္ဍိတမဟာဓမ္မရာဇာဓိရာဇ်ဒါ။ မည်တော်ရှိသော။ အမရပူရရွှေမြို့တော်
တည်။ ဘိုးတော်မင်းတြားကြီး၏ မြေးတော်စက္ကဝတ်မြဲပွဒတ်ထမူလည်း ဖြစ်ထသော။ သမုဒ္ဒိရာ
ကမ်းထိပ်ဆိပ်နှင့်ကကွ။ မြို့မ နိုင်ငံခရိုင်ရှိသော။ ဧဒ္ဒဝတီရှိုင်ပြည်ကြီးကို။ ရွှေလက်ဂဝတ်ဆန့်ဖြန့်း
နွယ်ဘုပွင့်။ လှမ်းတွက်လင့်၍၊ မဟာမုနိ။ ကြိနာတချုပ်ရှင်တော်မြတ်၊ သိဠိခဝတ်ကို။ အမရရွှေမြေရော
တော်စေသော။ ကြွမ်း တတ်ယေါကျာ းတန်းနိုးအားဖြင့်။ သိရိဝဟာဓမ္မာဘိဓယာသိဟသူရ။ မည်
ဂတော်ရှိသောခမည်း ကော်မြတ်စစ်မယ်တော်ချစ်တို့၏ ရွှေရင်နှစ်မြတ်ပဏိဂဓဘတ်ရပ်။ မနောခုတ်
တမူလည်း ဖြစ်ထသော။ ။ သိရိပဝရသုဓမ္မမဟာရာဇာဓိရာဇ။ မည်ဂတော်ရှိသောထရာမင်း
မြတ်သည်။ ။ဂကာဓာသတ္တရာဇ်ဘကာ ခု။ နယုန်လဆန်းခုရက်စနေနေ့အခါစကြာရထနာဒေါ်ခါဂ
ရှုံးရရှုံးစကြာဝဒေးမင်းဖြစ်။ နန္ဒရစ်ထိုကဲ့သို့။ ပြည်ပပြည်တွင်း။ လုံးရင်းပိုလ်ပြု။ ပဒုမကြာ ပွား။ ချာ
ချာပတ်ဦးမိုးမြဂ္ဂတ်ချုတ်။ အရတ်အရတ်ကျက်ကျက်တမြိုင်နက်။ ကောင်းကြီးမင်္ဂလာ ကျော်ပြာစေလျှ
က်။ ပြည်လုံးကြက်သရေ။ မြို့တောဝင်းပတ်။ နန်းလုံးနတ်ဖြစ်သော။ တောင်မိဘုရားခေါင်ကြီးနှင့်တကွမ
နောအမွှတောက်တော်မူသတည်း။ ။ရွှေတောင်တက်ပြီ။ ကြုံကြီး ဝိရိယ။ ညာဏ်သာဟဖြင့်။ ယတောခုဂ
ဏ မယတောပရာဓ။ ယတောဓမ္မသာသနာတော်နှိက်ထုံလွှပ်ခြင်းမရှိသောအစလေသဒ္ဓါ ဖြင့်။ သင်္ဂြိုဟ်က။
ပရိဘောကဥဒ္ဒိသကာ။ စည်းခိုကူထွတ်ပြာသဒ်တန်းဆောင်းကျောင်းစသော။ ပရိတဦးအပေါင်းတို့ဖြ
င့်။ ဖြိုးမြင့်အသဘာပါရမီတော်ကား။ သနုဝ္ဂီရာတက်ရန်။ သဲမှုန့်သောဓမ္မ။ မယာအလျှင်ဖြစ်သတည်း။ ထို
အခါ မဏ္ဍိမပိုက်။ ဝဏ္ဏတိုင်းခဝသာသီပြည်။ ထိုဆိပ်ဝိမင်းတို့ အရိုက်မပျက်။ နန်း ညွန့်တက်ဖြစ်သောစ
န္ဒရဂန္ဒသျှိန်။ ဓေလ်ရပဲဒ်နစဝသာမင်းတို့မှလည်း။ နတ်ပမိုဦ့အော့။ သုံးရော်ပုံရှိ။ မျိုးဘုန်းရှိတို့။ ရှိရိုးစွ
တ်ခ။ ဆက်သစေခြင်း။ တလွှားကုန်အောင်။ ပြည်တောင်တီးဆောင်းမင်းအပေါင်းတို့။ ပျပ်ဝပ်ညွှတ်ကို
င်း။ ရှိုင်းရာဖြစ်ခြင်း။ ခညာပုညာ။ ညဏ္ဍရသ္ဒီရဲရဲညီသောအားဖြင့်။ ချော်ဆိပ်ဂသာကြာ။ ကြယ်တကာ
တို့အလယ်။ လမင်းပြည့်ဝန်းထွန်းတော်ပ၏သို့ဖြစ်သတည်း။ ။ဘုန်းတော်ကြီးမြတ်။ တို့တော်ထွ
တ်ဘား။ မိုးနတ်ပလွှန်။ ဒရာဇာသို့။ ရွယ်ချွန်မင်္ဂလာ။ ဆင်စကြာကို။ ဘယ်ညာလက်ချိန်။ ငိုးဝင်းတိန်မှုဝ

ရဒိနှ်ဝန်းရစ်။ ကျွန်းလျှန်းလှစ်သျှက်။ သယ်ရွယ်တော်ဖြစ်။ ဥပရစ်ဘုန်းထူးနန်းညွှန့်ဦးက။ ကျေး၍။ လက်ပိန်လွှန်လေသည်ကား။ ။မနောပုဗ္ဗင်္ဂမာ။ မှာမနောသေဋ္ဌာ။ မနောမယာမနသာစေပသန္နေန။ ကျွန်းဟသည်ကား။ ။ဒါနံဒတွာသီလံသမာဒိယိတွာဥပေါသထကမ္မံကတွာ။ ကြေရတနာ။ ရုံထိုက်ရာဝေဘာအချိုးတရေး။ ။ဆုသို့အဘိဒိကျမ်းပါဠိနှိက်။ ရွှေလုံးတော်သိနည်းနာယိသောအားဖြင့်။ နောင်ပါမင်းဖြစ်တော်မူသောအခါ။ ဘုရား ပွင့်ရာမဟာဗောဓိမဏ္ဍိုင်အား။ ပြီးမြင့်တော်မူမည်။ မနောပဏိဓိရှိတော်မူလင့်ဦးသကား။ ဗာရာဏသီဝေသာလီစသောအနေခံမျက်နှာမြေခံမျက်နှါတရွှေး။ ရဋ္ဌာဇေဋ်ဓိ။ နေသတ္တိရှိ။ ဗရာဓိတို့။ အား။ ရှုစားဖွနည်းတော်မူလျှင်။ မျက်မြင်ကြောန်မှန်ဂသောအားဖြင့်မဏ္ဍိမဟိုက်မဂဓရာဇ်ဝိုင် ၚ ရေသဘိအရပ်နေရဋ္ဌာရာဖြစ်အနီ။ ဘဂမင်းပယ်စား။ မြေမျက်နှာတက်။ ရှေးဂပါနှောင်းပျက်။ သွားအက်တော်စဉ်။ မဟာပထဝီမြေဘိကောင်းနှစ်။ အဓိန်ဖြင်သော။ မင်္ဂလါဥကင်။ သရိက်ပြင်တက်။ အမြင့်အတောင်တရော။ အဝန်းထက်ဝက်။ ခက်မဝင်စည်တည်သောအားဖြင့်။ အရပ်တက်ဝန်းခြင်သစ်ပင်နွယ်မျက်လက်ယာရစ်ရှေးရှုမျက်နှာမူလျက်။ ဝဇိရာသနပလ္လင်တကဲ့ပြင်ကဲ့သို့ဖြစ်၍။ အလုံးစုံသောသဗ္ဗညု ဘုရားတို့။ ထိမ်မှောင်မိဆိဂကိလေသာအပေါင်းကို။ အရဟတ္တမဂ်ဉာဏ်တော်ဖြင့်။ ပယ်ဖျက်အောင်မြင်တော်မူရာ။ မဟာဗောဓိပေါ်ဓိမြတ်အား။ အေးထောင်းတော်ဒိရိမဟိသောက။ ဒေဝါနံပိယတိဿ။ ကာဘိက်စကြဝတေးမင်းတို့ကဲ့သို့။ အထွန်ကြည်ညိုစွာသော ရွှေလုံးတော်ဖြင့်။ ပြီးမြင့်ပူဇော်လိုရကား။ ရွှေငွေပတ္တမြားသုံးပါး ချယ်ဖျစ်။ နှစ်ထရျက်သောမီးတံခွန်တန်ဆောင်မြထာပန်းကုံးပန်း ခိုင်ပေါ်ပေါ်စရာသောဒေဝဓမ္မနှ်ါတပ္ပဝတ္တုအပေါင်းကိုပရိက်လှူဂခြံပြည့်စုံစေဦး၍။ ဂွနှန်း နွယ်လါမင်း ထကာဘတို့မဇ္ဈိဦရဲမဘုမြိ းသေါ ဂုဏ်ာတိဓ။ ပြအပ်သောတံခွန်ရှိရကား။ ။ဖြူသောအဆရုံးကြေညာသွားဖွဲ့ရှစ်။ နှဲ့င်းနှစ်သွေးရွှေရေးငွေရေးပိုးပရုံသွေးရွှေးရွှေးနီရောင်ကြာညိုထောင်အားဖြင့်။ တခုဇေါးဘယ်ချော်သွယ်ကြိုးရစ်နွယ်သောပတ္တမြားရှင်မျက်စိ။ ဘဝါ။ မြေလက်မြိတ်စက်ပကာတိ။ တွေးတွေးညိုချိကိုယ်လုံးဖြူလျက်။ သဂ္ဂတော်ပဉ္စဂွေးဂတွေးချိဂသော။ ဘိရိစခွ ရ။ ကပြည့်နှေ့ညး။ လအ်အခါ။ ကန္နိုရာကြာဖြူ။ သင်းခွေပန်းအဆင်းရှိသော။ နိဗ္ဗန္နပဗ္ဗယနာဂရေဇ်အချုန်ရတနာစကြာဆင်မင်း။ တခွတ်ခင်းလျက်။ ဘိရိပဝရမဟာရာဇ်ဂွာရထနာဒေဝီ။ မည်တော်ရှိသောတောင်မိဘုရားခေါင်ကြီးနှင့်တကွ။ ဘုရားသခင်သာသနာတော် ၂၃၅၆ နှစ်ရောက်ပြီး။ ကောဇာသက္ကရာဇ်ဘ၈၃ခု။ သရဝဏ်နှစ်။ ဂျဋ္ဌကာလ။ သရဒအခါ။ ။ မဟာဗောဓိမဏ္ဍိုင်နှိက်ဖွင့်တော်မူသော။ ဘုရား မြတ်စွာကိုရည်မှတ်တော်မူ၍အမှူမောဒနာ။ ကြေညာသတို့ဖြင့်။ အဟုန်မစဲ။ လှူဖွဲ့သဘင်ရင်တော်မူသည်။ ။အခုန်ဖွန်သောကိုယ်တော်အဖြင်ဖြ။ သမ္မာသမ္ဗုဒ္ဓ။ ဘုကြီးရှ၍။ ဝေနေယတို့အား။ ယောကြားကယ်ချွတ်နိုင်သော

ဘာသများစွာသိသရောလည်း။ ပါရမီဆယ်ပါးတရားအတွက်ထိုင်သိုဘော ။ ဆုတောင်းပတ္တနာတော်
နှင့်တကွ။မယ်ဘော်။ခမည်တော်။ဘိုးတော်။ဘွားတော်။ဘေးတော်မင်းတရားတို့အားလည်းအမျှဝေ
တော်မူသည်။ ။မဟာပထဝီ ဤ ါမြေကြီးကား။ငါ ဝါ သက်သေဖြစ်စေသောဟူ၍လည်းရွှေကရားဖြင့်
ရေစက်သွန်းချ၍ပိုင်တန်းတော်မူသည်။ ။ဤ ါသို့မြင်မိုရ်ရှိမိုရ်။ရပိသသီ။မိုးလုံးညီ၍သို့။ကပ်လုံး
ကမ္ဘာ။ပြောပစရာ အနန့်ရှည်စွာတည်ရာဖြစ်စေ၊အမရပူရရွှေနန်းတော်မှ။ မဟာရေဒီနွှအဂ္ဂမဟာခမ္မ
ရာဇဂုရုမည်သောပုရောဟိတ် ။ မြေနန်းတော်ဝန်မဟာမင်းလှသာဂသူဟူသောအမတ်ကို ။ အရေမကာ
သောအချင်းအရင်တို့နှင့်တကွ ။ စေခန့်တော်မူ၍မဏ္ဍိုပထိုက်မဟာဗောဓိမဏ္ဍိုင်ရှိက်။ ဤ ါကျောက်စာ
သံဒိုင်း လိုသို းမှတ်ဒိုက်တားစေရသတည်း။ ။မင်္ဂလာဗဟို။ မြလျှံညီသား။ မြင်းမှုရိုရ်တပိုင်း။
ထင်းကျွန်းမှိုင်းလျှက်။ မြန်းဘိုင်းဖူး။ လက်ယာဒုဝယ် ။ ပြောင်မြူပစ္စယာ၊ရဲး နဂနှင့်။ အမရနန်း
မြင့်၊မြူဝန်း ဖွင့်သည်။ ဆင်မင်းသခင်။ ဆဒ္ဒန်ရှင်လျှင်။ အောင်မြင်ဇုန်သည်ငါးမာန်လှည်းသား။ ဥဇည်
ချက်ချာ။ မြေဖျက်နှာတက် ။ ဝဇ္ဇရာသန။ နန်း မဉီကာင်။ သမိုက်ပြိုင်တက်။ ပလ္လင်ဘုံရွှေ။ ဇဍီဝဟာ
ကို။ဘွားငွပတ္တမြား။သုံးပါးခြယ်နှစ်။ပြောင်ပြောင်ရစ်သား။ ဒိုးပျစ်မြိုတာ။ရတနာတန်းဆောင်။ ပန်း
တောင်ပေါ်ပေါ်။ ထွင့်ဒေဘံဒိုးစွန်။ ထီးတံခွန်ဖြင့်။ သရဝဏ်နှစ်။ သတ္တရစ်ကောဇာ။ ထောင်ရာမွှဲ့ကျ
မ်း။ရှစ်ဆဲ့သုံးတွင်း။ မိုးဆုမ်းဆောင်စ။ သရဒဝယ်။ မဂဇထိုင်းမြေ ။ ဇုဂိုလ်ယုံစေ၍။ ဖြစ်တွေကြောင်း
လျှာ း ။ လှူတော်များ ကို။ မှန်ကြားမင်္ဂလာ။ မှော်ကွန်းစာဖြင့်၊ မဟာသမ်ယတ။ မဟာသိမိုရ်ပါဋ္ဌိနက်
ထွဲ။ရွှေဘွဲ့ပွင့်။ စည်သူဆင့်၍။ ရှင်ပင်မိနိတော်။ ရွှေခွန်း ခေါ်သည်။ မတ်ကျော်ကဗိမြတ်ပဏ္ဍိလျှင်။
နောင်ပြိုသာသနာ၊ကမ္ဘာရာမြေ၊တည်တွန်း ဂဝဟု။ ကြက်သရေသွင်းရှိုဝ်း။ စာရင်းထိုးသည်။ ။
မောက်မြို့ရွှေစာသံပိုင်းတည်း။ ။မဏ္ဍိုမထိုက်။ မဟာဗောဓိမဏ္ဍိုင်သံပိုင်းတော်ကို။ လောကာထ
ကျွနာအဂ်ါ ၄ ပါးနှင့်ပြည့်စုံသူစား ၅ မြို့စား နေမျိုးဘိမိရဇာသူအမတ်ထိုခန့်အပ်တော်မူ၍ဆုခွန်ဒိုထါမ
ဟူရာကျော်အပြင်ရှိုက်။ ကောင်းမွန်တင့်တယ်စွာ။ ကောဇာသက္ကရာဇ်သာဂဒရု။ တန်းဆောင်မုန်းထ
ပြည့်ကျော်ရက်အင်္ဂါနေ့၊ တွင်းမှတ်ရေးသားပြီး ပြည့်စုံသည်၊ သကရာဇ်ဘာသာမြန်မာဘာသာ
ပေါက်တစကားပြေ၊ စာကြောင်းရေ ၇၅။ ကျောက်မျက်နှာအလျှား အရှည် ၂ ဒံ၃ ။ အနံ ၁ ဒံ၅

TRANSLATION.

On the Obverse.

I adore the Buddha, who has attained Arhatship, and who is possessed of supreme intelligence.

May there be victory!

As all Buddhas gained victory at the foot of the Bodhi Tree, so also may our noble master, the king of rigteousness, obtain victory by virtue of his homage to this great Bodhi Tree.

Our king of righteousness, Lord of many white and also of celestial elephants, is descended from the high and numerous solar race of kings, and his virtuous royal father, grandfather, great grandfather, &c., who all professed the true faith, were, according to historical accounts, of the noble Śákya family, who are the fountain of all piety and liberality. In bestowing gifts he is never satisfied; he observes the laws, he regards the laws, the law is his mirror as well as his banner. He pays constant homage to the three jewels, viz. Buddha, his laws, and his church. He worships various kinds of pagodas and shrines, and constantly bears in mind as well as makes inquiries about the Bodhi Tree where Buddha conquered Mára (Satan), and where he put an end to all lusts and ignorance.

I will now relate the facts *in extenso*. About 2,570 years from the commencement of Kali Yuga, Gaudama, who had knowledge of all the laws, verily attained his Buddhaship. He was begotten of the Queen Máyá and King Sudodana, and after retirement from the country of Kapilavastu he attained the knowledge of the way to Nirvána at the foot of the Banyan Tree. His laws and his disciples still exist in the world, as recorded in the Puránas of Gaudama. Our king made inquiries from the Yogis and Bráhmans who came from India, as well as from traders who returned from the same country in the reign of his royal grandfather, the lord of the celestial elephant. It was described to him that a Bodhi Tree was in existence on a level rising ground on the bank of Narinzara river, at Gayá in the Magadha kingdom; that it was, like a king of the forest, 100 cubits high, the stem alone being half that height; that there were evident marks of the southern branch having been cut (the branch came off of itself according to the desire of Gaudama when it was about to be carried to Ceylon); that the temple built by Thiri Dhamma Aśoka, King of the whole island of Jambudwip, on the spot where Buddha's Wazira thana throne (Vajrásana) stood, was still standing, and that the Burmese inscription on stone, made when the aforesaid temple was repaired by the lord of many white elephants in B.E. 657, was still to be seen.

Our king saw that the above description was one and the same with the description given in several books, just like the Jumna is one with the river Ganges, and after carefully weighing the facts he came to the conclusion that the Banyan Tree described was no other than the birth-mate of our Buddha.

I shall state the above still more fully. The spot of ground on which the Bodhi Tree stands rises gradually from the surrounding fields to the height of 26 cubits, and occupies an area of 18 payzahs, which is covered with silvery white sand, overgrown with elephant grass, and the surface of which is as smooth as the face of a drum. The surrounding trees bend to the right as if paying homage. The Bodhi Tree is so situated that its stem served as a back to the Buddha's throne, and its leaves as an emerald umbrella. On the Wazira-thana throne innumerable Buddhas have, from infinite period, obtained omniscience after meditating upon the 36,000,000 laws of Vipasanna, or upon Mahá Wazira Nyana.

This throne appears first when a new world is formed, and disappears last when the world is destroyed, and is called Bodhi Mandine, because, apart from its lasting nature, it is like the kernel of the earth, which is 240,000 yozanas deep.

Having thus heard of this most wonderful tree he devoutly paid homage to it from a distance, even as did the kings of Kalinga, and Thiri Dhamma Asoka, Pathaynadi Ko-sala, and Dewanam-piya-tissa. Soon afterwards our illustrious master, who bears the title of Thiri Pavara Sudhamma Mahárájá-di-Rája, the lord of white elephants, and of the celestial elephant, the colour of which is like that of the full-moon in the month of Tazoungmone and like the Kumudra lily which flowers in the same month, sent by land and water, *viá* Arakan, his Purohit, Mahárájínda-ekka-mahá-Dhamma Rájaguru and his minister, Myay-nanwoon, with innumerable offerings for the Bodhi Tree, in the era of religion 2365 and B.E. 1183. Before doing so, he, together with his chief queen, Thiri-Pavara Mahárájinda Ratna Deví, performed the ceremony of dedication by praying with gold and silver flowers set with precious stones, and with parched rice, umbrellas, flags, and spiral flags made of gold and silver. He then poured out water into the earth, making the earth a witness of his good deed. He also prayed that he might hereafter become a Buddha to save the creatures that are drowned in the endless whirlpool of existence. Also, he shared the merit that would accrue from his good deeds to his royal parents and ancestors.

May this inscription last to the end of the world like the Meru mount, the sun, and the moon.

This inscription was written by the minister Mahá Zaya Thinkyan.

On the Reverse.

As the sun, by means of its innumerable rays, gives light to the four islands, so has Buddha, the conqueror of the passions, turned the wheel of the law, and has thereby enlightened the darkness in human minds. May he grant victory to our king of righteousness.

And as the sun, by turning round in heaven, dispels the darkness below, so has our king by turning the wheel of power and justice driven away all dangers from his subjects May he (the king) grant victory to his subjects.

I adore the Buddha, who has attained Arhatship and who is possessed of supreme intelligence.

Our beloved lord, Gaudama, who attained Buddhahood after struggling hard during 400,100,000 worlds, first obtained an oracle from the lord Dípankara, in the Tharamanda world, that he would verily become a Buddha; since then the oracle was repeated by Kondinya and twenty-two other Buddhas, and he finally attained the knowledge of the four truths under the Bodhi Tree, and fed mankind with the cool water of his law, and gave them salvation. For the salvation of those who had not the fortune to see him he left instructions that his law should be preached to the remotest part of the world. Accordingly it shines like a flame of fire and with sweetest fragrance in the towns of Prome, Pagán, Myinzaine, Tsagine, Panya, Ava, Moutsobo, and Amarapura, and throughout our dominions.

The lord of that country, by title Thiri-Pavara Mahárájádi-Rájá, is the great-grandson of his most illustrious great-grandfather, whose power was like a flame of burning fire; grandson of the lord of the celestial elephant, the founder of the Amarapura city; and son and jewel of the great king Mahá Dhamma Bijaya Sinha Súra, who, with greatest ease, annexed the great country of Arakan to his dominions, and removed from there to Amarapura the Mahámuni image which is endowed with life.

In B.E. 1181, on Saturday, the 13th, waxing of Nayoon, he ascended the throne with his south (or chief) queen, amidst great rejoicings of the people.

His piety and fervent devotion was not the least lessened by his elevation to the highest position, and he shines amongst kings like the Lichavi kings of Vesali in India, and like the moon amidst stars. His power extends far and wide, and he is possessed of an elephant which is like the Eráwún elephant of the king of heaven.

Bearing in mind the verse in Adi Kyan, "Danumdatwa, Silansammadiyitwa, obosatakamum kartwa," he determined whilst he was a prince that he would patronize the Bodhi Tree when he should become king, and made constant inquiries about the Bodhi Tree from the Bráhmans, Yogis, Dasantris, and Bairágis who came from Benares and Vesali. On being entirely satisfied that the Bodhi Tree still stands on a perfectly level ground, 18 payzahs in extent, on the bank of Narinzara River, at Gayâ, in Magadha, and that its height is 100 cubits, half of that being the length of the stem alone, and that the surrounding trees bend to the right as an act of homage, he was very anxious to make offerings to it like his royal ancestors Asoka, Piyatissa, and Kalinga.

In the era of religion 2356 and B.E. 1183 he prepared flags, flowers and parched rice of gold, silver, and precious stones, and with his chief queen, Thiri-Pavara Mahárájinda Ratna Devi, performed the ceremony of dedication amidst great shouts of rejoicing of the people. He prayed that he might become Buddha to give salvation to the perishing souls, and that he might be perfect in the ten virtues, and he shared the merit of that good deed to his royal parents and all his royal ancestors. He made the earth to bear witness to his good deed by pouring water on it from a golden kettle.

After dedication, which will be remembered to the end of the world, he sent his Rájaguru and the Myaynan minister, Maháminhla Thagathu with hundreds of followers, to the Bodhi Tree in India to present his offerings there, and to put up this stone inscription.

(Here follows a verse to the following purport.)

In 1183 B.E. the lord of Burma, the lord of the white and the celestial elephant, sent men to present his valuable offerings and to put up a stone inscription, at the Bodhi Tree, and the Minister Mahá Thankaya wrote this inscription that it may last as long as the land and the water.

The Minister Naymyo Thiri Rajathu, who was sent to India to inscribe the above on Mahura stone, completed the work on Tuesday, the 11th waning of Tazoungmone in B.E. 1183.

Number of lines 85 in Burmese and Sanskrit, prose and poetry.

The stone is 2 cubits 8 hands 3 inches long and 1 cubit 1 hand 1 inch wide.

This record was set up during the reign of Hpagyi-daw, on the full moon of Kártika (November), in the year 1822 A.C. It shows that influential Burmese officers of State visited India just before the first Burmese war of 1824. As stated above (p. 211), it takes the first date of the old Burmese inscription to be 657 and not 667, as it has been read by Ratna Pála, Colonel Burney, and Mr. M. Hla Oung. I called the attention of the last-named gentleman to this, but he could not reconcile the difference, and attributed it to a mistake of the later inscription-writer.

Small Burmese inscriptions. Nos. 16-17.

There are two other Burmese inscriptions at Buddha Gayá, one on a votive stúpa stuck up as a finial on the balustrade in front of the Báradwárí, and the other on the pedestal of a statue at the foot of the Bodhi Tree. General Cunningham has published *facsimiles* and translations of both of these, and I copy the translations from his work (*a*).

No. 16, on a votive Stúpa.

1. In 1185 (A.D. 1823) the 2nd day of the waxing moon of Wakhoung.
2. Shime-pu, resident of the place called Kwun-tshwai, wrote this stone-writing.

No. 17, on Pedestal of Siva and Párvati.

1. In 1171 (A.D. 1809), the 13th day of the waxing moon Thedengyat, Mahá * * *.
2. Master of the lord-elephant, great lord of life, the royal gift * * *.
3. * * presented and made offerings. May men and angels applaud!
4. The persons who came are Nga-po-tu and Nga-Kway :—

Neither of these is of any interest, but the last is worthy of note as shewing how utterly careless the pious travellers were who defrayed the expense of the record.

(*a*) Arch. Surv. Report III, 105, and plate XXXII.

It is certain they were Buddhists; they had nothing to do with Hinduism; they came to behold the secred Bodhi Tree and presented their offerings to it; but, in recording their gifts, they did not care to see that they were glorifying the Hindu divinities Śiva and Párvatí, by placing their inscription at their feet. And if in the present day such mistakes can be committed, or such disregard shown as to the nature of the receptacle of inscriptions, it may be safely presumed that people of old were not more particular. Such mistakes were possible, and it would be unsafe to jump at conclusions from the mere fact of an inscription occurring on a rail or a post.

CHAPTER VI.

CHRONOLOGY.

HISTORICAL CHRONOLOGY NEGLECTED ALIKE BY THE HINDUS AND THE BUDDHISTS—DATES ASSIGNED BY DIFFERENT NATIONS TO BUDDHA'S BIRTH AND DEATH—DATES ARRIVED AT BY CALCULATIONS AND INTERCALATIONS—MYTHICAL CHARACTER OF BUDDHA—PROBABLE DATE OF HIS NIRVÁṆA—DATE OF THE AŚOKA RAILINGS—GREAT TEMPLE—FERGUSSON'S OPINION ABOUT ITS DATE—THEORY OF THE BURMESE ORIGIN OF THE TEMPLE—THEORY FOUNDED ON THE STUCCO ORNAMENTS—THEORY FOUNDED ON THE NINE-STORIED PLAN OF THE TEMPLE—THEORY FOUNDED ON THE ARCHES—THEORY FOUNDED ON THE SUPPOSED DATE OF AMARA DEVA—THEORY FOUNDED ON THE CONSTRUCTION OF THE PORCH—AŚOKA'S VIHÁRA—LIMITS OF THE AGE OF THE GREAT TEMPLE—HIOUEN THSANG'S ACCOUNT OF THE BUILDING OF THE TEMPLE—THE STORY OF THE BRÁHMAN BROTHERS—GENERAL CUNNINGHAM'S DEDUCTIONS—CONCLUSION.

No nation of antiquity devoted more attention to the division and reckoning of time than the Hindus. Alike for the smallest fractions of a second as for ages comprehending millions of years they devised standards and ways of measurement. Of eras, epochs, cycles, and ages, both civil and astronomical, they had also a large variety, each having its well-defined date of origin. It was held, too, a distinguishing mark for a great sovereign to establish an era, and many were the kings of ancient and mediæval times who sought that means of perpetuating their memory. But unfortunately Indian writers never brought their systems of chronology to bear upon history; and, in the absence of chronology, their history has degenerated into the most inconsistent fables and legends. With a literature far more extensive than that of Greece or of Rome, and spreading over twenty thousand volumes, they have not a single work which gives a faithful chronological account of twenty consecutive reigns in ancient times.

Neglect of dates by Buddhists.

The Buddhists were somewhat better in this respect. They recorded many dates. But as Hindus by birth, feeling, manners, customs, and habits, though professing a different faith, they retained their national indifference to chronology bearing on history; and, on the whole, the chronology of Buddhism is as unsatisfactory as that of Hinduism. It is impossible, therefore, to establish on any safe, solid, unquestionable basis the chronology of the place which forms the theme of this work. Almost every date is doubtful, every question open to contradiction, every fact susceptible of very discordant and different interpretations. It is the object of the following pages, therefore, not to solve difficulties and settle debatable points connected with its history, but to place before the reader the salient points of the different questions at issue, and to indicate what seems to the writer as likely to afford the most probable solutions.

Date of Buddha.

The first question of date, in a work professing to describe the hermitage of Buddha, should be the age of that personage. But the information available on the subject is so discordant that it opens a protracted vista of over two thousand years.

Hindu sources of information.

Detesting with all the warmth of sectarian hatred a pervert who had forsaken their ancestorial religion and proved the most successful opponent, the ancient Hindus, from whom we should first look for information, never took the trouble to record the history of Buddha, much less to assign him a particular date. They have named him in many of their works, but only to mislead. To quote the language of Max Müller, they have made him "the father of his father, and grandfather of his son."(a)

Tibetan dates.

The Tibetans, who early embraced the religion of the saint, and still profess it with the greatest ardour, seem never to have attempted to ascertain the date of the founder of their religion. According to Csoma de Körös, they have no less than fourteen different dates recorded in their scriptures for the day of that founder's death, and, for ought we know to the contrary, there may be several others. The dates range from 2422 to 546 B.C., the specific dates being 2422, 2144, 2139, 2135, 1310, 1060, 884, 882, 880, 837, 752, 653, 576, and 546. (b)

Chinese dates.

The people of China first accepted the religion of Buddha at about the close of the first century before the Christian era, and the oldest Buddhist book in their language dates from 67 years of that era; but, notwithstanding the accuracy with which the Chinese generally record the dates of historical events, they have no fixed date

(a) Ancient Sanskrit Literature, 263.

(b) Csoma's Tibetan Grammar, pp. 199 to 201.

current among them for the death of Buddha. According to Tchao-chi, quoted by Ma-touan-lin, the earliest date is 1130 B.C. From facts mentioned by Fa Hian, that date would range between 1070 and 1020. The authorities consulted by Klaproth fix the date of Buddha's birth at 999 B.C. and his death at 949 (*a*), thus giving the saint a career of 50 years.

Burmese, Siamese, and Ceylonese dates.

The Burmese, according to the chronological tables given in Crawford's embassy, brought him down to 628 B.C., the death being set down at 589, the span of life in this case being 40 years. According to the first Burmese inscription at Buddha Gayá (p. 209) the date of death should be 218 years before 263 (B.C.), the date of Aśoka's accession, or 481; but according to the second (p. 215) it is 543 B.C. The Siamese dates, though not the same, approximate closely those of the Burmese. The Ceylonese have an only date, and that places his death in the year 544 B.C., or in the year preceding that in which Vijaya founded a new dynasty in Ceylon. (*b*) This last was for some time accepted as the true date, and much might be said in support of its accuracy. The geneological tables given in the Ceylonese chronicles and in the Hindu Purāṇas, as also in some of the Buddhist Avadánas, assigning a probable average reign to each prince, and the use which has been made of the event in civil chronology, plead strongly in favour of it; and some of the Nepalese Buddhists accept it as the correct date.

Dates arrived at by modern research.

Modern antiquarian researches have, however, of late questioned its accuracy. The learned Professor Max Müller rejects all the systems as alike unworthy of trust, and thinks that "to try to find out which of these chronological systems is the most plausible seems useless, and it can only make confusion worse confounded if we attempt a combination of the three." (*c*) After a careful survey of all the facts bearing on the question, he is disposed to believe that there is an obvious intercalation of 66 years in the reckoning of the Ceylonese chroniclers, which being eliminated, the true date of Buddha's death would be 477 B.C. (*d*) This deduction, however, is open to the objection that it does not reconcile contradictory statements, and

(*a*) Prinsep's Indian Antiquities, I, p. 30.
(*b*) Turnour's Mahawanso.
(*c*) Ancient Sanskrit Literature, p. 263.
(*d*) Ibid. p. 298.

entirely rejects all those facts and statements which are opposed to it. In fact, it cuts the gordian knot, and does not unravel it. General Cunningham has lately found, in the temple of Súrya at Gayá, an inscription of the fifteenth century which professes to be dated in the era of Buddha's death (a); and by calculating by the name of the day of the week and the moon's age therein given, he comes to 478 B.C. as the true date. The difference between the two reckonings amounts to only one year, which may be easily overlooked. The calculations on which the General's conclusion is founded are, however, yet in need of verification, and when verified it would not advance the question in the least, as there is nothing to show that the era adopted by the inscription writer of the 15th century was more authentic than those of Ceylon, Burmah, Tibet, or China.

Advancing from the last, some German antiquarians have brought down the date of the Nirváṇa to the 4th century before the commencement of the Christian era; and to crown all M. Wassiljew, in his 'Buddhismus,' has repudiated the very existence of Buddha as a historical entity. He says—"Le Buddha n'est, pour ainsi dire, pas une personne; lui aussi est un terme technique ou un dogme. Bien que diverses légendes indiquent une personnalité précise, néanmoins elles contiennent si peu d'éléments vraiment historiques que cette personnalité même se transforme en un mythe." (b)

Amidst such divergence of authorities and opinions it would be futile to expect a satisfactory conclusion. The tendency of recent research has been rather to widen this divergence than to bridge the chasm; and, under the circumstance, it is perhaps best to leave the subject where it is. All that can now be safely affirmed is that the weight of evidence is in favour of the opinion which would place the career of Buddha between the sixth and the fifth centuries before the Christian era; and in the preceding pages this idea has been adhered to without any special leaning either to the date of Ceylon or to that of Professor Max Müller.

Date of the railings.

The next date I have to refer to is that of the railing round the great temple. Of all the architectural remains that have come to notice at the place, the railing is unquestionably the oldest, and a satisfactory solution of its date is a matter of

(a) Arch. Surv. Report, III, p. 126.
(b) *Apud* Senart's Essai sur la Legende du Buddha, p. 7.

importance. But on this subject we have nothing more positive than a tradition of the seventh century for what happened nearly fifteen hundred years before. The narrator of the tradition, however, is a trustworthy person, and the circumstances mentioned by him are borne out by collateral evidence. The narrator is Hiouen Thsang. After describing the destruction and the subsequent resuscitation of the Bodhi tree by the order of the chief queen of Aśoka (p. 97), he says:—"Le roi, pénétré de respect et d'admiration, l'entoura d'un mur en pierre, haut d'une dizaine de pieds. Cette enceinte subsiste encore aujourd'hui." (a) This "stone wall," existing to the middle of the seventh century, has been supposed to be the same with the railing. The height given is the same, and the character of the railing is such as *à priori* to suggest the idea of its being of the same class with the Sánchí and the Barâhat structures of the kind. The tradition, besides, is one of those which are seldom likely to be apocryphal. A remarkable building, as soon as erected, is associated with the name of the builder, and the association lasts as long as the building, and not unoften for a long time after it. During the existence of the building scarcely any opportunity presents itself for a disassociation, or the imposition of a new name, particularly when the old name happens to be a popular and universally respected one; and even the attempts of powerful sovereigns to change such names have not unoften proved abortive. The great Akbar, unquestionably the most powerful and most popular sovereign of India, failed to change Agra into Akbarabád, and his grandson Shah Jahán's Shahjahánábád never could cope with Delhi. We may, therefore, without any great stretch of the imagination, assume that the "stone wall" which Hiouen Thsang saw existing in his time was the same which Aśoka had put up; and that Aśoka did put up something it would not be presumptuous to accept as a fact. If any faith is to be reposed on his biographers he lived at Buddha Gayá for five years, and devoted much of his wealth to its embellishment (cf. p. 97). He was the greatest patron that Buddhism ever had, and the public voice gave him credit for no less than 84,000 Buddhist structures of various kinds; and, though we are not called upon

(a) Memoires sur les Contrées occidentales I, p. 463. General Cunningham translates a part of the passage quoted above into a "stone wall 12 feet in height," but the word in the French version is *dizaine* (10), and not *douzaine* (12).

to lay any faith on that number, we may fairly presume that the person who erected the monuments of Sánchí and Baráhat did not neglect the most sacred spot on earth in the history of his religion. Under ordinary circumstances it would be the first to engage his attention. Of all the sovereigns of ancient India he is the only one whose age has been most satisfactorily proved. He reigned from 263 to 235 B.C.; and if the assumption, first adopted by General Cunningham and never since questioned, that the railing which Hiouen Thsang saw, and the remains of which exist to our day, is due to him, its date would be the middle of the third century before Christ. The character used in some of the inscriptions found on this railing affords collateral evidence of great weight in favour of this conclusion (p. 182). That character has not yet been found in any record of a later date than the second century B.C., and its presence on the railing must place the railing to an age previous to that date.

Exception, however, may be taken to the assignment of the rails to Aśoka on the ground of the inscriptions naming other than Aśoka as donors; but as the nature of the donations referred to by them has not been defined in them, and I have elsewhere shown that the donations meant were other than the stones on which they occur (cf. p. 184), it appears to be of no moment. It would doubtless have been highly satisfactory had the name of Aśoka been met with on one of the rails; but, in the absence of such a proof, we must rely upon the best available, and that by no means is an unsatisfactory one.

Date of the Great Temple. Fergusson's opinion.

The most important monument at Buddha Gayá is unquestionably the Great Temple, and, according to General Cunningham, it is, next to the rails, the oldest. Mr. Fergusson, however, whose opinion on such matters carries great weight, demurs to this. In his letter to Mr. Grote, quoted above (p. 108), he expresses his positive opinion that "the building *we now see* was erected in the first year of the fourteenth century." This is slightly modified in his 'History of Architecture' (II, p. 474), where he observes "a temple was erected, according to an inscription found on the spot about the year 500, by a certain Amara Deva, and was seen and described by Hiouen Thsang in the seventh century; but, having become ruinous, was rebuilt by the Burmese in or about the year 1306, as shown in woodcut No. 982. From its architecture there can be little doubt that its external form, and the details of the stucco ornaments with which it is now covered, belong to the latter epoch, and so do all the parts which are arched, and all the true arches. The frame-works of the building, however, and those parts constructed with horizontal arches, seem to belong to the earlier erection." In his most recent work he substantially retains this opinion. After adverting to Hiouen Thsang's account and the Wilkins' inscription, he continues:—"From the data these accounts afford us we gather with very tolerable certainty that the building we now see before us (woodcut No. 16) is substantially that erected by Amara, the Brahman, in the beginning of the sixth century; but the niches Hiouen Thsang saw, containing golden statues of Buddha, cannot be those now existing, and the sculptures he mentions find no place in the present design; and the amalakas of gilt copper that crowned the whole, as he saw it, have disappeared. The changes in detail, as well as the introduction of radiating arches in the interior, I fancy must belong to the Burmese restoration in the beginning of the fourteenth century. Though these consequently may have altered its appearance in detail, it is probable that we still have before us a straight-lined pyramidal nine-storeyed temple of the sixth century, retaining all its essential forms—anomalous and unlike anything else we find in India, either before or afterwards, but probably the parent of many nine-storeyed towers found beyond the Himalayas, both in China and elsewhere."(a)

Theory of the Burmese building the temple.

To notice these arguments seriatim. The first position about the Burmese rebuilding the temple in 1306 is clearly a mistake, caused by the erroneous translation of the record on which it is founded. Adverting to it, General Cunningham justly remarks:—"In this statement I must take exception to the word *rebuilt*, for which I would read *repaired*. * * * That the Burmese *rebuilt* the temple in A.D. 1305 is, I am confident, a gross mistake, owing partly perhaps to the ignorance as well as want of precision in the original writer of the Burmese inscription, and partly to the looseness of the English translations given by Ratna Pála and Colonel Burney. According to Ratna Pála, the original temple erected by Aśoka 'having fallen into *disrepair* was *rebuilt*;' 'again being *ruined*, it was *restored*,' and after a long interval, being once more '*demolished*,' the Burmese minister

(a) History of Indian and Eastern Architecture, pp. 69-70.

was employed to *repair* the sacred building. It was thus, says the translator, '*constructed* a fourth time.' Here the confusion between *disrepair*, *ruin*, and *demolition* is fairly balanced by the confusion between *rebuilding*, *restoration*, and *repair*. In Colonel Burney's translation I find the same tantalizing want of precision. According to him the original temple of Aśoka having been *destroyed* for a long time was *repaired*. I need quote no further, but will simply state my opinion that the temple was not rebuilt by the Burmese at any time, but simply *repaired*."(a)

This opinion, formed by General Cunningham on *à priori* reasoning, has since been fully borne out by Mr. M. Hla Oung. His version, given on page 207, invariably uses the word *repair* instead of *rebuild*, and in support of this rendering he has given me the most satisfactory reasons. In a letter to me he says:—"The Burmese word, which I translate 'repaired,' is *pyoo*, 'to do.' The same word occurs throughout, except the first repair by a Panthagoogyee, where the word used is *pyin*, 'to repair.' *Pyoo* would have been of doubtful import had not the *pyek*, 'disrepair,' which occurs throughout, made it all clear that *pyoo* means to do the necessary repairs." In the face of these facts, it would be futile to urge that the Burmese *rebuilt* the temple in 1305. It was in 'disrepair,' and they simply repaired it.

Evidence of the stucco ornaments.

The assumption about the external form and the details of the stucco ornaments being due to the Burmese repairs is equally untenable. In support of it Mr. Fergusson appeals to the peculiar character of the architecture; but as he does not define what that peculiarity consists in, it cannot be discussed. That the form is not modern is evident from its being a copy of the Nálandá temple, which dates from before the Christian era. The nine-storeyed arrangement, the niches, and the stucco ornaments, are all exact counterparts of what are to be seen there, and the doubt expressed, therefore, of Hiouen Thsang not having seen the niches as we have them now is quite uncalled for. The fact of the stucco ornaments, both at Nálandá and at Buddha Gayá, having deteriorated by successive repairs has been already noticed (p. 111), and, judging by it, the only conclusion which can be fairly arrived at is that the Burmese repairers only spoiled the details of the ornaments by their clumsy handling, but did nothing to alter in the least either the external form or the

(a) Arch. Surv. Report, III. pp. 92-93.

internal arrangement of the temple. They devoted only a few months, not quite a year, from 667 to 668, to the work, and in an out-of-the-way place like Buddha Gayá, in the beginning of the 14th century, they could not have got a sufficient number of masons to do much more than patching up broken mouldings and giving a coat of whitewash to the building.

Thus then the temple was not built in the beginning of the 14th century. Nor was it built a century or two before that time. The recent translation of the old Burmese inscription clearly shows that some time before the 14th century the King of Thado had caused it to be repaired. With reference to this personage Colonel Burney says:—"*Thado-men*, or king of Thado, was the family title of a race of kings whose capital was at Tagoung, a city which once existed on the left bank of the Erawadi in north latitude 24°." (*a*) General Cunningham doubts this, and would have the name to be that of an Indian prince. In either case the fact remains that a considerable time before the 14th century the temple existed, and was repaired by some pious king or other.

Coming to the 6th century the theory of the nine-storeyed arrangement being due to that century, and of being "the parent of many nine-storeyed towers found beyond the Himalayas, both in China and elsewhere," is not much more reliable. Reverend Samuel Beal, in the Introduction to his translation of Fa Hian, says:—"Hitherto (A.D. 335) natives of India had been allowed to build temples in the large cities, but now, for the first time, the people of the country were permitted to become Shamans; and, as a final proof of the rapid growth of the religion, we find that at Loyang alone (Honanfu) there had been erected (350 A.D.) 42 pagodas, from three to nine-stories high, richly painted, and formed after Indian models." (*b*) The nine-storeyed arrangement must have been common enough in India long before to be carried to China before 350 A.D., and such being the case that arrangement can be no proof of the temple under notice being due to the 6th century. Under the circumstance I am satisfied that General Cunningham is perfectly right in coming "to the conclusion that we now see before us the very temple which Hiouen Thsang visited and described in A.D. 637." (*c*)

(*a*) Asiatic Researches, XX. p. 170.
(*b*) Travels of Buddhist Pilgrims, p. xxiii.
(*c*) Arch. Surv. Report, III.

The argument based on the existence of the radiating arches has been already shown (pp. 109f.) to be fallacious, and nothing more need be said about it.

Theory of Amara's building the temple.

The theory about Amara Deva, the Bráhman, having built the temple in the 6th century is founded on Mr. Wilmot's inscription. But as I have, I fancy, most clearly shown that the inscription is a myth, and never had any tangible existence (p. 204), all superstructures built upon it must tumble down along with it. My opinion regarding that inscription was first published in 1864, and it was well known to Mr. Fergusson, for he commented in that year on the paper in which it appeared; but in 1876 he put forth his theory without saying a word to show that my opinion was erroneous, and that the inscription was really authentic. Nor has any other orientalist, European or Indian, questioned the accuracy of my opinion. I labour under the disadvantage, therefore, of not knowing where I am mistaken, and what are the arguments on which Mr. Fergusson has rejected my opinion, and, accepting the authenticity of the inscription, based his theory on it. It might be that he was not called upon to notice the objections of an obscure individual like me; but, situated as I now am, I can only say that the theory is founded on a *pititio principii*, and induces a most inconclusive conclusion.

Theory founded on the porch.

The inscription apart, it is difficult to reconcile the theory of the temple having been built in the middle of the 6th century with the statement of Hiouen Thsang, that the temple had existed for some time before the porch was added, and that the porch was seen by him in A.C. 637. The date of this porch has been, I think, very satisfactorily shown by General Cunningham. His arguments on the subject I shall here quote at length:—"To the third period of the temple's history I would ascribe the addition of the two-storeyed pavilion to the eastern face, which, as we know from Hiouen Thsang's description, must have been built some time before A.D. 637. I infer also from the story of Sasángka's minister placing a lamp in the inner chamber of the temple before the figure of Mahádeva *on account of the darkness* that the front pavilion and all the vaults and arches had already been added before A.D. 500 or 600, say about 500 A.D. To this period I would refer the repairs of the plaster of many of the mouldings, which must have been done some time between the date of the original building and that of the great second plastering by the Burmese in A.D. 1305. To this period also I would refer the basalt plinth which we now see in front of the temple, and perhaps also the basalt pedestal of the great temple itself. The mouldings of both include a *cyma*, which is not found in the original *brick basements* of either the Nâlandâ or Buddha Gayâ temples, but which is the most striking feature in the mediæval *stone basement* of the Nâlandâ Temple.

"Now, the stone basement or portico of the Nâlandâ Temple is beyond all doubt an after addition to the original brick temple. This is clearly proved by its being built against the mouldings of the plastered brickwork, instead of being bonded with it. The junction is made so awkwardly that the ornamental band of moulding is left rough, and the hollow between the end of the stone and brick mouldings is filled with plain bricks. On this subject Captain Marshall, who appears to have examined the building very closely, makes the following observations:—'The whole temple was made of the large brick or tile that appears to have been universally employed in building these *Buddhist* structures, and, speaking generally, the whole building had been raised at the same time; but in more than one instance, from break in the bond, it was manifest that portions were either the result of an after-thought, or, at any rate, had been built at some subsequent date.' At what date this addition was made to the Nâlandâ Temple may be approximately fixed by the masons' marks which I found on some of the granite blocks of the portico. Fig. 8 of Plate XXXI reads *Nala*, and fig. 9 simply *la*, the initial letter being wanting. Both are incomplete, but I have no doubt that they were intended for *Nâlandâ*, being the masons' marks made at the quarry to show that the stones were destined for *Nâlandâ*. Fig. 10 reads *Sriva* or *Sâva*, or perhaps simply *Sava*. Now the forms of these letters are certainly earlier than those of the 7th century, as exhibited in the Tibetan alphabet and the coins of *Sasângka*. The granite portico of the Nâlandâ Temple was, therefore, added before A.D. 600, or, say, not later than A.D. 500, which agrees with the date assigned to the basalt pedestal and basalt plinth of the Buddha Gayâ temple, showing the same peculiar moulding." (*a*)

Accepting this conclusion to be correct, we must suppose that the attack of Śaśânka against the temple and the destruction of the Bodhi tree must have

(*a*) Arch. Surv. Report, III, pp. 100-1.

taken place long after the erection of the porch and the alteration in the interior arrangement of the sanctuary. The story about the minister of Śaśánka putting a lamp in the sanctuary to make the image of Mahádeva visible (p. 84) would be otherwise inexplicable. A short time after Śaśánka, Púrṇa Varma renewed the Bodhi tree and built a wall 24 feet high round the court-yard of the temple for the better protection of the tree and the temple from inimical attacks. This was done in A.D. 610, and the wall was in existence in the time of the Chinese pilgrim who saw it.

Fa Hian's notice.

The evidence of the porch of the 5th century can leave no doubt in any person's mind that the temple must be older. Now a century before the erection of the porch, *i.e.* in 401-404, Fa Hian visited Buddha Gayá, and in all the principal spots associated with the penance of the saint he found monuments still existing. Among others he specially notices "three Sanghárámas" or monasteries "in the place where Buddha arrived at perfect reason."(*a*) These were "occupied by ecclesiastics, who were supplied with the necessaries of life by the people, so that they had sufficient of everything and lacked nothing." He also noticed "the four great pagodas, or those erected on the place where he (the saint) was born, where he obtained emancipation, where he began to preach, and where he entered Nirváṇa." Regarding their age, he remarks:—"The sites of these four great pagodas have always been associated together from the time of the Nriváṇa."(*b*) In Mr. Laidlay's Pilgrimage of Fa Hian, page 282, the existence of the towers is more clearly indicated; it runs thus:—"The four great towers(*c*) erected in commemoration of all the holy acts that Foe performed while on the world are preserved to this moment since the *ni houan* of Foe."(*d*)

Lowest limit of age.

The second of these pagodas, there can be no doubt, was the same with the Great Temple. It was sufficiently old then to be worthy of the epithet "great," or of much higher respect than the others which surrounded it. The time necessary for this halo of antiquity

(*a*) Beal's Buddhist Pilgrims, p. 125.

(*b*) Opus cit. p. 126.

(*c*) Confounding the statements of one Chinese pilgrim with those of another, in 1864 I took the 'great tower' here mentioned to be the one which Aśoka had built. I now correct the mistake.

(*d*) Ibid. p. 126.

to be brought on it could not have been at the least under two centuries. This would bring us to the second century; but we cannot even rest there. The Gupta inscriptions noticed above (pp. 191-192), though not referring to the erection of the temple, forcibly impress the idea that the temple must have been existing in the second century, and we must, therefore, proceed to the first for the age of the monument, and that may be looked upon as the *terminus ad quem*.

Highest limit of age.

On the other hand, Hiouen Thsang informs us that the ground on which the Great Temple stands was originally the site of "a small vihára" (*un petit vihára*). This is converted into "a chaitya" in the chapter on the life of Aśoka in the "Divya Avadána." It is there said that after hearing from his tutor, Upagupta, the history of the place, Aśoka "presented a hundred thousand suvarṇas for the Bodhi tree, and for the erection of a chaitya by its side."(a) The 'Aśoka Avadána,' which was translated into the Chinese in Circa 265-31 A.D., and must be at least nineteen hundred years old(b), does not use these words, but it repeatedly affirms that the king did build chaityas in the neighbourhood of the sacred tree. The question remains uncertain, therefore, as to whether Aśoka built a vihára or a chaitya. In other places of Buddhist pilgrimage, such as Sánchí and Baráhat, Aśoka built chaityas, and a chaitya would at first thought appear to be the most likely structure which the king would design for Buddha Gayá. But a hemispherical mass of solid brickwork, such as a chaitya must have been in his time, is of all structures the least likely to crumble down in a century or two; and a sacred edifice of the kind is what a Buddhist would be the most unlikely person to break down and build a structure of some other kind on its site. A vihára, on the other hand, such as was built in those days,—a chamber or chapel for prayer meetings and lectures, built of bricks with clay cement,—was susceptible of rapid dilapidation; and in its case the necessity of rebuilding, or renewal, would soon arise, and such a structure may be *renewed* and not *repaired* whenever necessary without any offence to religion. It might be added also that a chaitya was usually raised for the deposit of some relic of the saint, or,

---

(a) Burnouf's *Histoire du Buddhisme Indien*, p. 388. "*En conséquence le roi donna cent mille (Suvarṇas) pour l'arbre Bodhi, et fit elever en cet endroit un Tchaitya.*"

(b) My Sanskrit Buddhist literature of Nepal, p 16.

in other words, to create a sanctuary; but where the most sacred of all earthly objects, the Tree of Knowledge, was already present, it was not necessary to resort to any secondary means; whereas a chapel in its neighbourhood would be at once useful and appropriate. I am disposed to think, therefore, that it was a vihára, and not a chaitya, which Aśoka built to the east of the Bodhi tree. The railings afford some corroborative evidence in favour of this supposition. Wherever a railing has been seen round a chaitya, it is always circular; but the one at Buddha Gayá was rectangular, and it presupposes the structure enclosed by it to have been other than of a circular form. (a) It might be said that the necessity of enclosing both the chaitya and the Bodhi tree within the same railing led to a departure from the ordinary rule; but there is nothing to show that such was really the case. That it was not a temple may be affirmed without any hesitation. Temples imply images, but, as I have already shown (p. 128) that image worship had not come into vogue in the time of Aśoka, no room could be required for its performance. It may be safely accepted as facts that the spot on which the Great Temple now stands was once the site of some structure, not a chaitya, which had been built by Aśoka, and that the old monument was for some cause or other removed to make room for the temple. If we allow 150 years for the duration of Aśoka's monument, we have the beginning of the first century B.C. to be the *terminus a quo* for the present temple.

Mean limit of age.

So far the chain of evidence may be accepted to be tolerably complete, or as much so as we can reasonably expect in a case of this kind, though some of the links are not quite so strong as could be wished. This gives us a period of two hundred years, from the beginning of the first century B.C. to the close of the first century A.C., within which we must look for the date of the Great Temple. Now, according to the Burmese inscription of 1305, the first repairer of Aśoka's vihára was one Penthagoogyee, whose identity is not defined. Colonel Burney takes the word to mean a religious person. Mr. M. Hla Oung says—"*Gyee* (*lit.* great) is applied to a person who is worthy of veneration, and *Penthagoo* is a common

(a) The celebrated Mahá Vihára of Ceylon, built by Devánám-piya-tissa, about 300 B.C., had an enclosing wall forming a rectangle of 115 yards by 72. *Apud* Beal's Buddhist Pilgrims, p. 159.

name for a pious layman who is zealous in the promotion of religion;" the result in either case being the same—a pious man. According to Hiouen Thsang this was a Bráhman, who, by order of the god Mahesvara, transferred his faith to the law of Buddha, and testified his zeal for his new religion by erecting the large temple. It would not be unreasonable to suppose that this Bráhman was the same with the Penthagoogyee, the pious layman of the Burmese record.

Story of the Bráhman brothers.

The story of the conversion of the Bráhman and his erection of the temple is thus given by the Chinese pilgrim:—"On the ancient site of the temple the king Asoka had at first erected a small vihára. Subsequently it was a Bráhman who reconstructed it in grand proportions. Originally he was a Bráhman, who, having no faith in the law of Buddha, adored the god Mahesvara. Having learnt that the god was to be found in the mountains of snow (Himálaya), he proceeded with his younger brother to address to that god his vows. The god said to him—'In general only those who make vows after performing some meritorious act can hope to be successful. It is not to me that you should address your prayers, for it is not I who can grant them.'

"'What act of merit shall I perform,' inquired the Bráhman, 'for obtaining the object of my vows?'

"'If you wish,' said the god, 'to plant the root of righteousness, you should seek the field of perfect goodness. The Tree of Knowledge is the place where may be seen face to face the fruit of knowledge. Return quickly on your feet, stop before the Bodhi tree, erect there a grand vihára, excavate a large tank, and render to them all sorts of offerings. You will then for certain obtain what you desire.'

"After having received the order of the god, the two Bráhmans were imbued with a feeling of profound faith, and returned together. The elder brother constructed the vihára, and the younger excavated the tank. Moreover, they completed their devotion by making rich offerings, and sought with ardour the object of their vows. They obtained them in effect, and subsequently became the ministers of the king. Whatever they received as emoluments or rewards, they gave them away in charity. When the vihára was completed they appealed to accomplished artists to produce an image of Tathágata, representing him in the attitude in which he was when he was just becoming a Buddha. Months and years passed away in vain, for none responded to their call. At last it was a Bráhmaṇa who came forward and addressed the congregation of the clergy, saying—'I shall produce the marvellous figure of Tathágata.'

"The clergy said to him—'Now, what do you require to construct the image?'

"'Only some aromatic paste,' replied he. 'Let it be deposited in the centre of the vihára, with a lighted lamp for me to work with. When I have entered the place, I shall make myself a close prisoner within the door, and it should not be opened for a period of six months.'

"The body of the clergy conformed to his orders. When he had thus passed over four months, and when consequently the six months had not been completed, the clergy were impelled by curiosity and admiration. Having opened the door to see his work, they beheld in the middle of the vihára the statue of Buddha, seated with his arms crossed, and in an imposing attitude. The right foot was placed above, the left hand was closed, and the right one was hanging down. It was seated on the east side, and had an air the most majestic that had ever been beheld on earth. Its chair was in height four feet and two inches, and in breadth twelve feet and five inches. The statue was in height eleven feet and five inches; the two knees were eight feet and eight inches apart from each other; and the distance from one shoulder to the other was six feet two inches: the signs of a great personage were completely shown on it. This figure appeared affectingly life-like, only the upper part of the left breast had not been completely modelled and polished. But the clergy could not see the artist, and this proved that the statue was the result of a divine miracle. All the clergy heaved deep sighs, and ardently prayed to behold the author of the statue. Among them was a Śramaṇa, who was always distinguished by his uprightness and sincerity of heart; he saw a dream, in which he beheld the aforesaid Bráhmaṇa, who thus spoke to him—'I am Maitreya Bodhisattva. I had been under the apprehension that no artist had been born who in his mind could conceive the figure of the saint. It was therefore that I myself came forward to represent the image of Buddha. If the right hand is hanging down (this is the reason). When formerly the Tathágata was on the point of seeing face to face the fruit of Bodhi, the demon appeared to tempt him. The spirits of the earth were eager to put him on his guard. One of them had come forth to the front to assist him in overcoming the demon. The Tathágata told him—'Fear not in the least; by the force of patience I shall vanquish him.' The king of the demons asked—'what witness have you?' The Tathágata lowered his hand, and, pointing it towards the earth, replied—'That is my witness.' At that moment the second spirit of the earth suddenly came out to serve as a witness. That is why now the hand of the statue is directed towards the earth, in imitation of the former action of Buddha.'

"The clergy, having become apprised of this divine miracle, could not by any means repress their sense of regret. At the same time they covered with precious stones the upper part of the chest, which had not been completed, and placed on the head a magnificent diadem, set off with garlands ornamented with pearls, for the glory of the statue." (a)

General Cunningham's deductions.

The story is of interest on many accounts, particularly as illustrative of the Buddhist belief regarding the first statue set up in the Great Temple; but the only circumstance of any historical value in it is the reference to the Bráhman in whom we recognize the Penthagoogyee of the Burmese inscription, and General Cunningham has worked it out with great tact and ingenuity. I need make no appology, therefore, for quoting his remarks at length. He says—"Amongst all this confusion it is pleasant to turn to the simple narrative of the Chinese pilgrim, from whom we learn that the original temple of Aśoka being a small one, it was rebuilt on a grand scale by a Bráhman. No clue is given as to the date of the new temple, but I am inclined to think that it may be assigned with some probability to the first century B.C. In his account of the great temple of Báláditya at Nálandá, which was 200 feet high, Hwen Thsang expressly states that in size and magnificence it resembled the great temple near the Bodhi-drûm. Now, this temple of Báláditya, which was identified by me in 1861, was partially excavated at my recommendation in 1863, and afterwards more completely by Mr. A. M. Broadley in 1871. I visited Nálandá in January 1872, and made a careful examination of this great ruined temple, the walls of which are still standing to a height of more than 50 feet. Large masses also of the fallen walls are still intact. From all these remains I am able to vouch for the accuracy of Hwen Thsang's statement

(a) Memoires sur les Contrées occidentales, I, pp. 465 to 468.

that the Nâlandâ Temple, with respect to size and magnificence, was comparable to the great temple near the Bodhi-drûm.

"Both temples are square in plan, both rise from a raised terrace or platform, both are built of bricks faced with stucco, and both are ornamented with rows of panels containing figures of Buddha. But the agreement with Hwen Thsang's description goes still further. The height of the Nâlandâ temple, he says, was 200 feet. Now we know both the breadth and height of the Buddha Gayá temple; and, as the Nâlandâ temple resembled it, we may conclude with some confidence that it was built in the same relative proportions of height to base. The base of the Nâlandâ temple is 63 feet square, and that of the Bodhi-drûm temple is just 50 feet, its height being 160 to 170 feet. According to this proportion the height of the temple of Bâlâditya at Nâlandâ would have been a little over 200 feet, which agrees exactly with the measurement given by Hwen Thsang.

"Now the Nâlandâ temple was certainly not either repaired or rebuilt by the Burmese. On the contrary, we know that the last alterations and additions to it were made to the entrance doorway by Raja Mahipâla (*a*), as recorded in an inscription discovered by Captain Marshall when making the excavation previously alluded to. As Mahipâla lived in the beginning of the 11th century, we gain no less than three centuries for the antiquity of this style of temple over the date adopted for it by Mr. Fergusson.

"I return again to the account of the temple given by Hwen Thsang. According to him the Bráhman builder of the temple had a younger brother who excavated a tank. Neither its name nor its position is given, but it was probably the nameless tank which now exists to the west of the temple. It is specially unfortunate that the name of the Bráhman is not mentioned by Hwen Thsang; but as the date of Bâlâditya is fixed by him to the first century B.C., so we may place the building of the Bodhi-drûm temple about the same time, or perhaps a little earlier than Bâlâditya, as the larger temple was probably the latter one. I have a suspicion that the Brâhman and his brother may, perhaps, be the same as the two brothers, Sankara and Mudgaragâmini, who founded the first monastery at Nâlandâ.

(*a*) The addition was not made by Mahipâla, but, during his reign, by an oil-seller.—See my translation of the inscription in the Journal of the Asiatic Society, Vol XLI, part I, page 310.

When they are first mentioned, they are called simply 'the two Upâsika brothers who laid the foundations of the famous monastery of Nâlandâ;' but afterwards the elder brother is called 'King Sankara,' and Nâgârjuna is said to have studied in the Nâlandâ Monastery of Sankara shortly after its foundation. This King Sankara must therefore be identified with Hwen Thsang's Sho-kia-lo-o-tie-to, or Sankaráditya, whom he also makes the first founder of the Nâlandâ monastery. This is a mere suggestion, but it seems not improbable that the two enthusiastic brothers who built the Nâlandâ monastery on the site of Sâriputra's birth-place might be the same two brothers who had previously built the great temple near the Bodhi-drûm. But quite independent of the question of their identity, I look upon the fact mentioned by Hwen Thsang of the similarity of the two great temples of Nâlandâ and Buddha Gayá as a fair evidence that the two buildings belonged to the same period; and I accept the pilgrim's statement that the Nâlandâ monastery was built seven hundred years before his time as a plain fact, which he must have obtained from the annals of the monastery itself. Bâlâditya must therefore be placed towards the end of the first century before Christ, or early in the first century after Christ." (a)

Conclusion.

It is undeniable that there are some weak points in this identification; but it is the best under the peculiar circumstances of the case. The main fact, the similitude of the Nâlandá temple to that of Buddha Gayá, is unquestionable; and the assumption, therefore, that they are of, or of about, the same age may be fairly received as probable. The materials now available cannot help us to any more positive conclusion, and by accepting it we do not exceed the limits—first century B.C. to close of first century A.C.—within which we have to look for the date of the temple. The tradition about the Bráhman brothers is one of those which are not much open to the charge of fabrication, inasmuch as it is on the face of it not an interested one. Had any body wished to take the credit of the temple to himself he would have given his own name to it; or, if he had wished to attribute it to some of his favorites, he would have named him, and made him a Buddhist of old standing, instead of leaving out his name and calling him a converted Bráhman. As a mere tradition of a fact in which none took any particular interest, such a condition is

(a) Arch. Surv. Report, III, pp. 93-5.

not necessary. On the contrary the omission of names and circumstantial minutiæ shows that the narrator is honestly reciting what he has heard, and thereby imparts to his narration an appearance of authenticity. The story besides has the support, such as it is, of the Burmese inscription, which is of some consequence. And if on the strength of these arguments the story be accepted as true, the conclusion arrived at by the learned archæologist follows as a matter of course. Whether it is really so or not must abide the result of future and more satisfactory research.

INDEX.

2 K

BUDDHA GAYÁ

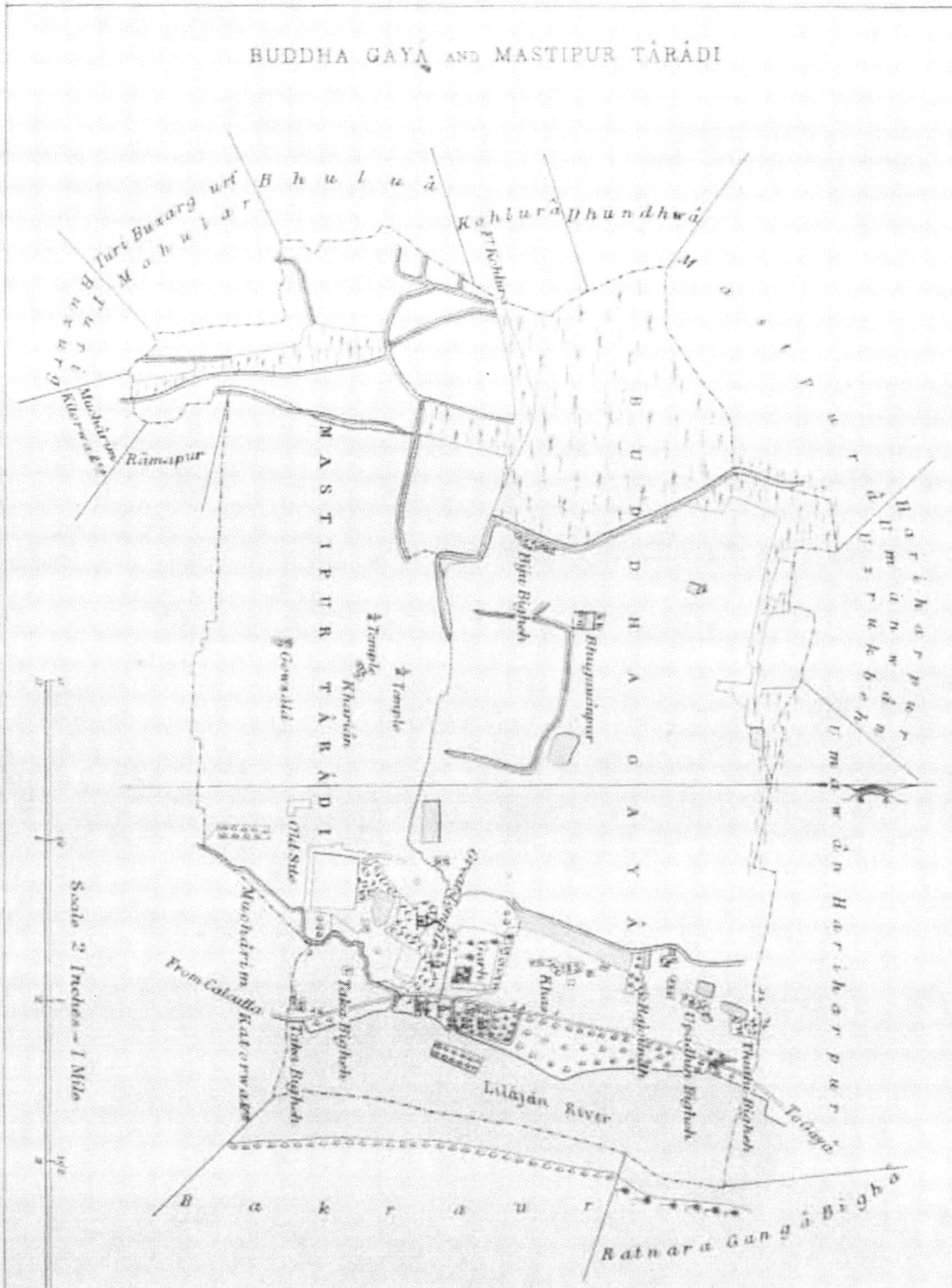

Reduced from Captain H. V. Stephen's Survey Maps

Lithographed at the Surveyor General's Office, Calcutta, May 1878

AUTOTYPE.

MÀRA'S ASSAULT ON BUDDHA, from a Fresco Painting in Cave No. 1. AJANTÀ.

PLATE III

BUDDHA GAYA

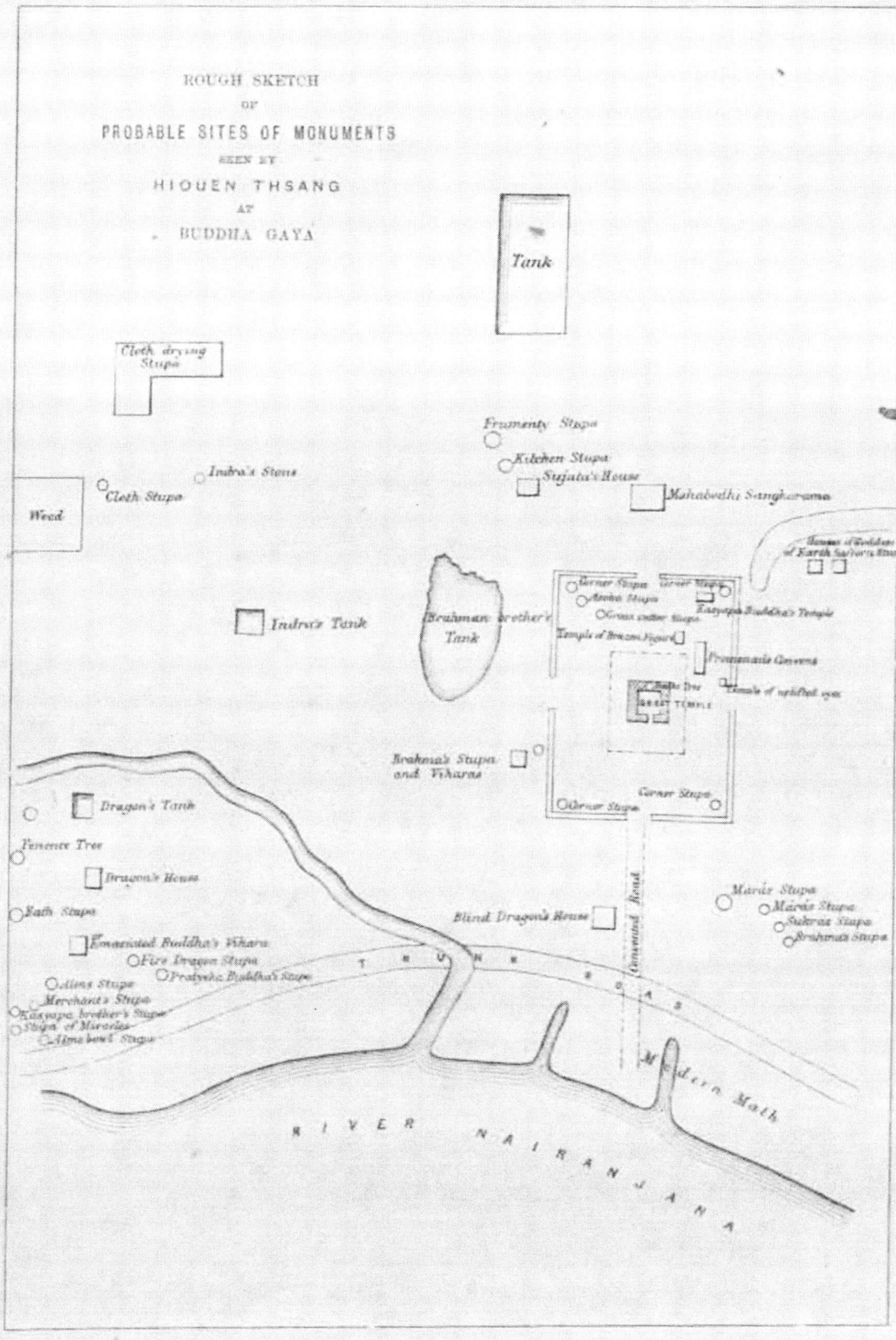

PLAN OF SITES NOTICED BY HIOUEN THSANG AT BUDDHA GAYA.

PLATE IV

BUDDHA GAYÁ.

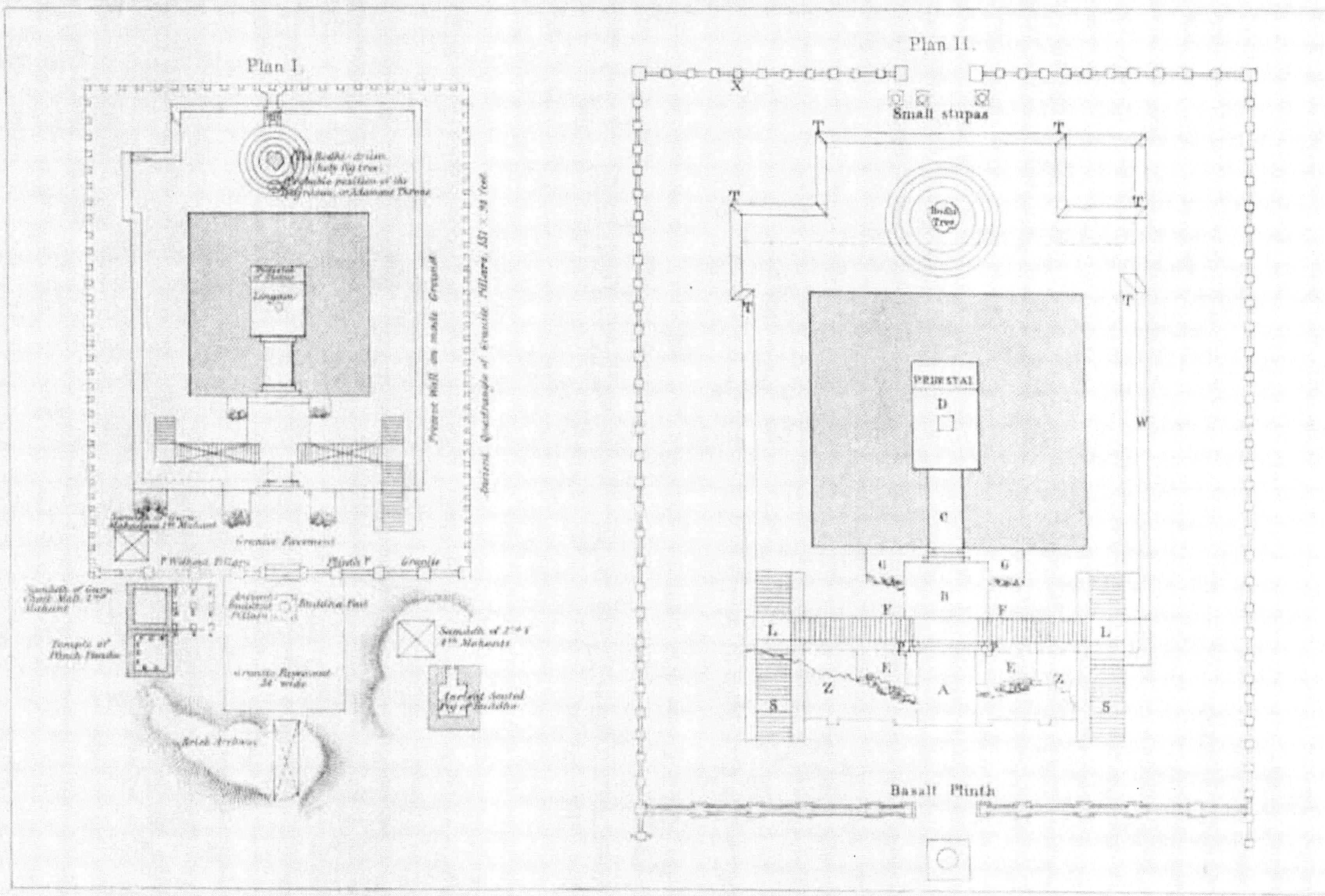

GENERAL CUNNINGHAM'S PLANS OF THE GREAT TEMPLE AT BUDDHA GAYÁ

Plate vi.

AUTOTYPE.

PANCHA PÂNDAVA AND SAMADHS.

AUTOTYPE.

SOUTHERN FACADE OF THE GREAT TEMPLE.

BUDDHA GAYÂ.

Plate viii.

SOUTHERN FACADE OF THE GREAT TEMPLE

NICHES OF THE GREAT TEMPLE TERRACE. S.

BUDDHA GAYA

A. P. Bagchi, del.

NICHE FROM THE SOUTH SIDE OF THE GREAT TEMPLE.

(Restored.)

BUDDHA GAYÁ

A. P. Bagchi, del.

Printed in Colors at the Surveyor General's Office, Calcutta.

BUDDHA FROM THE SANCTUM OF THE GREAT TEMPLE

BUDDHA GAYÁ.

A. F. Saghili, delt.

A. THRONE FROM THE SANCTUM OF THE GREAT TEMPLE. B, C, & D. PANELS FROM ASOKA PILLARS.

BUDDHA GAYÁ.

A. F. Baghchi, delt.

STATUETTES FROM THE GATE-WAY OF THE MATH.

BUDDHA GAYÂ.

Plate xiv.

AUTOTYPE.

HOUSE ON THE GARH.

BUDDHA GAYÂ.

Plate xv.

AUTOTYPE

EASTERN FACADE OF THE GREAT TEMPLE.

ARCHES OF THE GREAT TEMPLE IN 1863.

AUTOTYPE.

ARCHES OF THE GREAT TEMPLE IN 1877.

ANCIENT TEMPLE AT KOÑCH.

PORCH OF THE GREAT TEMPLE.

BUDDHA GAYA.

Fig. 1.

Fig. 2.

Fig. 4.

Fig. 3.

A. F. Bagchi, del.

Printed in Colors at the Surveyor General's Office, Calcutta

FIG. 1, PADMAPANI, NOW CALLED TARA DEVI.

FIG. 3, DHYANI BUDDHA, FROM THE PANCHA PANDAVA TEMPLE.

FIG. 2, BUDDHA AS A TEACHER, FROM THE COURTYARD OF THE MONASTERY.

FIG. 4, PRITHIVI DEVI, FROM COURTYARD OF THE MONASTERY.

BUDDHA GAYA.

Fig. 1.

Fig. 2.

Fig. 3.

A. P. Bagchi, delt.

Printed in Colors at the Surveyor General's Office, Calcutta.

FIG. 1, VISHNU WORSHIPPING BUDDHA; FIG. 2, NAGAKANYA AND CHILD; FIG. 3, BUDDHA, DISCIPLE AND ATTENDANT.

BUDDHA GAYÁ.

Fig. 1.

Fig. 2.

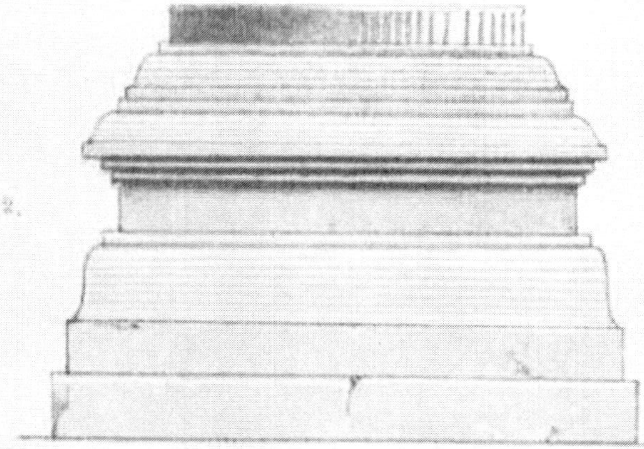

Fig. 3.

Fig. 4.

A. N. Bagchi, delt.

BASES OF PILLARS.

BUDDHA GAYA.

A. P. Bagchi, Del.

FIG. 1, BUDDHA- FROM A NICHE IN THE NEW WALL. FIG. 2. BUDDHA, FROM A NICHE IN THE NEW WALL.

FIG. 3. PADMAPANI, BY THE SIDE OF THE EASTERN GATEWAY.

FIG. 4, DANCING GIRL, IN A NICHE ON A VOTIVE STUPA FIXED ON THE NORTHERN SIDE OF THE NEW WALL.

FIG. 5. A DEVOTEE, BY THE SIDE OF THE EASTERN GATEWAY.

FIG. 6, BODHISATTVA, FROM A NICHE IN THE GATEWAY OF THE MONASTERY

PLATE XXIV

BUDDHA GAYA

F. Bagchi, Del.

HERMIT AND DEVOTEES FROM A NICHE IN THE NEW WALL.

BUDDHA GAYÁ.

A. P. Bagchi, delt.

Printed in Colours at the Surveyor General's Office, Calcutta

FIG. 1. BANGLE. FIGS. 2, 3, 4, & 5. NECKLACES. FIG. 6. CROWN.

BUDDHA GAYA.

Fig. 1.

Fig. 2.

Fig. 3.

A. P. Bagchi, delt.

FIG. 1, MÁYÁ DEVÍ CALLED GÁYATRÍ DEVÍ, FROM THE MATH.

FIG. 2, BHAIRAVA, FROM MATH.

FIG. 3, MÁYÁ DEVÍ CALLED CHHOṬA THAKURAN FROM THE PANCHA PANDU TEMPLE.

BUDDHA GAYÁ.

Fig. 3.

Fig. 4.

Fig. 1.

Fig. 2.

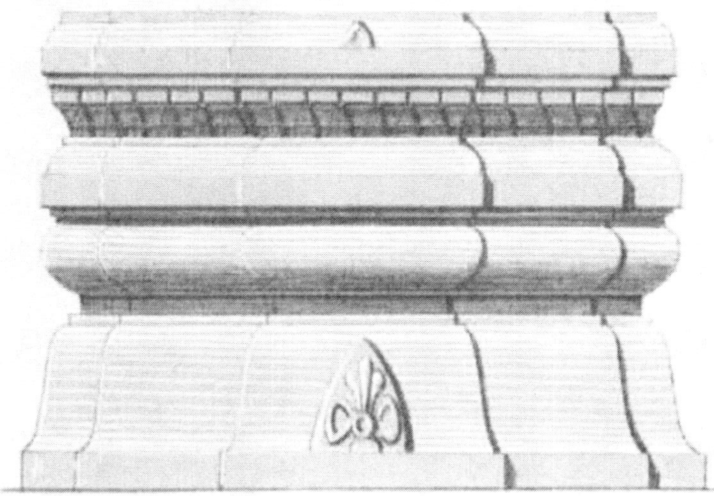

A. F. Bagels, delt.

Printed in Calcutta at the Surveyor General's Office, Calcutta.

FIGS. 1 to 3, BASES OF PILLARS. FIG. 4, BODY OF A MODEL TEMPLE.

BUDDHA GAYÁ.

A. P. Bagchi, Delt.

Printed in Colours at the Surveyor General's Office, Calcutta.

PADMAPÁNI.

BUDDHA GAYÁ.

A. P. Bagchi, delt.

Printed at the Surveyor General's Office, Calcutta.

MÁYÁ DEVÍ IN THE INDIAN MUSEUM, CALCUTTA.

BUDDHA GAYÁ.

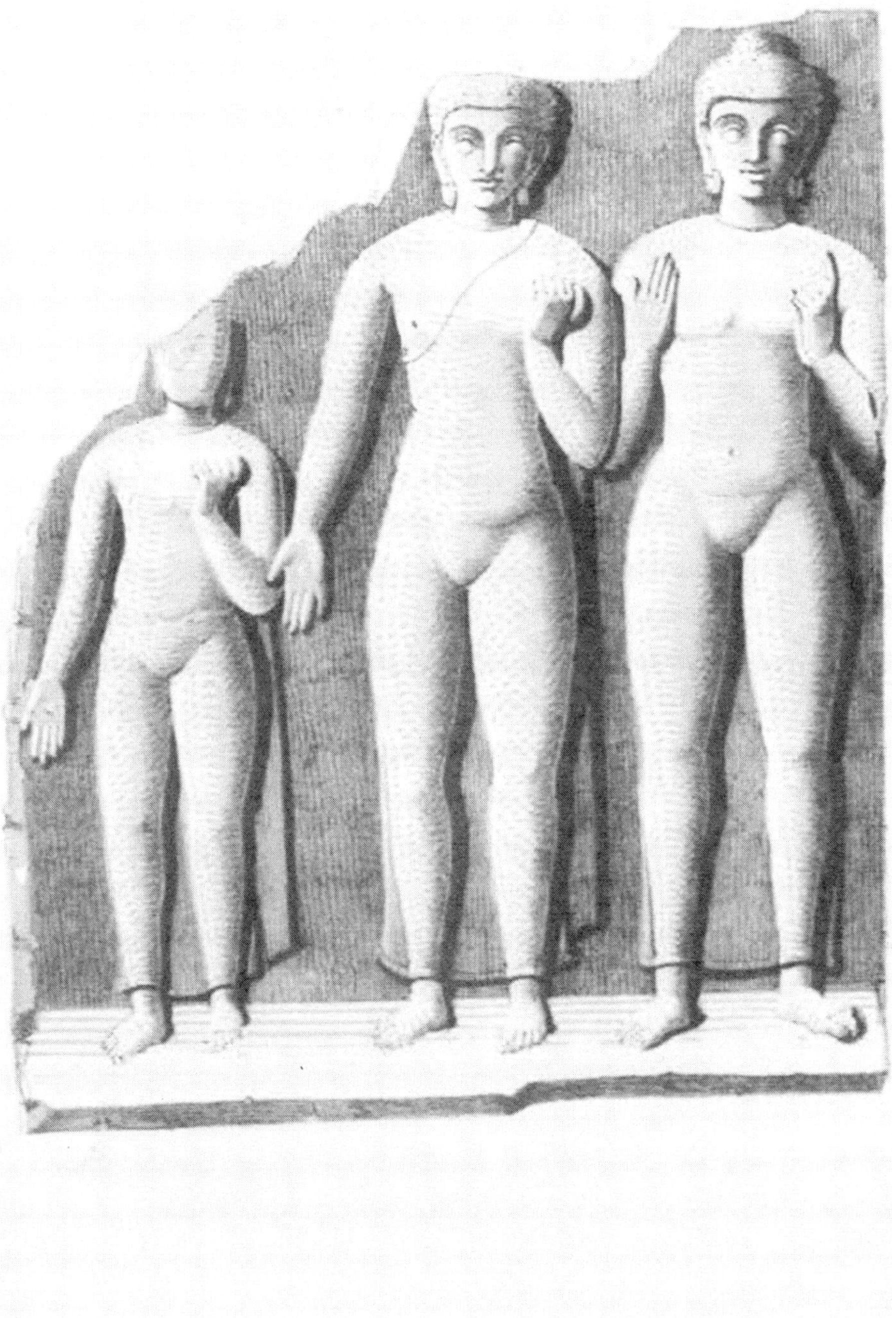

A. P. Daguns, Delt.

Printed in Colors at the Surveyor General's Office, Calcutta

BUDDHA AND DISCIPLES, FOUND IN A NICHE OF THE NEW WALL ROUND THE GREAT TEMPLE

BUDDHA GAYA.

Fig. 1.

Fig. 2.

Fig. 3.

Fig. 4.

[illegible] Dast, Del. Printed at the Surveyor General's Office, Calcutta.

[illegible] ON A CAR DRAWN BY SEVEN HORSES.

FIG. 2. THREE-HEADED [illegible] ON A CAR DRAWN BY THE [illegible]

FIG. 3. GODDESS WITH EIGHTEEN ARMS.

FIG. 4. [illegible]

BUDDHA GAYÁ.

Fig. 1.

Fig. 2.

Fig. 3.

A. P. Bagchi, delt.

FIG. 1, BUDDHA FROM THE MATH.

FIG. 2, VAJRAPANI ALIAS VAGISVARI DEVI, FROM THE TEMPLE OF VAGISVARI DEVI.

FIG. 3, PADMAPANI ALIAS SAVITRI DEVI, FROM THE COURTYARD OF THE GREAT TEMPLE.

BUDDHA GAYÁ.

A. P. Sagrin, delt.

Printed at the Surveyor General's Office, Calcutta

AŚOKA RAILING, RESTORED.

BUDDHA GAYÁ.

Fig. 1.

Fig. 2.

Fig. 3.

Fig. 4.

Fig. 6.

Fig. 7.

A. P. Bagchi, delt.

BOSSES ON RAIL-POSTS.

BUDDHA GAYÁ

Fig. 1

Fig. 2

Fig. 3

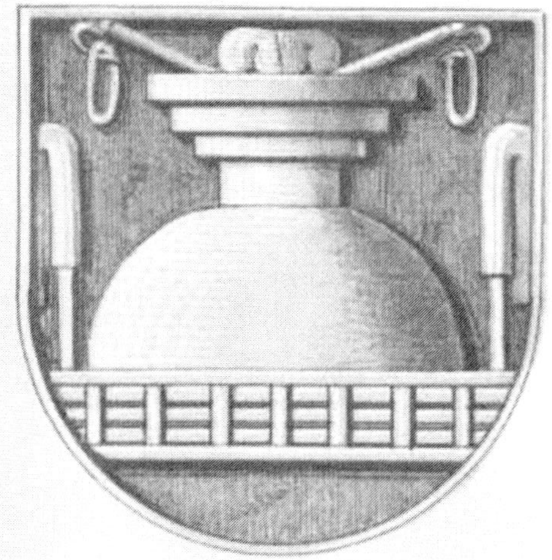

Fig. 4.

Fig. 5.

Fig. 6.

S. P. Bagchi, delt.

BOSSES ON RAIL-POSTS.

BUDDHA GAYÁ.

Fig. 1.

Fig. 2.

Fig. 3.

Fig. 4.

Fig. 5.

Fig. 6.

A. P. Bagchi, delt.

Printed at the Surveyor General's Office Calcutta.

BOSSES ON RAIL-POSTS.

BUDDHA GAYA.

Fig. 1.

Fig. 2.

Fig. 3.

Fig. 4.

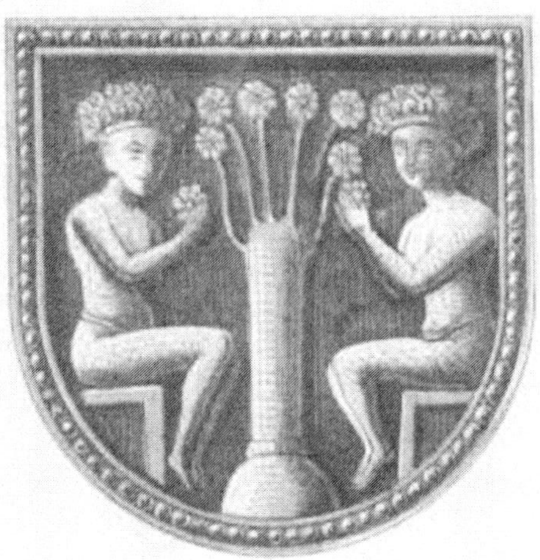

Fig. 5.

Fig. 6.

A. F. Bagchi, lith.

BOSSES.

BUDDHA GAYA.

BOSSES ON RAIL-POSTS.

BUDDHA GAYÁ.

Fig. 1.

Fig. 2.

Fig. 3.

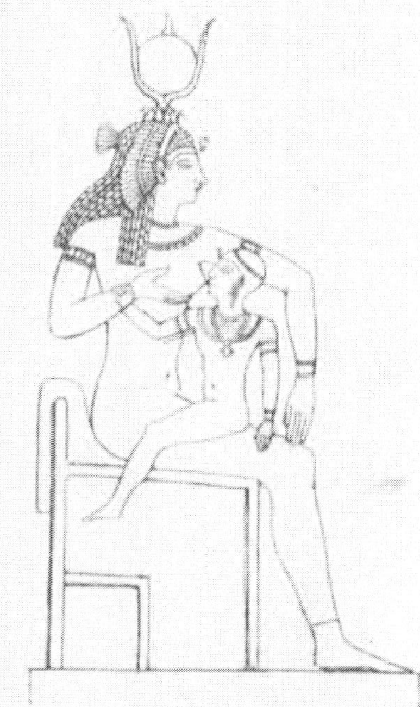

A. F. Bagola, delt.

FIG. 1, YASODA, NOURISHING KRISHNA. FIG. 2, MARY NOURISHING JESUS. FIG. 3, ISIS NOURISHING HORUS.

BUDDHA GAYA.

Photozincographed at the Surveyor General's Office, Calcutta.

FACSIMILE OF AN INSCRIPTION IN THE INDIAN MUSEUM.

BUDDHA GAYÁ.

A. P. Bagchi, delt.

Printed at the Surveyor General's Office, Calcutta.

FIGS. 1 TO 7 CHAITYAS. FIGS. 8 AND 9 KALASAS FOR CHAITYAS.

PLATE XLII

BUDDHA GAYA.

A. P. Banglu, delt.

Printed in Lithog. at the Surveyor General's Office, Calcutta.

VOTIVE STUPAS.

BUDDHA GAYÁ.

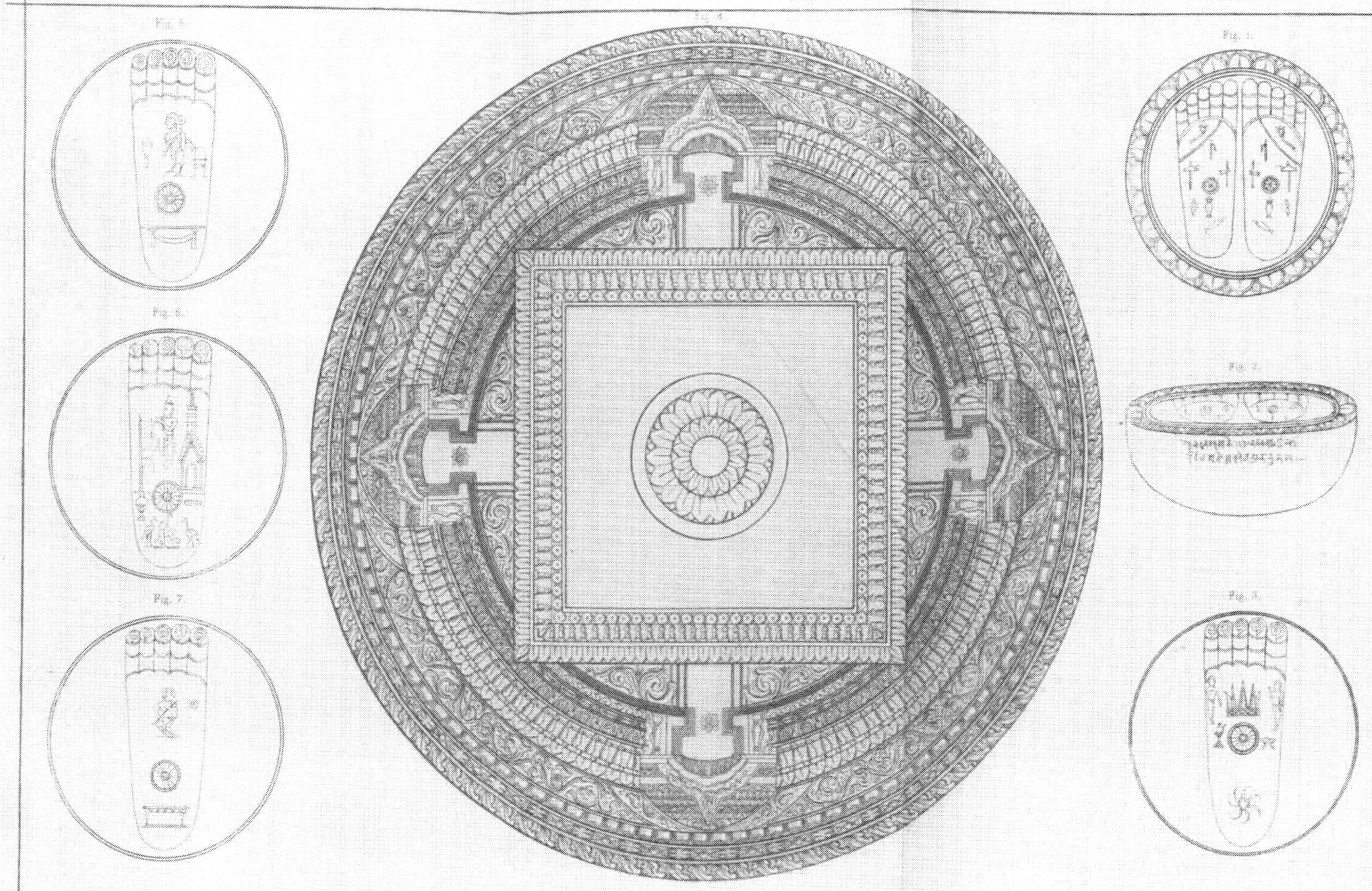

FIGS. 5, 6 & 7, FOOTPRINTS OF BUDDHA.

FIG. 4, VAJRASANA, THE ADAMANTINE THRONE OF BUDDHA.

FIG. 1, BUDDHAPAD.

FIG. 2, INSCRIPTION ON BUDDHAPAD.

FIG. 3, FOOTPRINT OF BUDDHA.

PLATE XLIV

BUDDHA GAYÂ

A. P. Bagchi, delt.

BOSSES ON RAIL-POSTS.

BUDDHA GAYÂ.

Fig. 7.

Fig. 8.

Fig. 9.

Fig. 10.

Fig. 11.

Fig. 12.

BOSSES ON MEDIAL PILLARS.

BUDDHA GAYA.

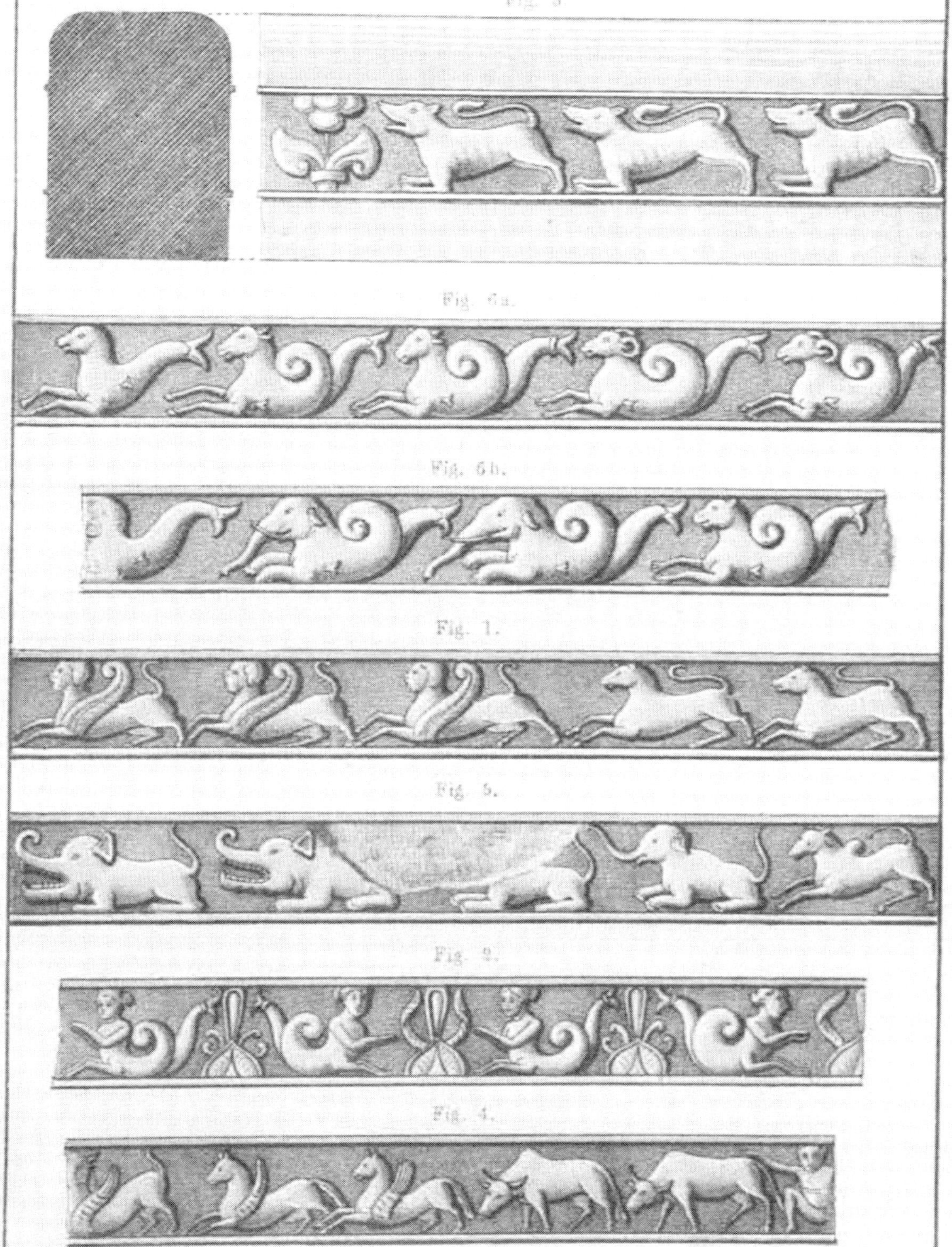

A. P. Vogeli, delt.

FRIEZES ON COPINGS.

BUDDHA GAYA.

Fig. 1.

Fig. 2.

Fig. 3.

Fig. 4.

A. P. Bagchi, delt.

Printed at the Surveyor General's Office, Calcutta.

FLORAL DEVICES ON COPINGS.

PLATE XLVIII.

BUDDHA GAYÁ.

Printed at the Surveyor General's Office, Calcutta.

FIG. 1. A CORNER PILLAR OF THE ASOKA RAILING.

FIG. 2. A LENTIL IN THE INDIAN MUSEUM.

FIG. 3. A COLUMN, IN THE INDIAN MUSEUM.

FIG. 4. A SILL IN THE INDIAN MUSEUM.

BUDDHA GAYÁ.

A. P. Bagchi, delt.

Printed at the Surveyor General's Office, Calcutta.

FIG. 1a, b, c, AND FIG. 2a, b, c. DETERIORATIONS OF MOULDINGS BY REPAIRS.

FIG. 3. NICHE OF PORCH. FIG. 4. ELEVATION OF TERRACE. FIGS. 5 to 11. MOULDINGS OF PORCH.

BUDDHA GAYÁ.

GATE-PILLAR OF THE AŚOKA RAILING.

BUDDHA GAYA.

From the Pavement.

From a Coping in the Indian Museum.

A1 B1 A2 B2 A3 B3 A4 B4

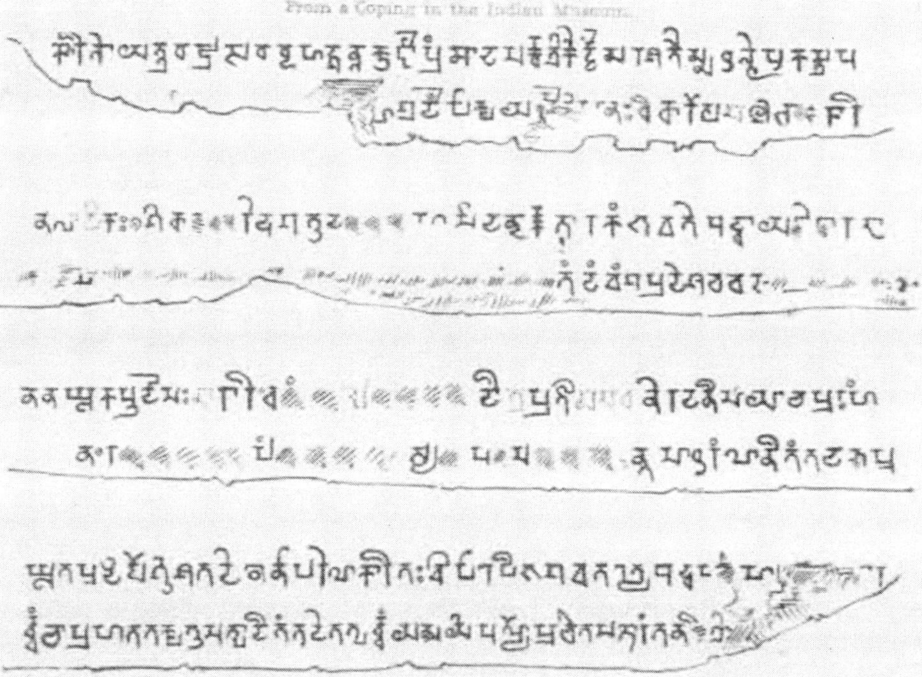

From the base of a statue found by Major Mead.

A1 B1 A2 B2

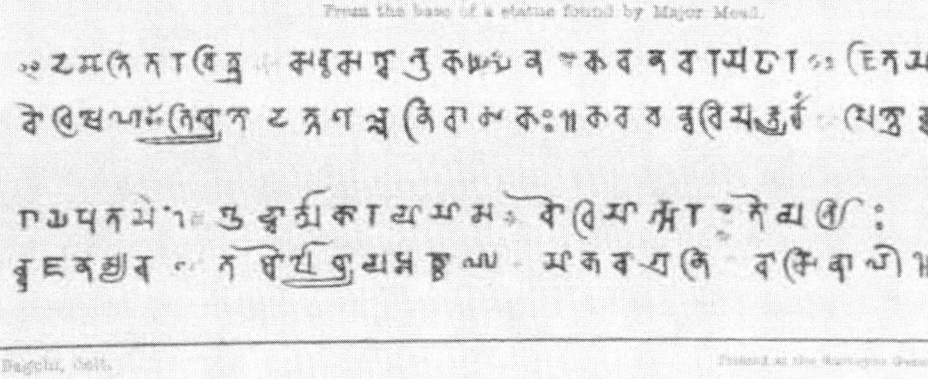

A. F. Bagchi, Lith.

Printed at the Surveyor General's Office, Calcutta

INSCRIPTIONS.